Ann D. Roberts

Alaska Gardening Guide

Volume 1
Alaska
Vegetables for
Northern
Climates

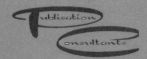
Publication Consultants

PO Box 221974 Anchorage, Alaska 99522

ISBN 1-888125-54-3

Library of Congress Catalog Card Number: 00-105349

*Front Cover. Horticulturist Pat Wagner poses with a giant cabbage grown in the Matanuska Valley,
near Anchorage, Alaska. The record for one entered in the Palmer State Fair is 98 pounds, grown in
1990 by Leslye Dinkel. Photo by Don H. Dinkel.*

Manufactured in the United States of America.

Dedication

This book is dedicated to my mother, Carolyn Jane Becker Drury, who died of cancer in March of 1983, at the age of 68. Before her death she had spent a lifetime homesteading and gardening in Alaska, and was a member of the North Pole Country Garden Club. She served two years as president of the Alaska State Federation of Garden Clubs and two more years as organizer and chairman of the Pacific Regional Convention of State Garden Clubs, held in Fairbanks the summer before her death. My main regret is that she did not live to see Alaska Gardening Guide in print, although she encouraged me to write it, and things I learned about gardening from her are woven into the very fabric of this book. I seldom speak of her death; or perhaps I would rather pretend it had not happened. But I always knew she loved me and was there for me, and I feel her loss particularly at times like these, when I long to show her that I did indeed complete what I set out to do.

This book is dedicated as well to all the gardeners and farmers of Alaska, whose experiments and experiences gardening in the far north both made this book, and formed the reason for writing it. It is by sharing the expertise of hundreds of gardeners and researchers that both commercial agriculture and home gardening becomes feasible in the subarctic.

Last, but certainly not least, I dedicate this book to the One who made the plants we are trying to grow so well. Without Him, there would be nothing to write about at all. I am thankful that I have been able to enjoy all He has provided.

Acknowledgments

I would like to thank those credited by name within the pages of this book. Some of them will be taken by surprise, since I was not able to interview them personally, but gleaned their wisdom from their writings and as reported by others. Some have moved away and some are deceased. I was able to consult some in person, such as Mary Armstrong, Ed Bostrom, Eloise DeWitt (deceased), Jim Holm, Dr. Charles W. Knight, Clair Lammers, Grant Matheke, Dr. Jenifer Huang McBeath, Lee Risse, Dr. V. E. Romanovsky, Dr. Stephen Sparrow, and Judy Weber. Many others I interviewed by telephone, including Jim Douglas, Walt McPherson, Joe Orsi, Victor M. (Jack) Spratt, Jr., and Wayne Vandre.

My particular thanks goes to my father, Dr. Horace F. Drury, who proofed my earliest manuscript, and helped me with many of the more scientific explanations, such as that for the phenomenon known as photoperiodism that is such an important factor in subarctic growing success.

Though they did it so long ago they may not remember, I also thank Dr. Donald H. Dinkel, Ray Morgan (deceased), Carroll Phillips, and Richard "Skeeter" Werner, all of whom proofed various chapters-in-the-making, as well as those who lectured to the first Master Gardener's class in Fairbanks, many years ago.

Special thanks are due Michele Hébert, Dr. Patricia S. Holloway, and Virgil D. Severns, for their willingness to answer my frantic calls as deadlines neared, and for being kind enough to wade through the complete rough draft and offer insightful and expert advice, pointing out where explanations could be made clearer.

Many of those mentioned in the book also contributed photographs or slides to illustrate it, and Barbara Fay was kind enough to allow me to reprint her herb chart. Most of the other photographs came from the Alaska Cooperative Extension staff, and the Georgeson Botanical Garden Collection, for which I will be forever grateful!

I was the beneficiary of the gardening successes of many, without ever knowing their names. I thank them all the same - they know whom they are. Perhaps they will recognize their advice where it appears within. And now, as you use this book, you too will be the beneficiary of those who contributed to it, and know how inadequate our thanks must be.

Foreword

Michele Hébert

Land Resources Agent, Alaska Cooperative Extension

As a teacher of the Cooperative Extension Service Master Gardener program, I am always in search of a good guide. I have many books about gardening. What has been missing from my library has been a comprehensive book about vegetable gardening in Alaska—Till now!

Ann Roberts is a true gardener. She was born with dirt under her nails, has a passion for growing things, and years of Alaska gardening experience. Gardening was in her family genes and the growing passion was passed on from one generation to the next just as surely as dandelions pass on yellow flowers. Helping with the family garden was not enough; Ann wanted to understand all the science from soil chemistry to soil biology. She spent years — asking questions, taking classes like the Cooperative Extension Service Master Gardener program, and doing her own research. There was more than a desire to grow things well.

Her enthusiasm took her a step further—to write a book and share her wealth of knowledge with others. I am especially thankful for the amount of work that has gone into *Alaska Gardening Guide*. She has written from her own knowledge and summarized information from agricultural professionals and gardeners from across Alaska. These individuals have spent years experimenting and working to overcome the challenges posed by the unique growing conditions at Alaska latitudes.

This excellent guide for vegetable gardening in Alaska brings together practical information and scientific knowledge. It is full of how-to, scientific explanations, and resources for further information. It gives the reader the know-how to overcome the climatic challenges and take advantage of the benefits of gardening in the far north. I look forward to sharing the book with my Master Gardener students in years to come.

Alaska Gardening Guide is an excellent tool for both new and seasoned gardeners—and it is about time!

Table of Contents
Alaska Gardening Guide
Vol. I: Alaska Vegetables for Northern Climates

Part One: Alaska Gardening Basics

Part Two: Beyond the Basics

Part Three: Plant Specifics

Appendices

Garden belonging to Tone Deehr

Hawks Farm and Garden Center in North Pole, Alaska.

Garden belonging to Les Vierick

Holm Town Nursery, Fairbanks, Alaska

Preface

And God saw every thing that he had made,
and, behold, it was very good. Genesis 1:31a, KJV.

Many years ago, in 1867, when then Secretary of State William H. Seward consummated a deal with Russia to purchase Alaska for about two cents an acre, people laughed. They called Alaska names like Seward's Folly, and Seward's Icebox. Even today, you can still run across references to those nicknames for Alaska in social studies textbooks.

Virgil D. Severns

Portage Glacier, Alaska.

That was a long time ago, but many people have never quite forgotten the picture of Alaska as an icebox. Even people who know for a fact Alaskans don't live in igloos still conjure up winter images when they think of Alaska. Anyone who has been to Alaska, on the other hand, is more likely to envision forests and mountains.

True, there are not very many huge rolling fields covered with corn as far as an eye can see, but there certainly are vegetables. Not very visible, perhaps, but tucked away in backyards, or hidden inside makeshift greenhouses, the vegetables are there. And, we are told, bigger and better than are found in many other places, due in part to the long, long summer days that help make up for the dark days of winter. We have even been told by visitors, as well as by in-house experts, that the flowers are brighter, the colors more intense, again thanks to the "Midnight Sun."

Yes, there **are** vegetables in Seward's Icebox — and berries, and fruit, and melons. Read on and see ….

The garden in Kotzebue (above) has various soil-warming polyethylene covers which are removed during the heat of the day to prevent overheating of the plants. Garden (below) in Ambler, Alaska.

Chapter 1

Subarctic Gardening

Be still, and know that I am God: ...
I will be exalted in the earth. Psalms 46:10, KJV.

T he emphasis in this book (and the reason for writing it) is to focus on how gardening in Alaska is different— what special knowledge is needed to succeed here, what new techniques will help meet some of Alaska's unique growing challenges. If it is also of help to other northern gardeners outside of Alaska, then so much the better!

First the Bad News

And there is no denying there are challenges to gardening in Alaska. With the exceptionally long days of sunlight (too much of a good thing), some biennials, such as beets, complete their normal two-year cycle of growth in one year. They bolt to seed before the storage roots have matured. Head lettuce sends up a seed stalk before it has had time to mature a firm head. Melon roots cringe from the cold soil and fail to grow well. Slugs invade gardens of Southeastern Alaska, and are known to be spreading in Southcentral Alaska. While potentially productive windblown silt covers farmlands in Alaska's Interior to a depth of over 100 feet in places, only a few inches may overlie rock or gravel in other areas. Permafrost lurks just beneath the surface of much of the state, keeping the soil cold, or melting to form sink holes ranging in size from a gentle dip, to a hole big enough to bury a house.

Prof. Tom Osterkamp, ret.

This is a common sight in Alaska. Where permafrost containing excess ice thaws under pavement and in roadside ditches, the result is damage such as these long longitudinal cracks.

Then the Good News

Yet there is great agricultural potential here, both for farming and for small backyard gardens. According to Dr. Donald H. Dinkel, former Plant

Physiologist at the University of Alaska, vegetables grown in Alaska have "very high quality, with high-sugar content, low-fiber content, and excellent yield." And there is land, much more than is now being farmed or gardened. E. N. Severson, Agricultural Statistician for the

Georgeson Botanical Garden Collection.

Dr. Donald H. Dinkel, shown here, is "outstanding in his field" in more ways than one, and was always way ahead of his time with his plant experiments at the University of Alaska Fairbanks Agricultural Experiment Farm.

United States Department of Agriculture, wrote in 1972, "Alaska holds the distinction of being the largest state in the Union with the smallest acreage devoted to agriculture."

Pick-your-own operations are on the rise, and roadside stands and farmers' markets can be found in more and more areas. State fairs in the Matanuska and Tanana Valleys serve as showcases for the state's vegetables.

And best of all, thousands of gardeners in Alaska, and the experts interviewed for this book, have already come up with answers to many of the challenges mentioned earlier. Just glance

ACE staff

Lois Mendenhall (upper) beams over her prize-winning green beans at the Tanana Valley State Fair. Her beans went on to win class champion. Farmers' Market in Fairbanks, Alaska (lower).

over the table of contents, or scan the index, to be made aware of how much help there really is.

Dividing Alaska

Alaska is such an immense state, stretching over 1,200 miles north to south and (until 1983) four time zones east to west, that the temperature and weather conditions encountered go from one extreme to another. It is difficult, if not impossible, to address all the possible gardening challenges of such a varied area. This book concentrates on the major growing areas, Southcentral, the Interior, and Southeast.

Obviously, there are many gardeners in other areas of the state. It is hoped that they will be able to identify with one or more of these areas, and to select from various chapters those ideas most applicable to them. Examples would be gardeners near the Arctic Circle who may be able to use the directions for warming cold soil with clear plastic (see Chapter 10), or bush gardeners who might be interested in learning about constructing battery-powered electric fences for moose control (see Chapter 9).

Hot Springs

Not everyone newly-arrived in the state realizes there are over 100 hot springs here, in addition to the well-publicized glaciers. A few of the better known ones in the state are Manley Hot Springs, Chena Hot Springs, Circle Hot Springs, and Pilgrim Hot Springs.

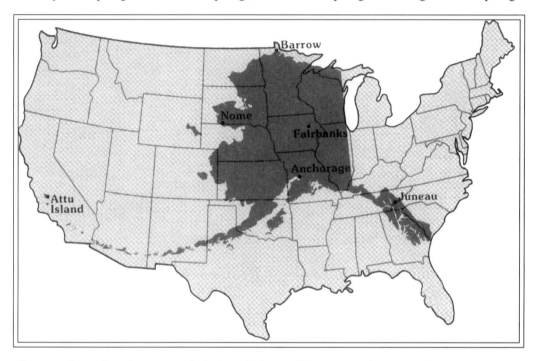

This map shows the relative size of Alaska, which is well over twice the size of the state of Texas.

Soil near hot springs is not necessarily warm, but there is great potential for heating with piped-in hot water from the springs. Potatoes and grains are reported to be doing well at Pilgrim Hot Springs near Nome, and other garden vegetables are grown there as well. The main problem, in fact, seems to be plants that grow too well—weeds, that is!

Major Population Areas

In the remainder of this book, it should be understood that, unless otherwise noted, the regional terms employed refer to Alaska. Thus, for example, Southeast refers to South-eastern Alaska, not the southeastern part of the United States.

Southcentral

Southcentral contains the best known farming area of the state, the Matanuska Valley, which extends from the Knik and Matanuska Rivers on the east, to the Susitna River watershed on the west, and includes a few farms around Anchorage. Southcentral also includes the Kenai Peninsula.

Interior

A potentially much larger, but still relatively undeveloped farming area is located in the Interior. The Interior extends from the Brooks Range on the north to the Alaska Range on the south, and includes Delta Junction and the villages of Tanana and Fort Yukon. Fairbanks is located in this area, often referred to as the Tanana Valley. The growing season is shorter than in Southcentral, with much more severe winters, but warmer summers. Rainfall is generally the lightest here of the three regions.

Southeastern

Gardening in Southeastern Alaska is severely limited, due to a variety of factors. Cloud cover, heavy precipitation, and slugs discourage gardeners here. In addition, many towns are built on steep rock hillsides, where lack of soil and erosion of existing soil are problems.

Virgil D. Severns

Pilgrim Hot Springs, as seen from a bush plane.

Organization

This book is arranged in three parts. First is a section on planting basics for the beginning gardener in Alaska, whether or not he has ever gardened elsewhere. Second is a more in-depth section dealing with specific problems encountered in the various areas in Alaska, such as cold soil (Chapter 10), or heavy precipitation (Chapter 11). A final section gives individual suggestions for raising particular vegetables. Obviously, all vegetables cannot be covered in great depth, but, hopefully, it will give a start with the most common ones.

Resources for Gardeners

Alaskans have two excellent gardening/farming resources. One is the Alaska Cooperative Extension, University of Alaska Fairbanks (ACE), discussed in more detail in the next section. The other is the University of Alaska Fairbanks itself, which includes the School of

Agricultural & Land Resource Management with its Agricultural & Forestry Experiment Station in Fairbanks and Palmer Research Center in Palmer. In Fairbanks, the horticultural program of the Experiment Farm is now the Georgeson Botanical Garden. The Garden's director, Dr. Pat Holloway, and her staff, supplied much excellent guidance and many of the photographs included in this book.

Alaska Cooperative Extension

Throughout this book, frequent references to the Alaska Cooperative Extension, University of Alaska Fairbanks (ACE) will be found. This is a cooperative effort of the University of Alaska Fairbanks and the United States Department of Agriculture. ACE interprets and disseminates research from the University of Alaska, and for many years its booklets and pamphlets were the only available information source for gardeners and farmers alike. Its publications have been a major source of information for this book.

ACE photo by Don Quarberg.

The lower fields at the University of Alaska Fairbanks are test plots too, and the results of research conducted here will aid farmers state-wide in growing better field crops.

But it has been more than just a source of printed words. The personnel of its many offices throughout the state have been eternally patient about answering questions and clearing up misconceptions. The majority of photographs in this book came from their archives. This book would have been impossible without their willing cooperation, because it was an attempt to draw on the knowledge, not of one person, but of many experts in the field of gardening in the subarctic. It is hoped this book will prove useful to gardeners, not only in the state of Alaska, but in other northern states, and Canada as well.

In Appendix C is a list of addresses for the Alaska Cooperative Extension offices, to facilitate contacting the nearest one for specific help with gardening problems, or for literature referred to in this book. Most of their publications are free; for some of them there is a

Georgeson Botanical Garden Collection.

The Georgeson Botanical Garden is more than a pretty garden to prove to tourists that flowers and vegetables grow in Alaska—school children of all ages come to learn here, and variety testing benefits the whole state. Volunteer labor from the community contributes to much of the building and maintenance.

Georgeson Botanical Garden Collection.

These flower and vegetable beds at the Georgeson Botanical Garden serve multiple purposes. Among other things, every bed is actually a test plot, some of which are research projects for students attending the University of Alaska.

small charge to help defray expenses. A fairly complete listing of their publications can be found at their web site on the Internet (URL in Appendix C). Many of their booklets can be ordered online.

Master Gardeners

In 1978, Wayne Vandre, then Horticulturist with the Alaska Cooperative Extension in Anchorage, was instrumental in setting up a Master Gardener Program, patterned after similar programs in other states. In 1981, the program was expanded to Fairbanks.

Interested people, who have gardened at least one year in Alaska, may, for a modest charge, take a course of about 40 hours of horticultural instruction. In return, they agree to volunteer back 40 hours of time passing on their knowledge to the rest of the public.

The Alaska Cooperative Extension, University of Alaska Fairbanks is a cooperative effort of the University of Alaska Fairbanks and the United States Department of Agriculture. This view through their door shows some of the many pamphlets and instruction booklets they provide free to the public.

The course includes such things as vegetable culture, lawn care, greenhouse growing, insect pests of Alaska, herbicides, plant diseases, and food preservation, as well as a bit on houseplants and the special challenges they face in Alaska. The Master Gardeners tour local gardens and greenhouses, where they are shown first hand what they have learned about in class, and are given hands-on experience.

After completing the course, given in late winter and early spring, the participants sign up for a wide variety of activities aimed at helping other gardeners in the community. Many Master Gardeners give far more than the required 40 hours of volunteer time. Some of their activities include teaching classes and answering questions (in malls, garden centers, or commercial greenhouses, to name a few.) They may be found in farmers' markets, and at fairs, manning a table piled high with literature to help gardeners. Some contribute to gardening radio spots or television programs, some volunteer at the Georgeson Botanical Garden, and some are available to answer phone calls coming into ACE, or even to make house calls to help diagnose a particular plant problem.

Dr. Ray Gavlak lectures on the latest research in subarctic gardening to would-be Master Gardeners.

Michele Hébert

ACE staff

Teresa Killion looks on as Glen Risse makes a point to a Master Gardening class. The class is visiting Risse's Greenhouse.

ACE staff

Master Gardener, Derinda Weber, mans an informational composting booth at the Tanana Valley State Fair.

The Master Gardeners also build and maintain a Demonstration Garden at the Tanana Valley State Fair in Fairbanks, to show visitors as well as locals the latest good gardening practices. Photographs of them throughout this book aid in demonstrating particular methods such as raised row planting.

Eventually, the plan is to spread the Master Gardener Program over the whole state, with advanced courses offered to Master Gardeners who have completed the beginning course. Southeast, considered by some to have the least favorable climate for gardening in Alaska, has some of the most active and enthusiastic Master Gardeners' groups. If this book cannot help with a certain problem, feel free to call the nearest Alaska Cooperative Extension Service office to determine if they have a Master Gardener who can help.

Chapter 2

Plant with a Plan

Where there is no vision, the people perish: ...
Proverbs 29:18a, KJV.

It is possible to drop a few seeds at random, water occasionally, and finish the summer with a respectable vegetable crop. It is also possible to finish the summer with an even more respectable weed crop.

The new gardener in Alaska has to take into consideration factors often unheard of in the contiguous United States—such as plants that bolt to seed, not because of warm temperatures, but because of long days (actually short nights). On the other hand, some problems wrestled with further south pose little, if any, problem here—such as potato bugs, cabbage loopers, and Japanese beetles.

Regardless of what one may have been led to believe by pictures of the lush Matanuska Valley with its giant cabbages, a garden in Alaska does not spring into being, complete with neat rows of green fed by dark, rich soil. The best gardens are actually begun as much as a year before, with the selection of a site.

Garden Location
You will want to consider at least three factors in choosing your garden location: sun exposure, slope, and soil types. Some gardeners, particularly those of the Interior, must add a fourth—accessibility to water.

Sun Exposure
The amount of sun a site receives is especially important in northern areas like Alaska, because the rays are already so weakened by the slant at which they arrive. The additional atmosphere sunshine must pass through filters out and greatly reduces heat as well as ultraviolet rays, both needed by plants for optimum growth. A garden will need at least six hours of direct, unshaded light each day.

Buildings, trees, fences—all can shade the garden. Of these, trees are often the greatest problem, because they also draw moisture and nutrients with roots that may extend out into the garden area. Common remedies are root pruning and total removal.

To root prune, dig a ditch all around the garden area, about two or three feet down. Remove the cutoff root ends from the garden. Before you choose this option, you should understand something of the nature of tree growth in Alaska.

As mentioned earlier, Alaska's soils are cold (even frozen) 10 to 20 feet down. In fact, in many newly cleared areas, you may not even be able to plant until the soil thaws. Because of this, trees in Alaska do not send down taproots. Instead, most spread their roots horizontally, close beneath the surface. When a root is pruned, too much of the tree's support

Virgil D. Severns

This garden in Kotzebue utilizes a plastic windbreak (to left of greenhouse).

system may be removed. Check on where the tree would fall if a major anchor root should accidentally be chopped off.

If the tree's probable landing area is unacceptable, it may be best to select the second option and remove the tree entirely. In this case, there may be the added complication of the tree in question belonging to a neighbor.

Before refilling the ditch, Michele Hébert, Land Resources Agent in Fairbanks, suggests that a barrier (preferably metal) be inserted to keep roots from regrowing into the garden.

Windbreaks

Before removing all obstructions, take into account how much wind the garden area is likely to receive, and from which direction. Certain areas of Alaska (Delta Junction, and many coastal areas, for example) are subject to high winds much of the year. It might even be advisable to add trees or fences for windbreaks.

In Alaska, as anywhere, wind direction and strength will vary considerably for different seasons. In general, major winds are from the east, varying from Southeast in the Panhandle, to east in Southcentral, to a more northeasterly direction in the Interior and coastal areas like Nome. The winds tend to be stronger in Southeastern Alaska, and more variable in the Interior, due to the terrain. A windsock in a garden site may help to determine the prevailing wind direction.

If a windbreak is needed on the southeast side of a garden, consider construction of a clear barrier of glass or plastic, which will not block out too much sun. Even if there does not seem to be much wind from the north, it is often an advantage to have a building at the north end of the garden. A south wall is a favored spot for cold-tender plants, as well as for attached greenhouses.

Finally, what should be done when everything has been considered, and part of the plot must be in the shade anyway? Turn the shade to your advantage, planting cool-weather

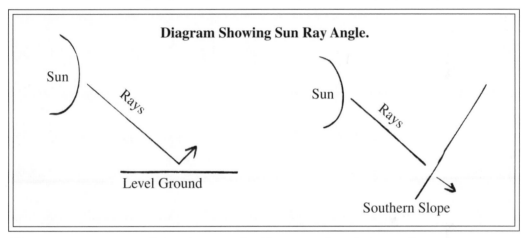

Direct sun rays are more efficient than rays that hit at an angle and glance off.

crops which appreciate the cooler temperatures provided there. Some of these would be cabbage, broccoli, and true spinach. Very quick-growing vegetables, like radishes and leaf lettuce, can be planted in a row that spans sun and shade. The shade should help slow the growth at one end and provide an extended harvest without the bother of planting twice.

Slope
Level land will be easy to till, but if your land has a slight grade, a south slope is best. Any slope will provide drainage, but a south slope will have the additional advantage of good sun exposure, and will most likely not be in a frost pocket. Air is like water; cold air tends to flow downhill. The top of a slope may have higher temperatures and less frost (or less severe frost). Even when they get as many total hours of sun, north slopes are cooler. This is due, again, to the slant at which the sun's rays arrive, or strike the ground. Direct rays are more efficient than slanting rays that hit at an angle and glance off.

Terracing
If your slope is so steep as to threaten erosion with the first heavy rain, you may want to

bench terrace. Virgil Severns, retired Agricultural Extension Agent, suggests a minimum of 20 foot wide terraces which may need to be made with heavy equipment, but which will have the advantage of being easily worked with machine tools.

Narrower terraces, for hand cultivation, can be built by hand or rear-tine tiller. Begin at the top of a hill, flattening the top edge by loosening the soil and spreading it level for about three to four feet. Skip six or eight inches on the downhill side, and repeat for the next bench.

Cover the outer six to eight inches of a ledge with the dirt to help level it, but do not till. If

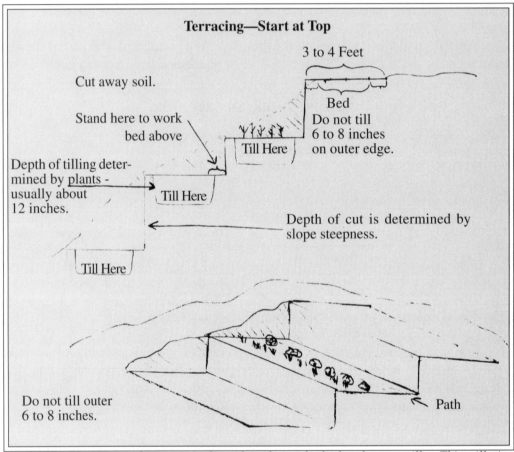

For hand cultivation, make terraces about three feet wide, by hand or rototiller. This will give you six inches for a drainage ditch, a 24 inch wide bed, and six inches of untilled hillside to prevent crumbling at the edges.

edges are loosened, terraces may break up and wash away. To cultivate by hand, walk on the inner edge of the terrace below, which can be scooped out a bit for drainage.

It is possible to till a five-foot width to allow for small machine cultivation, but you would then be growing in subsoil because you would be cutting the inner edge of a terrace more deeply into the hill. A photograph showing terracing can be found in Chapter 11, as well as alternate directions for building them.

Soil Types

The area you choose may have more than one type of soil. For information on soil types typical of Alaska, see Chapter 3. Investigate a proposed site to determine what soil types there are to work with. Once a location is chosen, do a soil test.

Soil test kits are available in most gardening supply stores, or through the mail. Or, if a soil test with fertilizer recommendations is preferred, have the soil tested by the Alaska Cooperative Extension (ACE). Your request and $20 will bring complete instructions for preparing a sample. Addresses will be found in Appendix C. See Chapter 3 for more details on soil testing and Chapter 4 for fertilizer information.

Make soil tests in the fall, if possible. Results from ACE may take three to five weeks during the spring rush, which can hold up planting for those who test in the spring. Once the fertility of the soil is known as well as the types of soil structures present, one can plan better how to utilize areas of a garden; for example, planting carrots in the sandy area, potatoes in the section with the low pH.

Fall is also a good time to improve soil by digging in compost, manure, or peat. If lime is added in the fall, however, protect it from erosion by raking it in. This will also increase its reaction with the soil.

Making Your Plan

Don't guess a plot's size; actually measure it. Draw it on paper, preferably graph paper, showing any little jogs or odd-shaped corners. A scale of one inch per foot of garden is a useful size. Indicate sun direction, prevailing wind direction, shade from buildings, trees, etc. Some vegetables, like cole crops, are more tolerant than others; some even prefer the coolness provided by shade.

If there was a garden there before, keep in mind previous plant locations. Some disease and insect pest problems may be lessened by crop rotations (growing certain vegetables in different parts of the garden each year.) See more information about this in Chapter 8.

Crop Rotation

According to Mr. Severns, crop rotation is "probably not nearly as important as in many places Outside." In other states, rotation is practiced mainly for insect and disease control. Certain pests and diseases attack particular plant groups, and may be discouraged when they discover their favorite plants have been moved. Except for root maggots and potato scab, there is little need to rotate crops here for disease or insect control.

On the other hand, shallow rooted crops may never make use of more than the top few inches of soil. Root crops use up nutrients from deeper down. Some plants (like corn) are very heavy feeders; some (like peas) return benefits to the soil. So crop rotation is practiced in many Alaska gardens simply to obtain the most value from the soil.

To determine a useful crop rotation, it may be wise to mentally, or even on paper, divide the garden plot into smaller subplots. Some growing areas you might plan for are these:

1. Perennials:

These include asparagus, rhubarb, and berries. This area you will want to dig deep and enrich well, as it will not be disturbed again. This area will not figure into a rotation plan, except perhaps when tilling in a strawberry bed to start fresh. Do not plan on raised beds for perennials north of the Alaska Range.

2. Legumes:

An example would be peas. Legumes enrich the soil, and are light feeders themselves, so would be a good choice to precede the heavy feeders. Note: Even in Alaska, there is some transfer of the fixed nitrogen from legumes (and other plants that form nitrogen-fixing nodules) to surrounding plants. According to Michele Hébert, Land Resources Agent for the ACE, to get optimum enrichment, the legumes should be tilled back into soil as green manure. For more information on nitrogen fixation in Alaska, as well as a short list of non-legume nitrogen fixers, see Chapter 4, **Nitrogen**.

3. Heavy Feeders:

Celery, onions, leeks, tomatoes, squash, and corn are heavy feeders. The last three are best grown through plastic. This area should receive the fullest enrichment, and would therefore be first in your rotation.

4. Second-Heavy Feeders:

These include brassicas, greens, turnips, kohlrabi, and radishes. These could follow heavy feeders.

5. Root crops:

Here we are speaking of root crops except potatoes, and those mentioned already. These should not be in soil that is freshly manured. They could follow legumes or heavy feeders, because they derive nutrients from a different zone than do leafy plants.

6. Potatoes:

Potatoes will tolerate a more acid soil, so will do well where many other vegetables would fail, such as too close to trees, or in newly cleared ground. Because of their acid preference, the ground should not be limed. Even though manure is on the acid side, do not add fresh manure, as it may encourage scab in potatoes.

By fertilizing heavily and improving the soil each year where group three plants will be, and by rotating crops, a gardener can more evenly utilize his garden's space, without too large an expenditure of time or money at one time.

Irrigation

Unless you live in one of the wetter areas of Alaska, now is the time to choose an irrigation method: sprinkler, surface irrigation, or subsurface irrigation. Probably the majority of gardens in the Interior are watered with sprinklers where accessible to running water and by hand-carried buckets where not. The main objection to sprinklers seems to be the problems that arise when soil-born disease organisms are splashed onto the leaves of plants such as bush beans.

On the other hand, the cooling effects of water on leaves may temporarily benefit some plants that might otherwise bolt to seed in very hot weather. Another use for sprinklers is seen when an unexpected cold snap in the night leaves a garden white with frost. The plants can sometimes be saved if wet with a fine spray continuously until the sun melts the frost on the leaves.

But the main reason the experts recommend sprinklers in the Interior is due to the cold well water. When the air is warm, it is able to warm the cold drops of water considerably before they reach the plants.

Surface irrigation may involve ditching between the rows, or actually lowering the row itself. The latter method is not recommended in any area with excessive rainfall. In rainy areas, the ditches will more likely be looked upon as drainage ditches to divert water away from plants.

ACE photo by Don Quarberg

These tomato plants were caught by a hard frost when outside temperatures dropped to 19° F.

Cold water temperature is not the only problem with surface irrigation systems. The decision to surface irrigate on a slope may affect the direction of rows. If the rows go across the slope, surface irrigation may wash gullies in the rows; if with the slope, it may cause erosion. One possible solution is to angle rows from the upper corner to the opposite lower corner. If water tends to collect at the bottom of a slope, it is there that one may want to plant water-loving plants, like rhubarb, to benefit from the runoff.

There are numerous types of surface irrigation systems available commercially, ranging from soaker hose through which water seeps continuously, to double-wall types, to expensive hoses with tiny individual tubes directed to each plant. The double-wall type is recommended over a plain soaker hose, due to more even water distribution. The latter tends to distribute too much volume close to the source, with less farther down the line. Be sure to read in Chapter 10 about the improved turbulent flow hoses. Drip irrigation systems are sometimes installed on the surface of the ground, and sometimes covered lightly with soil, when they perhaps should be called subsurface irrigation

Subsurface Irrigation

Subsurface irrigation could involve underground pipes and emitters, or be as simple as earthenware flowerpots (or punctured coffee cans) sunk in the ground next to single plants. Be sure to move flowerpots inside for the winter, or water in them will freeze and break the pot.

With both subsurface irrigation, and surface irrigation, investigate the possibility of warming the water somewhat before it reaches the plant roots. Pumping water into a barrel for the sun to warm before pumping or hauling it to the garden may be one solution. See Chapter 10 for a discussion on using solar-warmed water to warm cold soil, and also for information on irrigation under plastic mulch. Included in that same chapter is a discussion of the types of irrigation tubings available. Many are obtainable in kit form from local garden supply centers.

This picture of a drip irrigation hose shows the emitter where the water dribbles out. If the hose is buried in the soil, emitters should usually be on top. There are many types of drip irrigation systems available. Some others are discussed in Chapter 10.

Deciding What to Grow

Before you can decide how much of what to plant, there are a few questions that should be answered:

1. *What kind of garden do I want: flower, herb, or vegetable?*
If you want to eat your garden and have it too, consider planting flowers in the vegetable garden. Many herbs lend themselves well to companion planting. See Appendix A for a companion planting guide.

2. *How serious do I want to get about gardening?*
Some vegetables, like cool-weather cabbages and broccoli, require less work than others. Eggplant really should be blacked out every night to force fruit to set, (see Chapter 12) and melons may require the extra expense of a greenhouse. A small garden can be cared for by hand, but a large one may be difficult without more expensive cultivating equipment, or free labor from family members.

3. *How much of each vegetable do I need for my family, and how much will I need to plant to obtain that amount?*
The planting guide in Appendix A may help you answer this question. It is taken from ACE publication, *16 Easy Steps to Gardening in Alaska* (#300G-00134). Notice the

chart also includes usual spacing recommendations needed to plan rows. Spacing guides sometimes tend to run a little wide. If soil is in very good condition and full of humus and organic matter, it will be possible to plant closer without detriment. Just be sure to leave room for the mature size of plants at their final thinned distances.

This is a good time to send off for seed catalogs; some take six weeks to arrive, then it may be six more before an order is filled. Some addresses can be found in Appendix A. Those planning for next year's garden during this year's growing season will find many seeds available locally. It is important to select short season (early maturing) varieties—see Chapter 12 for more information on selecting seed for northern climates.

While waiting for the catalogs, use the answers to the preceding questions to help decide what vegetables to grow. One way to pick vegetables is to start with two lists: the musts and the maybes. The former list will include plants that you will find room for no matter what; the latter can be fit in as space permits. Grow only vegetables your family likes or are willing to try. Better to start small with a few well-liked vegetables, than to plant everything, tend the garden all summer, and then have to throw half away when your family refuses to eat it.

Check the spacing guide to determine how close to plant, then draw labeled rows on the plan. Some other factors to be considered in spacing rows are conventional vs. wide-row planting, flat vs. raised rows, and hand vs. machine cultivating.

Conventional and Wide-Row Planting

Conventional planting calls for single rows of vegetables with paths between. While some gardeners find single rows easier to weed, the method does result in a considerable portion of the garden being devoted to paths.

Wide-row planting is an attempt to get around this; several rows are planted with plant spacing between each row instead of row spacing. This allows for higher productivity in the same size garden. With some crops, there are many more plants; as much as six times more per square foot in a wide row than in a single row. Paths can be the same width as usual, but there are fewer of them.

Time and effort are saved, too. When seeding, it is not necessary to space as exactly as in a single row. The first thinning (see specifics later) can be done quickly from a standing position. So many more plants at a time can be reached that you can weed or harvest the equivalent of up to 15 feet of a single row without moving.

Competition is lessened and growth facilitated. Vegetables growing closely in a wide row act as a living mulch, shading out competing weeds, and also help maintain moisture in the soil. Temperature and moisture conditions are more constant than in single rows.

Wide-row planting also helps protect plant roots. Foot traffic on paths tends to compact soil and harm roots of bordering single rows. In wide planting, most of the plants are not next to paths, so are not disturbed.

Still, wide-row planting is not for everyone. For one thing, there will seem to be a lot more hand weeding in the rows (at least in the beginning) because machine cultivators cannot be used. A combination of both methods, planting some single rows and some wide rows, may be more practical. Large or spreading plants, like rhubarb or giant cabbages, might as well be in single rows because of the wide spacing required between plants anyway. Fenced peas are always grown in single or double rows.

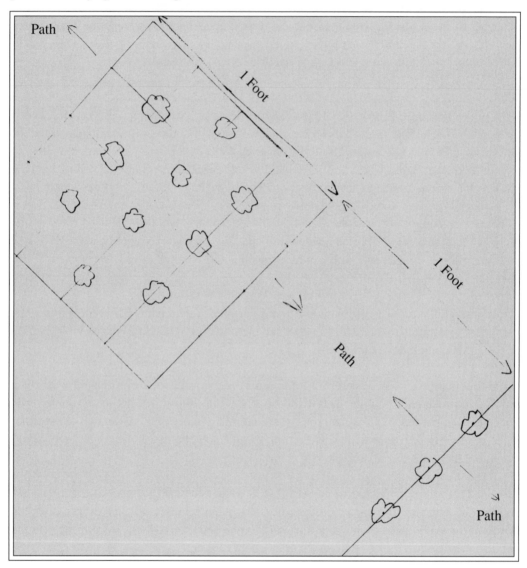

Diagram to illustrate the difference between single and wide row.

If wide-row planting is chosen, here are the steps that might be followed:

    1. Mark the wide row with stakes and string. If planning a row the width of a rake, only one edge will need to be marked with string.

    2. Drag the rake the length of the row, holding one edge of it next to the string. Iron

rakes are about 14 to 16 inches wide, which is a good width for a wide row. To make it wider, run the rake down the row again to double the width. Whatever width you decide on, you should be able to reach easily to the center from each side.

3. Broadcast seeds evenly. Onion sets and garlic cloves can be pushed into the soil with a finger. Transplants are set as usual, but set them apart in all directions the distance recommended within the row, not the distance given for between rows. Example: cabbages would be 18 to 24 inches apart. Set them in staggered formation, two plants across the row, then one plant in the middle of the row 18 inches further down the row, two more 18 inches beyond, and so on. See the planting guide in Appendix A for the specific distances recommended for each vegetable.

4. Firm the seeds into the soil with a hand or the back of a rake or hoe.

5. Rake soil over them from the side of the row, leveling the seedbed as you go. Generally, cover seed to a depth of two or three times their diameter. Small seeds should be barely covered.

6. Firm the soil again gently and sprinkle. Keep the seedbed moist until germination.

7. The first thinning can be done with a rake when the seeds are only $1/4$ to 1 inch tall. Pull the rake gently across the row, letting the

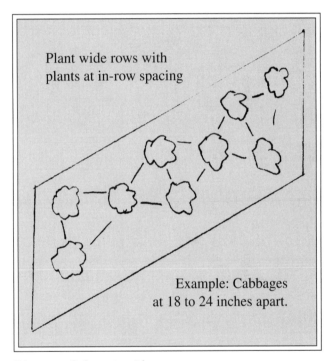

Plant wide rows with plants at in-row spacing

Example: Cabbages at 18 to 24 inches apart.

Diagram of plants in wide row.

teeth sink into the soil about $1/4$ inch. This will not only thin the seedlings, but will also be the first cultivation and weeding of the row. Exceptions to this thinning: beans, peas, sets, and transplants. Being larger, these can be planted more nearly with proper spacing.

8. Later thinnings by hand can be done while weeding, and the thinnings eaten. Thin plants gradually over the weeks to stand apart in the wide row the distance in all directions they usually stand in single rows. A note of warning: a common mistake gardeners make the first time they try wide rows is to over plant. The equivalent of a 20-foot row will fit into four feet if you are thinning to five plants deep.

Raised-Row Planting

If you garden in Southeastern Alaska, with its heavy rainfall, you will probably seriously consider raised rows. If so, do think about making them wide rows, too. Made wide, the edges are less likely to crumble into the paths and not as many raised rows will be needed. Raised rows are also an excellent planting technique for annual vegetables in the rest of Alaska, as they make a definite difference in the soil temperature. This is a consideration that becomes increasingly important the farther north one gardens.

Raised rows can be temporary—tilled in when the season is over and re-mounded the next season. Re-mounding in the fall will hasten drying and warming the following spring and perhaps speed up planting time.

Raised beds are recommended for carrots. Not only is the bed warmer, but the looser, deeper soil allows the roots room to grow thick and straight.

Raised rows can also be permanent raised beds, boxed in with two-by-fours or even railway ties. If this option is chosen, fertilizer will be spread only in the beds, thus saving money by not fertilizing the paths. However, you may have to dig the fertilizer in by hand, unless your beds are wide enough to accommodate a tiller. Step-by-step directions for making raised beds will be found in Chapter 11, because they are so well adapted to solving the problems of the wet weather gardener. If used north of the Alaska Range, raised beds should never be planted with perennials (see Chapter 13).

Cultivation

If a small garden is planned, you can probably get by with hand weeding and enjoy it. But if a very large garden is planned, consider machine cultivation. While a push-type cultivator may do, some will want to rent or buy a rototiller. Each spring the newspaper ads are full of people offering tilling services. If using a tilling service, look for one with a rear-tine tiller with a furrowing attachment. As explained in Chapter 11, this can be a great help in making raised beds.

Owning a tiller will enable you to plant rows far enough apart to use the tiller for cultivating between rows. If so, wide rows are doubly important, as the wide paths will cut down on growing space. See Chapter 9 for more ideas on weeding.

ACE staff

This garden in Eagle, Alaska uses temporary raised beds to warm the soil.

Completing the Plan

In using the planting guide for spacing, use half the between-row distance indicated for the first row at the edge of the garden. When changing to a vegetable with another spacing, use ¹/₂ the wider spacing. For example, celery is listed at 24 inches between rows, and carrots at 18. Leave 12 inches (¹/₂ the wider spacing of celery) between the rows of celery and carrots. If the celery is planted at the edge of the garden, it will be 12 inches from the edge. If carrots go there, they will be 9 inches from the garden border. An exception would be made by those planning to keep a rototiller swath around the garden to discourage encroaching weeds and grass.

A final note on laying out your rows. You have already considered shade from buildings

Boxed-in permanent raised beds make up this garden on the Chena River.

ACE staff

This rototiller has been used for weeding between the rows.

ACE staff

Mary Armstrong, a bedding plant grower in Delta, is careful to plant rows of short plants where they will not be shaded by taller ones.

and trees. Now, consider shade from plants themselves. If corn rows, for example, run east/west, they may shade the next few plant rows to the north.

Selecting Your Seed

The last step in planning concerns the actual variety selection, which can be made when seed catalogs arrive. There are a few plants that probably will not grow well in certain parts of Alaska, for various reasons.

For example, the short season and long days of the Interior preclude growing soybeans. Eggplant is marginal for the same reason, although new varieties are being tested which may not be as sensitive to light. See Chapter 12 for more specifics on the effects of this long-day phenomenon, photoperiodism. Popcorn needs a longer season than it can get in most of Alaska. Early planting inside can overcome long-season requirements for many plants, which is why you should be doing this preliminary planning months in advance of planting. Starting plants ahead is covered in Chapter 5.

Many problems can be sidestepped by planting varieties that have been tested for Alaska. Appendix B lists recommended varieties for Southcentral, Interior, and Southeastern Alaska. These lists are revised and updated every year or two and can be obtained from ACE.

Most varieties recommended (some actually developed in our state) are carried within Alaska by local garden centers and variety stores. Other companies with more national distribution are carrying more of the recommended varieties each year. Be sure to read Chapter 12 for more information on variety selections, and plan to grow short season crops.

Chapter 3

Assessing Your Soil

... some seeds ... fell upon stony places
... and because they had no root,
they withered away. Matthew 13: 4-6, KJV.

After you have decided to have a garden and made up your mind what you want to plant, the next step is to take a good look at the soil and see what needs to be done to improve your chances of success. This is a process that would have to be gone through anywhere in the world, but in the far north, there will almost certainly be one or more unique problems to contend with. Over much, but not all of Alaska, the first of them will be permafrost.

Permafrost

Permafrost is ground that remains frozen all summer. Although many people living in more southerly regions have never heard of it, it is not at all uncommon. In fact, it has been estimated permafrost underlies one fifth of the world's land surface. It is a potential problem for gardeners in most of Alaska, much of Canada, and even in some parts of the northwestern continental United States.

In Alaska, permafrost occurs as a continuous sheet north of the Brooks Range, extending from a few inches below the surface down to as deep as 1,000 feet. As one goes south, however, it gets progressively thinner, the melted layer on top gets thicker, and holes or gaps begin to appear in it.

In Interior and Western Alaska, the permafrost is often less than 100 feet thick and the thawed layer on top may be as much as several feet in depth. It may be completely absent in places, particularly on the sun-warmed southern slopes of hills and along the inner sides of riverbeds.

One homesteader in the Fairbanks area found permafrost beginning 35 feet down. His neighbor a few miles away had to drill his well through 90 feet of permafrost. When the neighbor later sold his home and rebuilt 500 feet away, he encountered no permafrost whatsoever.

Farther south, in Southcentral and Southeastern Alaska, permafrost occurs only sporadically, in isolated and often widely separated masses. In the Panhandle and along the Aleutian Chain, and on other islands, it is usually completely absent, but may occur in any region in which the average annual temperature is freezing or below. Of course, average temperature means just that. Summer temperatures may be quite high—90° to 100°F. in Interior Alaska, for example—as long as the winters are long enough or cold enough to bring the average down.

The key factor to look for in a known area of discontinuous or sporadic permafrost is insulation of the ground surface—something that can keep the ground from thawing out completely during the summer. Sphagnum or peat moss is the most efficient insulator, usually helped out by heavy spruce woods or thick underbrush. Often a good indicator of frozen ground is surface moisture. A boggy or swampy surface is almost a sure sign that the ground is too frozen to permit drainage.

The good news is that if the surface insulation can be removed or cleared away, the permafrost can then melt down to a level which will permit good natural drainage and which will

Prof. Tom Osterkamp, ret.

This now abandoned house was damaged when heat from the house entered the ground through the floor, melting the underlying permafrost. Because the excess ice in the permafrost was not distributed evenly, the house twisted and buckled as it settled. Less damage was sustained by the unheated carport.

cause no problems. Of course, this may take a couple of years, but the result could be excellent garden soil. Much of the Agricultural Experiment Station land in Fairbanks is underlain by permafrost which by the early 1980s had melted down to 16 feet and which has caused no trouble for many years.

On the other hand, it is sometimes better, on poorly-drained soils, to avoid thawing the permafrost at all. The solution here would be raised beds. See Chapter 10 for details.

It is important to note there is nothing wrong with moss as such. In fact, in the right place (broken up and thoroughly mixed with the soil) it may be just what a garden needs. Just do not allow it to form an insulating mat on the surface. If ground is frozen hard, it may be necessary to scrape the moss off to one side and allow soil to thaw for a year or two before putting it back and spading it in or rototilling it under.

Ground Ice

Of particular importance in the north is the ground ice often found in permafrost. Of different origins, there are about five types of ground ice, but what is important to know is that the ground can hold more ice than it can unfrozen water. When the ice melts it causes the ground to sink. This can result in deep pits and hummocks.

About $1/4$ of the Fairbanks area, for example, is underlain with permafrost with large ground ice masses, and some fields show pits and heaves. This heaving is not seen as often on the actual flood plain, since coarse-grained sediments without ground ice are there.

When Chena Hot Springs Road was rebuilt and straightened some years ago, the contractor was unaccustomed to working with permafrost. According to Dr. V.E. Romanovsky of the Geophysical Institute, they dug down deep, but ending up laying fabric (used to hold the road together) directly on ice. The fabric was covered with sand and gravel and finally asphalt, but the damage had been done. Since the ice had been exposed to the warmth of summer, the permafrost began melting, and of course, the road began dipping in places, while deep sinkholes formed in others.

Even though frozen ground may exist three feet below the surface after clearing and extend two or three hundred feet down, except for roadways, there will normally be few settling problems. But permafrost does cause other problems for gardeners—cold soil and poor drainage being the most critical. These problems are covered in more detail in Chapters 10 and 11, respectively.

Soil Types

In general, Alaska's major soil for gardening purposes is a very fine-textured silt. The silt tends to be thicker in valleys and on lower slopes. It is blown in by wind, and has been found piled as high as 100 feet. Subsequent rain causes holes (like pouring a cup of water into a glass of fluffy talcum powder), which in turn form "pipes" for many feet down. Most soils here lack active clay material, and most certainly lack fertility.

Much of Alaska does not even have much silt, having instead one of the following:

• **tundra;** (there are several types) most often seen as hummocky treeless peat covered with wild flowers and lichens and usually underlain with permafrost;

• **bog**; muskeg with thick peat over soil so wet it may quiver when stamped on;

• **half bog**; a thinner layer of peat over water-mineral soup which can, however, support trees; or

• **rock**; as in the Ketchikan area, where you may have to import much of your garden soil.

In Southcentral, the silt is underlain mostly by a gravely layer, which can mean constant rock picking for the gardener. Many gardeners in Anchorage have solved the problem by building growing boxes and having them filled with good screened topsoil. A word of caution for buyers of topsoil—be sure you are not just buying a truckload of silt, or pure peat.

In the Interior, the silt will more likely be on a layer of very sandy soil, in which case it may be best to condition it with the addition of peat until time can be found in which to build it up with plant residues, compost, and manure.

As low as Alaska is on clay, there are still those who have heavy clay soils, which turn to mud in the spring and delay planting. Gardeners who have clay soils can take heart in the fact that clay is potentially the richest of all soils, once the food locked up in it is released. Be careful to leave it alone, unless it is just right for tillage. Walking on it when it is wet, or

This garden was planted in native soil with no fertilizer.

tilling too soon, can pack it down and ruin what aeration and texture it has. Do not work it either when it is so dry the surface is cracked.

Lee Risse, a commercial greenhouse operator in Fairbanks, maintains that people are too eager to get into their gardens in the spring. If you try to work your soil too soon, you will only succeed in balling it up. He suggests you squeeze a handful of soil. If it forms a ball (which then falls apart when dropped), it is probably ready to work. The soil is too wet if, when you open your hand, it stays in a ball with clear indentations from your fingers.

Heavy Clay Soils

When your clay soil is right for working, do everything possible to break it down to enable roots to better penetrate it. If, as are most Alaska soils, your clay soil is too acid, the addition of lime can also improve its texture. The calcium in the lime helps small clay particles clump together into crumbs or granules. The larger the soil particles, the more air spaces in the soil. Other good additions are horse manure, preferably strawy, or really well-decayed material— the latter because there is often too little air in clay for it to rot down satisfactorily.

Clay soil compacts tightly and holds water. An addition of sand may help to drain moisture, which should help warm up the soil. Peat can also be added, but remember that peat holds water too, and water will tend to keep the soil cooler. Double digging, explained later, may also be helpful.

While attempting to improve a tight soil, avoid growing small-root crops in it, such as

ACE staff

These sickly brassicas, shown one month after planting, suffer from a severe nutrient shortage.

carrots, which may become malformed. Very strong roots, like Jerusalem artichokes, may help break it up. Most kinds of greens are recommended for clay soils.

Light Sandy Soils

This type of soil needs building up instead of breaking down; stabilizing, not disturbing. Most sandy soils dry out quickly, become dusty in hot weather, blow away, and are always hungry. On the other hand, they are easy to work, well drained and aerated, and will warm up earlier in the spring.

Sandy soil will eat up an immense amount of semi-decayed material; half matured compost or sappy green stuff. If the plot has perennial weeds, it can be double dug well at the start. Bulky material spread in the bottom of the trenches when double digging will help hold the soil together. (See directions for this procedure later in this chapter.) Once dug, it is better to give top dressings only, as anything put in soil moves quickly downward. If placed too deeply, fertilizers may be washed away from the roots. Manure, compost, leaf mold, or other organic material left on the surface will build up a more stable topsoil, gradually working itself in where roots can make use of it.

Light soils can make full use of the colder types of manure (cow and pig). Green manuring is also good (see Chapter 4). This kind of soil should not be left too long without a crop of some kind on it, or fertilized too far in advance of sowing or planting. Root crops do well in light soil.

Silt Loam Soils

As mentioned before, most Alaska gardening soil is a fine-textured glacial silt. It tends to be low in organic matter, have poor soil structure, and pack when wet. Its thickness varies from very thick in river valleys, to just an inch or two in some areas. If it is present, it can be improved with the addition of organic matter. Where it is too thin, as in much of Southcentral Alaska, where it is often just a thin layer over sandy gravel; or in much of Southeastern Alaska, where it can be a thin layer over rock, other arrangements may have to be made to provide workable soil. Good soil can be brought in and dumped on the garden.

In Southeast, because of steep slopes and erosion problems, make provisions to keep soil from washing away in heavy rains. One way to do this is with permanent raised beds, described more fully in Chapter 11.

Other Thin Soil Types

Many areas of Alaska have more peat or muskeg than silt. Gardeners in these areas again may find it more profitable to import their soil. Peat has little or no nutrient value. It is widely used to improve soil structure, however, and will help a light soil retain moisture. Beware of using too much peat moss in your soil mixture, because of its lack of fertility. Because peat is acid (peat in the Tanana Valley has tested a pH of 5 to 5.5), you will probably need to add lime as well.

Double Digging

All soil types can be improved by double digging, or trenching, a technique that will loosen tightly packed soils, allow additions of organic material in sandy soils and silt loams, and provide an opportunity to remove perennial weeds, large rocks, and gravel pieces to replace with other materials. In general, the process involves removing the top layers, breaking up the subsoil with a spading fork, and then replacing the top layer, so as not to bury any topsoil.

Remember, if you only dig, and do not incorporate amendments into the soil, the soil that all that work has made more friable may well settle back again, more solid than it was before being disturbed. If the only object is to stir up the ground to make the soil easier to plant, a rototiller is what is needed, and is certainly recommended for very large gardens. But if you wish to improve soil in a small area, double digging a little at a time may be the best way to do it.

The tools needed for double digging are simple—a shovel or spade is all, and a pitchfork is nice to have, but optional. For marking a plot, you may want string and stakes.

Renee Lozier lays out rows with string in the Alaska Cooperative Extension's Demonstration Garden. Also helping are Master Gardeners Carol Lovejoy, Julie Hedgecoke, and Darlene Dupont.

Master Gardeners, Darlene Dupont, Julie Hedgecoke, Michele Hébert, and Renee Lozier move dirt onto plastic at the Tanana Valley Fairgrounds.

Begin by laying out a plot, and marking it down the center, dividing it into two equal sections. At the end of one half, put in four stakes to mark the extent of one trench (any width you want, but usually about 18 inches or the width of the bed if you are making permanent beds).

Fork over the soil, removing weeds, roots, and rocks. Then with a spade, move loose earth from this first trench on to the ground (or sheet of plastic) next to (but not covering) the adjoining section in the other half of the plot. Keep the spade vertical and take only thin slices of soil (not more than three or four inches thick). This will make digging quicker and easier.

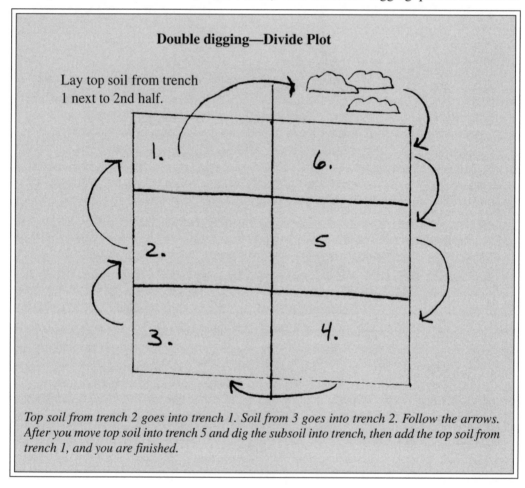

Top soil from trench 2 goes into trench 1. Soil from 3 goes into trench 2. Follow the arrows. After you move top soil into trench 5 and dig the subsoil into trench, then add the top soil from trench 1, and you are finished.

Continue forking and spading, always pulling out every scrap of weed root as you go. When all earth is loosened and removed for the depth of the spade, you will probably have reached the subsoil, which is harder and dryer than the soil just shifted. Loosen this well, to the same depth again, pulling out roots, but do not remove subsoil from the trench. If you have plenty of time, leave the trench exposed to weather for a day or two before continuing.

The first trench is the hardest, because you have to move the topsoil the farthest. For the rest, move the soil forward into the empty trench. As you dig, work in manure or some other organic material (see Chapter 4 for ideas); deeply in a clay soil, nearer the surface for a light one. At the end of the first half, move to the second section, taking out the first-trench material and moving it into the vacant trench and so back again down the second section until the initial heap of earth is reached, which goes into the last trench.

If you find a lot of old bricks, glass, or large stones in the topsoil, you can use them for the foundation of a permanent path. If the path runs through the plot, increase the length of the trench to include the path area and throw the stony material onto it as you dig. Of course, do not do this if paths will be temporary, and you plan to rototill next year. If the plot borders on a weedy area or lawn, the path will act as a barrier between creeping roots and cultivated ground. Later you can roll a surface of ashes or chippings into it.

There is less reason to dig deeply into the subsoil in Alaska, since the coldness of the soil in ground-level beds will keep most plant roots from reaching very far down anyway. For deeply rooted plants, and especially ones like carrots, piling up soil in raised beds will supply the room needed for the deep roots, and if done right, these beds will be warm enough to encourage longer roots. See Chapter 11 for more information on raised beds.

Ed Bostrom makes gardening easier by using a rear tine rototiller. Attachments are available to extend the usefulness of rototillers even further.

It is very important to enrich the top six inches of soil in any way possible, due to its natural infertility and poor structure. For this reason, when rototilling compost and organic additions into it, you may wish to check to see that the tiller is set for shallow digging, so you do not inter good organic materials. A rear-tine rototiller can greatly ease initial soil digging and enriching, as well as later weeding. Attachments such as furrowers can extend their usefulness even more.

All About Soil pH

Soil acidity is measured with a pH scale, reading from 0.0, very acid (sour) to 14, very alkaline (sweet). Neutral, with soil neither acid nor alkaline, is 7. Note that scales included with home test kits seldom include the rare extremes and, in fact, may use a color matching scale instead of specific numbers.

Since pH is a logarithmic function, a pH of six is ten times more acid than 7, and a five is a hundred times more acid than a 7. Most Alaska soils range from a pH of 3.5 to 8, with the higher numbers being much more infrequent.

The acidity of the soil plays an important part in determining fertility. In other words, no matter how much fertilizer is applied, the plants may still starve. Very acid or very alkaline soil will tie up nutrients out of reach of the hungry plants. If present in soil, all elements needed by plants can be utilized at a pH between 6 and 7. All macronutrients (nitrogen, phosphorus, potassium, sulfur, calcium, and magnesium) have reduced availability in acid (low pH) soils, and some of the micronutrients and nonessential elements such as aluminum can become toxic to plants. Conversely, high pH can lower availability of some macronutrients and such micronutrients as boron, zinc, copper, manganese, and iron.

An example of this is seen with the very important nutrient, phosphorus. As the soil pH drops, and nears five, phosphorus begins to be locked up by combining with aluminum and iron in the soil. A similar effect occurs at a pH above 7.2, this time in combination with calcium.

Soil with too low a pH can be corrected with the addition of lime. Lime improves gardens in other ways as well. Besides neutralizing soil acidity, and unlocking nutrients, it aids nitrogen fixation (see Chapter 4), improves soil structure of clay, and helps soil organisms which break down organic matter (again, see Chapter 4). If dolomite limestone is used, both calcium and magnesium will be supplied to the soil. Chapter 4 explains how to raise or lower the soil pH for best growing conditions, and describes the various types of liming materials available.

But before attempting to alter soil pH, you need to know more about the soil. Too much lime can be as damaging as too little, and excess lime can be very difficult to remove. One way to find out more about a particular soil is to take a soil test.

Soil tests can be taken with a home kit, sold in most garden supply stores and commercial nurseries. Directions are included with the kits. These usually test for the three major nutrients; N (nitrogen), P (phosphorus), K (potassium), and for soil pH. Various meters are also available, including some for moisture and light.

A more accurate test can be obtained from a testing service. Many land-grant colleges (the University of Alaska Fairbanks is one) have soil testing programs of some type. Alaska's is in Palmer at the UAF Agricultural Experiment Station Soils Laboratory.

The soil-testing program is educational in nature, providing information on selecting the correct fertilizer, amounts of fertilizer and lime needed, and the best times to apply them. For $20, the Palmer Plant and Soil Analysis Laboratory will analyze your soil for nutrients and determine the pH. The Alaska Cooperative Extension Service then makes interpretations of this information as well as recommendations.

An additional note about pH levels: the Palmer laboratory actually conducts two tests for pH; one for water pH, which indicates the soil pH, and one for buffer pH. This latter test tells how much lime is needed to raise the pH to the optimum level. A standard soil test then will include pH, lime requirement, N, P, and K. By special request, levels of organic matter, soil

Michele Hébert

These leaves demonstrate the toxicity of the micronutrient, boron.

texture, trace elements, and tissue analysis for major and trace elements can be obtained.

Greenhouse owners should be aware of the special greenhouse test that includes a test for soluble salts that can build up to toxic levels in greenhouses. For more information on what is available, and prices, contact the Palmer Plant and Soils Laboratory (address in Appendix C).

Taking a Soil Sample
In order for a testing service to do a good job, the home gardener must first take an accurate sample. Improper sampling will give misleading test results, and lead to inaccurate recommendations. A separate soil sample must be taken from each different area. For example, separate samples from the garden, the flowerbed, the lawn, and the greenhouse will be required. In addition, a large garden or lawn area may contain different soil types or condi-

tions. There may be low spots, sandy areas, various slopes, etc. Because of the variation, separate samples for each unique soil condition should be considered. In the case of small gardens or flowerbeds, this would not be necessary.

The Alaska Cooperative Extension suggests a garden sample be made up of at least five sub-samples from various parts of the garden, with 15 to 20 sub-samples from a ten-acre field. They also advise not sampling soon after a lime, fertilizer, or manure application, or when soil is excessively wet, snow covered, or frozen.

Collecting the Sub-Sample

Tools needed for sampling are a spade, a clean plastic pail, a knife (or trowel), and a paper bag. Avoid metal pails, as the metal may react with the damp soil and throw the results off.

Taking Soil samples.

Remove sides, leaving a 1 inch strip.

Make a V trench, slice 1 inch thick.

Dig a V-shaped hole 5 or 6 inches deep. If you do not sample deeply enough, you risk getting a sample of the organic duff that is breaking down on the surface, which is often more acidic than the soil at six inches. If you dig much deeper, you may be testing soil your plant roots will not even reach.

Take a one-inch slice from one side of the hole. Trim the sides of the slice, leaving a one-inch strip on the spade. Slide this strip into the pail. Repeat the procedure over the area to be sampled. Using your hands, break up clods in the pail and mix well. A stick or wooden spoon might be better, but again, avoid metal implements that might alter the results.

Remove about two cups of mixed soil from the pail and put it into a paper bag, labeling the bag to show where it came from. The rest of the soil should be discarded. Do this for each separate area to be tested, mixing sub-samples in your pail and transferring them to a separate labeled paper bag. It is a good idea to draw a little map of your garden showing where samples came from for future reference.

Drying the Samples

All samples should be air dried right away. Storing damp samples (even for only the few days before they are actually tested) can cause the results to be inaccurate. To air dry, spread each two-cup sample separately on clean newspapers about $^1/_4$ inch deep. Avoid handling the sample more than necessary. Do not apply artificial heat of any kind. A fan may be used to help dry the sample, but heat from an oven, stove or furnace can alter the results. Return the sample to the bag, and write your name on it.

If you have sent for (or picked up) the soil test packet from your Cooperative Extension Office (#SGV00044), it will include the paper bag and full instructions. It will also include a *Soil Sample Information Sheet* (#SGV0044A) to fill out for each sample. The information asked about the sample is very important. The more you can supply about a particular soil sample, the more accurate and complete will be the recommendations that come back.

Some information that may be included: past fertilizing, liming or manuring history, what grew there previously, and whether the area is intended for lawn or vegetables.

In some cases, what **kind** of vegetable may be important. For example, potatoes may develop scab if limed as for other vegetables. You will find a number in the upper right corner of the information sheet, which should also appear on the bag to help identify the sample.

Mailing the Sample

At the time of this writing, the fee per sample for the standard test was $20, which is less than the actual cost of testing. To order the kit, enclose $20 in the form of a check payable to the Alaska Cooperative Extension. After receiving the kit and taking your sample, mail both directly to Palmer (address is in Appendix C).

Chapter 4

Improving Your Soil

But other (seeds) fell into good ground,
and brought forth fruit ... Matthew 13:8a, KJV.

Anyone can tell you plants need sunlight, warmth, and water, but good fertile soil is every bit as important. Alaska's soils are generally classified as infertile, and much of the research done over the years by agricultural scientists in the state has been directed toward improving this condition.

Alaska's soils are hard to categorize because there are so many variations over such a wide region. Factors such as organic content, acidification, moisture range, and temperature play a part in determining how a particular soil will react to a particular level of fertilization. For example, a fertilizer that would make the soil in Ketchikan fertile might have very little effect on the soil in Nome. Then, too, there is usually a time lag before soil test results reflect fertilizer and lime applications.

According to Paul F. Martin, retired Research Soil Scientist in Palmer, "Application of 10 or more pounds of phosphate per acre may change the soil test value for available phosphate only one pound per acre." This is because the rest of the added phosphate is locked up in insoluble compounds (see Chapter 3). Crops vary in their food requirements and their ability to obtain these elements from the soil, so what is good for one crop may not be so for another.

The availability of one nutrient is often dependent upon another. An excess of one can alter the balance and produce a deficiency of another. In tests made in Delta in the summer of 1980, it was shown rather dramatically that high rates of phosphorus or nitrogen are wasted unless applied in combination. Or to put it another way, "a chain is only as strong as its weakest link."

As mentioned in Chapter 3, soil pH is a big factor in determining the availability of nutrients, so it should perhaps be considered first.

Changing Soil pH

Assuming a soil test has indicated a specific soil pH, consider crops planned and their preferences. Fortunately, while each type of plant has a preference for a certain pH, most also have a rather wide range in which they do well and give profitable yields. This sometimes leads to confusion in reading tables of recommended pH values—they may differ widely and yet be true. But rather than working for a single precise ideal pH for an entire garden, which may be unattainable, it may be better to know in general what is in different areas of the garden and to select plants for those areas accordingly.

Dr. George Allen Mitchell, a soil scientist and Assistant Professor of Agronomy in Palmer, reports that he sees many cases of over liming, due to gardeners attempting to raise their soil pH to a neutral 7. According to him, this is not desirable for most crops, and he advises a pH range of 6 to 6.5, slightly acid. If part of a garden is more acid than this, one may want

Virgil D. Severns

In a vivid reminder of Alaska's lack of soil fertility, this photograph shows an uneven application of fertilizer on a field of grain.

to put acid-loving plants in those areas rather than try to raise the pH and perhaps be faced with an opposite problem with other plants.

Vegetables for this acid area might include berries, peppers, eggplant, radishes, and potatoes. The potato is an example of a plant that will grow well in a very wide range of pH, but which is usually grown in more acid soil because scab diseases seem less of a problem with a pH of 5 to 5.4. Gardeners may wish to use the above plants in a rotation so this area will never be over limed, and the other garden areas can be limed to suit other vegetables.

As can be seen from the soil pH chart (Appendix A), there are some vegetables that may need more lime. Again, these can make up their own rotation to avoid having to plant an acid-lover where ground has been well limed.

Most of Alaska's soils are too acid, and several things contribute to making and keeping them that way. Ground near alder, spruce, and birch trees will be acid (due to acid leaf litter), as will newly cleared areas. Adding peat to improve soil texture will make soil acid. The same thing applies to adding leaves. Adding certain fertilizers will also increase the acidity of your soil (see **Nitrogen** later in this chapter). The point of all this is, some lime will very likely need to be added, just do not overdo. Get an occasional soil test to check up on the soil's progress. It is not easy to lower soil pH once it has been over limed.

Choosing a Lime Source

The chief sources of lime are limestone (rock) and shell deposits. Both consist largely of calcium compounds. Although calcium itself is an essential element for the growth of many plants, actual requirements are not great. The chief reason for the use of lime is control of soil pH. The hydrogen and aluminum in the soil make the soil acid. The calcium neutralizes excess acids, thereby raising the pH.

Natural ground rocks include limestone (usually about 90% pure), and dolomite lime, which provides magnesium along with its calcium. Neither leave harmful residues in the soil and they give long-lasting benefits, but are slow acting. Ground limestone is graded by particle size, and the percentage of each size is printed on the label. The smaller the particle size, the faster it will react to raise the pH.

The Alaska Cooperative Extension, University of Alaska Fairbanks (ACE) recommends wood ashes be used as a supplement. Wood ashes vary with their origin (type of tree), but, in general, they contain 45% calcium carbonate lime equivalent, as well as 5% to 10% potassium. Do not store wood ashes exposed to the weather, or much of their nutrient value will be lost through leaching. Too thick a surface application is not advised; ashes become quite sticky when wet.

There are limestone deposits in Alaska, but they are, as yet, undeveloped. Unfortunately, most of them are on lands withdrawn for parks, so may never be developed. In the meantime, the freight cost for shipping limestone in from outside Alaska far exceeds the original cost of the lime.

Hydrated lime (slaked lime), and quicklime (burned lime) are faster acting but may burn seed or seedlings, so are not recommended for already planted gardens. Some think these latter also destroy soil bacteria. If hydrated lime is used, multiply by five instead of 7 in the formula given later for determining how much to use.

Tests were conducted on processed crab waste from Kodiak. The conclusions were that this calcium carbonate-chitin material has value as a liming agent, and would be of help on the strongly acid soils of Kodiak, but that relatively large amounts would be needed for effective pH change. The most effective rates tested were four or five tons per acre.

Marl (shellfish deposit) is available in Southcentral for liming. There is a large deposit located in Palmer.

Raising pH

There have been several formulas given to determine how much lime is needed to raise pH by one unit. If a testing service tested your soil, they probably made recommendations for you. If not, here is one formula: if using dolomite lime, subtract the actual pH from what you want the pH to be, multiply the result by 7, and the answer is the approximate number of pounds of dolomite lime needed for 100 square feet of garden, or one cubic yard of potting soil. In other words, it takes seven pounds of dolomite per 100 square feet to raise pH by one unit. The liming effect should last about three years. If the soil is very acidic, however, it is not wise to add all the lime needed in one season, as a sudden increase in lime may result in a temporary over lime situation until the lime reacts.

Several factors influence the amount of lime needed. Silt and clay soils of the same pH will need more lime than sandy or light soils. More organic matter also increases the amount of lime needed. High rainfall, as in Southeast, tends to leach lime and more frequent applications will be needed.

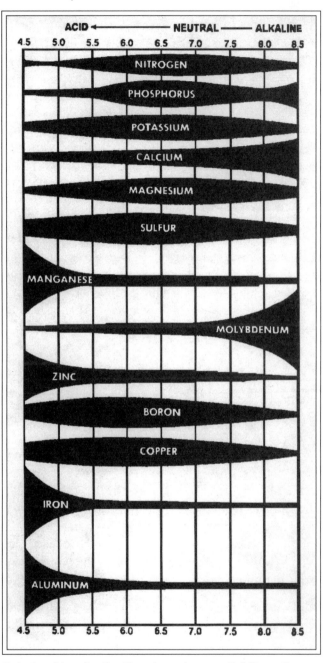

Relationship of soil pH and nutrient availability - Source, Schulte, E.E. and K.A. Kelling. 1984. Aglime, Key to Increased Yields and Profits. University of Wisconsin, Cooperative Extension Service Publication #A2240, 1984.

Lowering pH

It is well to keep in mind that not all soils in Alaska need lime. There are several soils in central and northern Alaska that are alkaline. For example, soils near Wiseman and Prudhoe Bay have tested above 8. To lower pH a little, add peat or use cotton-seed meal for fertilizer. To lower it a lot, over too large an area to totally replace the soil, elemental sulfur can be applied. Sulfur is a caustic chemical, so get help from an ACE Agent; do not try to apply it alone.

A fairly recent publication, *Soil Fertility Basics* (#FGV-00242A) by J. L. Walworth, former soil scientist with the Palmer Research Center, includes a chart of optimum crop soil pH ranges. This chart was combined with a chart he published in *Field Crop fertilizer Recommendations for Alaska, Vegetables* (#FGV-00643) and included in Appendix A.

Plant Nutrients

About 16 elements needed by plants have been identified. It is possible there are other trace elements we do not know about yet. Of those identified, air and water supply three, and the rest must be supplied by soil. Alaska's soils are generally low in the three major soil nutrients; nitrogen (N), phosphorus (P), and potassium (K), also called potash.

Nitrogen

Under natural conditions, animal droppings and fallen leaves supply nitrogen, although leaves may actually cause nitrogen depletion at first because some kinds have a very low nitrogen content, and the organisms involved in decomposition need to use all the nitrogen they can get just to carry out the process of decomposition. Eventually, of course, the nitrogen contained in leaves will be released and be available to plants, although it may take several weeks or even months.

Free nitrogen is present in large amounts in the atmosphere, but cannot be utilized as such by most garden plants. It must first be combined chemically with oxygen to form nitrates or with hydrogen to form ammonia. This can be done inorganically by electric discharges. A surprising amount is fixed (converted to usable form) by lightning flashes in thunderstorms and carried into the soil by rain.

More important to gardeners, many bacteria have the ability to fix atmospheric nitrogen. Certain plants, especially legumes such as peas, beans, vetch, alfalfa, clover, and others have formed mutually useful alliances with some of these bacteria. The bacteria live in small nodules on the roots of the host plants and, in return for their housing and other considerations, generate enough usable nitrogen to supply both themselves and the host plants. Not only do legumes (provided the proper bacteria are present) require very little nitrogen fertilizer for their own growth, but also (when they die and are spaded under) they release their stored-up nitrogen for the use of other plants.

Non-Legumes

Most legumes do this work, but some non-legumes do so, also. Among the non-legumes that fix nitrogen are species of alder, *Shepherdia* (soapberry), *Elaeagnus commutata* (silverberry), and *Myrica gale* (bog myrtle or sweet gale), which are native to Alaska. Proof of the nitrogen-fixing powers of alders can often be seen in the darker green, more luxuriant growth of grasses growing close to them. Nitrogen from the leaves of stands of alder can average 50 to 100 pounds per acre per year. However, one would hardly want an alder in the middle of the garden, so it might be wiser to investigate the legumes.

Using Legumes

For a long time, many garden experts believed that legumes could not fix atmospheric nitrogen in Alaska, due to cold soil and short seasons. This perception was encouraged by the fact that many gardeners in Alaska have never seen nodules on any of their legumes. But research conducted on Alaska Agricultural and Forestry Experiment Station Research Farms at Fairbanks and near Delta Junction by Dr. Stephen D. Sparrow, Verlan L. Cochran and Dr. Elena B. Sparrow, has proven the experts wrong.

According to an abstract published in *Agronomy Journal* in 1995, "Results of this study indicate that the potential for N_2 fixation by introduced forage legumes in subarctic climates is high, despite relatively short growing seasons and low soil temperatures."

What may be even more exciting to Alaskan gardeners is another finding; "Amounts of N_2 fixed by red clover, sweetclover, pea, lentil, and white lupin, especially at Fairbanks in this study, were similar to or higher than typical values reported for these species in temperate climates."

A word of caution: the amount of nitrogen fixed by legumes in gardens is dependent in part on the type of legume, soil pH, effectiveness of the bacteria, nitrogen content of the soil, and available phosphorus and potassium in the soil, according to L. J. Klebesadel, Research Agronomist with the United States Department of Agriculture in Palmer, Alaska.

The most common garden legumes are peas and beans. They leave the soil richer in nitrogen than before they were grown and their roots should always be left in the ground when the crop is harvested. It is definitely a good idea to chop up the vines and incorporate them into the soil as well. Some gardeners practice a crop rotation to take advantage of the enrichment, growing corn or another heavy feeder in the space occupied the year before by peas.

Legume Inoculation

The nitrogen fixing power of legumes can be enhanced by supplying the plants with the appropriate bacteria. While the Alaska study discussed earlier found very little benefit from inoculation with bacteria on the Fairbanks plots, there was a significant difference noted at the Delta plots. The study concluded that the Fairbanks plots did not derive much benefit mainly because "both pulse and forage legumes had been grown at Fairbanks for many years prior to this study, and rhizobia populations in the soil were apparently high enough to provide good nodulation and N_2 fixation for most of the legume crops." Nevertheless, Dr. Stephen Sparrow advises Alaskan gardeners, whether in Fairbanks or not, to always inoculate their legumes "because it is cheap and is good insurance."

When purchasing inoculant, be sure to get the one specified for a particular crop. Commercially available, Rhizobium bacterial inoculant is recommended for adding to pea and bean seed at planting time (the non-legumes listed in the earlier section titled **Non-Legumes** utilize different bacteria, such as *Frankia* for alders). Usually, the procedure is to dampen the seed, then sprinkle the inoculant and stir to coat evenly. There is also a granular type available, which is simply poured in the planting trench after the seeds are sown.

For those growing grains in Alaska, inoculated Canadian field peas nodulate well here. The small-grain crop grown with it has also been shown to benefit from the peas' nitrogen fixation. But, as Dr. S. Sparrow says, "The real benefit comes when the N-fixing plant dies and the N is released from its tissues due to decomposition. Therefore, at least in Alaska, the benefit to non-nitrogen fixing plants comes in the year or two following the N-fixing plants."

As for why the typical Alaskan gardener does not see nodules, it is probably because the typical Alaskan gardener employs a fertilization program that removes any need for the legume to make its own nitrogen. The test plots in the research study were fertilized with potassium and phosphorus, not nitrogen.

Nitrogen Cautions

It is possible to have too much nitrogen, especially when applying high-nitrogen chemical fertilizers. Excess nitrogen causes plants to make very lush, sappy growth with an unnatural dark green color. If used on beets, for example, the result will be beautiful greens and infinitesimal beets. To use up excess nitrates quickly, grow leafy crops that need plenty of nitrogen.

Another problem associated with nitrogen is the possibility of increasing soil acidity with it. When ammonium forms of nitrogen are added to soil, they become nitrates that drop the pH of the soil. Within limits, the higher the rate of fertilization, the lower the pH goes. Urea forms of nitrogen go to ammonia first, then to nitrates. The problem can be avoided by adding nitrogen in the form of calcium nitrates, or potassium nitrates, both of which, unfortunately, are more expensive. When applying nitrogen, be sure to water it in well.

Nitrogen is a most difficult nutrient to test for, because it is so easily lost, and because it can be added by the weather or decomposition of organic matter in the soil. The amount a soil test indicates is present in the fall may be very different from the amount present in the spring.

Phosphorus

Phosphorus is important for strong root systems. It is also said to hurry maturity, increase fruit development, and increase vitamin content of plants. Unfortunately, phosphorus is probably the nutrient most lacking in Alaska's soils. For years, the Agricultural Experiment Station in Fairbanks has been recommending fertilizers with a higher P number than N. They have also recommended that some of the P be in a water-soluble form, or as triplesuperphosphate. On the basis of tests conducted during the years 1959 through 1961, they now recommend that the fertilizer not contain nitric phosphates. The tests included soil in the Kenai Peninsula, and the Matanuska and Tanana Valleys. In nearly every case, 10-30-10 fertilizer was shown superior to fertilizers with equal N and P numbers, and fertilizers with nitric phosphates proved inferior to those without.

A dramatic example was a test involving lettuce grown in the Tanana Valley that yielded 3.6 times more without nitric phosphates than did lettuce grown with them. The Research

Soil Scientists involved, Dr. Winston M. Laughlin and Paul F. Martin, believed that "the poor results obtained with fertilizers containing nitric phosphates may be related to their low water solubility since many Alaska soils are extremely low in phosphorus. In addition, many soils have the capacity of fixing phosphorus applied as fertilizer. Thus these results indicate that fertilizers should be selected that are relatively high in P and those containing nitric phosphates should be avoided."

Phosphorus "fixing" is different from nitrogen "fixing" by bacteria. In the latter case, the bacteria fix, or convert, free atmospheric nitrogen and make it more available to plants. Soils that fix phosphorus, on the other hand, tie up phosphorus so plants cannot use it. It is now suspected that, in some Alaska soils, phosphorus fixation may be due to the presence of allophane, which is a component of many volcanic soils. Samples of the following soils

These broccoli leaves show a deficiency of phosphorus.

showed relatively high levels of phosphorus fixation: Simeonof Island, Talkeetna, Homer, Willow, and older soil in Kodiak. Relatively low in P fixation were samples from Fairbanks, and a soil sample of a very recent ash fall on Kodiak Island. Soil scientists Dr. George A. Mitchell and Dr. Jay D. McKendrick surmise that "it may be that either weathering or accumulations of organic matter contribute significantly to the phosphorus fixation capacity of volcanic ash."

Potassium

The third major nutrient supplied by the soil is potassium (potash). It is needed for strong stems and to help fight diseases. It is said to improve the keeping quality of fruit, decrease water and boron requirements for plants, and aid plants in utilizing nitrogen.

It has been found that the more soluble potash there is in the soil, the more the plants will take up. Overeating potash will keep the plant from taking up other elements it needs.

If plants are grown organically, a mixture of organic potash sources: plant residues, wood ashes, manure and compost for quick short-term potash; and mineral rock powders (rock potash, granite dust, greensand, or basalt rock) will provide for slower long-term release. As with rock phosphate, an acid soil may help with this release.

Over 35 years ago, commercial potato growers in Alaska faced a near wipeout of their crops. Scientists at the Agricultural Experiment Station spent over 10 years on the mystery. It was finally solved—a potash deficiency. They came to these three conclusions:

1. At least 200 pounds of potash (expressed as K_2O) per acre should be applied for potatoes at planting time.

2. When enough potassium is not available in the soil, spraying the leaves with Sulfate of potash, or muriate of potash, can help.

3. Sulfate of potash is superior to muriate of potash.

AMOUNTS OF NITROGEN PHOSPHOROUS AND POTASH IN ORGANIC FERTILIZERS*

Organic fertilizer	Lbs/100 lbs Nitrogen (N)	Dry Organic Phosphorous (P_2O_2)	Material Potash (K_2O)
Seaweed	1.3	1.0	5.0
Wood ashes**	0.0	1.3	8.0
Starfish	5.0	8.0	2.0
Peat moss	3.0	0.0	2.0
Horse manure	0.6	0.2	0.5
Chicken manure	1.6	1.3	0.5
Sawdust	0.0	0.0	1.0
Cooked fish scraps	8.0	13.0	4.0
Salmon meal	10.0	3.0	4.0
Crab meal	6.0	2.0	2.0
Bone meal	4.0	24.0	0.0

*Secondary and minor elements are also available from these materials, such as calcium (Ca), magnesium (Mg), sulphur (SO), iron (Fe), manganese (Mg), boron (BO), molybodenum (MoO), copper(Cu), zinc (Zn), and chlorine (CI). These are often lacking in Alaska soils.
**A more important function of ashes is their liming effect.

From Gardening in Southeastern Alaska (#HGA-00237) by former Southeastern Alaska district Extension agent, Kathy Jelesky McLeod, adapted in 1971 by Alan C. Epps, Extension Horticulturist.

Organic gardeners may wish to consult the table on the left, from ACE's' publication *Gardening in Southeastern Alaska* (#HGA-00237).

Three other elements are required by plants in relatively large amounts: calcium, magnesium, and sulfur. These may be deficient in certain soils in Alaska.

Calcium and Magnesium
Calcium and magnesium are alkaline, and can be added easily by using dolomite lime. The two need to be balanced, as an excess of one will lead to reduced intake of the other.

Sulfur
Elemental sulfur is acid forming and is often used to lower pH. As discussed earlier, a few

soils in Alaska have been found to be slightly alkaline. Sulfur can help correct over-liming problems, but as mentioned before, is a rather caustic chemical and somewhat difficult to apply. Consult with your local ACE office.

In addition, there are seven micronutrients that are essential to good plant growth: boron, chlorine, copper, iron, manganese, molybdenum, and zinc. Of the seven, deficiencies have not been found in Alaska so far with chlorine, copper, or zinc .

An earlier ACE bulletin on fertilizers (#P-33) noted that "EXTREME CARE must be used when applying micronutrients to guarantee against over-application. Even small amounts may be toxic. Some water sources in the state contain sufficient amounts of boron to be toxic to certain plants. If in doubt, contact your Extension Agent."

Chemical vs. Organic

It is not the purpose of this book to advocate one type of fertilizing program over another. It is only to present information on fertilizers that are available in Alaska, and to indicate the recommendations of the experts. It is assumed the readers are intelligent enough to make up their own minds about what they want for their gardens. This understood, then, here are the definitions on which this chapter is based:

This tomato's blossom end rot was caused by a calcium deficiency.

Chemical Fertilizer: A fertilizer that is a combination of a natural earth product and a strong acid, i.e., processed chemically. (Example: Superphosphate is 50% rock phosphate and 50% sulfuric acid.)

Organic Fertilizer: A fertilizer that is made of plant and/or animal residues, either fresh or having accumulated and been preserved over a long period of time. (Examples: leaf mold, marl, peat, manure, etc.) ACE has an excellent flyer for organic gardeners titled *Make Your Own Complete Fertilizer*, (#HGA-00131).

Natural Fertilizer: A fertilizer that consists of a natural earth product which may have been processed mechanically, but which is not treated with acids or other substances to increase its solubility. (Example: finely ground rock phosphate.)

In this book, for the purposes of simplification, natural fertilizers have been lumped together under the term organic fertilizers.

Chemical Fertilizers

The most commonly available commercial fertilizers are labeled with the percentage of the three major soil elements, N, P, and K, in that order. For example, a bag labeled 8-32-16 contains 8% nitrogen, 32% phosphorus, and 16% potassium. If it is a hundred-pound bag, this will mean it will have 8 pounds N, 32 pounds P_2O_5, and 16 pounds K_2O.

Fertilizers with high percentages of these elements are better buys because there is less filler being shipped from the manufacturer. Fertilizers with all three elements are called complete fertilizers. It has been recommended that the numbers total at least 40% to avoid spending money on too much filler.

Alaska's soils need a high phosphorus fertilizer, as mentioned before. This means the second number should be highest. Often used is 8-32-16, or 10-20-10. MagAmp fertilizer, recommended for many years by the late Mann Leiser of Alaska Greenhouses, Inc. (in Anchorage) analyzed 7-40-6 plus 12% magnesium. Unfortunately, the 50 pound bags gradually became so expensive, that production stopped in 1997. According to his son Wayne, who owns and operates Dimond Greenhouses, MagAmp was not a water-soluble fertilizer and was slowly released by bacteria in the soil (lasting outdoors for three growing seasons), so he recommended it for organic gardeners even though it was a commercially produced fertilizer.

ACE staff

Heavy rainfall areas should have the fertilizer application divided in two—half to be applied during seedbed preparation or transplanting, and the other half for later in the season. This will help prevent all nutrients from being leached away before the end of the growing season. On raised rows (without plastic), apply only to the top of the rows, for the same reason. It will leach down soon enough.

This squash leaf gives silent proof of too much boron (boron toxicity).

Organic Fertilizers

It should be remembered that when adding any fresh organic matter to soil, the effect will be a temporary loss of plant fertility. The soil microorganisms that break down organic matter use soil nutrients themselves, making the plants wait until the bacteria break down in turn.

In general, organic matter that has at least 1.5% nitrogen has enough to take care of its own decomposition. Those with less will need additional nitrogen added when composted or when tilled under.

Care must be taken to maintain proper soil pH when adding organic matter. Most organic material will be slightly acidic, but wood ashes test at a pH of around 9 or 10, bone meal 10, and some manures about 8.

Manure

Manure is the oldest and most common fertilizer in much of Alaska. If manure is used exclusively, 20 tons will be needed per acre, which is roughly 10 pounds per 100 square feet, or one pound per square foot. This may seem like a lot, but remember that fresh manure is quite heavy. ACE's *16 Easy Steps to Gardening*, advises a minimum application of ¹/₂ pound per square foot, with four times that amount for a newly cleared sandy site. Do not, however, use any manure on soil that will be planted to potatoes within the next two years, as it can encourage potato scab.

In Southeast, because of already wet soils, manure should not be applied in large quantities. This is because of the great water-holding ability of manure and bedding, and because of the tie-up of nutrients while it is decomposing. But a little is better than none, for, as well as providing plant food and organic matter, it acts like an inoculant and stimulant to the soil microorganisms.

ACE suggests composting the manure first, adding small amounts of well-composted material to the soil at a time, and adding inorganic (chemical) fertilizer and lime when spreading the composted material.

With any manure, it is a good idea to investigate the source. Some manures may contain disinfectants used to wash down stalls. The bedding can make a difference, too. Too much sawdust added to the garden at one time can create a nutrient problem, due to its high-cellulose content and low nitrogen. Manure with sawdust bedding may better be composted for a few years first. Some manure contains weed seeds, which can be a real challenge for the gardener. Composting the manure at temperatures between 145° and 160° F is recommended for killing weed seeds and pathogens and breaking down cellulose.

Like wood ashes, manure should be stored under shelter to reduce leaching. Another way to prevent loss of nitrogen in the form of ammonia, (fermentation), is to mix 100 pounds of rock phosphate into each ton of manure while piling it up. The phosphate combines with the nitrogen to form an excellent fertilizer. There is less loss when manures are applied to the soil fresh, but with Alaska's short season, it is difficult to apply and let sit for the 8 weeks recommended before planting. In our cold soils, 8 weeks may not be enough for it to rot satisfactorily.

Appendix A contains several organic fertilizer charts that may help you. Remember, however, that how manure is stored, length of that storage, percentage of moisture, and how the manure is spread and incorporated into the soil all play a part in determining the nutrient content of that manure.

Nitrogen is the most easily lost of the primary nutrients in manure, both through volatilization of ammonia and through leaching by rainfall. About 50% of the nitrogen that is provided by the manure, however, is available to crops the first year, with the balance becoming available in subsequent seasons.

Much greater percentages of potash are available the first year than nitrogen or phosphorus. According to Dr. Charles W. Knight, Associate Professor of Agronomy at the University of Alaska Fairbanks, this is because potassium (being water soluble) does not form an organic compound, and will quickly leach out of the manure and become available to plant roots. Phosphorus (phosphate) on the other hand, forms an organic compound that must have time to decompose, so is fairly stable in manure.

Types of Manure
Cold Manures
Cow and pig manures are classified as cold manures. These ferment slowly with less chance of burning tender plant roots. Steer manure is also available dry in bags. Be sure to mix it well into the soil. Left on the surface, it can form a hard crust difficult for water to penetrate.

Hot Manures
Hot manures are sheep, chicken, rabbit, and horse. These are better dug into the soil in the fall, or composted before applying directly to the plants. Horse manure is good for heavy soils as its dry nature counteracts the wetness of clay. Uncomposted, as mentioned earlier, it will probably introduce weeds into your garden because the weed seeds go right through the horse without being digested. Horse manure is particularly notorious for spreading chickweed.

Poultry manure is the most concentrated of manures, and special care must be taken in applying it. In fact, two or three tons may be all that is needed per acre (25 to 30 pounds per square rod.) It has been estimated that 100 hens will produce four tons of droppings per year. The editors of the *Organic Gardening Magazine* advise adding two pounds of phosphate to this amount to prevent loss of nitrogen, as well as adding phosphoric acid.

Virgil Severns, when he was the Cooperative Extension Agent in Nome, cautioned against using dog or cat manure, which can be very dangerous. Tapeworms and other parasites from dog manure can infect humans. Roundworm eggs can persist in the soil for many years, and hookworm larvae from the feces of both cats and dogs cause skin sores in humans. Particularly dangerous would be root crops like carrots or potatoes grown in soil fertilized this way.

Manure Tea
For side-dressing plants (see later, this chapter), use manure tea, which is liquid manure. To make, simply fill a bucket with water, drop in some chunks of manure (a few cupfuls) and let it sit a day or two in the sun until the water is warmed and dark. It is helpful to give it a stir with a stick now and then, while it is steeping. To use, it is usually diluted with water to the color of weak tea, but there is no reason it cannot be served to the plants a little stronger. It can even be fortified with extra phosphorus by adding a capful of fish fertilizer to each bucketful. The same thing can be done with compost, for compost tea. The compost is

usually put in a burlap bag and suspended in the water, but the manure sinks to the bottom so there is little need for the bother of a separate bag to hold it. When the tea has been used, refill the bucket with water and reuse the manure—it will be good for two or three fillings, until the water no longer darkens. For a larger garden, a more convenient setup would involve adding a spigot near the bottom of a large barrel and covering the top with a piece of plastic. In this case, materials should be in a bag so as not to clog the spigot.

Other Organic Amendments

Liquid Fertilizers

In addition to such homemade concoctions as the above, there are several organic liquid fertilizers on the market. The main ones are fish fertilizer and liquid seaweed. If fish fertilizer is chosen, be sure to get a deodorized one, especially if you have pets. Some dogs will be convinced a fish has been buried for them to find, and it may become a problem keeping the garden from being excavated. Seaweed is highest in potash. Some gardeners have reported that liquid seaweed seems to improve cold-hardiness of seedlings grown indoors for transplanting.

To make manure tea, the manure can be put in the water, where it will sink to the bottom, but for compost tea, the compost is first put into a burlap bag.

Bloodmeal

Bloodmeal (ground blood from slaughterhouses) can be bought in bags from fertilizer stores. It is very high in nitrogen and, as such, should be applied sparingly. Too much on some plants will cause lush foliage at the expense of fruit. Bloodmeal is used directly in the ground or is sprinkled on the compost heap where it helps speed up decomposition. When applied to the ground, it should be mixed with the soil, as it tends to crust when wet. Insects are attracted to it when it is left sitting in opened bags. Some people mix it with water to apply.

Bone Meal

Bone meal is available in fertilizer stores in small boxes or in bulk. There are two kinds: raw, which breaks down slowly in the soil; and steamed, which breaks down faster due to the absence of fats. Steamed bone meal is very high in phosphorus. It can also help lessen acidity.

Cottonseed Meal

Also available in bags from feed and fertilizer stores, this amendment has a good nitrogen content, though not as high as bloodmeal. It has a low pH, so is recommended for acid-loving plants.

Fish Scraps

These are reported high in nitrogen and phosphorus. To keep fish from making a compost heap smell, cover with a sprinkling of soil. Fishmeals have about 10% nitrogen, with crabmeal at 6%.

Grass Clippings

These can be worked into soil or added to compost. They usually contain about 5 to 10 times as much nitrogen as phosphorus.

Greensand or Granite Dust

These natural rock powders are used to supply potash, in much the same way that rock phosphate supplies phosphorus. The major difference is that greensand does not have to be worked into the soil, but it seems to be more effective if mixed with manure and rock phosphate and turned under. The three together make a complete fertilizer. Amounts to apply are similar to rock phosphate. Unfortunately, greensand and granite dust are not always locally available in Alaska, and their heavy weight makes shipping costs prohibitive.

Leaves

Leaves are a good source of humus and minerals such as calcium and magnesium. They also contain N, P, and K; the nitrogen being as high as 5%. They can be dug in, composted, or made into leaf mold. To make leaf mold, shred (if possible), put into a container with limestone (unless using the leaf mold on acid-lovers) and keep them damp. With our short season, it is advised that gardeners start the mold in the spring and use it half done in the fall, or the amount of time it will be frozen after winter may make it take as long as three years to break down.

Leaves should not be put on the compost heap without shredding, if at all possible. Unshredded leaves lie in layers, excluding moisture and air, and decompose very slowly from the bottom up. If you do not have a shredder, leaves can be shredded with a rotary-mower, using a wall to contain the pile.

Phosphate Rock

This is a good source of phosphorus and also has many valuable trace elements such as calcium, boron, and magnesium. The great debate centers on whether it breaks down adequately in our cold soils. It is a slow-acting fertilizer, which in warmer states will last many years from one heavy application, without burning plants. The rate suggested there is 20 pounds to 100 square feet, and it is strongly recommended that it be mixed with manure and dug in. Tests in the Soviet Union some years ago showed it to be much more effective when actually mixed with manure, as opposed to spreading it separately. Some think our acid soils help in breaking down the rock, and may help counteract the cold soil temperatures. No specific research has been done for Alaska's conditions as yet, so use your own judgment.

Seaweed, Kelp

These are high in potash and trace elements. They can be washed first to remove salt, but Walt McPherson, when he was ACE Agent in Southeast, reported that there had been no problem with salt even in areas of heavy use, so he no longer recommended washing. It is possible that the heavy rains are doing the washing. In Southeast, some gardeners use seaweed as a mulch for winter protection of perennials. As a fertilizer, it is worked into the soil or composted.

Sewage

There are two types, activated (sewage with air bubbled through), which has 5% nitrogen and 3 to 6% phosphorus, and digested (sewage which has been allowed to settle over filter beds), which has about 2% nitrogen and phosphorus. Not all of the nitrogen in either will be available right away. Sludge is usually acid, but it is not known how fast it breaks down in cold soil. One advantage it has is that it has other nutrients (trace elements), but perhaps too much sulfur. If sludge high in toxic metals is accidentally applied, remember it will be less toxic at high pH's, so lime may help.

Raw sewage should never be used. Treated sludge does not seem to be dangerous, and is said to be very clean in the Fairbanks area. Virgil Severns advises that one contemplating using sludge should investigate it thoroughly—it may not be as safe on vegetables as on grains fed to animals before being consumed by humans. Dr. George Allen Mitchell, Soil Scientist, writes from Palmer that "it is unlikely that heavy metals would be a problem in any Alaska sludges. These metals come from heavy industry, which we don't have. As long as it is treated it should be safe on vegetables." Indeed, tests of sludge in the Fairbanks area in recent years have found very low levels of heavy metals.

Starfish

An excellent source of phosphorus, starfish can be composted or cut up and buried with the plants when setting out transplants. They are reported to be an excellent fertilizer to feed rhubarb .

Wood Ashes

These are alkaline, and one of their main advantages is their liming action. But they have value as a fertilizer, too, being high in potash and having some phosphorus. Ashes should not be allowed to come in contact with tender seedling roots or germinating seeds.

Fertilizer Recommendations

Specific chemical fertilizer recommendations may be obtained from ACE bulletin on fertilizers, *Soil Fertility Basics* (#FGV-00242A), and organic gardeners might want to pick up *Organic Fertilizers* (#FGV-00349) by C. L. (Johnson) Falen, former Extension Assistant at the Palmer Research Center, ACE. For organic growers, there is also the bulletin *Make Your Own Complete Fertilizer* (#HGA-00131) mentioned earlier. Do remember, however, that recommended amounts are only general guides, providing good results in the majority of Alaska's situations. Climate and soil conditions will vary and may affect the success of these amounts. For example, plants growing in full sun will need more than those growing in shade, because they are growing faster. To be really specific for a garden, a soil test is required and recommendations given based on the individual situation.

The recommended amount of chemical fertilizer for a garden for which there is no soil test available is three pounds of a complete fertilizer per 100 square feet broadcast and worked into the soil before planting.

Application Methods

There are several methods for applying fertilizers, which can be classified according to when the application occurs.

Before Planting

Broadcast fertilizer evenly over the entire garden, then rake it in or till shallowly. This method is often used for large fields, or for manure applications. Remember that while fertilizers are generally put as deep as 12 inches in warmer climates, our cold soils dictate that fertilizer be dug in no deeper than about six inches. To broadcast dry fertilizers, toss handfuls (or use a trowel) on the ground, trying for even coverage. For very large areas, a push-type spreader may be used. If so, delay tilling until after, so the spreader wheels do not sink in the loosened soil.

During the Planting

Another way, which will use less fertilizer, is to spread the fertilizer only in the seed row or planting hole, mixing it with dirt so the fertilizer will not come in contact with the seeds. Usually, it is best to be sure the fertilizer is a bit below the seed. In rows, a furrow one-inch deeper than the planting furrow can be made about $1/2$ to 1 inch away from the seed furrow. This is sometimes called "banding." A band of fertilizer can be put around larger individual plants when setting them out.

After Planting

Fertilizer applied later in a growing season is said to be "side-dressed." Dry fertilizers can be spread a few inches from the row or around individual plants, either banded in a furrow, or worked lightly into the soil. Side-dressings with dry fertilizer should always be watered well to make the nutrients available to the plant. When watering in the fertilizer, wash off any that may have gotten on the plant. Chemical fertilizers can be very caustic and burn enough to kill the plant entirely. Organic fertilizers are easy to side-dress in liquid form and are not likely to burn the plants. Liquid fertilizer, chemical or organic, can be applied with a "dip" which hooks into the watering system and releases measured amounts automatically when watering. See Chapter 5 for a photograph of a Master Gardener using a dip.

Green Manures

Green manuring means to grow a crop and then turn it under the soil to decompose, instead of harvesting it to eat. If the purpose is to add nitrogen to the soil, grow a legume. If the purpose is to add humus, grow some type of grass. Buckwheat (and most other green manure crops) should be cut before setting seed, or introduction of a new weed into the garden may occur. Annual rye grass is often used as a green manure crop because it grows fast and will not survive the winter even when not cut in time. Many grasses can be mown several times during the summer (at perhaps six to eight inches) before they are turned under, adding more organic material each time. Cuttings can be left on the soil, or added to the compost heap. In areas where winter erosion is a problem, the crop (called a cover crop in this instance) can be left to hold the soil until spring.

The main problem with green manures is, in order to grow them, part of the garden must be

Ann Rippy, Conservation Agronomist with USDA, Natural Resources Conservation Service works with Deborah Koons, of the Fairbanks Soil & Water Conservation District, filling a wire fencing compost bin at the Demonstration Garden at the Tanana Valley Fair grounds.

out of production. If planning to try a green manure crop, consult your local ACE Agent about the best varieties for your area. Dr. Dinkel warns that there may be a problem any time a cover crop or organic amendments such as leaves or plant residues are tilled in. He suggests adding some chemical fertilizer to help the addition break down quicker and to replace nitrogen tied up in decomposition.

Composting in Alaska

Decomposition of organic materials needs bacterial and fungal action in a warm, moist place. Breakdown of materials here can occur slowly because of cool air and soil temperatures, if precautions are not taken. In the Interior, where there is summer warmth, but not ideal moisture, it can take as long as three years unless you select a sunny site, mix the right amount of water and materials, control particle size, and turn weekly (or even daily if you are using Ed Bostrom's method).

Aerobic composting (turning the pile to incorporate oxygen) is faster and preferable to anaerobic composting, which means the materials are breaking down very slowly in the absence of oxygen.

Compost

ACE staff

An empty greenhouse often does double duty, holding the compost pile during the winter months.

Compost is decomposed plant and animal residues, perhaps with a little soil. It is useful for soils with low organic matter. It provides better aeration, root penetration, water infiltration, and increased water-holding capability in sandy soils. It also reduces crusting of the soil surface. It contains nutrients, but the kind and amount will vary, depending on what was put in and how much loss has occurred through leaching and evaporation. Compost tea, similar to manure tea, is one way to use your compost.

The Compost Enclosure
The enclosure used for compost will vary according to where in the state you live, or more accurately, the precipitation of your area. It will also be determined in part by whether you plan to overwinter your compost and continue making the same load in the spring, or whether you plan to start it in the spring and spread it on your garden half-finished, if necessary, in

This is not a picture of hot manure. (right) The rising steam reveals how hot compost can become when properly made, even when it consists of only grass and brome hay.

Ed Bostrom

ACE staff

A temperature (left) of 145° to 160°F in the center of the pile will kill most weed seeds and reduce or eliminate pests and pathogens.

ACE staff

Gary Koy (right) turns a compost pile in the Denali National Park. He was participating in a federal grant with the Natural Resources Conservation Service to study the feasibility of composting dog wastes.

the fall or spring of the following year. One can, of course, skip the enclosure altogether, and pile materials up in a heap, but a covered enclosure will keep it from spreading all over the yard, while reducing moisture loss and leaching.

For overwintering a compost heap, closed containers like cement enclosures or tight wooden boxes are not a good idea. The liquid at the bottom will become a solid block of ice that may not even thaw completely in summer. In any case, if the bottom of the box has drainage, take a tip from Pam Young, a gardener in Fairbanks, and rig it to drain into a container. This compost tea can then be used as a liquid fertilizer.

In Southeast, and perhaps even Southcentral, you can probably use a slatted open box, or a chicken wire enclosure with good results. However, if you live in one of the dryer areas, like the Interior, it would be a mistake to use an open-type box. Rainfall is so sparse in the Interior it is important to conserve all moisture possible, unless you plan to be continually hosing down the compost. Four tight boxes with removable fronts are what the late Eloise DeWitt of Fairbanks used. Commercial greenhouse operators often use an empty greenhouse to compost during the winter months.

Building the Compost Pile

The pile should consist of layers of uniform thickness. For cold climates like ours, a maximum width of four feet is recommended. The height should be a minimum of three feet. The bottom layer should be coarse material like old stalks and big weeds, and be about six inches deep. Subsequent layers might include three inches of manure, shredded leaves, or grass clippings. Kelp will also do, but if it is dried kelp, additional moisture will be needed. The real trick to a hot compost heap, maintained Mrs. DeWitt, is "a lot of manure and a lot of green stuff."

Build sides and ends a little higher than the center, to form a saucer on top to help hold the water. This will be especially important in the Interior, and may not be so desirable in Southeast. Now wet the pile well. Use warm (not hot) water if possible; it may increase the initial bacterial action, especially in more Arctic regions.

The temperature of a compost pile is a very important indicator of microbial activity. Temperatures of 145° to 160° F in the center of the pile will kill most weed seeds and reduce or eliminate pests and pathogens. An inexpensive, long stemmed compost thermometer can be purchased at most gardening stores.

The best covering for the heap in Alaska is clear or milky plastic, which allows the sun to warm the heap and helps to retain that heat. With the plastic covering, moisture levels are kept more constant and evaporation is prevented (for the Interior) and rainfall shed (for Southeast).

ACE used to recommend leaving the covered heap for 10 weeks, then forking it over and placing the edge materials in the center of the new heap. They are now recommending, for aerobic composting, the pile be forked over for the first time in two or three weeks, and then every five to eight days in Southeast, and every 7-10 days elsewhere in Alaska. The top is then dished as before. They also suggest sprinkling a little extra fertilizer through the heap as it is re-piled. Most of the following summer may be needed to finish the compost, so it is a good idea to start a new one each year to have a continuous supply.

Eloise DeWitt did not attempt to overwinter her compost. By the end of the summer it had broken down enough to apply to the garden, but she let it stay in the boxes until the following spring. She removed the fronts in the spring to let the compost thaw. It was ready by June 1 to fertilize her transplants as she set them out.

Leaves and other garden refuse she had collected for the next year's pile was spread on the ground to keep down weeds. By spreading it out, she eliminated the problem of finding her pile of leaves frozen in the middle when she was ready to begin composting in the spring. She raked up the loose leaves, tossed them into her shredder, and then into the bin. She had nearly finished compost in one summer, even though she did not

Numerous mounds of compost, in varying stages of decomposition, dot Ed Bostrom's fields.

turn the pile at all (she did "cheat" a little with her earthworms, discussed later in this chapter). Energetic gardeners who want to turn their piles should be able to speed up the process considerably.

Using Compost

Compost is removed from the bottom of the pile first. If you wish, you can screen the compost through a coarse one-inch screen to use as potting soil or in seed flats, and return the larger material to the pile. Rub the compost as you screen it, and most will go through. The finished compost can be used for a mulch, a soil amendment, potting soil, a seed starting mix, or to make compost tea.

What to Compost

Organic materials such as sod, grass clippings, leaves, weeds, manures, sawdust, shredded newspapers, wood ashes, twigs, hedge trimmings, and garden plant residues are all good compost materials. Lots of wood ashes can be used, but remember they will raise the pH level of your compost. Layers of ashes should be no more than three inches thick. The calcium in wood ashes aids in decomposition .

Avoid diseased and insect-ridden plants in case the decomposition is not complete. There is also the chance weed seeds will not all be destroyed. Steer clear of invasive weeds such as quackgrass. Garbage can be added, but avoid grease, fat, meat scraps, plastic wraps, and bones. Fats are slow to break down, and meat can attract dogs or develop unwelcome odors.

Do not use any unchopped woody waste, or pet feces. It is possible to compost dog manure, but there are very specific rules to follow, and you are urged to contact the Fairbanks Field Office of the USDA Natural Resources Conservation Service (telephone (907) 479-2657) for more information and free help in designing a compost system to meet your specific needs.

It is well to remember that the more surfaces the bacteria can work on, the faster will be the decomposition. Hence, you should chop as much as possible before adding to the heap. A shredder is one way to go, but a lawn mower will do a good job of chopping up soft things like leaves, as mentioned earlier, if done against a wall or other obstacle.

Ed Bostrom

Dale Hulsey turns a compost pile to incorporate oxygen and speed the decomposition.

For compost made without the plastic covering in an area with a lot of rainfall, you may need to lay poles across while building the pile. Remove them when the pile is all stacked up, and the resulting holes will provide the air that decomposition needs.

High-Speed Farm-Scale Composting

Ed Bostrom, of North Pole Acres, is the acknowledged composting expert in Alaska. In fact, he received a grant from the Alaska Science and Technology Program to experiment and develop a composting program that would produce high quality, weed-free compost in the shortest time possible. His method involves daily mixing or turning of the compost, but produces finished compost in 14 to 21 days.

Ed Bostrom

North Pole Acres (left) participates in a grant program to develop a composting method which produces high quality, weed-free compost in the shortest time possible.

First spoiled (right) brome hay is put down in long windrows.

High nitrogen grass (left) is added to the hay mounds.

The grass (right) and hay are mixed by machine. Here a tedder rake does the job.

Ed Bostrom

Ed Bostrom (above) found that a rotovator did a better job of mixing the hay and grass.

The long mixed mounds (above) are heaped into high piles with the help of a tractor.

Dale Hulsey (above) drenches the new pile. It is very important to wet the compost thoroughly.

The stick (left) in each pile provides a handy place to keep track of the date it was built, and each day it is turned.

Large -scale composters (right) will want to turn their piles by machine.

Regina Cambilargiu (below) uses the shredder in the final step in composting at North Pole Acres.

Ed Bostrom

Ed Bostrom

ACE staff

Finished compost can be used as a soil amendment, mulch, or screened for a seed starting mix, or potting soil.

The method he developed is meant for large-scale operations, though it would be easy to adapt for smaller endeavors. For all composting, four ingredients are needed:

1. Carbon
2. Nitrogen
3. Water
4. Oxygen

Mr. Bostrom's system begins with collecting and laying out brome hay in long windrows. The moldy or weedy hay not fit for sale is the carbon source.

Next, grass that has been mown and collected in plastic garbage bags is dumped and spread out over the hay. In Ed's case, the grass used is well fertilized, so it is particularly high in nitrogen and is the source of the second ingredient for good compost.

On this farm-size operation, the grass and hay are mixed by machine. A tedder rake pulled by a tractor was originally used to mix the organic material. The tedder rake worked, but a tractor-operated rotovator was discovered to work even better. It mixes the grass and hay in about four or five passes. Ed does not add manure or other amendments (his personal goal is an animal-free product).

After the compost is mixed, the tractor's front-end loader helps to scoop up the long mounds into large compost heaps. For best efficiency, piles should be at least four feet high.

The compost heaps must be well watered. This is very important. The piles are soaked until they are very wet throughout. This of course, provides the third ingredient for good compost.

Within 24 hours, the interior of each pile will reach 160° F. Because Ed, over a long period of time, makes so many piles, he puts a stick in each pile where he can mark the date when it was turned and thus keep track of his operation. After that first 24 hours, the piles are turned and drenched again. They can be turned by hand, or machine. The outer layers must be turned into the center for even decomposition. This stirring of the piles incorporates the oxygen that is the fourth and final ingredient for good compost.

Each pile differs depending on weather and the moisture content of the grass, but in general, each pile will be hosed down well each day (after turning) for three to five days (until it continues to maintain its moisture). The heaps will continue to heat up each day until the composting is finished, usually in 14 to 21 days.

Decomposition is complete when the interior of the pile has cooled to 100° F. If the outsides of the piles have been consistently turned to the inside, pathogens and weed seeds have been destroyed. The compost may be used right away, but Ed prefers to let the piles overwinter. As soon as the ground dries in the spring, he spreads them out to partially dry. When conditions are just right, a shredder is used to grind the compost to an even consistency.

Then the compost is bagged and used with all the horticultural crops grown at North Pole Acres, as well as in their potting soil.

Mulches

Mulches, other than clear plastic ones, are not ordinarily recommended for cold Alaska soils. By shielding the soil from the sun, they keep soil temperatures low. However, in the warmer Interior, they can sometimes be used for weed control, if special precautions are taken. For a discussion of the technique, see Chapter 9.

Mulches can, however, be used in the winter for the protection of perennials; especially if there are not at least six inches of snow by the time cold weather sets in. In that case, mulch perennials with at least six to eight inches of leaves or other mulch (current research says to avoid straw). Unfortunately, winter mulches invite rodents and glaciation. Therefore, if there is enough snow, you may want to forgo the mulch.

Earthworms

Earthworms are included here under fertilizers because of their soil-improving qualities.

Most of Alaska is without earthworms, but they have been found as far north as Anchorage, and more recently (with the warmer winters of the past few years) even in the Fairbanks and Manley areas. Some gardeners first noticed them in conjunction with rotting trees in the woods, or found them under rocks in weedy places. One gardener, Victor M. (Jack) Spratt, Jr., of An-

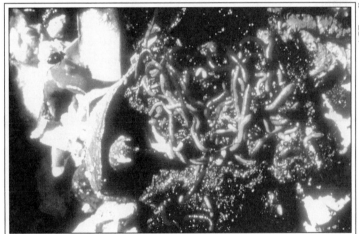

ACE staff

Typical red earthworms, these are not the shorter northern version.

chorage, relocated them to his garden in the late 1970s where they multiplied manyfold. By the mid 1980s soil in flowerbeds against his house did not need to be cultivated, and the worms were multiplying in his vegetable garden .

These native Alaska worms are much shorter ("sawed off," says Jack) than their counterparts in more southern states. They are only a few inches long, and aside from that, resemble redworms. A few handfuls were obtained from Jack and imported to Fairbanks in the summer of 1980. As far as is now known, the worms themselves do not survive Alaska's harsh winters—but their eggs do.

It is possible to keep earthworms in the Interior (and perhaps even farther north) by overwintering them inside. The late Eloise DeWitt kept her little worm farm going for years. Her redworms lived in buckets of pure aged manure with a piece of plastic film loosely laid over the top to keep moisture in. Earthworms cannot survive if their skin dries out. They were fed occasional greens during the winter. Corn meal was also appreciated, though more expensive.

In the spring, instead of pouring the worms out on the ground, where they may die or disappear, she put dandelion greens on top of the earthworm castings. Her redworms, which seemed partial to dandelions, would rush to the surface of the soil. They were then easy to scoop out and remove to a fresh bucket of manure. If, for some reason, they do not come up, or dandelions are unavailable, dump the castings on trays, sort through, and remove the worms to a fresh bucket of manure.

The earthworm compost is then ready to use on the garden. An added benefit is that the compost is full of worm eggs which, as mentioned before, survive the cold winters better than the worms themselves. Eloise believed that many hatched in the garden, so she had worms working in the garden all summer, yet never diminished her supply, which increased all winter too. Her greenhouse plants never received any fertilizer after the first starter solution (see Chapter 5), yet were beautiful and healthy, thriving in almost pure earthworm compost.

Here are a few more hints from Mrs. DeWitt to help you raise healthy earthworms for a garden. The worms also like apple peels, cabbage leaves and potatoes. To keep potatoes from sprouting, cook them a little first. Be sure buckets have holes for drainage. If floors are heated, be sure to set the buckets up away from the heat. Do not allow the plastic to be too tight, or the worms will become too wet and drown.

Mrs. DeWitt did not advise using earthworm castings for potted houseplants. The castings have a mucus in them, which dissolves when you water the seedlings, which will make the soil sticky like clay. There is no problem, however, in the garden.

One greenhouse operator reported that worms ate the root hairs of his tomatoes, but worms will eat compost first, so the humus in the greenhouse soil may have been destroyed by steaming of the soil, a common practice in commercial greenhouses for weed and disease control.

More information and help on gardening with earthworms can be found in ACE bulletin, *Composting with Worms* (#HGA-01020). Ordering information is in the Appendix, or order it free over the Internet. Their Internet address (where they maintain a list of ACE publications) is in Appendix C.

Chapter 5

Off to an Early start

Therefore the Lord God sent him forth
from the Garden of Eden,
to till the ground from whence he was taken.
Genesis 3:23, KJV.

Whether you are a beginner, or an old hand at gardening, if you have decided to start some of your own plants from seed this year, this chapter is for you. If you do not plan to start your own, you may want to read this chapter anyway, for some tips on hardening out the seedlings you buy, and for planting and caring for your garden outside.

Perhaps nowhere is it as advantageous for a gardener to be an early bird as it is in the north. Alaska's growing season is short—a head start can lengthen it enough to make the difference between a great harvest and a mediocre (or, in some cases, even nonexistent) one. Some plants, like celery and most tomatoes, have no chance to mature at all if started outside from seed. Others, like cabbage and head lettuce, will produce more, sooner, if pre-started too.

First-time gardeners may want to rely on local commercial greenhouses for their pre-started plants. There are certainly some advantages. You need only walk down the aisle choosing sturdy, healthy-looking plants. You don't have to scheme about where to fit in one more flat of plants, or which type of light to buy. No need to fuss with spindly, leggy cauliflower, or worry about damp off. And best of all, you will never have to face a half dozen flats of wilted plants that you spent weeks nursing along and then forgot to water for a couple of days.

On the other hand, you will be limited to the varieties available locally, dependent on greenhouses whose suppliers do occasionally have a crop failure, or who run out of a vegetable you particularly want, and you will miss the joy of "doing your own thing"—of being able to say, "I grew it myself from seed." Then too, much of the "work" of seed starting can be minimized by modern technology now available to the small home gardener.

How Early is Early?
One of the most common mistakes made by newcomers to Alaska gardening is to start

transplants too early. Recommendations made by seedsmen farther south do not take into account our long daylight hours. Cauliflower, in particular, tends to get stringy and root-bound when started too early. According to Professor Emeritus Dr. Donald H. Dinkel, interviewed when he was Horticulturist at the Agricultural Experiment Station at the University of Alaska Fairbanks, younger plants recover more rapidly from the inevitable setback of transplantation and usually catch up with older, larger plants. Assuming adequate light and normal home temperatures, the Alaska Cooperative Extension Service, University of Alaska Fairbanks (ACE) has published its recommendations for early starting in *Seed Starting and Transplanting*, (#HGA-00032). Information from this and other ACE bulletins were combined to make the *Early Starting Dates* chart found in Appendix A.

How early depends, too, on when you plan to set out the plants. Frosts in Alaska, as anywhere, can come early or late. There is no month in the Interior that does not have a record low below freezing. Over the long term, the last spring frost falls around May 13th. But the date of the last expected frost, when it is fairly safe to set seedlings out, is generally considered to be June 1 throughout most of Alaska. If you live in a microclimate that allows you to set plants out earlier, you will need to make adjustments. Adjustments should also be made for plants that will be put into a heated greenhouse before June 1. The late Eloise DeWitt of Fairbanks, for example, started tomatoes March 1 for moving into her greenhouse in early April. A rule of thumb for tomatoes is to set out budding plants (ones with five to seven sets of leaves).

Sorting Seeds

If you have followed the suggestions of previous chapters, February or March should find your seeds beginning to arrive by mail. Seed packets will probably not have shown up in grocery stores yet, but year-round greenhouses and nurseries may have a supply. As the packets arrive, sort them into piles according to when they will need to be sown. Set aside the pile of those you will be sowing direct in the garden. These will probably include peas and beans, carrots and other roots, and leaf lettuce and other greens.

With some seeds you have a choice. Kohlrabi and Swiss chard could be pre-started or sown direct. In some areas, lettuce will make heads from seed sown outside, and zucchini under plastic may make it from seed. You may want to wait to order seed potatoes, strawberry plants, or onion sets until later, then have them shipped using an express method. See Part Three for more planting information for specific plants like these three.

Remember not all seeds should be started at the same time. If you follow the chart of starting dates, you will be starting a new batch of seedlings every few weeks (or months in some cases). Some will go into flats to be transplanted to individual containers later, and some will go directly into the individual containers closer to the planting-out date (because they do not transplant well.) Again, for specifics, consult Part Three. Seeds earmarked for early starting can be filed in envelopes by planting date, using the early start chart for dates.

Alaska gardening experts almost universally recommend keeping a gardening log. If you began one with a map of your plot and fertilization program, you may now want to add seed varieties, year bought, when sown, when germinated, etc. The record will be invaluable to you next year because everyone's situation is unique.

No chart can advise exactly when to plant or when frost will hit a particular garden. Because of the temperature and light conditions of your home, you may find you have to add or subtract a week from the chart to have transplants the right size at the right time for setting out. Your record should also include which seed companies you ordered from and how their service was. If you intend to save excess seed for next year, date the seed packets, unless they arrived already dated.

Commercial greenhouses, like this one of Lee Risse's near Fairbanks, grow bedding plants for quick starts in home gardens.

Germination Testing

If you have saved seed from a previous year, you may wish to make a germination test to see how viable it is. It is a little discouraging to sow a slow germinating seed such as celery or carrots, for example, wait weeks, and then discover it is not going to come up at all. If you should find out, by testing ahead of the season, that your seed has a very low germination rate, you can adjust your seeding concentration to make allowances for it.

To test for germination, spread out a paper towel in a shallow pan (a pie plate or cookie sheet will do), wet it and scatter a sample of seeds over the pie pan as uniformly as possible. Ten seeds would do if there are not many to spare, but twice that many would be better.

Cover with another paper towel and wet thoroughly. Keep this seed sandwich wet or at least damp (but not swimming in water) for a couple of weeks if necessary, although for most plants three to five days will be enough. Every day, peel back the top towel and have a peek, then carefully replace.

Be sure to keep the test going long enough to allow slow starters to germinate. Then, when everything alive has had a fair chance, a glance will tell whether to plant twice as much seed as called for or three times as much, etc., or whether it might be better just to throw out the old seed and start over.

Dr. Pat Holloway, with the Georgeson Botanical Garden, offers a refinement on the above method used at the labs of the Agricultural and Forestry Experiment Station in Fairbanks. The seeds are sprinkled across the short end of the bottom paper towel, then the towels are rolled up from the long side, making a long roll with seeds in only one end. The end without seeds is placed in a glass containing a few inches of water, where it acts as a wick to keep the seeds moist but not drowning. Added benefits of this "rag doll" method include saving space, and the fact that the roots grow downward toward the water, making it easy to separate and count the germinated seedlings later.

Preparations for Seed Starting

Containers

Inexpensive containers can be purchased from garden supply stores, or obtained free by utilizing empty containers you have on hand.

Purchased Pots

Store-bought pots come in a variety of styles. Larger ones, about five inches by seven inches, can be used as flats to start seeds for later transplanting into individual containers. Individual containers in sizes about three inches by three inches are available, and especially recommended for seeds that do not transplant well (more on them later).

Plastic containers with about six cells of $1^1/_2$ inches by $2^1/_2$ inches are also good choices for seedlings transplanted from flats. Then there are large plastic trays, about $10^1/_2$ inches by 21 inches, which are available both with drainage holes (to be used as "flats"), and without holes (to set other containers in to keep drainage water from marring counter and table surfaces).

In general, most people plant a lot of seeds in flats, where they can be distributed evenly, then later transplant the tiny seedlings to individual pots before they become crowded. Directions for doing this are often confusing because the final setting out into the garden plot is also referred to as "transplanting." To avoid confusion, this book refers to this final transplanting as "setting out," and all references to transplanting refer to moving the plants to second (usually larger) containers indoors. Once the seedlings have been moved to other containers, they may be referred to as transplants.

While pressed fiber pots are used a lot in warmer areas, their use is discouraged in Alaska. The pot does not break down sufficiently in our cold soil and short summer. They also dry out very quickly, which can be a disaster when hardening plants out on a breezy day. There is even some research to indicate that roots of many plants have difficulty penetrating the sides and bottom of the pot.

If such pots are used anyway, it may help to slit them three or four times from top to bottom and around the bottom before filling. Be sure to water them very well before setting out in the garden, and cover the top with soil, or the pot will act as a wick to draw water away from the roots. Some gardeners recommend removing the pot completely prior to planting, by soaking to soften, and then peeling the pot off gently.

All of the above purchased pots must be filled with a seed starting mix (discussed later). But

A variety of containers are available commercially.

another kind of pot has possibilities here. It comes as a small compressed pellet, which expands upon the addition of water. No additional soil need be added. One is sold under the brand name Jiffy 7®. It is fine, even desirable, for pumpkin and squash plants that do not transplant well, but they may be too small and limit the roots of such plants as cauliflower and cabbage.

The most available varieties of the compressed pots have a mesh netting on the outside to keep them together. This netting should be removed prior to planting them out in the garden, as it is not biodegradable. The other disadvantage with the pellets is, again, how quickly they can dry out. When these or the pressed pots dry out (especially if outside on a breezy day) they tend to tip over easily, breaking the tender plant growing in them. Several companies now have expandable pots without mesh. Jiffy 9® is one without the mesh. It is a little smaller than the two-inch Jiffy 7®, and is bonded with a gel. It should be left untouched for several hours after expanding to give the gel time to work.

"Found" Pots

A few examples of recycled pots would be milk or yogurt cartons, and cottage cheese and margarine tubs. The important things are that the container be able to be sterilized, be drainable, and be waterproof enough to hold together for a few months under damp conditions. Some people have tried egg cartons and found that, in general, they are too small to hold enough soil, and they dry out extremely fast. In addition, if they are over watered in an attempt to keep the soil moist, the cardboard containers tend to mold.

Used half-pint milk cartons can be collected in the winter from schools and cafeterias. Clean with a bottlebrush and a solution of one part bleach to nine parts water, let dry, and fold for storage by slitting the bottom on three sides. A rubber band will hold the flattened containers neatly. Non-foldable containers can be sterilized and stored by nesting, but be sure to punch drainage holes in them. When the milk cartons are unfolded again for use, there will be no need to punch holes, as the water will drain out the slits around the bottom after it is tucked up a little way into the carton. The loose bottom makes setting out later easy, but care must be exercised that it does not open prematurely and dump the plant. The growing roots will help hold it in if the pot is not disturbed too often.

ACE staff

Planted flats grow in a commercial greenhouse. Some have been broadcast evenly over the entire surface, and others, like those in the foreground, are sown in drills.

The milk cartons and yogurt containers are a good size for individual transplants, and cottage cheese and margarine tubs are useful as small flats.

Flats

Flats are shallow containers where numerous seeds can be started at once. Commercial greenhouses later thin the seedlings by snipping off some at ground level, and then, when the rest are larger, transplanting the sturdiest ones to individual containers where their roots will have more room to grow.

Most seeds are viable (able to germinate) for several years if stored properly, but they seldom have a 100% germination rate. Therefore, even if you ran a germination test (as discussed earlier) it is still advisable to reserve some seeds in case something happens to the first sowing. If nothing does, there will be seed for the next year. Simply tape the packet closed and store in a cool, dark, dry place—even room temperature is fine The exact number desired could be sown in individual containers, but chances are some will not germinate and some will be less than perfect specimens. With a small flat full (or a row in a larger flat), it will be possible to pick the best to transplant, and even have some to give away to friends who did not order in time.

As mentioned before, plastic trays are available in handy sizes for flats, or you can make your own. A good size is 14 inches by 24 inches and three or four inches deep, but any size to fit your space will do. It can be made from scrap boards and plywood. Whatever the size or material, it must have a narrowly slatted bottom, or holes drilled in the bottom for drainage. Be sure to protect the surface on which it stands.

Take a tip from commercial growers and label your plants right from the beginning with plastic waterproof stakes—you can make them yourself.

Whatever size flat or container, it will need a label. Some cole crops, in particular, look just like other cole crops until quite late in their growth. Many gardeners can attest to the time they bought a dozen each of cabbage, broccoli, and cauliflower plants—and grew a garden full of cauliflower, because even professional growers can be fooled.

Labels

Labels are inexpensive. They can be reused by writing on them with watercolor markers, but the markers may bead off, or wear off before the season is over. If you just plan to label "cabbage" with a permanent marker, the label can be reused on cabbages next year, but if you want to indicate variety and planting date, you may want to repurchase labels each year, or make your own. To make your own, cut plastic in roughly the same shape as store-bought labels from any plastic lid that is fairly flat. Be careful not to use strips of cardboard for your labels. Stuck into damp soil, they may mold and cause your seedlings to do likewise. Some gardeners save plastic lids that come with coffee and other cans. Others use margarine tub lids. Point one end of the label, and you are in business.

Seed packets on sticks do not make very good labels, despite their apparent popularity. If used outside, they tend to wash out after a few rains. In the house, if you plant as outlined earlier, you will need the packets to store next year's seed.

Labels with accurate dates and variety information on them can be used later to aid in transferring information to your gardening notebook.

Susan Delisa labels broccoli in Lee Risse's greenhouse on Chena Hot Springs Road, Fairbanks.

Soil

The planting medium you use bears a direct relationship to the gardener's number one nemesis—damping off.

Damp Off

Damping off is a generic term applied to several diseases of seedlings caused by fungi (primarily *Pythium*, *Phytophthora*, and *Rhizoctonia*) that all attack seedlings. But, as Dr. Holloway says, "Most people don't care which one is the culprit - dead is dead!" The fungus usually attacks at the base of stems (at the soil level), but it can also attack a seed just as it begins to germinate, in which case the seedling may fail to appear at all. Plants already germinated look fine one day, then wilt and die the next.

"Wirestem" is also a fungus, seen as a thin darkened stem on cabbages, cauliflower, and broccoli. In this case, the plant may continue to grow for some time before succumbing to the fungus.

Fungal diseases are often associated with unsterilized soil and are encouraged by the moisture in seed germinating mediums. This is the main reason for recommendations to start seed in man-made materials—in soilless mixtures.

Sterilizing Garden Soil

It is not a good practice to use your own garden soil to start seeds inside unless you sterilize it. According to Virgil Severns, former Alaska Cooperative Extension Agent in Nome, baking the soil at 160° F for one hour will kill most harmful organisms. Wayne Vandre, retired Horticulturist with the ACE in Anchorage, recommends 180° F for $\frac{1}{2}$ hour. Beware of high temperatures, which will burn up organic matter and drive off nutrients. Older gardening books sometimes suggest formaldehyde - be aware that this is no longer legal!

"Soilless" Mixtures

Since both of the above sterilizing methods cause disagreeable odors and take valuable time, many gardeners purchase a ready-mixed soil substitute instead. Some commonly used materials are vermiculite (a micaceous mineral), sphagnum moss, sand, or perlite (an expanded volcanic rock material), or combinations of the above. One commonly available commercial mix is called Jiffy Mix®. Another is available with earthworm castings in the mix. The Alaska Tree and Garden Center in Fairbanks reports good results with Sunshine® because of the wetting agent it contains. This makes it a little easier to work with than dry media. Vermiculite (used in Punch N Grow®) is all

This broccoli plant in upper right shows damping off caused in part by too much manure.

right for germinating seeds, but, by itself, lacks nutrition for plants, so will not support growth long. Nutrients must be added after plants emerge. It is perhaps best used mixed with other materials.

Recent warnings from the Environmental Protection Agency should be heeded. Since some potting soils containing vermiculite also contain asbestos, a known carcinogen, but are often not labeled as such, they are urging that all garden products containing vermiculite be treated as though contaminated with asbestos. Precautions for handling include using the material outdoors, wetting it and keeping it damp, and being careful not to allow dust from the material to be brought inside on clothing.

91

You will not need very much soilless mix for seed flats, so the expense will probably not be a problem. But when you are ready to transplant to individual containers, you will need considerably more soil. This time, you will probably want to use some of your own garden soil in the mix, to save money, and because the plants are hardier now and not as susceptible to soil pathogens. For this reason, it is a good idea to bring a few buckets of soil from the fall garden into the house where they will not freeze.

One of the reasons for transplanting into a mixture containing real soil is that the soilless mixtures are necessarily lacking in many nutrients the plants need, even when fertilizers have been added. The seed comes equipped with its own stored food, but the supply is soon exhausted. Those wanting to add their own fertilizer to the soilless mix, should use a complete fertilizer with trace elements.

Flats filled with a soilless mixture await seeding.

Treating Seeds

If you suspect damping off will be a problem, the seeds can be treated with a fungicide. Some of the most common are Thiram Seed Protectant®, Benomyl®, Banrot®, and Captan®. To use, put no more than the tip of a toothpick full into the seed packet and shake.

Some seeds come already treated with Captan®. It is poisonous, so should be kept away from children and pets. Treated seed should never be used for food. By law, treated seed is dyed bright colors (hot pink, bright green, etc.) to show it has been treated and to prevent accidental poisoning. Unfortunately, some (such as beans) look enough like jelly beans to attract the children they are supposed to be protecting. As with any pesticide, read labels and follow directions.

If you do not treat your seeds and damping off begins to occur later, Captan® powder mixed with water can be squirted on dirt and at the base of stems. Do not worry if some gets on the leaves, as Captan® is also a foliage fungicide, so should not harm them.

By following sanitary practices with soil and containers, many gardeners never feel any need at all to treat seeds with fungicides. Later in this chapter, and in Chapter 14, you will find more hints on how to provide a growing environment that encourages healthy plants.

Sowing Seed Indoors

Some precautions you can take while planting will also help you avoid the damping off problem. Air circulation is very important in preventing damping off. Do not try to save soil by only partially filling your flats and containers. Fill flats right to the top and gently

Covering flats with plastic will help hold the moisture in. In this photograph, pansies are covered with black plastic because they need dark to germinate. Several herbs need dark as well.

press to firm. Be particular to firm edges and corners. Then fill again and smooth off the top with a straight edge. Filling the flat to the brim avoids a dead-air space around the base of the plants.

If you are using a dry mix like Jiffy Mix®, mix with water until you can squeeze drops of water out. Do not save excess mixture—it may sour and ruin your sowing.

Sprinkle your seeds evenly (large seeds can be planted more precisely, one at a time). Try not to sow too thickly, as crowded seedlings also cut down on good air circulation. Cover the seeds with a thin shaking of dry mix. In general, the tinier the seed, the shallower it should be planted. Lettuce seeds will even germinate in the light, with no covering at all. ACE advises a depth of two to three times the diameter of the seed, as a rule of thumb. Press lightly to ensure good contact between soil and seed, but do not compress. If the soil was very damp, it

93

will need no more watering. If not, water lightly from the top. Do not over-water. Seeds surrounded with water will lack the oxygen they need to germinate. Do not do this first watering from the bottom, as it can float soil and seeds up and out of the pot.

If flats are watched carefully, and watered gently when needed, they can be set in a dark warm place, preferably with bottom heat (see later, this chapter). But, especially in the dry interior (and elsewhere if you have a dehumidifier), you will save yourself a lot of work and worry if you cover the flats with something to hold the moisture in. Some flats come with

ACE staff

Here a gentle spray is used to water the tiny seeds in a flat.

preformed, reusable plastic lids. Otherwise, damp paper or burlap can be used, but probably the simplest thing is plastic wrap, held on with a rubber band.

Alaska Tree and Garden Center advises pricking several holes in the plastic with a toothpick for air circulation, but this will not be necessary with the preformed plastic dome lids. The plastic should be removed as soon as the seeds germinate, at which time you will want to move the flats into the light.

Providing The Basics

Water

A small bulb sprinkler is an ideal tool for watering flats and pots without washing away tiny seeds. Avoid water that has been treated with a water softener. Some seeds are very sensitive to sodium buildup, and may not germinate, or seedlings may grow poorly. Another way to water, once the tiny seed has sprouted, is with bottom watering.

Bottom Watering

The simplest method for bottom watering is to set all flats or pots in a larger flat that does not have drainage holes. Put water in the outer flat and let it seep up through the drainage holes in the pots to the plant roots. This causes the roots to reach down toward the water and the plant forms a more extensive and sturdy root system. It also avoids washing away tiny seeds as might be done with surface watering if the spray nozzle is not fine enough. Some gardeners also believe this lessens chances of damp off, encouraged by a continually wet surface. When bottom watering, however, be sure plant roots are not sitting in excess water for a long period

Here capillary tubes are being used with Twin-Wall® hose to irrigate greenhouse plants.

of time. Rather than keeping the pots in a watering saucer all the time, pots can be set in water, and then returned to their place when the soil surface has darkened.

Capillary Watering

A variation on the bottom watering method is capillary watering. This is a system designed to enable you to automate your plant watering to save you worry, time, work, and let you be gone from home for longer than two days at a time. A system can be purchased ready-made or designed on the spot with the help of a greenhouse supplier.

In general, the capillary system consists of an 18-inch by 24-inch tray of high impact styrene plastic. The tray has channels to hold about two quarts of water. Sand, or the edges of a cloth or synthetic mat, extend into the channels, soak up the water, and release it to the seedlings through the bottoms of their containers. Some systems come with a large reservoir to automatically supply the trays with water, and bridging strips to carry water to other trays to enlarge the system. How long it can be unattended will depend on many variables, such as the humidity of the home, and the age of the plants (larger plants require more water.)

A warning is in order, if cloth capillary mats are used. Some greenhouse owners have reported that they often grow algae, which in turn attracts fungus gnats. The adults lay their eggs on the cloth surface and the hatching larvae have a banquet. See Chapter 8 for more information on fungus gnats.

Whatever system of watering is used for seedlings, it will probably not be needed until the seeds have germinated, if you covered them with plastic. The plastic should not be right against the soil. In fact, it may be necessary to prop up the plastic a bit if moisture condensing on it threatens to drown the tiny seeds. Once germination begins, never let the soil dry out, especially in the case of small seeds.

Heat

Most seeds will germinate well at a temperature of 70° F. Cole crops will also germinate well at 55° F. Germination temperatures are important, because, for example, if the soil temperature is 45° F, one might be able to sow carrots, but you had better hold off on the beans, which may rot in the ground long before the soil temperature is warm enough for them to germinate. For perennials, wait until the soil temperature outside is at least 50° F.

Bottom Heat

Many gardeners have reported greatly increased success with germinating seeds by employing some type of bottom heat. Whatever the air temperature is, the soil temperature is what will determine the speed of germination. A heating pad, heating coils, radiator, and a warm floor have all been used to accomplish this. Just take care not to put tender seedlings on a radiator that is too hot, and watch for increased drying effects.

Air Temperature

Once the seeds have germinated, air temperature again becomes important. Legginess (tall plants with skinny stems) "results from a light shortage, warm temperatures, and over watering," according to Ellen Ayotte, District Home Economist in Fairbanks interviewing Agricultural Agent, Virgil Severns. ACE recommends temperatures of 65° to 68° F by day, and 5 to 10 degrees cooler at night. The lower the temperature, the less stem elongation. It may be difficult to lower home temperatures that far at night, but the problem can be approached another way. There is a choice of slowing height growth (elongation) at night by lowering temperatures, or by simulating continued day (with its higher temperatures) by increasing the length of light exposure.

Light

Not all plants respond well to extra long days or nearly continuous light, but most vegetable seedlings are not harmed by it. If seedlings are started in a greenhouse in Alaska, they will get a great deal of light anyway, as our days begin to lengthen. In the house, continued heat in the night stimulates plants to continue to grow, as in the day, seeking light. By keeping the lights on, the plants' energy goes into photosynthesis, the conversion of light, water, and carbon dioxide to plant foods, rather than elongation.

Legginess is also the reason your growing lights should be very close to the plants. About three to five inches is recommended, depending on the light intensity. Transformers are available to make artificial lights brighter so they will not need to be so close to the plants. Young, immature plants, even those that prefer a short day, require more light than mature plants. Seedlings should be closer to the source of light than developed plants.

Plants should be grown in a sunny window only if the temperature can be kept down, as high temperatures near the glass pane will cause legginess. Use a thermometer to monitor and do not let the temperature go over 76° F (65° F is best). You will find you spend a lot of time turning plants to keep them growing straight (they lean toward the light), and they will probably be leggy anyway; the sunshine we get in early spring is just not bright enough.

A mirror placed behind plants in a window may help them, by reflecting light back on the plants. Other ways to increase light intensity are to add more lamps, replace old tubes, and move plants to the center of the tube. A light fixture mounted with chains will make it easy to raise the lights as the plants grow. Or boxes and boards can provide different levels for the plants, to be lowered as they grow.

In general, tests have shown that windowsill lighting, as opposed to a greenhouse with only natural lighting, is not adequate, while overheating is a major problem. So as soon as your greenhouse is warm enough, you may want to move your seedlings there, while waiting for warmer temperatures outside.

Reflectors

If possible, the light should have a reflector. One of the more inexpensive types of fixtures is the type sold as a workshop light. The inside of the hood should be painted, preferably flat white. Shiny metal or glossy white finishes do not produce maximum diffusion of light. If lights are mounted under a shelf or table, with no hood, the underside of the table or shelf can be made the reflector by painting it white. In any case, the reflective surface should be no more than one foot above the light fixture, or much light that travels upward will be lost as far as the plants are concerned.

Lamp Types

Nearly any type of fluorescent lamp can be used with plants, whether it is sold specifically for that or not. But it may be helpful to know that fluorescent tubes are more efficient at increasing dry weight yields in plants when combined with 5% incandescent light than when used alone. Of commercially available fluorescent lamps tested in 1959, warm white (supplemented with 5% incandescent light) produced the best yields. The Standard Gro-Lux® lamp only became commercially available in 1961, so was not included in the tests. However, it has since been shown to be an excellent lamp when combined with some incandescent lighting.

Even more favorable have been tests on the Gro-Lux® Wide Spectrum, introduced somewhat later. This lamp seems to have enough energy in the far-red area of the spectrum to enable the extra incandescent lighting to be omitted, although at least one test indicated that plants using this tube also benefit from supplementary incandescent lighting.

Incidentally, sunlight can also provide the red light to supplement standard fluorescent tubes. Incandescent bulbs are not advised for use alone, as they distribute light spottily, and produce too much heat for most plants.

Light Intensity

A standard to work for might be 15 to 20 watts of plant-growth fluorescent light (10 to 15 watts for germinating seeds which need light), or 20 to 40 watts of combined standard fluorescents for each square foot of light-garden area. The lamps may last a long time, but will not keep maximum efficiency. If a light meter is available, take a reading when installing the tube. Test it each year (every six months if used year around), and change the bulbs when the reading goes down to one-half the original. If you cannot increase the light, cool the environment.

As spring moves into summer, be careful of windows with hot southern exposures. Watch, too, for crowding. The ACE notes that another cause of legginess in plants is planting them so close they must compete too much for light. Crowded plants may be thinned or, if in individual containers, moved farther apart.

How long should the lights be lit? ACE reports that "Plants grown at cool (about 65° F) temperatures with abundant natural or artificial light for 14 to 16 hours per day should produce sturdy, thick-stemmed, dark green plants." If necessary, a timer will help you maintain a regular schedule.

Fertilizer For Seedlings

Most seedlings will need no fertilizer until planted in the garden, with the possible exception of those that remain in soilless mixes for more than a week or so. Even soil cannot guarantee adequate nutrition since soils differ drastically. A few plants that remain in the house for a long time, such as tomatoes and celery, may benefit from some liquid fertilizer. Some greenhouse owners use very diluted fertilizer every time they water. If you transplant into a mixture of soilless mix and garden soil, you may notice a sudden growth spurt and greening of your plants, due to the nutrient boost the plants receive from the soil. This is usually all most plants need before they are planted out, but many gardeners use a diluted liquid fertilizer when transplanting to larger pots.

You may want to skip ahead to Part 3, under tomatoes, to learn about Amisorb®, a biodegradable chemical that promotes nutrient uptake by plants. Early tests by the Georgeson Botanical Garden were exciting, to say the least.

Transplanting

As mentioned before, seedlings are usually transplanted into a potting soil mixture of some kind. One such formula consists of $1/3$ loam for nutrients, $1/3$ peat for moisture retention, and 1/3 perlite for drainage. Sand is too heavy for potting mixes. Because dampness retains cold, in the actual garden one might be using a slightly higher percentage of sand, to improve drainage and warm the soil. Eloise DeWitt, who taught a gardening class for the Tanana Valley Community College, suggested a potting soil of one part Jiffy Mix® and one part garden soil, with some perlite or vermiculite thrown in for drainage.

Before going into details on how to transplant, it might be well to repeat that not all plants **should** be transplanted. Cucumbers, squash, and melons have delicate root systems that are easily damaged and do not easily recover. It is better to start a few in each individual container, remove weak ones, and let them grow there until they are ready to go into the garden or greenhouse.

When it comes to actual transplanting, there are two schools of thought on method. The first might be called the conventional method, and the second, the dry soil method.

First the tiny plant is lifted by its ears and removed from the flat. Often this will be done by carefully removing the soil from the whole flat.

Conventional Method of Transplanting

In the conventional method, you wait until the seedling has its first true leaf. Usually the first two leaves on a plant are the cotyledons (seed leaves), which contain the food supply for the developing plant. The true leaves typically look quite different.

When the true leaves appear, prepare the pots for transplanting. Water the flats well. Then, using a pencil or plant label as a dibble, and holding the plant by its ears (leaves) instead of by its neck (stem), insert the dibble into the soil, loosening the roots and lifting the plant gently up, retaining whatever soil clings to the roots. This is called "pricking out" the plant, and commercial greenhouse transplanters become very expert and quick at it.

Make a hole in the new pot with the dibble (deep and wide enough to accommodate the root system comfortably) and drop the plant in gently, at the same level at which it grew in the original flat. Firm the soil lightly around it, water, and keep it out of direct sun for a day or two.

Dry Method of Transplanting

Dry method practitioners hold that the root system of a plant is too large by the time the true leaves appear. Plants are transplanted just as soon as they are large enough to handle. The soil is dried out by withholding water, instead of watering just before transplanting. The soil is dried just to the point where it falls away from the roots easily, not to where the plant begins to wilt. Then, instead of pricking out the plant, the whole small flat or portion of a larger one is removed from the container. If the dirt

Then a dibble or pencil is used to prepare a hole in the new container, and the transplant carefully set in. Most seedlings should be covered up to their necks in soil—in other words, deeper than they sat in the original flat.

does not come out easily, or stays in one solid lump, it is dried another day without the pot. When dry enough, it should easily fall apart exposing the individual plant roots.

Seedlings are then lifted by the "ears" and put into the new pot in a new hole made by a dibble. But this time, the plants are set up to their necks in soil. If you do happen to transplant cucumbers, squash, or melons (it is not recommended), they are the exception to this, and are only planted to their original level. The section on tomatoes, in Part 3 discusses another type of exception. After transplanting, water and shade for a few days.

With both methods, care must be taken not to expose tender roots to air or sun. Carefully wash off any dirt spilled on the leaves, and especially on the growing point. It is important to water when transplanting to settle the soil and eliminate air pockets near the roots. But remember that over watering encourages fungus diseases. According to many authorities, over watering is the prime cause of failures for beginning gardeners attempting to grow their own transplants for the first time.

Garden Timing

When it comes to planting out, many people tend to rush the season. You just cannot anticipate the last frost. Low-lying areas are particularly susceptible to late frosts. Even when the frosts are over, cold winds at ground level can do almost as much harm, especially to newly moved plants that are having to get established in a new environment, perhaps with some root damage as well.

Some Alaska sites, according to Dr. Dinkel, can be planted as early as May 10, while others may have to wait until sometime later than June 1. In general, however, for most of Alaska, June 1 (or Memorial Day weekend) is the usual date for setting out transplants, especially frost-tender ones.

Planting from seeds (direct seeding) can take place a bit earlier, gambling on the frosts being over before the shoots appear. Eloise DeWitt's recommendation, in her favorable interior site, was to seed directly in the garden after May 1 as soon as the ground is workable. For most areas, gardeners will tell you to direct seed around May 20 to 25, but Mrs. Fleugel of Fairbanks usually had most of her garden in, protected by clear polyethylene, by April 24. She planted in permanent boxed beds that were easily converted to mini-greenhouses by spreading plastic film over them until the weather was more clement. Some of her planting dates in a recent year were beets and salsify on May 1, little cabbages in cups May 3, and beans on May 30. You will find most longtime gardeners advising that you plant beans last; they need a warm soil to do anything anyway.

Warm soil is the key when it comes to planting out. No matter how warm the air temperature is, seeds will not germinate or grow well if the soil is still cold. Soil temperature charts indicate that few vegetables will germinate below 40 degrees, and most of those that need 60 degrees or higher are seldom planted from seed in the north anyway. Remember that this is soil temperature, which generally lags behind air temperature. It becomes very important to obtain a thermometer (you do not need an expensive soil thermometer) and check your soil temperature before planting out.

Carrots are noted for being one of the earliest things you can plant—the late Scotty Clark of Ruby, and Mrs. Bergman of Fort Yukon both planted theirs the previous fall! The late Dick Morris of Fort Yukon used to gift friends with 6 or 7 inch long carrots with $^3/_4$ inch diameters in June, which were probably fall planted. Other gardeners have noted mixed success with this technique. A few other things that can be planted very early are potatoes, which take a long time to show up above ground, and peas, if planted a little deeper than usual. The reason for the deep planting is only partly for frost protection; it is mostly to conserve moisture. Melt-water from winter snows often fools the early gardener into thinking there is no need to irrigate, a fallacy that can cause needless grief, especially in Interior gardens.

Hardening Off Seedlings

Direct seeding aside for the moment, seedlings need to be prepared for the outdoors before being moved there permanently. They have been in a protected environment and are very vulnerable to any type of change, whether wind, temperature, or ultra-violet rays of the sun. The process of acclimating them to the out-of-doors is called hardening off, and involves getting plants used to their new home gradually by putting them outside for longer and longer periods. Some gardeners advise withholding water a bit, too. The usual period of hardening off is a week to ten days, so count back that far from the day you plan to set them out permanently.

Do not be alarmed if your plants change. ACE warns that leaves may turn slightly yellow with tinges of red at the edges, but that this is normal. Depending on variety, some may bronze more than others. Most plants will quickly recover, however, after being planted in the ground.

If your plant pots are in larger flats, moving them each day will be greatly simplified. Some of the plastic flats on the market are not really very sturdy, so be careful when handling a full flat. Ideally, you will be moving the flat to a shady spot outside that is well protected from winds. Leave the flat there for about an hour the first day, increasing the time each day. In a day or two, put the plant in partial shade, and in a few days, the plant will have graduated to full sun. Always protect the plants from drying winds and temperatures below 45° F. Toward the end of the ten days, the plants can be left out overnight.

If at anytime during this period you notice the plants looking very sick or ragged, you may be trying to harden them out before the air temperature is warm enough for them. Return them to the house for another week or so, and then try again. Be sure to check carefully for signs of drying. Hardening plants out seems to increase their demand for water greatly, and while you may have been watering them every other day inside, outside you may need to water them every two hours, or three or four times a day. Pressed fiber pots and expanded soil pots will probably need watering even more often. Actually, you may have noticed a conflict here. You are **supposed** to withhold water somewhat while hardening out. Just remember that outside it is easy to overdo the drying. When you are checking for drying, check also for insects.

Plants you are planning to put into a covered frame or greenhouse will not need hardening out. Plants you are going to set through plastic, but which will be exposed to the weather above the plastic, should be planted last, allowing the air temperature to warm as much as possible. Some gardeners like to have some plastic over these plants as well, until the weather is definitely warm. See Chapter 10 for more information on planting with plastic, and for other ideas on warming cold soil for earlier planting.

Lee Risse, a commercial greenhouse owner, offers some suggestions for taking some of the work out of transporting your seedlings back and forth. Put plants on a snowmachine trailer, wagon, or wheelbarrow. Wheel it into the garden each morning. Cold nights just mean wheeling it back into the garage. On nights that are not too cold, a hoop and plastic (like a covered wagon) will protect the plants. Be sure, though, not to let the mini-greenhouse become too hot. The ideal, of course, is a greenhouse where you can control light and temperature. You can then lower the heat for hardening off, without having to move the plants at all.

The Starter Solution

When you are ready to plant the hardened-off seedlings in their permanent home, mix up a fertilizer starter solution. One recommended by ACE is one or two tablespoons of high phosphorus fertilizer (such as the 10-52-17 that former Alaska Cooperative Extension Agent, Virgil Severns, uses) in one gallon of water. Alaska Tree and Garden Center suggests 9-45-15. Others available are 10-52-10, and Rapid Gro® which is 23-19-17, perhaps a bit low on phosphorus. The reason for a high phosphorus level being important is that this is the nutrient especially required for good root systems, and is not naturally a very available nutrient in most Alaska soils. See Chapter 4 for more information on fertilizers.

Many gardeners use fish fertilizer (readily available in Alaska) or manure tea for a starter solution, perhaps with some steamed bone meal worked into the soil to boost the phosphorus level. Whatever you use, you will need $1/2$ to 1 cup of solution per plant. Eloise DeWitt preferred to mix the solution half strength and use one or two cups of

Master Gardener Lou Andreis demonstrates that newly set out transplants need plenty of water, whether planted through clear plastic or not. A half-strength starter solution of liquid fertilizer is applied at the same time with the aid of a hose attachment.

it per plant. She reluctantly added two tablespoons of spectricide or diazinon because of a severe root maggot problem, but only for the brassicas, and later the onions. See Chapter 8 for other ways to foil the root maggot.

Setting Out Your Seedlings

There are three steps for setting out your hardened plants.

1. Soak the plant well.

2. Prepare the hole. Dig it roomy enough for the root mass. Plant seedlings as deeply as possible, right up to the first leaves, or in the case of tomatoes (which

send new roots from each node), even deeper. The exception is the cucurbits—melons, cucumbers, and squashes. You may want to mix in fertilizers and soil conditioners below the root zone. If a soluble fertilizer is used as a starter solution, pour about one cup into the hole and let it mostly sink in. NOTE: Even if not fertilizing at this time, do not omit this step of watering the hole—it can mean the difference between failure and success when planting out.

3. Insert the plant in the hole, firming soil around it. Some gardeners water it in to eliminate air pockets around the roots; others warn that this may cause the soil to crack later, leaving spaces for air. Therefore, if you water from the top, check later in the day to see if you need to firm the soil again.

Seedlings should be set down in basins (shallow depressions in the soil), especially water-loving ones such as celery and broccoli, unless you have an overabundance of rain and very poor drainage. The basin will help hold water, as well as make a handy place to side-dress fertilizer later in the season.

A bulb planter can be very handy for digging your holes. The soil should be prepared ahead by tilling in some manner. Push down on the planter, while twisting. You will find it easy to

Sharpen the cutting edge before twisting your bulb planter down through the plastic to make holes for your transplants.

remove the core of soil through the top of the planter, or by shaking the planter. The bulb planter is even more useful when planting through polyethylene, as you might be doing with such plants as pumpkins. You may want to sharpen the cutting edge before twisting it down through the soil, plastic, and all.

Dr. Dinkel has a word of advice for protecting young seedlings their first few days in their new home. On a hot sunny day, the zone of stem sticking out of the plastic may burn off. He suggests you put the empty pot next to the stem to shade it and shelter it from wind. Avoid planting in the heat of the day; late afternoon is best.

Direct Seeding

By the time you have begun to set your started plants outside, you will already have planted most of the seeds that did not need an early start.

Seeds may be planted as soon as the soil can be worked, provided it is not too wet. Ideally, the soil should be naturally damp. Do not let the soil dry out too much. Unless irrigating is convenient, do not work up the soil ahead of time. The best way is to work up the garden and plant it the same day. An exception should be made in the case of a gardener who fertilizes with fresh manure in early spring. Planting then will need to be delayed for a few weeks. See Chapter 4 for more information on this.

You can prepare your seed drill with a hoe, using the point for a single row, or the flat side for a flat bottom drill. The flat bottom drill is suggested, for example, for peas, where you plan to sow two rows close together. Pea seeds are placed in the outer edges of the drill, and a fence erected between them later. See Appendix A for a planting/spacing guide, and Chapter 2 for directions for wide-row planting. Chapter 11 covers the making of raised beds.

Eloise DeWitt advised Interior gardeners to plant in a trench, six inches wide at the top, not filling it completely with soil. This way, water will go into the trench and seeds will not dry out so quickly. When the plants were bigger, she put a hose down and let it run quite fast to fill the trenches. This way, the paths stay drier. She did not sprinkle after the seedlings were large, because of the cold temperature of the water, although Virgil Severns reports that sprinkler drops warm up considerably on their way to the plant through warm summer air. For planting in other areas, which receive more rainfall than the Interior, see Chapter 11.

Succession Planting

If you have never done it before, succession planting simply means that a few weeks after you have planted, say, radishes, you will plant some more. Do not wait until you are harvesting the first crop, and do not make a full planting each time, but just a portion every few weeks. The purpose is to extend the ripening period of short season crops, and avoid a harvest rush with everything maturing at the same time. In the case of radishes a single planting means harvest in a little over a month, and then nothing for the rest of the summer.

Northern climates do not lend themselves to succession planting for as many vegetables as do more southerly areas, but that is not to say it cannot be done. Dr. Dinkel suggests radishes, leaf lettuce, turnips, and spinach for succession planting; beet greens are also a good choice.

105

Eloise DeWitt used to obtain a second crop of peas from the same vines (see Part Three for details on method) and others extend the harvest by sowing early and late varieties at the same time (or, as in the case of corn, early and extra early varieties!). As mentioned in Chapter 2, you may also be able to extend a harvest by letting rows span sun and shade.

Finally, many Alaskan gardeners have learned that the clear polyethylene that helps retain moisture for seedling flats, and protect early plantings in the garden, is also great for extending the season just a bit in the fall. When the weather station warns of a light frost, gardeners hurry to pull plastic over their flowers and vegetables in the hopes of staving off

ACE staff

Here clear plastic helps protect plants from an early frost.

frost for one more night. Even coverings of old newspapers can help, but polyethylene seems to work best.

A Final Reminder
Label your plants, or record varieties on your garden map for future reference. You may want to date when each was planted out, and take notes on weather conditions and plant development as the season progresses.

As for growing a successful garden, Part Three gives hints about individual vegetables for the rest of the growing season, while the next chapter shifts ahead to harvest time. Having a problem? Skip to Part Two for help with specific gardening challenges.

Chapter 6

Storing Your Harvest

Thou crownest the year with thy goodness;
and thy paths drop fatness ...
the valleys also are covered over with corn;
they shout for joy, they also sing.
Psalm 65:11,12 KJV.

The harvest is your reward for all the planning, weeding, and tender loving care that went before. This is the pay-off, when you reap your profits by picking produce that will see you through a winter of over $1 a head lettuce and tasteless store-bought strawberries. Yet, surprisingly enough, this is where most gardeners fall short—giving away their summer labor of love by wasting their gardens' bounty.

How to Waste a Garden

There are many ways garden vegetables can be wasted. By letting radishes grow past their prime, you will end up discarding the woody red balls. If one ripe cucumber is left on the vine, others will fail to develop, and the harvest will be limited to that one. The adage "bigger is better" is seldom true of garden vegetables. Letting peas grow fat and tight in their pods before harvesting may fill more freezer containers, but no one will eat them when thawed out and cooked next winter.

Another way to waste a harvest is to use an improper storage method. Textures of some vegetables may break down when frozen. Certain produce stored in the same root cellar with other produce may pick up odors. One rotten potato can spoil all the potatoes. And some vegetables need a temperature setting that would ruin other vegetables.

Disposal of Excess

Your garden harvest can be disposed of in a variety of ways that do not include long-term storage. Give vegetables away to friends, neighbors, and charitable organizations. Feed livestock, or pick up a little extra pocket money by selling what is not needed.

Many communities now have a Farmers' Market where you can sell your excess, and some gardeners keep mental lists of private customers for their summer extras. In recent years, more and more farmers have been planting extra large areas for pick-your-own businesses.

Occasionally produce vans can be seen parked on roadsides, and not all of these are selling produce shipped up from more southern states. The Department of Agriculture can inspect produce, enabling sales to the military, and local stores are often eager for some really fresh produce to sell.

A few more exotic ways to use your harvest, offered by Virgil Severns, are "pumpkin" pies made from squash or carrots, and jack-o-lanterns from oversize vegetables (such as turnips). Each year, fairs give ribbons and cash prizes for vegetable art and centerpieces, not to mention categories for largest or oddest of various vegetables. Out of apples? How about bobbing for turnips?

Storage Methods

The best storage method is no storage—eating vegetables fresh, just picked and raw, or

Di Griffin displays her vegetables at the Tanana Valley Farmers' Market in Fairbanks.

freshly (and lightly) cooked. Barring fresh use, the next step is to determine the best method of storage for the particular vegetable. The rest of this chapter is devoted to general harvest tips and various storage methods. For more detailed information, consult a local Alaska Cooperative Extension Office. Some offer fall short-courses in canning, freezing, and "putting things up". Michele Hébert, Land Resources Agent with the Alaska Cooperative Extension, University of Alaska Fairbanks (ACE) reminds gardeners to be sure to select storage type varieties, and let them mature fully (carrots, potatoes, squash).

Harvest Hints

Before we consider storage methods in more detail, there are three points on harvesting to consider.

1. **Harvest delay means reduced harvest**. When a plant has mature fruit, it has no need to produce more. If you let that large cucumber stay on the vine to see how big it will get, the vine will not set more blossoms, nor expend much energy growing and maturing any smaller cucumbers already on the vine. If one delays picking peas, the vines will stop producing—once its reproduction is assured, why should it set more seed?

2. **Storage never improves garden produce**. What is ready to pick today, may be already beyond prime tomorrow. Once past prime, no storage method can improve it. Peas that are too starchy will not lose their starch by being frozen. Raspberries that have fallen to the ground will not be eaten fresh **or** preserved.

Non-gardeners are willing, even eager, to pay for the right to pick strawberries on farms such as this.

Mrs. Eloise DeWitt suggested that four crops (peas, beans, strawberries, and raspberries) be picked every third day, with the picking days staggered if possible. Others find raspberries need picking even more often.

3. **Delay between harvest and storage can lower nutrient values, appearance, and quality of the produce**. In fact, delay can mean total loss! Harvested vegetables should be prepared immediately for storage, if not planned for use the same day. Peas shelled and saved a few days at room temperature because of an over-full refrigerator may shrivel and spot before blanching arrests enzymatic action.

Instead of trying to harvest more than can be comfortably processed at one time, harvest a little each day, setting aside what the family can use right away, and preserving the rest. You will be surprised at how quickly the larder is filled, and you will be cutting losses of produce and nutrients, and assuring your family of high quality eating.

Preservation Methods

The following is a list of options for harvest storage. It includes a brief description of each method and what equipment and procedures it will entail, as well as which vegetables are best suited to each method. It does not attempt to be an exhaustive study of the various methods, which would be beyond the scope of this book. Use this section to decide on appropriate preservation methods for the produce to be stored, and to obtain an overview of these methods.

If you choose, for example, to can or freeze, you will want to look for a canning manual

ACE staff

A fresh salad from your own garden—how better to enjoy the fruits of your labor?

or freezing guide for more specifics for the vegetables you wish to put up. ACE has many good publications, classes, and recipe booklets to help you. The addresses and phone numbers of their various offices in Alaska, including Internet addresses, are in Appendix C. With the exception of root cellars (which require special construction techniques in the north), and leaving plants out all winter (which is seldom recommended where winters are so severe), most recommendations made for preserving in warmer climates can apply here as well.

Packing

By wrapping certain vegetables in paper, moisture loss is reduced. If the wrapping material is absorbent, moisture loss is slowed, and excess moisture (that might support disease organisms) is absorbed. A few vegetables that can be handled like this are cabbage, head lettuce, and green tomatoes. ACE estimates that wrapping lettuce in paper towels and storing at 32° to 35° F may extend the storage life for four to six weeks. Green tomatoes, wrapped in newspaper and stored at 50° to 60° F should be checked weekly for ripening and spoilage.

Another type of packing involves storing root crops in layers of moist sand, sawdust or peat. If carrots are stored this way (above 40° F) cut the stem down to ¼ inch and alternate carrots to make best use of the space, but be sure they do not touch. Cover with about two inches of clean, damp (but not wet) sand and make a new layer on top. If beets are stored this way, leave roots on, and at least ½ inch of stem. Do not wash the beets.

Cabbages are sometimes shrink-wrapped in plastic film for storage. 33° F should keep the cabbages in good condition for up to four months, especially if they are winter varieties with tight mature heads.

In general, temperatures in packed storage should be below 40° F, with high relative humidity (85%). Too dry will cause evaporation, drying, and shrinking. Too wet will support disease organisms. Temperature fluctuations shorten storage life.

Whole Plant
Another way to slow moisture loss is to hang the whole plant, such as tomato or cabbage, by its roots. Remove smaller roots and dirt. Some gardeners also remove most of the tomato leaves, and some have found removing the roots slows moisture loss even more. For cabbage, dry outer leaves at room temperature for a few days first. Celery and brussels sprouts can be kept by planting their roots in soil or peat in a cool place and watering occasionally. Avoid getting water on the plants. Temperatures for whole-plant storage should be around 35° to 40° F. Humidity should be a little higher than with dry storage.

Refrigeration
An extra refrigerator can give you better control over temperature. Lowered temperatures slow moisture loss and reduce bacterial action. Vegetables normally stored in the refrigerator can be stored this way, such as radishes (remove tops and roots), turnips, head lettuce, cabbage, and zucchini. By using an extra refrigerator, temperatures can be kept just above freezing, which might be colder than normally desirable for a regular refrigerator.

Canning
Canning may be done with cans, as the name suggests, but it is also done with canning jars. If planning to use cans, a can sealer will be required. There are different types of cans, depending on what is being canned. The different types are listed in the chart on the following page. An exhaust step will be required when using cans for canning.

To use jars for canning, jars and lids are required, which these days usually means two-part lids, consisting of a flat center lid and a rim that is used to tighten the lid.

Canning always involves cooking, although one can also freeze in certain canning jars (see **Freezing**, this chapter). This is important to remember—you will not be able to can **raw** vegetables or berries. Even pickles will be cooked in the pickle-making process.

Many vegetables can be canned successfully, but it is important to use the proper method and processing time. Basically there are two methods: boiling-water-bath canning, and pressure canning.

Hot-Water-Bath Canning

High acid fruits, tomatoes, and pickles are the only foods that should ever be canned with this first method. To safely can tomatoes this way, the pH factor should be 4.5 or lower. (The lower the number, the higher the acid content.) Add no water, which would dilute the acid, and avoid overripe tomatoes, which generally have lower acid. Be wary of tomatoes that have been bred especially for low-acid content. If you combine other vegetables or meats with the tomatoes, you will have to use the other method, with processing time determined by the food requiring the longest processing time. The boiling water should be two inches above the tops of the jars or cans when processing.

Type of Can	Recommended For:
C-enamel	corn, hominy
R-enamel	beets, red berries, red/black cherries, plums, rhubarb, pumpkin, winter squash
Plain	most all other fruits and vegetables

Pressure Canning

Low acid foods, i.e. all common vegetables except tomatoes and pickles, need a temperature higher than boiling water, which can be obtained in a pressure cooker with an accurate gauge to control pressure at 10 pounds (240° F). Most current cookbooks or canning guides will give you proper processing times for either type of canning.

Headroom

When canning in jars, you should leave space between the top of the food and the lid of the container. This headroom allows for bubbling of hot liquids, or expansion of solids during processing. The amount of headroom needed varies with the type of food being processed, and will usually be indicated in the canning guide.

The seal is formed by the vacuum created as processing drives air from the headspace, so no headroom means no seal. If, by filling the jars too full, too little headroom is left, the contents may bubble out with the air, sticking to the lid of the jar and providing a channel for bacteria to enter. Solids or seeds may be caught under the sealing compound on the lid and prevent the formation of an airtight seal.

Too much headroom, on the other hand, can be just as bad, preventing the jar from sealing if the processing time is not long enough to exhaust all the excess air in the jar. To avoid discoloration of food at the top, be sure food pieces are covered with liquid.

Only $^1/_4$ inch headroom is required for tin cans since they are sealed before final processing.

Spoilage

Spoilage may be caused by a variety of bacteria or fungi that are normally present almost everywhere—in the air, in water, and even on the surfaces of healthy vegetables growing in the garden. The organisms themselves are harmless—you could (and sometimes probably do) swallow them and they would be completely destroyed by stomach acids. But given a source of nutrients and a surprisingly short time at a suitable temperature and pH, these organisms grow and multiply rapidly, producing as waste products, substances that are highly toxic to people and animals.

The toxin of one species in particular, *Clostridium botulinum*, is one of the most deadly poisons known to man. The botulism, which it causes, may wipe out whole families or even larger groups who have eaten contaminated food. While these organisms can grow and function in the complete absence of oxygen, and can survive boiling water (212° F), fortunately for us they cannot survive in an acid environment and are totally destroyed by high temperatures (249° F), provided the heat has time to penetrate to the center of the container.

Spoiled vegetables are not just unpleasant; they are extremely dangerous. Discard leaking jars, or cans and jars with bulging ends. The bulging would be due to gas formed by spoilage. If you open a container and liquid spurts (again, due to trapped gas), or there is an "off" odor or mold, immediately discard the contents. DO NOT TASTE! Do not dispose of it where other people, children, or pets might find it.

As for what may be canned—nearly any vegetable suitable for eating cooked will can well. However, broccoli, brussels sprouts, cauliflower, and cabbage become discolored and stronger flavored when canned, so they, along with berries, are more often preserved by freezing when possible.

Pickling

Pickles are most often made from cucumbers, but many other vegetables (and fruits) make good pickles too. The pickling juice is high in acid, so the jars can be sealed with the boiling water bath.

It is important to use good quality ingredients and proper proportions of vegetables, salt, vinegar, sugar, and spices. Iodized salt may darken the pickles, so for pickling only, you will probably want to purchase non-iodized salt. You should look for pickling, dairy, or kosher salt, either coarsely or finely ground. Do not use table salt. Even if it is non-iodized, the additives in it that keep it free-running in damp weather make pickling liquids cloudy. Rock salt and other salts used to clear ice from sidewalks are not food-pure and should never be used.

Vinegar should have 4 to 6% acidity. Less can lead to soft pickles. For a less sour pickle, do not dilute the vinegar, simply add more sugar. Either white or brown sugar may be used, white giving the product a lighter color. Use fresh spices for best flavor.

Vegetables or vegetable pieces should be uniform in size. ACE advises removing all blossoms from cucumbers, or enzymes from them may cause softening of the cucumbers during fermentation. Some vegetables that make good pickles are cucumbers, green tomatoes, zucchini, beets, carrots, green snap beans, onions, peppers, tomato relish, and other mixed vegetable pickles and relishes.

Drying

The organisms of decay and breakdown must have moisture to function. Drying causes the organisms to cease functioning, so the food does not spoil. Equipment is minimal if the sun is used for drying, but drying is much more even and efficient with special drying equipment.

One advantage of storing vegetables by drying is the shrinking effect of drying—a very little space will store a lot of food. Temperature in actual storage does not usually matter, but relative humidity must be kept low. Drying is a good storage method for the Interior, but special precautions must be taken for Southeastern rainy areas, to keep humidity away from the dried vegetables.

Sun drying is unpredictable, unless relative humidity is very low and temperatures high (over 100° F). If those conditions cannot be met, the vegetables may spoil (sour or mold) before drying is complete, and it would be better to choose an alternate drying method.

Blanching

Vegetables for drying must first be prepared by blanching. This means heating them enough to inactivate enzymes that are active in living plant tissue. If this is not done, enzymes will cause flavor and color to deteriorate during drying and storage. Vegetables to be frozen will also need to be blanched, as will be seen later in this chapter.

Blanching can be done with hot water or steam. Steam blanching takes more time, but usually results in less leaching of vegetable solids, and reduced vitamin loss. To blanch with steam, obtain a kettle with a tight lid, and a colander (or wire basket or sieve) that fits into the kettle. Heat about two inches of water to boiling in the kettle. Put the colander, loosely packed with vegetables, into the kettle and cover. Leave it there until the vegetables are heated through and wilted . If cut through, a piece of food should appear cooked (translucent) nearly to the center.

To blanch with water, use only enough to cover the vegetables. Bring the water to a boil first, then gradually stir in the vegetables. Keep the lid on the kettle, and reuse the same water for batches of the same vegetable.

There is an excellent booklet available from ACE, *Drying Foods at Home*, (#P-261), which was actually published by the United States Department of Agriculture. It includes charts for sun, oven, and dehydrator drying of fruits and vegetables, with recommended times for each different vegetable, as well as descriptions of advance preparations and blanching times. The book also has plans for making a dehydrator (either natural-draft, or electric). A good companion leaflet is our own state's extension pamphlet, *Let's Make Dried Fruit Leather*, which includes recipes for berry and rhubarb leathers.

Freezing

Freezing is one of the best methods of preserving from the standpoint of flavor and nutrient retention, and ease of packaging. As mentioned before, blanching is necessary for most vegetables. ACE lists sweet green peppers as an exception to blanching and other gardeners have found parsley will keep well frozen without blanching. Another reason for blanching is that it wilts or softens vegetables, making them easier to pack. Since blanching time varies both with vegetables and with the size of the vegetable pieces, consult a freezer guide for specifics. Fruits and berries are not usually blanched for freezing, as it causes too much texture breakdown.

Since foods expand when frozen, headroom will keep them from popping their lids in the freezer.

Freezer Burn

One problem often encountered with freezing is freezer burn. This is caused by the drying effects of the cold temperatures when food packages come loose and open, or when inferior packaging materials are used. You have probably tasted what happens when a half-empty box of ice cream is returned to the freezer loosely closed. To avoid freezer burn, wrap tightly and try to remove all air from the packages.

Some garden products can be frozen in a variety of ways. Berries, for example, can be frozen plain, with sugar, or in a syrup pack. Rhubarb can be frozen without blanching as whole stalks (wrap well in laminated freezer paper), blanched for one minute as one or two inch pieces and frozen with or without sugar ($^1/_2$ cup per quart of rhubarb), or pureed. To puree, dice and add 1 cup of water to $1^1/_2$ quarts rhubarb and boil two minutes (or until tender). Cool and press through a sieve or whir in a blender. Add $^1/_2$ cup sugar per quart of puree. Pack into freezer containers leaving $^1/_2$ inch headspace. Seal and freeze.

Freezer Containers

There are many different types of containers for freezing. Among these are plastic bags and ties, and plastic boxes with lids, in a variety of sizes. You can freeze produce in the boxes, then pop out the frozen blocks to store in larger plastic bags in order to reuse the more expensive boxes. There are also plastic-coated cardboard boxes with plastic liners, canning/freezing jars, seal and boil bags, tin cans, and laminated freezer wraps. Those choosing to freeze in jars should be sure they are jars designed for freezing. The best type has a wide mouth and a tapered bottom, allowing partially defrosted contents to slip out easily for further thawing.

The fact that freezing tends to break down berries can be used to advantage to make juices by freezing, thawing, and mashing (raspberries, for instance). The resulting liquid and pulp will store in much less space in the freezer, as a concentrate. When ready to use, the raspberry seeds can be strained out and the juice used to flavor other beverages. Incidentally, rhubarb is a great extender, picking up the flavors of whatever it is mixed with.

Vegetables that freeze well are peas, broccoli, cauliflower, cabbage, carrots, greens, celery, parsnips, corn, zucchini, turnips, rutabagas, tomatoes, green peppers, parsley, rhubarb, and ber-ries. Some varieties of green beans tend to be tough unless French-cut before freezing, while other varieties seem to freeze fine. This is true of other vegetables, also, and you will find that many seed catalogs indicate varieties that freeze particularly well. Remember that, except for berries, most of the above will need to be blanched first, so will be used later in the cooked state.

Dry, Cool Storage

Perhaps the easiest of all methods, dry storage keeps vegetables in the fresh state, but cannot be used well without some type of temperature and humidity control. Different vegetables have different temperature requirements, but in general, winter squash, toma-toes, pumpkins, sweet green peppers, cucumbers, and eggplant need 50° F; potatoes, 38° to 42° F, and most other vegetables require temperatures below 40° F, but above freezing. Potatoes can be stored in a very few areas on the ground, with a thick cover of straw. Carrots and beets stored at 32° to 40° F keep well in five to ten gallon containers, covered with a cloth to keep air moist. See the storage chart in Appendix A for more specific infor-mation. Because of temperature and humidity requirements, you may find it best to provide both warm, dry storage (for members of the squash and cucurbit family), and cool, moist storage for root crops.

Some of the vegetables that do well in dry, cool storage are pumpkins, potatoes, kohlrabi, winter squash, cabbage, carrots, onions, parsnips, and beets. Winter radishes, cucumbers, turnips, rutabagas, parsnips, and summer squash (zucchini) can also be kept this way if waxed first.

Waxing

Waxing can extend the storage life of vegetables kept in dry, cool storage (or under refrig-eration). The idea is to cover the vegetable with a thin layer of wax to cut off contact with air, stop normal respiration or oxidation, and retain moisture. The method reduces drying and shriveling and is most often used on root crops such as turnips or rutabagas.

To wax vegetables, collect a large metal pot or pail and a large wire basket that will fit in the pot. Wash and dry the vegetables. Trim off tops, but avoid putting scratches or cuts in the skin surface. Heat water in the pot, and keep it just below boiling. Melt an inch-thick layer of paraffin (such as is used to seal jelly glasses), mixed with 10 to 20% beeswax, on top of the water (it will float there). Room-temperature vegetables are put in the basket and dipped quickly through the layer of wax, into the water, and out again. Thin-skinned veg-etables like cucumbers and summer squash should not be put into the hot bath. They must be treated with a wax emulsion, or liquid form applied cold.

To use waxed vegetables, peel wax off with the skin. Two cold-storage vegetables that should not be waxed are cabbages and onions.

Root Cellars

Root cellars are often used for dry, cool storage. Note that the name means a storage place suitable for root crops. It does not necessarily mean that it will be underground where roots grow. The work involved in digging an underground facility, as well as shoring up the walls, and the addition of supplemental heat, may make this type of structure a problem in the far north. You will not, especially in Interior Alaska or farther north, be able to dig a hole, bury vegetables, cover the hole up, and leave until you need a bag of potatoes or head of cabbage. The root cellar will almost surely need some type of heat and will have to be checked often to be sure the heat is being maintained. Air circulation and ventilation are very important, as well, to control humidity.

Because of these problems, many people (unless they are excavating under a cabin not yet constructed) find it easier to adapt a corner of an existing well-insulated structure, such as an empty garage or basement. To help you design such an adaptation, ACE offers these hints:

The structure could have thick (8- to 10-inch) walls filled with sawdust, or four to six-inch walls with conventional insulation, framed of rough lumber and less expensive building materials. Air circulation is needed next to the outside wall (i.e., the vegetables must not touch the wall). A fan to move the air would be advisable, as well as a double entryway with insulated doors, a form of supplemental heat, and an outside vent.

The late Ray Morgan, when he was Agricultural Agent for the ACE in Fairbanks, emphasized the need for adequate ventilation to control humidity. Without some method of letting out excess moisture, mold will form, he notes. While a vent might be sufficient in the Interior, coastal areas tend to have higher humidity and a fan may be needed in the vent pipe. However, humidity should not be allowed to fall too low, or moisture loss will lead to shriveling of root crops. For most vegetables an all-purpose humidity level around 85% will suffice (see chart in Appendix A for vegetable-specific recommendations). Water may be added to the cellar at times by pouring some on the floor (a good reason to have vegetables raised on pallets). A bucket of wet sand can be placed on the floor to raise humidity, but it will be adequate only if very little is needed. Actual temperature and humidity will be determined by which vegetables you plan to store. Lower temperatures, in general, require higher humidity.

You will need a light for use when you visit the cellar, because many vegetables (like potatoes) must be stored in the dark. Avoid windows if possible, using vents and fans if necessary for ventilation. Besides admitting light, windows also speed up heat loss, not something to be desired in far northern root cellars. Heat is lost faster through ceilings than walls, so ceilings should have at least twice the amount of insulation. A vapor barrier should be placed just under the inside wall and ceiling coverings.

To convert a corner of a heated basement, a room must be constructed with fully insulated interior walls. An existing window can be modified to let in cold air to cool the room when necessary, while the insulated interior walls and door will keep the cold from penetrating the rest of the basement, or warm air from the house being lost out the storage room window. Put boards between stacked boxes for air circulation, and make the front face of bins removable for easy cleaning.

Be sure to hang a thermometer and check it frequently. A sling psychrometer is an inexpen-

ACE staff

The series of photographs on these two pages shows the building of a root cellar in Fairbanks. Here (left) the site to be excavated is marked.

Next the hole is dug. This one is deep enough to accommodate walls of eight foot boards standing vertically.

The lumber being used is rough-cut and treated on one side with a copper-based wood preservative.

Here the late Ray Morgan and a helper build the walls. Note the white insulating board used on the outside of the walls.

ACE staff

Mr. Morgan and his helper are finishing the roof. Note that once again, insulation is added. ACE suggests double the insulation on the roof as in the walls.

After wrapping the whole in plastic, the root cellar is buried.

This photograph of a root cellar which was built into a hillside shows a vent pipe in the roof, and a door in the foreground.

This is another type of door, built for a freestanding below-ground root cellar.

119

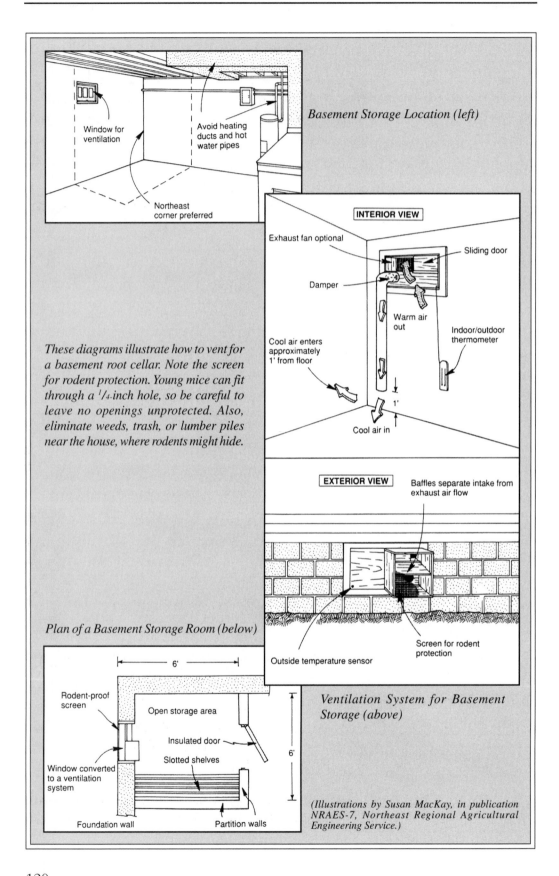

Basement Storage Location (left)

Window for ventilation

Avoid heating ducts and hot water pipes

Northeast corner preferred

These diagrams illustrate how to vent for a basement root cellar. Note the screen for rodent protection. Young mice can fit through a ¹/₄-inch hole, so be careful to leave no openings unprotected. Also, eliminate weeds, trash, or lumber piles near the house, where rodents might hide.

INTERIOR VIEW

Exhaust fan optional

Sliding door

Damper

Warm air out

Indoor/outdoor thermometer

Cool air enters approximately 1' from floor

Cool air in

1'

EXTERIOR VIEW

Baffles separate intake from exhaust air flow

Outside temperature sensor

Screen for rodent protection

Plan of a Basement Storage Room (below)

6'

Rodent-proof screen

Open storage area

Insulated door

Slotted shelves

6'

Window converted to a ventilation system

Foundation wall

Partition walls

Ventilation System for Basement Storage (above)

(Illustrations by Susan MacKay, in publication NRAES-7, Northeast Regional Agricultural Engineering Service.)

sive instrument used to determine both temperature and humidity. It is even possible now to automate an alarm to sound when the temperature rises too high or drops too low. Thermometers are made that can be hung upstairs, with sensors extending down to the storage room to eliminate the need to run up and down stairs checking. A well-insulated root cellar can be heated by opening the interior door slightly, or even simply by switching on a red (or well-shaded) light bulb.

The chart in Appendix A can help you decide on the proper temperature for your root cellar. It includes the recommended temperature, relative humidity, and approximate length of storage for fresh, dried, and frozen fruits and vegetables, and average freezing points for them. NOTE: Freezing points are not the same as for water. Your local Alaska Cooperative Extension office will have more information on preparation of specific vegetables for root cellar preservation.

Jellying
A final storage method, especially for fruits and berries, is making jellies and jams. A jelly is clear, with pulp and seeds strained out. Jams still have the pulp, but it is pureed. Preserves contain recognizable berries or chunks of fruit. Chokecherry seeds are poisonous, so chokecherries are recommended for jellies, never for jams or preserves. If using chokecherries, pick out leaves, remove stems, and simmer, but take care not to crush the seeds, which are then strained out. With most other berries, the choice of jelly, jam, or preserve is up to you.

There are four basic ingredients for jellying; they are fruit, acid, sugar, and pectin.

Only $3/4$ of the fruit should be ripe. The riper the fruit, the less pectin it will have naturally, so having 25% unripe fruit becomes very important when you do not plan to use any additional pectin.

With fruits low in acid, lemon juice is usually added. The proportions are one tablespoon lemon juice to one measuring cup of fruit juice.

Sugar helps in gel formation, adds to flavor, and serves as a preserving agent. It will not matter whether beet or cane sugar is used. In general, sugar will make up about 60% of the product.

In recipes without added pectin, light corn syrup can replace up to one-fourth of the sugar in jellies and up to one-half of the sugar in other products. With added powdered pectin, corn syrup can replace up to one-half of the sugar in any of the products. With liquid pectin, corn syrup can replace up to two cups of the sugar. Honey can replace up to one-half of the sugar in any recipe where no added pectin is used. In products made with added pectin, two cups of honey can replace two cups of sugar in most recipes; only $3/4$ to one cup of sugar should be replaced by honey in small recipes yielding five to six glasses.

Some fruits and berries have enough pectin naturally, but most recipes call for some additional to be added. Commercial pectin is available in two forms: as a powder or a liquid. The main difference is **when** they are added.

Powdered pectin is added to strained juice before heating. The mixture is rapidly brought to a full rolling boil, sugar added, returned to the rolling boil, and boiled for one minute.

Liquid pectin is added to juice and sugar after the mixture is brought to the full boil. Stir constantly while heating. After the pectin has been added, the mixture is brought again to a full rolling boil and boiled for one minute.

Sugarless diet jellies or jams can be made by using pectin, but with sugar substitutes. Because they lack the sugar that acts as a preservative, they spoil easily in temperatures above 40° F, so should be stored in the refrigerator or freezer. There are now several pectin-type

Ed Bostrom stirs up another batch of jelly. On his right, clean bottles wait for the hot syrup.

products available that require very little sugar or other type of sweetening products, according to Ellen Ayotte, former Home Economist with ACE in Fairbanks.

There are many books and booklets on the market that give complete recipes for jams and jellies, as well as directions for other preservation methods mentioned in this chapter. Contact any local ACE office (addresses in Appendix C) for a list of their latest publications on preservation of garden produce, and locally developed recipes for some of the more popular and abundant fruits and vegetables.

Chapter 7

Putting Your Garden to Bed

And the Lord God took the man,
and put him into the garden of Eden
to dress it and to keep it. Genesis 2:15 KJV.

When the last beet is harvested, the last ripe tomato eaten, the garden work is over ... or is it? Actually, some of your most important garden chores should be done in the fall during and after the harvest.

Fall Clean-Up

Even before harvest is over, you can begin to gather stray tools, and remove no longer needed supports and netting. It is particularly important that weeds, all scraps of plastic, and diseased or insect-infested plants be removed from the garden before tilling. Gather up all flats and potting equipment. Drain hoses before a surprise cold snap freezes the water in them.

Nettings

As vines are removed from them, plastic nettings can be taken down and rolled lightly around poles for storage, or folded. It is a good idea to label net sizes, to help in spacing supports the next year. Decide now if there is a need to replace any nets this winter. Mail order them now and avoid rush charges next spring.

If using more permanent-type nettings, such as chicken wire, it may not be desirable to remove them every year, but you will have to forego crop rotation. The edge of the garden may be the best place for permanent-type fences, to interfere least with tilling of the rest of the garden.

Improving Your Soil

While you can improve your soil in the spring, before planting (and many do), fall is also a good time. Fall tilling can be done to incorporate garden plant residues, as well as to add additional organic matter and nutrients with the addition of composts and manures, both green and otherwise. (Incidentally, if you have the humus content of the soil checked, aim for 5%, but 2% is good). Now would be a good time to lighten that heavy clay area with some sand, or improve the water-holding capacity of that sandy area with the addition of peat. It is also the perfect time to go back and read Chapter 4 for more ideas on improving soil.

Winter Protection

The soil should not be left bare for the winter. Soil is warmest under deciduous plantings (trees that drop their leaves and allow snow to cover the ground), with mulched soil a close second. Cover-cropped land is cooler, with bare soil (as found under evergreens) the coldest of all. Manure put on in the fall should be tilled under the same day, to conserve as many of the nutrients as possible, but then something else should cover the soil. One good possibility is leaves. Never waste leaves and grass clippings by burning them. Mulch with them in late spring, or compost them in summer, or spread them on in fall, but never burn them.

One reason for a winter mulch is to reduce the chances of alternate freezing and thawing which destroys the beneficial bacteria in the top two inches of soil, as well as the root cells of perennials. Snow helps insulate the soil in most of Alaska, but may not be there for some Southeastern gardens, where rain is more often the rule.

Cover Cropping

The idea with cover cropping is that the crop will provide a cover all winter and be tilled under in the spring. One reason for a cover is to prevent the soil from washing away or compacting in heavy rains. It also captures soil nitrates and other plant nutrients before the rain leaches them away. The nutrients are later released when the cover crop decays.

Cover cropping is difficult to practice in the shorter-season areas of Alaska. Planted after harvest, there is just not time for a respectable stand to develop before winter strikes it down. One can, however, grow a cover crop to be used as a green manure on parts of the garden that are not in production. Just be sure the crop does not go to seed if you do not want it returning as weeds the following year. As discussed in Chapter 4, annual rye is a good cover crop that will not survive the winter to plague you next year. Buckwheat is sometimes grown to choke out weeds. Again, with buckwheat, be sure it does not go to seed. Incidentally, young buckwheat leaves are reported to make good salad greens.

To till in the cover crop in spring, or a green manure crop, first mow it if it is standing. Ideally, a layer of well-rotted manure or compost should be spread over the stubble to help speed decomposition. Then, till the crop into the soil using a shallow depth setting if possible. Try to keep the organic matter in the top few inches of soil. Remember, in our cold soil, plants will not be reaching down very deeply for nutrients. This tilling should be done a few weeks before planting to allow time for decomposition. If soil remains wet late in the spring, you may not feel you have time to wait for the cover crop to decompose, so you may want to use a nonliving cover, as described under **Winter Protection** (earlier in this chapter), and in Chapter 9 under **Mulching**.

Final Tilling

Rock powders can be put on in the fall, but melting snow and rains will leach nitrogen and potassium so quickly that fertilizing for these two is best left until spring. By the same token, save wood ashes and compost until spring. If manure is applied in the spring, follow the cautions in Chapter 4 to avoid burning plants.

Under loose mulch, leave the soil rough, which helps it warm up and dry out sooner in the spring. Consider furrowing it deeply, or tilling a drainage furrow if there is a real problem with drainage. After tilling, spread the ground as thickly as possible with organic plant material such as leaves, grass clippings, vegetable leavings (non-diseased, of course), straw, or what have you. Even with our long winters and cold soils, much of it will decompose by the time the soil has dried enough to disturb, and you will be able to till it in easily. Some exceptions are vines (like squash, pumpkin, or peas) and corn stalks, which will decompose better if tilled in while still fresh. If left to dry on the surface, there may be a problem with them wrapping up in tiller blades.

Any leftover mulch can be saved for the compost heap. See Chapter 4 for ideas on how to be sure it is thawed when needed in the spring. Any time left before snow falls can be spent gathering compost materials, like leaves, for next summer. It is difficult to find leaf-covered lawns in July. Before putting away power tools, use them to help construct a compost heap. Again, see Chapter 4 for more details on building compost piles.

Maintenance

There is more time to repair hand tools now, before the spring rush to plant. Clean, sharpen, repair, oil (try boiled linseed oil for wooden handles), and put them away.

Follow the owner manual for specifics on power equipment. If the manual is gone, here are a few steps to follow:

1. Drain the gas tank and run the engine until the carburetor is dry.
2. To prevent accidental starting, disconnect the lead-in wire to the spark plug.
3. Drain the dirty oil and refill the crankcase with clean oil.
4. Clean mud, matted clippings, and other debris from all parts of the machine. A wire brush will help, especially underneath rotary mowers. Paint rotary mower undersides with oil.
5. Wipe off excess oil and grease from the drive chain, flywheel, axle, and wheels with a kerosene-soaked rag.
6. Remove the air cleaner and wash with kerosene. Replace the paper filter on models that have one. Reinstall the air cleaner.
7. Lubricate all drive chains with chain oil.
8. Grease all grease zerks and oil other lubrication points.
9. Tighten all nuts, bolts, and screws.
10. Remove rust spots with steel wool or emery cloth, and paint.
11. Clean and sharpen cutting edges of attachments.
12. Check rubber tires for damage and proper air pressure.

13. Remove the spark plug and check for fouling. Clean or replace.
14. Store protected from weather if possible.

Tool Storage

Your storage place may be as simple as a cardboard box or as fancy as a pegboard with tool outlines stenciled on it. What is important is that hand tools be free from dirt and stored out of the weather, and power tools have appropriate maintenance procedures performed on them prior to storage.

Be sure tools will be accessible when needed. For example, you may want to mix transplanting soil with your trowel in March and, while you may not have expected to use your rototiller so early in the spring, you may want to till a friend's garden that dried out sooner than yours. Store the tiller where you will not have to cross your still-wet garden with it.

Taking Inventory

There are several things to inventory and prepare for early spring. One is a seed supply, and the other consists of anything needed for starting plants indoors, if planning to grow your own transplants next spring. Chapter 5 may be a good one to reread now.

With harvest fresh in mind, make decisions regarding seeds to purchase for next year. Note extra seeds that may not need reordering, and make up a list of new ones to try. Later, when the seed catalogs start arriving, you will be ready to make up an order with minimum fuss. If you gardened for the first time this year, you may not be receiving very many seed catalogs yet, so send away for some now. There is a list of some of the more popular seed companies in Appendix A, which are keyed to the Variety Lists in Appendix B. Included are some of the firms specializing in northern varieties. Extra seeds you are saving should be wrapped airtight and kept in a cool place.

Among other things needed for seed starting, is an inventory of seed flats and containers. Make decisions now regarding whether or not you want to increase the supply for next year. Now is the time to order vermiculite or perlite to mix with your own soil for transplanting. If planning to do that, be sure to bring in garden soil before it freezes, to mix in the spring (when soil outside will still be under snow and frozen). Using part of your own soil when starting many plants can mean considerable savings over buying commercial potting soil.

Planning Next Year's Garden

If you do not have a map of your garden this year, showing where you grew what, now may be your last chance to make one, before you forget. It will come in handy when planning next year's garden, during the long dark days of winter, especially if you include notes on the success of different vegetables this year. See Chapters 2 and 4 regarding crop rotation, and Chapter 2 for more information on garden planning. While out in the garden, do not forget to take soil samples, as described in Chapter 3. That way, you will have the results back in time to apply lime in the fall, if needed, and certainly by the time you need them in the spring.

Chapter 8

Plant Pests

He spake, and the locusts came,
and caterpillars, and that without number,
And did eat up all the herbs in their land, and
devoured the fruit of their ground. Psalm 105:34, 35 KJV.

One of the nicest things about gardening in Alaska is the relatively few insect pests. According to Dr. Donald H. Dinkel, retired Professor of Plant Physiology at the University of Alaska, "The worst insects you will encounter are cutworms and root maggots." He goes on to say that few pesticides are needed.

Only about 19 insects, plus slugs, are even frequent enough to discuss here, and many of them may never even be observed in the garden, much less create a problem.

Basic to any attempt at control of insect pests, is knowledge of the insect's **seasonal** cycle, as well as its general life cycle. Entomologist David P. Bleicher, formerly of the Palmer Research Center, felt that this point was "very important when considering non-chemical methods."

Whether the controls you attempt are organic or chemical, they must be based on knowledge of the insect's habits and habitat. When speaking of chemical control of root maggots in particular, Mr. Bleicher added that "once this basic information is obtained, the presence of susceptible stages of the root maggots can be predicted and pesticide applications accurately timed, allowing for fewer pesticide applications and improved control." Of course, this could apply to any insect pest.

Control methods vary with the insect, but a general discussion of controls might be in order here. More specific recommendations will follow for each pest, as their seasonal and life cycles are discussed.

Insecticides

All insecticides available in Alaska come with a label meant to give some idea about their safety. In order of increasing danger, they may be labeled *caution*, *warning*, or *danger*. Those marked *restricted-use* can only be bought or used by, or under the supervision of, a certified applicator. Workshops for certification are offered each year through the Alaska Cooperative Extension, University of Alaska Fairbanks (ACE).

The science of pesticide use is constantly in flux. Federal agencies have been reevaluating insecticides once considered perfectly safe, and outlawing some, or severely restricting their use. Twenty years ago, the latest ACE publication on garden insect control (#P-137) listed only five insecticides. Some of those are not even widely used any more.

It would be irresponsible to give amounts of specific insecticides to apply in a book that may become outdated in a year or two as the federal government continues to refine the use of pesticides. General comments in this chapter will refer instead to less lethal remedies, such as pyrethrum (a plant based natural pesticide) and gardeners are urged to contact their local ACE office for the most up-to-date word on chemical remedies (addresses are in Appendix C.)

ACE staff

Insecticides are dangerous. Buy only enough for the current season, read labels carefully, and follow directions. The label is the legal document that always supersedes anything read in a book or brochure, but the **user** is responsible for the legal use of all pesticides. Never attempt to spray any plant already suffering from stress—especially drought or wind. Water well a few days before spraying, and wait a few days after a heavy wind.

This cabbage leaf shows signs of injury caused by the insecticide, diazinon.

Insecticides come in several forms. Emulsions and wettable powders can be diluted with water. Some, such as diazinon, do not keep well once mixed. Mix only what will be put to immediate use. Dusts and granular materials are applied in dry form. In general, a more concentrated chemical will be cheaper because of lower shipping costs.

Some Safety Precautions

Reread the label every time you spray or dust. Mix sprays on a solid, level surface. Work with pesticides only when fully dressed. If some accidentally spills on you, wash well with soap and water and wash clothes separately from other clothing.

Keep all chemicals away from children, preferably stored in a locked cabinet. Do not store leftover spray—dispose of it according to label directions. Empty containers should not be buried, but triple-rinsed and crushed to discourage future use. Use the rinse water from liquid concentrates by pouring it back into the spray tank as the water portion of the next mixing. Never try to reuse an insecticide container.

Protecting Honeybees

Some insecticides are more dangerous than others to bees. For example, carbaryl (Sevin®) can be carried back to the hive by bees and fed to newly emerging bees along with pollen. Gardeners can obtain a complete listing of pesticides and their relative toxicity to honeybees from ACE (addresses in Appendix C).

Other factors can be important too. Insecticides in dust form are more dangerous to honeybees, because the dust can be gathered with pollen and taken to the hive.

Avoid spraying when plants are in bloom. If you must, keep the spray away from blossoms and only spray when there is no breeze. If close neighbors keep bees, you should warn them ahead of time. They may even be able to help determine the best time to spray.

Alternate Insect Controls

Because insecticides are so dangerous, and render vegetables inedible for a period of time, many authorities advise their use only as a last resort. There are many more natural and less dangerous ways to defeat pests. These fall into two categories: prevention and cure.

Caution must be taken to protect honeybees from insecticides.

Prevention

Prevention, in turn, includes five aspects: healthy soil, crop rotation, clean gardening, natural repellents, and trap crops.

Healthy Soil

Research from universities as widely spread as Missouri, Florida, and Iowa has found a definite relationship between soil fertility and plant insect damage. Nematodes, for example, have been shown to be literally eaten alive by beneficial fungi that build up in soil that has been enriched with organic material.

Minerals are important for healthy soil too. The Iowa Agricultural Experiment Station found pea aphids feeding more often on plants weakened by soil mineral deficiencies .

One thing that contributes to insect preferences in plants is the fact that insects need carbohydrates to a much higher degree, than say, you, relatively speaking. Research at the Missouri Agricultural Experiment Station has indicated that plants grown in soils lacking organic matter produced excess carbohydrates. It appears that insects prefer these plants.

Crop Rotation

Crop rotations are very important in protecting many crops from pests. Some insects are adapted to feed on specific plants, and when those plants are removed or not available, the insect usually does not survive.

Wild mustard is a natural host of the root maggot. Do not allow it to grow near your garden.

Clean Gardening

Many insect pests overwinter in dead plant refuse. Fungi, which are spread by spores that multiply quickly, are often concealed in rubbish. To minimize insects and diseases, burn diseased plants and plant refuse. Compost plant residues either in a compost heap, or by sheet composting—tilling them into the soil in the fall. For root maggot control, it is especially important to remove cole crops that have been attacked, as soon as they are discovered. When harvesting, removal of the whole plant will help insure that the larval stage is unable to move into the soil to pupate and become the next year's adults.

Weeds also should be removed from the edges of the garden. Tansy mustards are host plants for the red turnip beetle, and weeds in Southcentral and Southeastern Alaska often harbor slugs. According to the late Dr. R. H. Washburn (former Research Entomologist in Palmer), writing in the *Agroborealis* of turnip maggots, "Any cruciferous plant with a tap root the size of a pencil seems to be a suitable host." The seed corn maggot is a more general feeder, and infests several other plant families as well.

Avoid handling healthy plants after touching diseased ones. Stay out of the garden when it is wet, as plants bruise more easily then and can become susceptible to mildew and rot. Diseases of green beans in particular are spread very readily by handling the wet plants, or splashing mud on them.

Georgeson Botanical Garden Collection

Repellents

Opinion is divided on the benefits of repellents. The most often mentioned is garlic. In more southern states, marigolds are used to repel nematodes. An exudate given off by the roots is the actual repellent, and it takes several seasons to build up enough in the soil to have any great effect. Some gardeners in Alaska grow marigolds for the blossoms' scent, said to repel aphids and, some think, root maggot flies. There is controversy about whether it is actually the blossom scent, foliage scent, or root exudate. Unfortunately, it seems to take a lot of flowers to do the job. Some marigolds have been bred purposely to lack the scent, so watch what you use. Signet or French marigolds are good ones to try. There

Blooms of a French marigold, like Safari Scarlet shown here, as well as Signet marigolds, have a strong scent that seems to repel insects from companion vegetables planted nearby.

are books available that include information on use of repellents when companion planting. Appendix A offers a companion planting chart, but use caution; some of the combinations may not work in Alaska, and some companion crops are capable of taking over the garden as weeds.

Trap Crops

A plant grown as a trap crop has the opposite purpose of a repellent. Nasturtiums, for example, are sometimes grown to attract aphids away from other plants and to themselves. If the flat, yellow-fleshed varieties of turnips are grown near round white-fleshed turnips, the latter seem to attract maggots, leaving the former relatively pest-free. The companion planting chart in Appendix A lists some trap crop plants to consider.

Cures

One problem with insecticides is that insects and fungi are often able to develop strains that are resistant to them. It is usually preferable to use the least dangerous method of pest control first. It may even be best, in the case of a limited infestation, to let the bugs have a few weaker

Georgeson Botanical Garden Collection.

Nasturtiums can act as a trap crop to lure aphids away from vegetable crops. These are Tip Top Mix.

specimens (since many insects attack weaker plants first). If the infestation should become major, here are a few ideas for cures, not necessarily in order of effectiveness.

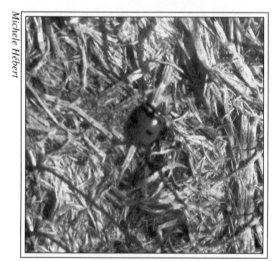

Michele Hébert

This photo, which is actually illustrating snow mold fungus, shows the beneficial ladybug.

Friendly Insects

Ladybugs (ladybird beetles) are native to Alaska, but in the case of a severe aphid infestation, you may find it advisable to strengthen their ranks by importing reinforcements. Release them gently in the morning or late afternoon; not in the heat of the day, which may cause them to fly away. Save some for a day or two in the refrigerator for later release. Unfortunately, ladybird beetles have been found to disperse too rapidly anyway, and are most effective if they can be confined in some way or if they are used in a greenhouse. Warning: An experiment with ladybugs in the University of Alaska greenhouse on the Fairbanks campus was a disaster. The beetles were brought in to deal with an acute aphid infestation in a greenhouse that is located on the second floor of their laboratory. Instead of dealing with the aphids, dead and dying ladybugs were found dispersed all over the building, stairways, etc.

Lacewings (aphid lions) and praying mantises also devour aphids, but the same problems occur with the latter as with ladybugs and they will not survive Alaska's winter unprotected. Lacewings arrive as immature crawlers, unable to fly away, and happily, survive our winters.

Botanical Insecticides
Botanical insecticides are insecticides derived from plants. They are toxic to insects (and in some cases, fish and other cold-blooded animals), but their toxicity for warm-blooded animals (like man) is low. They break down readily in soil and are not stored in plant or animal tissues. Care must be taken when purchasing botanicals such as pyrethrum and rotenone, as they are often mixed with more toxic synthetic compounds when bought as commercial dusts and sprays. They can be obtained in pure form as dusts or emulsions. According to Dr. Richard Werner, former Entomologist with the United States Department of Forestry, the emulsions usually have a synthetic oil spreader added to enable a more uniform application on the plant.

Mineral Oil
As a miscible oil spray, mix mineral oil with water in a solution that is 3% oil. This emulsion will discourage chewing and sucking insects, but may harm leaves unless sprayed only on perennials still in winter dormancy.

Insect Diseases
One example of an insect disease is *Bacillus thuringiensis* (BT), used to destroy the larvae of butterflies and moths (including cutworm larvae). Dave Bleicher concluded from early testing that, unfortunately, it was not effective with cutworms, at least in Southcentral. It is considered safe for humans and is available in liquid and powder forms, the powder keeping its effectiveness longer than the liquid.

Bug Juice Method
This consists of crushing a half-cup of the problem bugs and whirring them with two cups of water in a blender. The resulting liquid is then diluted (as much as thousands of times) and sprayed on the affected plants. Excess extract can be frozen for later use. Do not allow your bug juice to sit at room temperature, where it might become contaminated with salmonella bacteria as it decays. Do not use the method on pests of man, such as mosquitoes and houseflies, which may harbor human diseases.

It is not known for sure why this liquid repels or kills the insects. It is suspected that an insect, in dying, emits some type of exudate that repels that type of insect, or it may be that in the handful of bugs are diseased insects, and spraying spreads the disease and so kills the remainder. Cutworms, for example, can be infected with a naturally occurring granulosis virus. By making cutworm juice with these, one may actually be making a granulosis virus inoculant. Whatever the reason, the bug juice method does often seem to work.

Plant Juice Method

Homemade repellents can be concocted in much the same way as bug juice by collecting plants which are not poisonous, but which never seem to be bothered by insects. Choose plants with smooth leaves, blend with water, and dilute no more than five times. Spray the juice on plants that **are** bothered by pests. Marigolds, onions, and garlic (even though these last two do have their own pests) are often used for this method, partly because of their strong odors.

Hand Picking

This consists of exactly what the title indicates—picking insect pests off the plants by hand. In the case of cutworms, it can mean raking to expose the worms, then picking and disposing of them. Some gardeners keep a can with a little kerosene in it for this purpose.

Georgeson Botanical Garden Collection.

He-shi-ko green onion. Onions are often used as an ingredient in homemade repellents, because of their strong odors.

Others keep a handkerchief or rag handy to wipe their hands when they crush small pests such as aphids. Picking large insects off plants, when the infestation is small, is probably the most effective and simple way to deal with the pests.

Other Methods

There are other things to use, such as soapy-water solutions for aphids, or wood ashes for maggots, but such specific remedies will be mentioned with the insect pest with which they are most often used.

GUIDE TO ALASKA INSECT PESTS

Here are (alphabetically) the major insect pests you may encounter in your Alaska garden. Included are natural controls and organic solutions. As mentioned before, those planning to use a chemical pesticide should consult with the staff of a local ACE office (addresses in Appendix C) for the latest recommendations.

Line drawings are from *Integrated Pest Management Guide for Alaska,* published by ACE. Remember, when using chemical remedies, that aboveground plants should be washed thoroughly before eating. Follow label directions for the required waiting period between the last application and harvest of vegetable crops.

ANTS

Few ants ever attack or eat vegetable plants. Their damage is caused indirectly, by their fondness for the honeydew excretion of certain aphids and mealybugs. They protect these insects for the honeydew. There are many species of ants, and they come in brown, red, black, and yellow. Sizes range from very tiny to about one-half inch long.

Sprinkling steamed bone meal in the garden has been found effective in controlling ants. Organic

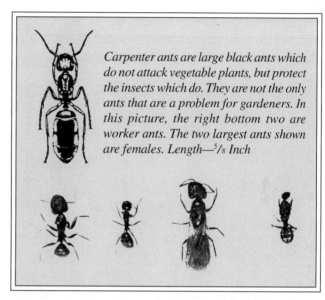

Carpenter ants are large black ants which do not attack vegetable plants, but protect the insects which do. They are not the only ants that are a problem for gardeners. In this picture, the right bottom two are worker ants. The two largest ants shown are females. Length—$^5/_8$ Inch

matter in the soil will increase soil moisture, which will also discourage ants. The herb tansy has been suggested for growing near doorways to keep ants out of homes. You might also wish to try a sprinkled barrier of Buhach®, a powder made from pyrethrum plants, which many Alaskans burn for control of mosquitoes. It is available in garden supply and variety stores. Look for it also in stores specializing in outdoor recreation.

The plant juice method applied to ants would call for grinding hot peppers, mixing in equal parts water, and adding a little biodegradable soap powder. You might also be able to use the ants' dislike of lemon juice to foil them.

APHIDS

Aphids, or plant lice as they are sometimes called, come in many colors, winged or wingless. They are small, pear-shaped, soft-bodied insects that suck plant juices and sometimes spread virus diseases. Most aphids secrete a honeydew that is greatly appreciated by ants, but which encourages molds or other fungi.

Winged adults fly up where they catch the wind and ride for great distances. Aphids, particularly in a wingless stage, can often be found massed almost solidly on the leaves and stems of their favorite food plants. In Alaska they are often seen in great quantities on birch trees. In the garden, they favor raspberries, peppers, eggplant, and various greens. When present in large numbers, they can quickly drain an infested plant's vitality, and leaves turn yellow and curl or twist.

While various aphid species have been severe pests in other areas of the United States and Canada, few have ever been any real problem in Alaska. Among those which have been a problem in the past are the apple grain aphid (mostly in Southeastern Alaska), the delphinium aphid (in the Matanuska Valley), and the birch aphid (in the Interior). Other species of aphids have been noted on a variety of plants, but have seldom appeared abundant enough to be damaging. This can perhaps be best explained by natural controls that seem to operate in Alaska.

The Georgeson Botanical Garden reports severe aphid infestations on turnips. According to Dr. Holloway, they can cause serious damage to young seedlings before transplanting, stunting plants (especially peppers).

Naturally occurring native predators, such as parasites and fungi, help to keep down the number of

Close-up of aphids in their winged adult stage. From Common Pests of the Interior Plantscape, ACE publication (#100C-0-073).

Length—¹/₁₆ Inch

Tiny aphids show up clearly on this willow branch. Aphids, which spread virus diseases, come in many colors.

ACE photo by T. R. Grams

aphids despite their extremely high reproduction rate. Drought conditions that may be unfavorable to the fungi are favorable to the predatory syrphid flies and the tiny braconid wasp parasites. In addition, small birds and the larvae of ladybird beetles do their part in controlling the aphid population.

For organic control, there is the obvious—importing extra ladybird beetles. Many years ago, the main method of control was covering plants with boxes and burning tobacco in a cup beneath them. You can also spray a tobacco-water mixture on plant leaves. In fact, just hosing down the infested plant (such as certain leguminous shrubs in Southcentral) with plain water can provide some relief to the plant. If you want to try a soap solution, be sure you use real soap, not detergent. Two possibilities are Dr. Brammer's Peppermint Soap®, available in health food stores (it is already a liquid) or Ivory Soap®. Rinse leaves with clear water after applying.

Like tobacco, tomato leaves may also help. Crush the leaves, soak in water, and strain. Or grind onions in a blender, dilute with equal parts water, strain and spray. Sugar esters may hold the answer for commercial greenhouse control of aphids. See **Whiteflies** later for more information.

Aluminum foil can be spread on the ground beneath affected plants. The sky reflections appear to confuse the insects, which then cannot seem to find the plants.

Diatomaceous earth is nontoxic, but can irritate if inhaled, so use it carefully. Simply mix with water and spray. Botanical insecticides used against aphids include pyrethrum, nicotine, derris, rotenone, sabadilla, and possibly ryania.

Other possible sprays include a solution of half-and-half rubbing alcohol and water. Some success has been reported with marigolds as a repellent (especially in greenhouses), or nasturtiums as a trap crop.

For chemical control, diazinon used to be recommended for greens and cole crops, malathion for anything except kale, Swiss chard, spinach, and lettuce, and dimethoate (Cygon®) for any vegetable. But science is evolving so fast (as well as regulations on pesticides) that it is very important now to contact a local ACE office before purchasing **any** chemical pesticides. Addresses are in Appendix C. Consult product labels for proper dilution. The insecticides are sprayed on foliage when the aphids appear, but before the leaves begin to curl from their attack.

NOTE: In greenhouses (especially those heated all year) aphids, as well as whiteflies and mites, can be a recurring problem. If chemical controls are used, do not use the same material repeatedly over a long time. About every third treatment should be with an alternative chemical to reduce chances of the development of resistance.

ACE photo by T. R. Grams

This parasitic wasp, family Specidae, is a solitary wasp that lives in colonies and feeds on caterpillars and small insects, thus helping control their populations.

CUTWORMS

Although there are about 956 species of the cutworm family in Alaska, there are only four species important economically. Of these, the red-backed cutworm is the most common and destructive in Alaska gardens.

The cutworm is a hairless moth caterpillar (larva) that dines on leaves and stems, often cutting stems off at ground level or just below. Fully grown, they are smooth and often greasy or shiny looking. Most are well camouflaged to match the soil or debris they hide in during the day. When disturbed, they curl up in a ball. The larvae usually feed at night (hence the family name of *Noctuidae*), but where there is overcrowding or lack of food, they may feed or migrate by day. The adult moth is sometimes called a miller.

The cutworm is able to survive winters even as far north as Point Barrow. The red-backed cutworm is also one of the most serious cutworm species in the prairies of Canada. In areas farther south, many species of cutworms have several generations each year, but in Alaska all species apparently have only one. All important Alaska species overwinter in either the egg or larval (cutworm) stage.

The adults of some species of cutworm have been found in flight as early as mid-June and as late as early October. The moth can easily be trapped in a black light trap in early spring and fall, but when it is most destructive (in midsummer), long hours of northern daylight make light traps ineffective.

ACE photo by Don Quarberg.

These cutworms were photographed in Tract N of the Delta Agriculture Project, in mown rape.

Length—1¹/₂ Inches

Light feeding by cutworms may mean just a few holes in plants, while heavy feeding may leave only a midrib and main stem of a mature plant. Young transplants are often cut off entirely, at ground level. The weeds, lambsquarters and chickweed, seem to be favorite food for cutworms. In fact, during a severe outbreak in the Matanuska Valley in 1943, cutworms actually did more good than harm in potato fields, almost eliminating the weeds without seriously damaging the potatoes.

Outbreaks of cutworms are cyclic, occurring at five to seven year intervals. Problems occur for a few years after the peaks, then cutworms practically disappear. Two factors seem to be implicated in their decline.

The first of these are the parasitic wasps called Ichneumon flies of the genus *Pseudoambyletes*. They parasitize the larvae of the red-backed cutworm. Unfortunately, the wasps seem to have such a strong preference for cutworms over other hosts, that when they build up in sufficient numbers the cutworms are almost eliminated; subsequently the wasps starve and die off, taking longer to build up again than the cutworms.

Insecticides, particularly carbaryl, can harm parasites that attack insect pests. One way to lessen the harmful effects would be to use the insecticide in bait form, rather than broadcast-spraying over the whole garden. Unfortunately, many cutworm species, including the red-backed, striped, and glassy cutworms, usually feed underground, and when given the choice, prefer succulent seedlings over bait, so baits often have little effect.

The second of the natural controls for Alaska cutworms appears to be a disease classified as a *Granulosis polyhedrosis* virus. It seems to be the main disease in Alaska cutworms and is sometimes an important factor in reducing populations of the pest.

When it comes to cutworm control in the garden, one thing to remember is that the adult moth dislikes laying its eggs on bare soil, hence the advisability of a fall cleanup involving tilling in all garden refuse at the end of the season. Wait as late as possible in the fall, when the moths are gone, to mulch the garden for winter. Fall tilling is not recommended for areas subject to wind erosion. Tilling early in the spring may help, by exposing cutworms for hungry birds.

ACE staff

Coffee cans serve as cutworm collars to protect plants in this Alaska garden. The large circumference of the can ensures that the plant will have plenty of growing room. Illustrated above right is one method of making and applying a cutworm collar around plants as a barrier to cutworms. Notice that the band is four inches in depth, with two inches of it pushed into the soil.

In the Matanuska Valley, it may be advisable to avoid unusually early plantings. There, one of the commonest species is the spotted cutworm that overwinters in the larval stage. A very destructive species in other areas of the United States, in Alaska it matures and pupates before most garden plantings are up, so ordinarily would have little opportunity to inflict much damage. It is occasionally troublesome in greenhouses when accidentally introduced in infested soil early in the season.

One of the simplest controls for cutworms is the barrier, or cutworm collar. This can be made of metal (a tin can with ends cut out), or cardboard (empty paper towel rolls sliced into about four inch slices), or even just a piece of stiff paper. Push the collar into the ground around the newly planted seedling, sinking it into the soil about two inches.

139

If metal cans are used, be careful not to use one that is too small around a plant that will grow a very thick stem, unless you plan a way to remove it before the plant grows too bushy. Some gardeners report that a nail or twig the thickness of a pencil pushed down near the stem of a plant will work. Apparently, the cutworm wraps itself around the stem and nail before beginning to chew, and the nail quickly discourages it.

Most cutworms hide during the day beneath litter, so garden litter can be a trap for the worms. You may even want to provide a place for them to hide, such as a square of burlap, four or five layers thick, pegged down. Be aware, however, that traps may not work well if they must compete with other mulches such as straw, which may be used in gardens in drier parts of Alaska. Mulches in wet areas may attract more slugs than cutworms, which is fine if that is their purpose.

Many cutworms can be found simply by raking an area and watching for fat curled worms. If a plant shows cutworm damage, dig in the soil near the plant stem for the cutworm. The red-backed cutworm is cannibalistic, so will usually be found alone. There are a few species of climbing cutworms that can be controlled with the same insecticides as aphids.

Insecticides are more effective when the treated area can be kept damp, as the cutworms will bury themselves in the dirt to keep moist if the weather is too dry. Irrigation may be necessary where soil is dry or overlain with a dust mulch. Chemical control calls for particular insecticides for all vegetables except corn, for which a different one is recommended. Consult with a local ACE office for the appropriate type. If using diazinon, remember it is only effective when worked into the soil, as prior to planting, or when setting out plants. In fact, diazinon was recommended in the past for insurance, especially where sod was turned over for a new garden.

To prevent cutworms from reentering treated ground a barrier is needed. Persistent chemical barriers around the perimeter might be used. Be aware that Sevin® is satisfactory only when applied to the foliage of larger plants—it is not very effective on below-ground feeders, according to the late Dr. Washburn. Again, check on the latest recommendations from ACE (see Appendix C for addresses and phone numbers).

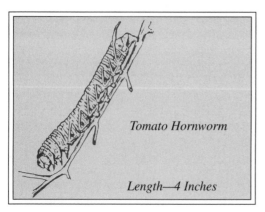

Tomato Hornworm

Length—4 Inches

FIREWEED HORNWORMS

As you might guess, this is a cousin of the tomato hornworm, shown left, which enjoys fireweed. If plenty of fireweed is available, it probably will not bother itself with garden vegetables. Its adult stage is the fireweed sphinx moth. It is common in the Matanuska Valley and at least as far north as the Yukon River. It has been seen in the Interior, but has never presented much of problem there.

The grown larvae are fully two inches long, heavy-bodied, pale brown to green or nearly black, with conspicuous, often red, spots along both sides. Their most distinguishing feature is a prominent, curved bright red horn on the anterior end. While their favorite food seems to be fireweed (they can devour a large leaf in minutes, chewing in a systematic manner from one end to the other), they have also been taken on potatoes and greenhouse tomatoes.

Hornworms are generally on a five-year cycle. Only occasionally will the population of fireweed hornworms be large enough to pose a threat to gardens. Because they are so large, hornworms are easy to spot and hand pick.

FUNGUS GNATS

Fungus gnats are tiny flies, black or dark brown. They are often seen in large numbers flying around high moisture areas. Their larvae are small, wormlike and pale colored, with a shiny black head. They favor soils high in organic matter and are often seen in greenhouses. While the adult flies are considered a nuisance in large numbers, it is the larvae that do the damage, feeding on tiny roots.

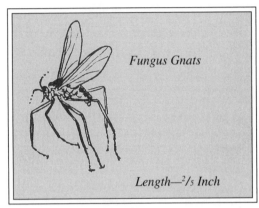

Fungus Gnats

Length—²/₅ Inch

Adults live only about a week, laying their eggs in the soil. When the eggs hatch soon after, the tiny larvae feed on decomposed organic material and plant roots. They will pupate after two weeks, emerging from their pupal cases in about four days. They are a particular challenge where cloth capillary mats are used (see Chapter 5), but may be a problem anywhere there is moisture and algae growth, such as in greenhouses and even drains. Strict sanitation is extremely important for control of this pest.

Hand vacuuming can be used, as well as sticky traps placed horizontal to the soil surface to trap egg laying adults, or even adults emerging from the pupal cases. Insecticidal soap, botanical insecticides, or any insecticide can be used, if it specifically lists the pest and the plant host you are treating. There are specific insect growth regulators available for fungus gnats.

LEAFHOPPERS

Leafhoppers, white, yellowish or pale green, about ¹/₈ inch long, are of the order of *Homoptera* (the same order to which aphids belong). They suck juices from plants such as potatoes and carrots, cause hopper burn, and are found on the undersides of leaves. Leafhoppers (which are jumping and flying insects) are common in Alaska, but not considered much of a problem for gardeners. Some spread plant diseases, but again, not often.

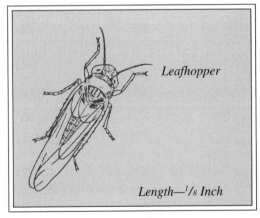

Leafhopper

Length—¹/₈ Inch

Botanical insecticides include pyrethrum, nicotine, and quassia. Chemical insecticides are the same as for aphids.

Leafminers leave visible trails through the leaf's tissue.
From Common Pests of the Interior Plantscape, ACE publication (#100C-0-073).

LEAFMINERS

These are the tiny larval stage of particular flies, moths or sawflies that burrow into the fleshy area between leaf surfaces. They leave visible trails through the leaf's tissue. This often weakens the plant and reduces its photosynthetic activity. The life cycles of leafminers vary according to species

Susceptible plants (which include many vegetables, flowers, and woody ornamentals) should be screened and infested plant leaves removed. Other suggested controls are the same as for fungus gnats.

LEAF ROLLERS

The most common leaf roller in Alaska is the birch leaf roller. But the raspberry leaf roller is the one that will concern gardeners. Leaf rollers are the caterpillars of small gray-brown moths, shown in the picture left. They stunt plant growth by webbing and rolling leaves as they feed.

Leaf rollers overwinter as eggs on bud stalks of host plants. The caterpillars hatch in mid-May to feed and roll leaves. Older caterpillars drop to the ground and pupate. Adult moths emerge in August to deposit eggs and begin the cycle over.

Most control methods rely on applications before the caterpillars have rolled the leaves. Consult a local ACE office for chemical recommendations. Dormant oil sprays may be effective on twigs when applied as the directions indicate. Remove infested plant parts.

ACE staff

Caterpillar stage of the leaf roller that feeds and rolls leaves (above).

Wing Span—$^1/_2$ Inch

MEALYBUGS

This is another pest that is not much of a problem in the garden—they are more likely encountered on houseplants, or in the greenhouse. You will know them by the webbing, like small tufts of cotton, found on the undersides of leaves and in the joints. Mealybugs are scale insects, wingless, with flattened oval bodies covered with a white waxy secretion. They move very slowly, due to very short legs.

Only a few species are native to Alaska, and none of these are of economic importance. Occasionally, however, introduced mealybugs are found in damaging numbers on both house and greenhouse plants. Where they are, leaves will be drooping, stunted or distorted. Controls are the same as recommended for aphids.

Mealybugs' presence will result in drooping, stunted, or distorted leaves.
From Common Pests of the Interior Plantscape, ACE publication (#100C-0-073).

Length—$^1/_5$ Inch

A simple remedy to try first is to spray with a strong stream of water, which will often dislodge them. When the infestation is low, alcohol (a drop on each bug) has been found effective. Apply with a feather or cotton swab. For larger infestations, kerosene emulsion or firtree oil, diluted as their directions indicate, can be applied as a spray or with a feather. Another simple solution to a large infestation in the greenhouse is to let the greenhouse freeze hard over the winter. The botanical insecticide recommended is quassia.

MITES

Resembling tiny red, yellow, or green spiders (but nearly microscopic in size), mites are not insects at all. Adults have eight legs; immature forms only six. Their eggs are tiny, colorless globules. They can survive in humid air with poor circulation, as well as hot, dry air.

Close-up of the tiny spider mite.
From Common Pests of the Interior Plantscape, ACE publication (#1CCC-0-C73)

Length—$^1/_{50}$ Inch

Adults and their young suck plant juices, resulting in a stippled or mottled pattern on leaves with silvery webs on the undersides. Heavier infestations distort leaves and reduce plant production.

Some mites, such as spider mites, make a webbing which covers the plant and may cause it to dry out. Other mites, such as eriophyid mites cause distorted fruit or galls on plant leaves.

Red spider mites in Alaska live on lower surfaces of plant leaves and puncture the leaf tissue with their mouthparts to extract the plant juices, causing the plants to lose vigor. Blotching or stippling of the leaves is caused by the resulting loss of chlorophyll and other cell contents. Leaves may turn gray or brown. Heavily infested plants can dry up completely and die. The adults spin fine thick webs over leaves and stems, which serve to

143

protect the mites. When mites are numerous, they may be found all over the plant, not just under the leaves.

In Alaska, the clover mite is the main species of economic importance. It is widespread throughout the northern United States and Canada, extending to the shores of the Arctic Ocean. It is a general feeder, causing injury to fruit and forest trees, and has been reported to occasionally cause severe damage in flower gardens in the Matanuska Valley.

Mary Armstrong, a bedding plant grower and gardener in Delta, reports the customary Delta winds blow red spider mites from nearby native vegetation onto garden plants. In Fairbanks, they seem to occur in large numbers on birdcherry (chokecherry) trees.

Georgeson Botanical Garden Collection.

These spider mites are busy making their characteristic webbing on a house plant, which may cause the plant to dry out.

Control is similar for all mites. One recommendation is to direct a forceful water spray on plants that do not have fragile foliage. Repeat every three or four days for two weeks. A 3% oil spray is also reported effective. In large plantings (orchards) an effective organic spray has been made of 20 pounds wheat flour to two quarts buttermilk and 100 gallons water, making a gravy which suffocates the mites, yet allows the leaves to breathe.

Rock phosphate or ground limestone may work as well—the important thing is to mix with a liquid that will help it stick to the leaves (as the buttermilk does). In the south, dusting with tobacco dust controls red spider mites on pineapple plants. Houseplants can be placed in a plastic garbage bag with a no-pest strip, but do not expect 100% control.

One tablespoon liquid dishwashing detergent to one cup vegetable cooking oil is said to work on spider mites and some kinds of whiteflies. Use 1-2 teaspoons mixed in one cup water in a sprayer, but test on a few leaves first, as it may damage some plants.

Botanical insecticides include pyrethrum, nicotine, and rotenone. Onions can be ground in a blender, mixed with equal parts water, strained, and applied as a spray. Water can be mixed with Diatomaceous earth for a spray. Be sure to avoid inhaling the irritating dust from this last.

In the greenhouse, and with houseplants, you may want to try hand picking, hand vacuuming, sticky traps, and spot killing with a cotton swab dipped in rubbing alcohol and rubbed on stationary pests. Also, close up easy entry points. Increasing humidity can discourage spider mites, as well as continuously removing webbing they use for scaffolding. A predatory mite, the Encarsia mite, can be used in a greenhouse to help fight a very high infestation.

If you choose to use insect growth regulators, be sure they are specific to the pest type and the type of plant involved. For example, for fruits and berries, apply miticides as directed on the product label for use on fruits and berries.

Chemical sprays are applied to the foliage when the insects appear, but before leaves begin to curl. ACE cautions against using the vines of peas and beans for food if they have been sprayed with chemicals. Consult with a local ACE office for which chemical remedies to use on which plants—they can be very specific. See product labels for proper dilution.

RASPBERRY FRUITWORMS

Raspberry fruitworms are pests of raspberries in most of North America. There is one species found throughout Alaska wherever raspberries are grown, and it is the common cause of wormy raspberries. A few places they have been found in Alaska are Haines, Eklutna, Circle City, Circle Hot Springs, and both the Matanuska and Tanana Valleys. They appear to be most abundant in the Interior.

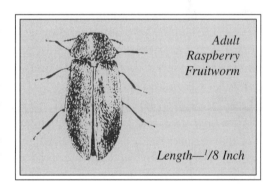

Adult Raspberry Fruitworm

Length—¹/8 Inch

Fruitworms are the larvae of a narrow-bodied, yellowish-brown hairy beetle about ¹/8 to ¹/6 of an inch long. The adults appear in spring, feeding upon fruit buds and unfolding leaves, often destroying the fruit buds and skeletonizing the leaves. They deposit their eggs on the buds, blossoms, or stems of the raspberry. When the larvae hatch, they work into the center of the fruits, feeding mostly on the central core, but sometimes on the fruit as well. The mature ¹/4 inch, slender, whitish larvae drop to the ground, pupating in the soil to emerge as adults the following spring.

Fruitworms cause only minor damage in Alaska, more on wild bushes than cultivated ones (there **are** more wild bushes than cultivated ones), but their presence in harvested fruit is objectionable and they are difficult to remove in cleaning.

Control centers on the adult beetle. Once the worms are in the fruit, control is impossible. The beetles may be treated with sprays or dusts containing rotenone (0.01% of rotenone in sprays, 0.75% in dusts). Three applications are recommended. The first would be about five to seven days after the first blossoms appear, with two additional applications 10 days apart. The Wisconsin Cooperative Extension advises spraying just before the first blossoms open, and again after the blossom period. Cultivating soil thoroughly in late summer may help by breaking up the pupal cases.

RED TURNIP BEETLES

ACE photo by T. R. Grams

Red turnip beetles cling to wild mustard. Their black stripes help to distinguish them from ladybugs.

Length—$^1/_4$ Inch

The adult red turnip beetle looks much like a large ladybug, but is bright red with three black stripes down its back and a black patch behind the head. It is sometimes mistaken for a Colorado potato beetle. Its tiny eggs are laid on the ground in loose clusters, sheltered by debris and soil lumps. They overwinter in this egg stage. In early spring, the larvae hatch and feed on weeds or other plants of the mustard family. Larvae are orange with black spots when small, turning black when mature. They have rough skins with a few short hairs. At $^1/_2$ inch long, they pupate on or just below the soil surface. Adults emerge in about 10 days.

According to the late Dr. R. H. Washburn, this pest occurs "from the Matanuska Valley in Southcentral Alaska to Rampart on the Yukon River. The largest population and the most severe infestations have been found in the Copper River Valley in the Kenny Lake area." In that area, the most common native host plant on roadsides and other disturbed areas is the tansy mustard group (genus *Descurainia*). See photos of wild mustard earlier in this chapter under **Clean Gardening**.

Both adults and larvae feed on members of the cabbage family. When the beetle population is small, turnips seem to be the favorite host plant. But populations fluctuate greatly, and when there are many beetles present, all members of the cabbage family grown in Alaska are severely injured. In Canada, the red turnip beetle is a serious problem in rape (especially in the Prairie Provinces) and in commercially grown mustard.

The larval stage is seldom a problem because it is present only in early spring when it feeds on weeds like mustards, shepherdspurse, and peppergrass.

Adults invade gardens in late June or early July, preferring cultivated crops of the mustard family, like turnips, cabbage, cauliflower, and radishes. The insects appear to travel great distances on the ground—they have wings but do not seem to use them. Dr. Washburn has written that "if thrown into the air, they drop to the ground and then get up and walk away."

The adults will feed for several weeks and then most will burrow into the soil a few inches to go into summer hibernation. In a few weeks they may again reemerge to feed. Mating and egg laying usually occur in late August. The adults do not survive the first hard frost.

Organic controls seem to center on the elimination of weedy host crops near the garden, such as the tansy mustards. In the case of serious infestations, the bug juice method described earlier might be tried, or a soapy water solution sprayed on the leaves.

Chemicals, if used, must be sprayed on foliage when insects appear, but before leaves curl. Consult with a local ACE office for chemical recommendations and precautions.

ROOT MAGGOTS

One genus of fly is the cause of the pests nearly all Alaskan gardeners and farmers have in common. These are root maggots, the larvae of several related flies.

The flies are slender-bodied, long-legged, and resemble the housefly. They overwinter as pupae about two to six inches beneath the surface. The adults emerge from the puparia

Light colored root maggots found on the ground at the base of a cabbage plant.

ACE staff

Length—¹/₄ Inch

and crawl to the surface in early June. Emergence takes place over a period of four to eight weeks. Adults mate and lay their eggs at the bases of plants in cracks on the soil surface. Hatching takes place in 3 to 10 days. The larvae move down and tunnel into root tissue as they feed. After completing their development, they migrate into the soil to pupate and the cycle repeats itself.

The turnip maggot, *Hylemya floralis*, attacks all crucifers such as brussels sprouts, broccoli, cauliflower, and cabbage; and root crops such as turnips, rutabagas, and radishes. These same crops are also attacked by the seed corn maggot, *Hylemya platura*, which is abundant in the Matanuska Valley, Homer, and other coastal sections of Alaska. Attacking onions is the onion maggot, *Hylemya antiqua*. Of the two that attack Alaska's cabbage family, the most common is the turnip maggot. This species, while not very serious in states farther south, is of great economic importance to Alaskan farmers and gardeners.

The turnip maggot is a native Alaskan. It has few effective natural enemies. Some braconid parasites are associated with maggot-infested plants, a particular beetle may feed on the eggs, and the Daddy Longlegs may have a role as well. But when the maggots hatch and tunnel into the root or stem of a nearby plant, it is difficult for predators and parasites to reach them. Decay often occurs in the tunnels of the maggots, and the injured plants are often infested with springtails (see later) and by very tiny root-feeding mites (see earlier).

The injury caused by the maggots also permits various fungal and bacterial diseases to gain entrance. The maggots often kill the host plant, but the water-conducting vessels of some may remain intact for some time, which means the plant may still be green (while under severe stress), even though injury is complete. One way to diagnose root maggot injury to cole crops is to note the red and yellow coloration of the lower or outer leaves. Plants not killed outright may be badly dwarfed. Cauliflower heads may be premature and very small.

Rarely, the seed corn maggot is a serious pest of potatoes, feeding upon newly planted seed pieces. Damaged pieces, and non-suberized ones (see Part Three, potatoes) are those most likely to be infested. Maggots also help transmit various potato diseases, especially blackleg.

Of crops affected by root maggots, cauliflower seems to be much more susceptible than cabbage. Broccoli, kohlrabi, and brussels sprouts are more tolerant, meaning that they can live with high maggot populations more easily than cauliflower. Turnips and radishes are very susceptible to injury, but some of the yellow turnips, such as Petrowski and Golden Ball, while not completely resistant, seem to be less attractive to root maggots. Rutabagas are quite susceptible, but often show an ability to recover from light or medium infestations. Some gardeners who were troubled by root maggots in turnips choose to grow kohlrabi instead, because the part we eat is not the same as what the insects eat.

To prevent the fly from laying eggs close to the stem of cole crops, a very close-fitting collar of tarpaper or light roofing paper can be fashioned, with a hole in the middle for the plant stem. The collar lies flat on the ground and should be applied when the young seedlings are first set out. Keep soil off the top of the disk, which should be at least four inches in diameter. Another simpler, though perhaps more expensive, method for foiling the offending flies is to cover plantings with fine netting, thus preventing the flies from laying their eggs at all (provided, of course, that the flies emerged from the soil before netting was spread).

Other management techniques include destruction of weedy mustards and unused cruciferous crops and debris. Infested plants should be immediately removed from the garden, as the maggots can move from one plant to another when plants are grown close to one another. Crop rotations are extremely important in root maggot control. The farther this year's crucifers are from last year's infested plots, the better the control. Avoid growing cauliflower and cabbage after root crops like turnips and radishes. Because of their higher planting density, root crops have the potential of producing enormous fly populations to plague garden crops in succeeding years.

If there is not a high pH problem in your garden, you might follow the advice of gardeners who have reported that spreading wood ashes around at setting-out time has helped. Victor (Jack) Spratt, an early Master Gardener in Anchorage, reports excellent control of root maggots in radishes when he uses a very heavy dose of ashes in the rows.

There is some debate over why the ashes seem to discourage the root maggots. Some feel it is an unpleasant surface to the fly on which to lay her eggs, and others think the ashes make the soil too strongly alkaline for the larvae. Those who hold the latter view suggest removing the dirt from stems already infested with root maggots, mixing in a heaping tablespoon of ashes with some of the soil close to the stem, then firming the soil back and watering. Another suggestion is to mix four parts wood ashes to one part each lime, rock phosphate, and bone meal. Stir in two cups of the mixture in a two-foot radius around susceptible plants when setting out.

Some ideas have been gathered from organic gardeners in Alaska, relating to maggot control on specific vegetables. They may not all work for everyone in every situation, but a few may be worth a try if you want to avoid the use of chemicals in the garden.

For seeded crops like radishes, turnips, and rutabagas, a natural plant powder called Buhach®, burned by many Alaskans to discourage mosquitoes, can be mixed with the soil

ACE staff

No one will want to eat this turnip after root maggots finish with it (right).

Root maggot damage is not limited to root crops. They destroy crucifers as well, and some varieties go after corn. (left)

A collar of tarpaper or light roofing paper (below) rests flat on the ground to prevent the root maggot fly from laying eggs close to the plant stem.

Root maggots play a part in the spread of the bacterial disease, black leg. (right) when planting. It is available in outdoor and garden centers, as well as variety stores. Some gardeners in Kodiak avoid root maggots in radishes by delaying their planting a few weeks. In Fairbanks, very early radish plantings have escaped maggot damage. Radishes planted in mid-July have also been worm-free.

If insecticide and tunnel-free onions are desired, try growing through plastic film. Lay the film over rows before planting, cut a small slit for each set, and poke the set into the soil through the opening.

Transplants of larger plants that do not like the "warm feet" that clear polyethylene provides, can be planted through the black plastic that is not normally recommended for Alaska's cold soils. Examples are broccoli and cabbage. The result should be weed management as well as root maggot control. However, it is important to remember that a fly that can accurately place eggs in cracks in soil or between plant stems and soil would also be able to place them between stem and plastic, so be sure the plastic is very snug around the stem. More detailed instructions for planting through plastic can be found in Chapter 10.

Root maggots have on occasion been controlled in cauliflower through use of a soapy water solution poured around the stems of plants just beginning to show evidence of infestation. Two other possibilities to try are garlic water, and interplanting with already blooming marigolds (see the companion planting chart in Appendix A).

When it comes to chemical controls, you should remember that the turnip maggot is not cyclic like red turnip beetles or cutworms. There may be a light infestation the first year, with heavier infestations each succeeding year that crucifers are planted. To insure a good crop, ACE advises treating garden plants every year, before the infestation is under way. One treatment at seeding time may be enough for the fast growing radish, but other crucifers must be treated two or more times (Dr. Dinkel suggests weekly treatments). You can reduce the number of applications, and obtain better control, by taking into consideration the **seasonal** cycle of the root maggot .

Hylemya male adults are the first to arrive, with the females following at a slower rate somewhat later. At the Matanuska Experiment Station, emergence of adults was found to begin anytime between June 4 and 19, a difference of 15 days. Eggs are not laid until two to seven days after the females emerge.

The eggs, and the larvae before they burrow into the soil, are the stages of the root maggot that are most accessible to pesticide applications. Adults fly so well they can easily escape to untreated areas, larvae (once they move downward) are protected by soil and surrounding root tissue, and the pupae are protected by additional layers of chitin. Therefore, it becomes very important to be able to establish just when egg and larval stages occur. Insecticide treatments before egg laying, or when all eggs have been laid, will be wasted money and effort.

Timing is important for all management techniques, but it is the most important consideration in chemical control of the root maggot. Therefore, look for eggs as a cue for action. When chemicals are suggested, ACE recommends three treatments (assuming you are unable to determine when the adults emerged) with the first at seeding or setting-out time, and the second and third treatments following at 7 to 10 day intervals. The last chemical treatment should be no later than 10 days before harvest, to prevent residue problems. The recommendation on the safe date may change, so call ACE (phone numbers in Appendix C).

Diazinon used to be the only insecticide approved for use on root maggots. It is absorbed through the maggot's skin or eaten, and acts on the nervous system. However, since the federal government is reevaluating insecticide use, gardeners need to contact a local ACE office for their latest recommendations and application advice.

SCALE INSECTS

Scale insects are softbodied but covered with a hard shell-like outer surface. Adults do not move as they suck plant sap with their mouthparts imbedded in the plant tissue. The plant will lack vigor and may have a coating of honeydew, which causes other problems.

After hatching, scale insects crawl around on the plant before they choose their permanent feeding location.

The stationary adults can be hand picked or killed by rubbing with a cotton swab dipped in rubbing alcohol. Some plants are sturdy enough to use

After hatching, scale insects crawl around on the plant before choosing their permanent feeding location.
From Common Pests of the Interior Plantscape, ACE publication (#100C-0-073).

Length—¹/₁₂ Inch

ACE staff

a high pressure spray of water to wash the insects away. Hand vacuuming can also be used, or sticky traps. Try insecticidal soap, botanical insecticides, or any insecticide that specifically lists the pest and the plant host to be treated.

There are specific insect growth regulators available. As with many other greenhouse and houseplant pests, it may also help to block their points of access to house or greenhouse.

SLUGS

While not an insect, slugs are nevertheless definite garden pests in some areas of Alaska, especially in wetter localities such as Southcentral and Southeast. They are gray or black, and resemble snails without shells. They have no legs and move by undulations of a "foot," aided by a mucus path they secrete, which hardens into a silvery trail. The trail enables the slugs to move from one level to another. Faster than snails, they can cover one mile in about eight days.

Slugs are nocturnal, meaning they feed at night (or on overcast days) and hide during the day. They are most active in warm weather, but most abundant in regions with moderate to cool climates and moderate to abundant rainfall. In Alaska they are most common in the coastal areas of Southeast, from Ketchikan to Haines and Skagway. They seem to have become well established in the Anchorage area as well, and are seen increasingly frequently in the Matanuska Valley.

Slugs are no problem in localities with very dry conditions, as long as there are no moist dark places where they can take shelter. They are occasionally seen in Interior Alaska, but do not usually pose a very serious threat to gardens. The few that show up (probably imported on greenhouse plants) can usually be handpicked quite easily. ACE suggests the use of fingers or an old teaspoon, dropping the slugs into a container with a half inch of salt in the bottom.

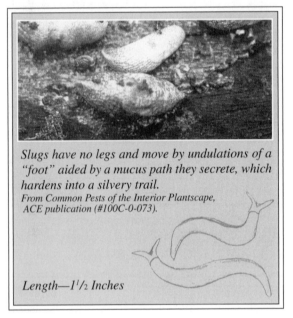

Slugs have no legs and move by undulations of a "foot" aided by a mucus path they secrete, which hardens into a silvery trail.
From *Common Pests of the Interior Plantscape,* ACE publication (#100C-0-073).

Length—1¹/₂ Inches

You can make your handpicking more effective by luring the slugs to where you want them. Provide substitute shelter by placing moist boards or other flat materials next to the plants. Slugs will crawl under to hide and you can dispose of them at your leisure each day. The method works best if other hiding places, such as weeds and lower leaves on cabbages, are eliminated. Leaf or hay mulches may add to your slug problem.

A bait often recommended is beer. The beer is placed in shallow containers (a disposable pie pan will do) in the soil so the top is even with the soil surface. Another pie pan should form a roof to keep out rain that might dilute the beer, making it less attractive to the slugs. A half-inch space is enough for the slugs to enter. Control is achieved when the slugs are attracted to the beer, crawl in, and drown. ACE recommends the beer containers be placed about three feet apart. Change the beer twice weekly or when diluted with rainwater (if not covered). If you are a nondrinker, and hate the thought of buying beer for slugs, try honey instead. Another type of bait is empty grapefruit halves placed near the favored plants. When the slugs crawl in, they can be disposed of easily.

Slug baits and sprays containing molluscicides are available, but are toxic to pets and people, so should never be used directly on food plants. They can be used on ornamentals, or adjacent to garden vegetables if precautions are taken to protect children and animals. Bait can be placed in the same type of containers described for beer, but this time the lid is mandatory to keep out pets and children, instead of rain. Metaldehyde baits may also be placed in a crushed metal can so slugs are able to crawl in, but not children's fingers. In damp weather, bait in pellet form will remain effective longer and be more economical than bait in loose form.

Another effective method is spraying slugs with household ammonia or vinegar. Only the slugs should be sprayed, not the plants, which may suffer tissue damage if directly sprayed. Botanical insecticides for slugs are white hellebore, and quassia.

For long-term control, rototilling gardens in both fall and spring will help by destroying both adults and eggs. This will be especially important in years of mild winters, which slugs can easily survive. Chickens, and especially ducks, feed upon slugs.

One final slug preventive is the barrier that keeps slugs out of the garden in the first place. Slugs have soft bodies, and are very sensitive to sharp objects such as sand, or dry materials such as ashes or lime. Slugs prefer a more acid soil than the ashes or lime provides. In addition, lime or ashes prevent their mucus pathways from being effective. Hence, a good control for slugs is the preventive expedient of ringing plants with lime or wood ashes, at least until it rains. Walt McPherson, when ACE Agent in Juneau, used a gravel drive for a barrier to one side of his garden, and sug-gested keeping weeds removed from around the garden to eliminate

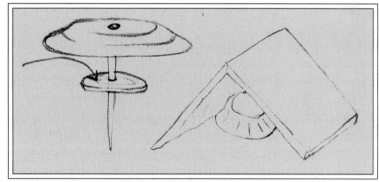

Slug trap using an inverted pie pan or two boards propped together can supply a shelter for slug bait. Then slugs can be disposed of daily.

hiding places for slugs. Some research done indicates that slugs prefer wilted weeds to growing vegetables, which may indicate a possible trap crop with which to attract slugs from the garden.

SPRINGTAILS

A very small, almost microscopic, soft-bodied, wingless insect, the springtail can leap enormous distances. Most only feed on decaying vegetable matter and fungi, but a few species feed upon germinating seeds or living plants. High populations

Springtail

Length—³/₁₆ Inch

can damage root hairs. They may also transmit rots and fungi.

There are many species in Alaska, but only a few, such as the armed springtail, are important here economically. One has been found infesting maggot-injured roots at Matanuska, and another markedly reduced stands of radishes, turnips, rutabagas and alfalfa in the Matanuska Valley in 1945. It was found that same year on seedling radishes at Homer and Circle Hot Springs, and on beans and other garden vegetables at College and Fairbanks. Springtails are not, however, considered serious garden pests in Alaska.

The garden springtail may be controlled with a dusting of lime containing two or three percent free nicotine. It has also been suggested that you alter the organic content of your potting soil, and eliminate areas of high moisture.

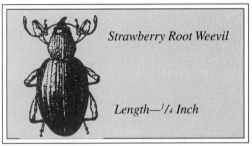

Strawberry Root Weevil

Length—¹/₄ Inch

STRAWBERRY ROOT WEEVIL

Both the adult and their young are a problem for small fruits and berries. The adults are small black or dark-brown beetles with a noticeable snout, who feed on plant leaves, giving them a notched look. The adults sometimes wander into homes, but they do not bite or live on stored food. The adult weevils overwinter in soil, emerging in late May or June. They lay their eggs near host plants.

The young, pale legless grubs, hatch and move to the roots and crowns of the host plants and begin feeding. Root-damaged plants look stunted or wilted. Some pupae and larvae also overwinter in the soil.

In addition to handpicking weevils and removing wilted or dead plant material, beneficial nematodes can be applied to soil. Look for labels listing weevils and follow label instructions. Follow label instructions as well for botanical or synthetic insecticides when leaf notching is seen. Be sure the label lists the plant type along with root weevils.

Strawberries in Alaska also have a pest that Dr. Dearborn called the Alaska strawberry snout beetle, because of its distinct snout. A small black weevil, it bores into and destroys ripening fruit, and is a particular problem when fruits lying on the ground are left on the plants until fully ripe.

Thrips rasp or scrape leaf surfaces, leaving gray or brown scars.
From Common Pests of the Interior Plantscape, ACE publication (#100C-0-073).

Length—¹/₁₅ Inch

THRIPS

Thrips damage beans, peas, onions and other garden plants by rasping and scraping leaf tissues, leaving gray or brown scars on the leaves. Both the fringed-winged adults and the wingless young thrips cause damage.

Pale yellow to brown in color, adult thrips overwinter in greenhouses, weeds, grasses and crop residues. In spring, they lay their eggs in leaf tissue. The eggs hatch in about a week. Young nymphs will feed for a week or so, then drop to the ground and pupate. Several generations can be produced in one year, depending on the location and species.

One of the best methods of control is to eliminate their favorite overwintering spots. You can also use mulches like aluminum foil to confuse them. Healthy plants are not bothered by a moderate number of feeding thrips, so if you keep your plants healthy and growing vigorously, they may be able to outgrow the thrips' attack.

High pressure water spraying can knock thrips off plants. One can introduce predaceous mites, or use insecticidal soaps or sulfur dust. If necessary to use a pesticide, choose a chemical labeled for the crop type and thrips and, of course, follow label instructions.

ACE photo by T. R. Grams

This shows severe thrip damage on potato plants.

WHITEFLIES

Another member of the *Homoptera* order, the whitefly, is not native to Alaska. It is essentially a greenhouse pest and not likely to survive the winter in Alaska if the greenhouse is shut down, but is easily reintroduced by plants brought into the greenhouse in spring. Adults are usually noticed first. When disturbed, they look like flying clouds of snowflakes. They are tiny (only $^1/_{25}$ to $^1/_{16}$ inch long), soft-bodied, fly-like insects with four white, waxy wings. The pupae are only $^1/_{35}$ inch.

The female may live a month in the greenhouse, laying as many as 100 eggs on young top growth. Worse than that, in only three generations, one female can result in 8 million female offspring. Older developmental stages of the fly are found on lower leaves. Eggs are laid in a circle, a few to 10 or more at a time. They are spindle-shaped with a short petiole at one end. They are white at first, turning gray, then black as they mature. Yellowish-green nymphs hatch out in five to 10 days. They have legs and antennae. They crawl a short distance, insert mouthparts into plant tissue, and start feeding. After

Length—$^{1}/_{25}$ Inch

Georgeson Botanical Garden Collection

Georgeson Botanical Garden Collection

Whiteflies (above) are shown on the underside of leaves, but the damage (left) shows up on the top side of the leaves.

This tiny whitefly (below) has been greatly enlarged to show detail.
From Common Pests of the Interior Plantscape, ACE publication (#100C-0-073).

the first molt, they no longer move, and become scalelike, flat, and transparent to green-ish-yellow.

Within three weeks, the nymphs have molted three more times and become yellowish-green with perpendicular sides. The edges of the body wall often have waxy thread-like projections, and there are two obvious black eyes. In a week or two, the winged whitefly adult will emerge through a T-shaped slit in the top of the last nymphal stage. Within two to seven days, the adult will begin to lay eggs and the cycle begins again. The white nymphal case remains on the lower plant leaves, often being mistaken for live flies or nymphs.

Adults and nymphs feed mostly on the undersurface of leaves by sucking juices. They secrete large quantities of sticky, glistening honeydew, giving rise to the development of an ugly black sooty mold. In severe cases, the plants may be completely defoliated.

Infestations may be easier to prevent then to cure. ACE recommends treating plants to kill whiteflies **before** bringing them into the greenhouse. Plants may be washed with a high pressure spray of water if care is taken not to damage fragile foliage. Young nymphs can be hand picked or spot killed with a cotton swab dipped in rubbing alcohol. A vacuum cleaner hose can even be used to remove visible pests, or one can completely strip off infested plant parts. Some people prefer sticky traps or introduce biological control organisms into the greenhouse. When purchasing an insecticide, botanical or not, look for a label listing the plant host, pest and site. In the greenhouse, eliminate or reduce points of access.

"Sugar esters" from a species of wild tobacco plant, *Nicotiana glutinosa*, called *N. trigonophylla*, may be the future answer for commercial greenhouses plagued with this insect. Sugar esters cause soft-bodied insects' outer coating to break down (they shrivel as they lose water), but are fairly nontoxic to hard-bodied beneficial insects.

A July 1998 article in *Agricultural Research* (USDA) explains that by using a fogger that produces droplets of 5 microns in diameter (so tiny they act like a gas), researchers were able to overcome the problem of whiteflies hiding on the lower surface of plant leaves as they feed and breed. On tests lasting only six minutes (dispensing about four gallons of water per hour) the fogger delivered less than half the sugar esters that the label recommended, but was 100% effective!

The main deterrents to the method are purchase of the fogger (it is available commercially from Shira Aeroponics, Ltd., of Rehovot, Israel) and the high cost of sugar ester extraction. More recently, however, Ava Chemical Ventures of Portsmouth, New Hampshire has produced a synthetic version of the active ingredient in natural sugar esters. According to the 1998 article, sythentic esters were expected to "be fully registered and commercially available by 1999."

WIREWORMS

Wireworms are thin, segmented, and unusually hard-shelled worms (really larvae of the click beetle). They are yellow-brown to dark brown, clumsy, and from $1/2$ to $1\frac{1}{2}$ inches in length. They feed underground, chewing germinating seeds, roots, underground stems, and tubers.

Wireworms are most likely to be a problem on poorly drained soil, or on land recently reclaimed from grass sod. They are not usually considered a major problem in Alaska, but gardeners are sometimes advised not to plant potatoes in recent sod areas because of them. Most of the damage from wireworms in Alaska has been due to them tunneling into seed pieces and newly-formed tubers.

The adult stage of the wireworm is a tan to black, hard-shelled beetle, $1/4$ to one inch in length, called the click beetle, or snap beetle. The click beetle gets its common name from the clicking sound it makes when righting itself after being turned upside down. The beetle bends its head and prothorax back. When its body suddenly straightens, the click is produced and the beetle is snapped into the air.

You are probably more likely to see these little black beetles in your garden, than the wireworms. They seem to have a preference for the cucurbit family.

These potatoes have been attacked by wireworms, leaving their characteristic holes.

Length—1½ Inch

C.H.Dearborn, Georgeson Botanical Garden Collection.

Control of wireworms centers on removing the conditions they prefer, such as aerating to improve drainage (see Chapter 11), tilling sod soils at one-week intervals for four to six weeks before planting (especially with potatoes), crop rotation, and fall cultivation. Admittedly, some of these suggestions will be hard to follow where growing seasons are short and wet.

A trap may also be tried if wireworms are a real problem. Put half a potato (minus its eyes, to prevent it from growing) by the affected plants. Run a stick through it into the ground (to mark the spot) and cover it with about an inch of soil. Remove the stick and potato in a few days with any wireworms that have taken the bait.

Consult with a local ACE agent for chemical recommendations.

Chapter 9

Plant Problems

But when the blade was sprung up, and brought forth fruit,
then appeared the tares also. Matthew 13:26, KJV.

The last chapter dealt with insect pests and slugs. But there are other plant pests, many of which are actually more of a problem to the gardener than to his garden. Among non-insect garden pests are fungi and disease organisms, small creatures such as rabbits, and not so small creatures such as moose. In addition, other plants can also present a challenge for the grower. This chapter will attempt to help you deal with the most common of these plant problems.

Plant Diseases

Wayne Vandre, retired Horticulturist with the Anchorage office of the Alaska Cooperative Extension, University of Alaska Fairbanks (ACE), defines plant disease as "any deviation from a normal condition." Thus, the term would cover conditions arising from such things as the environment (lack of water, for example), and physical conditions present (such as acidity in the soil). But, for the purposes of this chapter, we will consider the three main parasitic diseases: fungal, bacterial, and viral.

Fungi

Fungi can live in soil. There are two types—those that grow on dead organic matter, and those that grow on living matter. An example of the first type is the fungus often seen as a green "moss" on the soil of house plants (not to be confused with algae, which are different). It usually indicates the plant has been kept too wet, but it probably will not hurt the plant. To prevent, change the watering method (bottom water), or use a fungicide such as copper sulphate.

An example of the type that grows on living matter would be the fungus that causes damp off and wirestem, discussed earlier in Chapter 5.

Symptoms of fungal attack vary. Unfortunately, most of them can also be symptoms of other problems.

Leaf damage shows up as necrotic (dead) tissue between veins. Other necrotic symptoms

ACE photo by T. R. Grams

Here a cucumber leaf (left) shows the color mosaic that indicates the presence of a fungal disease.

ACE photo by T. R. Grams

This Sub-Arctic Maxi tomato plant (right) is suffering from fusarium wilt.

Wirestem (below), displayed here, is caused by a fungus.

ACE staff

are cankers (sunken depressions), and rots, which can also be caused by bacteria. Soft rots will exude an ooze that is gray or another dark color, even black. There may be an unpleasant odor. An example of hard rot is fruit mummification, where fruit hardens and fails to fall. Damping off, mentioned before, is a rapid rotting of tissue at the junction of soil and seed. For suggestions on seed treatment, see Chapter 5. The damping off organism is worldwide and occurs in all soils, even sand, but does not always kill plants.

Wilt is another disease caused by a fungus. It is essentially a clogging of the vascular tissue of the plant, resulting in plant starvation. There are two important ones, verticullum and fusarium, which occur periodically in Alaska. Many tomato varieties, in particular, have been bred with resistance to these two wilts. Seed catalogs indicate this resistance with the letters V or F after the plant name.

Two other symptoms of fungi are chlorosis (a subnormal development of green color) and mosaic (a blotchy, uneven leaf-color pattern), often associated with virus diseases as well.

Fasciculation (witches broom) is a common malady of spruce trees in Alaska. It is actually a rapid growth caused by a fungus. Fuschia can develop it too, with new shoots all coming at one point.

Mycelia are threads of fungus, and spores are the reproductive stage. "Rust" is an example of the spore stage. Sooty mold is associated with insects that secrete honeydew (whiteflies and aphids). The mold grows on the honeydew. It is mostly just unsightly, but when it is thick, it can block photosynthesis.

See Chapter 14 for more information on specific fungi that occur in greenhouses, and Part Three, **Potatoes** for specific fungi relating to potatoes, as well as beans, carrots, lettuce and cabbages.

Bacteria
If a plant wilts, and you cut the stem and find a gelatinous ooze that feels sticky, the damage was probably caused by bacteria. As with a fungus, bacteria-caused soft rot can have an odor, but hard or dry rot will have none.

One reason that the importation of apple trees is restricted is fireblight, a bacterial disease affecting members of the rose family, which includes apples. It has already been reported in Mountain Ash, an ornamental. Symptoms in Mountain Ash include the top curling in a "shepherd's crook." If a stem is cut, it will exude a sticky ooze. The disease is spread very rapidly by insects, but is not often found in roses, just fruit-bearing members of the rose family. Several chemical sprays and copper-based fungicides can be used to treat this bacterial disease. Some of these may be difficult to find locally because of the low numbers of fruit trees in the state, but can be ordered from outside the state quite easily. ACE is the authority on chemical remedies for plant diseases in Alaska. Consult them for the latest information on types and amounts recommended for specific crops. A full list of addresses and phone numbers is in Appendix C.

Viruses

As mentioned before, mosaic symptoms are often associated with viral diseases. Two common ones are tobacco mosaic virus (TMV) which affects tomatoes, and cucumber mosaic virus (CMV) which affects cucumbers and summer squash. Other symptoms are curling of younger leaves, which can also be a symptom of herbicide damage, too much nitrogen, or over watering. Tobacco users often spread this virus to greenhouse tomatoes, which is why commercial tomato growers forbid smoking in their greenhouses. If you have even handled a cigarette or tobacco, you need to wash your hands before working with or touching tomatoes.

Disease Prevention

As with most problems, prevention is better than cure. Prevention calls for one or more of these four steps: exclusion, eradication, protection, and immunization.

Exclusion

Exclusion really means just using basic sanitary procedures to see that the disease organism never gets near the plants. This is the most effective way to control disease. Two examples are disinfecting the soil and quarantining new arrivals.

ACE photo by T. R. Grams

Zucchini showing symptoms of cucumber mosaic virus.

Eradication

Getting rid of the disease or the plant carrying it would be eradication and would help in excluding the disease from the garden. In some cases, eradication involves pulling leaves off a plant and destroying them. To eradicate a disease, one may be using a fungicide, but do not expect it to reverse damage that is already done. It can only stop further damage and may not even be effective at first. This is because fungicides are designed for a particular life stage of fungi, and may have to wait for that life stage to appear before they can go to work.

Protection

When using a fungicide, the best thing would be to apply it before the disease hits. Protection could be the use of a fungicide, or preventive insect control, if it is an insect-spread disease. It might also mean providing proper air circulation, or avoiding over watering.

Gray mold, a serious disease of strawberries and raspberries, is caused by the fungus *Botrytis cinerea* (see photo in **Strawberry** section of Part 3). In 1994, Israeli researchers mixed one part three-month-old composted chicken or cattle manure with five parts water and let it ferment for two weeks. Spraying this "tea" onto tomato and pepper leaves significantly reduced gray mold on these plants.

Polish scientists report that five grams of finely crushed garlic per liter of soil can inhibit the growth of some serious soil fungi, lasting at least 10 weeks.

Immunization

This last means using varieties with inbred resistance to certain diseases, like tomatoes with resistance to fusarium wilt.

Mice

Moving up now to pests larger than slugs (see Chapter 8), we come to the mice problem. Shrews are often blamed for the damage done by mice, but shrews are meat eaters, and are not very interested in vegetables. Mice are something else. One simple way to cope with mice comes from the late Ray Morgan, former Community Development Agent with the ACE in Fairbanks. He advised taking large empty coffee cans and filling them ½ full of water. Sink them into the ground to within one inch of the top rim. Mice fall in the water and drown. It may be even more effective if you float some attractive mouse bait on the water.

This tomato seedling was cut off by a mouse.

Voles (small mouse-like animals) are particularly destructive of trees. They killed chokecherry trees in the late Dr. Irving's yard by "girdling" the trees (removing their bark all the way around the trunks). But the voles' first choice in food is seeds; nearly any kind will do. Jim Cox, in Fairbanks, decided to feed instead of fight. Just before the snow arrived, he dumped a pile of sunflower seeds beneath his trees and totally eliminated his problem. Despite large vole, mouse, and shrew populations, he reports absolutely no damage to trees as long as he provides them with plenty of sunflower seeds.

Rabbits

Rabbits are so well known for their jumping and burrowing ability that people tend to think only the highest fence, with a great deal buried, will discourage them. But the truth of the matter is that rabbits want an easy dinner. If the fence is 1½ to 2 feet high and buried about a half-foot into the soil, rabbits will generally look elsewhere for their meal.

Moose

Nearly everyone who plants a garden in rural or even suburban Alaska has trouble with moose.

These huge animals have been known to barge right through a five-foot chicken-wire fence, eating or trampling the best of the produce. This often seems to happen just before harvest time. Of course you could put up a high chain-link fence with posts anchored in concrete—but a much cheaper means of protection which seems to work quite well is an electric fence.

Electric Fences

This consists of a single strand of lightweight wire strung on special insulators about a foot above the top of a fairly high ordinary fence (such as might be used to keep out dogs, rabbits, children, etc.). For the latter, chicken wire, wooden pickets, or the kind of woven

This raised bed garden uses flagging to deter moose.

slats used to control snowdrifts along roads would be fine. Without the fence, the moose might not even see the single strand of electric wire and might break it down before it could deliver its shock.

The wire is electrified by a special device called a "fence charger" or "fence controller" which delivers a sharp jolt of high-voltage electricity to the wire about fifty times a minute. Although this can give quite a shock if you touch the fence inadvertently (as you probably will on occasion), really only a very low current (amperage) is involved and it is generally harmless to most people and animals. Some of the necessary materials for building the fence (charger, insulators, and wire) may not be obtainable locally, but are listed in the spring and summer catalogues of the large mail order houses.

Battery powered chargers can be obtained if house current is not available. In fact there are even solar powered chargers, but you can buy a lot of batteries with the difference in price! *WARNING: Under no circumstances should you try to apply house current directly to the fence.* It could kill you, and besides, it would be much less effective against the moose.

ACE staff

An electric fence keeps moose from Bruth George's garden near Fairbanks. You can see the white insulators holding the electric wire on top of red metal posts.

Here are two styles of moose fences made with poles. The middle fence owes its effectiveness to the height of the fence; the top fence (see inset) to the slant of the poles (top ones leaning out from the garden). Some gardeners employ both.

Test the fence from time to time to see that it is working, since it can be shorted out by weeds or by dirt on the insulators. To test, put the tip end of a long, live weed stalk (two to three feet long) on the electrified wire while holding the other end firmly. Then **slowly** slide the weed forward over the fence so that your hand approaches closer and closer. By the time your hand is within a foot or so of the wire, you should begin to feel a tingling sensation that will tell you everything is operating all right. The weed must be fresh so it will contain enough moisture to conduct current. Also, the ground must be damp enough to conduct the current back to the charger's wire. As a matter of fact, it is a good idea to keep the ground near the base of the fence damp, since dry dust is a good insulator. However, the

Georgeson Botanical Garden Collection.

This is all that was left after a visit from a neighborhood moose.

great weight of the moose would probably be enough to ensure good contact with moist earth under a surface layer of dust.

If your fence is not electric, try some of the tricks used in other states against deer, such as hanging human hair or purchased "scent" bags from your fence or nearby trees. Be forewarned, however, that this technique has been found to be ineffective where animal populations are high.

Jeff Lowenfells of Anchorage has tested bobcat urine as a moose deterrent. He reports that it works on cats as well as moose. If you want to try some yourself, you can order it from J&C Marketing, Box 125, Hampden, ME 04444, (800) 218-1749.

Joe Balch, a longtime Salcha, Alaska gardener, found an unique way to foil the moose. He hauled heavy metal surplus army cots (complete with springs) and positioned them above his vegetable rows. The bedsteads proved to be too heavy for the moose to move, so his carrots, beets, etc. were safe.

Weeds

A weed is just a plant growing where it is not wanted. Growing in the right place at the right time, the weed may be considered a beneficial plant. Indeed, many of our cultivated plants were once considered weeds in their native habitat. Before waging all-out war on weeds, consider a few good points they have:

1. They provide an absorbent covering that soaks in rain, preventing caking of the soil surface.

2. Weeds can be used for green manuring.

3. Weeds help hold topsoil together, preventing erosion.

4. Smaller weeds keep a moist soil surface around roots of cultivated plants.

5. They are often indicators of soil fertility or lack of it, as well as providing other information about growing conditions on a chosen site.

6. Their often-extensive root systems collect mineral salts from lower soil layers, where they might otherwise be washed beyond the reach of shallow crop roots. The minerals in weeds can be returned to the soil by composting.

7. Some weeds are edible, or have edible parts.

Weeds only become a menace when they endanger the well being of cultivated plants. There are several ways they do this. Some weeds, such as quackgrass, give off a toxic substance from their root systems that inhibits growth of other plants. Weeds compete with crops for moisture, nutrients, and light. They often host disease organisms and insect pests. And finally, they can make harvest difficult, especially where mechanical harvesters are used.

Weed Propagation

Some weeds spread by seed, others vegetatively, and still others, both ways. Lambsquarters is an example of the first, while chickweed is an example of the latter. In general, those that spread vegetatively will be the most difficult to control, but seed-spread weeds can be a real problem if they are continually allowed to reseed themselves.

The most important weed control measure that can be taken for seed-spread weeds involves timing. It is important to prevent them from going to seed. If you have an area you are letting lie fallow for a year, be sure to till it occasionally so weeds growing on it do not have a chance to go to seed. By the same token, if you purposely introduce a plant to crowd out the weeds, do not let it go to seed either, or it will become your new weed.

Creeping perennials, such as quackgrass, spread vegetatively by means of underground rhizomes. Each cut section of root with a node can re-root itself and establish a new plant. While there will be tremendous growth under the soil surface, most of it will be rather shallow, due to the coldness of Alaska soils. In other areas with warmer soil, broadleaf plants will generally have deeper root systems, but here they never reach very deeply. This is one of the few pluses of our cold soil. Where roots are shallow, weeding is easier.

Chickweed, considered by many to be the number one annual weed in Alaska gardens, is also spread vegetatively (and by seed), but it spreads mostly above ground.

Methods of Weed Control

There are four main means of control. These are biological, cultural, mechanical, and chemical. It is usually advisable to use more than one method in the total weed control program.

Biological Control

Animals, birds, insects, and competing plants are used for biological control of weeds. Believe it or not, it is **plant** competition that has been the most successful outside Alaska. Geese and ducks turned loose to eat weeds and slugs in strawberry patches, for example, have been known to decimate the patch in short order, eating strawberries and blooms alike, as well as other garden greens. Weeder geese seem to favor quackgrass and may leave all other weeds untouched.

If you have a large area to clear of weeds, and you can afford to have it out of production for a year, try buckwheat. Planted thickly, buckwheat is said to be able to give weeds enough competition to seriously weaken them, if not clear them out entirely. First weaken the weeds by alternately tilling and letting them grow back a few times. Then till, fertilize, and plant the buckwheat, seeding thickly. The buckwheat leaves can be used in salads as a green.

IMPORTANT: Do not let the buckwheat go to seed! (Wild buckwheat is a common weed in Alaska.) Keep cutting it off until ready to till it in as a green manure. Remember that a characteristic of buckwheat is that it continues to flower until cut down by frost, making it easy to miss the seed stage of the first flowering stalks. Do not let it go too long.

You can be the biological control. Many weeds are edible. A few examples are dandelions, chickweed, and lambsquarters. Be careful, however, for Alaska does have some poisonous weeds.

Cultural Control

Effective weed management involves planting only clean seed, free from weed seeds. Avoid introduction of new weed species. Uncomposted manures and straw mulches are two common offenders. Weeds are easily introduced into greenhouses in soil brought in with plants. If a new weed species is accidentally introduced, eliminate it from the garden or greenhouse before it can spread.

Controlling weeds around the edges of the garden is another way to help control them in the garden. This can be done by tilling a strip of up to five feet wide all around the garden, or the strip can be made weed free with a nonselective herbicide as discussed later. It is possible to control most seed-sown border weeds by merely mowing or using a grass whip to keep them from going to seed. Encourage children to pick dandelions in bloom before seed heads form.

Rotating crops can be a way to control weeds. Try rotating from a crop that is difficult to keep cultivated, to one that will be constantly cared for. An example would be planting potatoes where a crop grew through clear plastic the year before. Another example might be rotating strawberry plants from a weedy strawberry patch to a more weed-free area. In fact, it is very desirable to plant strawberries into areas that have been under careful cultivation for some time. On a larger scale, such as a farm, rotate from a weedy row crop to a cereal or grass crop.

One more tip is in order. Plant the garden immediately after preparing the soil. Many weed seeds germinate faster than many garden seeds. Planting right after cultivation may help to minimize competition and give tiny seedlings a fighting chance.

Mechanical Control
Mechanical control, perhaps the oldest method of weed control, includes hand-pulling, hoeing, mowing, burning, smothering (mulching), flooding, tilling, sawing, and even bull-dozing (of trees). In the case of beachgrass in Southeastern Alaska, it can even mean chopping at roots with a hatchet or axe.

A weed can be destroyed either:

- by removing it completely from the garden (roots and all)

- by exposing the plant roots in such a way that they dry out before they can re-root in the soil

- or by merely weakening the plant by continually chopping off the green leafy parts needed for photosynthesis (the conversion of light, water and carbon dioxide to plant foods) to take place.

In this latter case, the plant is forced to use up its stored supplies of food to send up new shoots. Even if the roots themselves are never disturbed, if the aboveground parts of the plant are repeatedly cut off, the root-stored food will eventually be depleted and the weed will die. This is very important to know when dealing with a plant that spreads vegetatively. You may not be able to eradicate all roots and underground parts from the soil, but you can still defeat the weed just by outlasting it.

•Timing Your Weeding
The best time to do any weeding is when the weeds are small. .. "hairs," says Dr. Dinkel, formerly with the University of Alaska Experiment Station. He recommends growing in straight rows, marking the rows (the way many grow radishes in their carrot rows to mark where the slower germinating carrots are), then cultivating before the plants even come up. Prompt early weeding will greatly reduce later weeding chores.

•Weeding by Hand

If planning to hand-pull weeds, pick a time when the soil is moist, so the weeds will come up easily with their entire root systems intact. Lambsquarters and fireweed are two of the easiest weeds to eliminate by hand pulling. The large taproots of dandelions may necessitate the use of a trowel to loosen hard-packed soil so the whole root can be removed. If the taproot is broken off and left in the ground, you may find a new plant replacing the old within the week. While the soil should be moist, do not plan to water too soon after weeding if leaving the weeds to die by the rows. Watering before the weed roots dry out may result in the weed re-rooting where it fell. This is especially true for chickweed, which can grow new roots from bits of stem. In fact, chickweed should be removed entirely from the garden.

Add young weeds to the compost heap for later recycling back to the soil, but avoid adding weeds with mature seed heads, unless you can be sure the compost temperatures will reach the 140° F needed to kill weed seeds.

•Hoeing

Some weeds are easier to hoe than hand-pull. Chickweed falls into this category. Sharpen the edge of the hoe for best results. Dr. Dinkel's staff preferred his homemade "hula ho," fashioned from an old broomstick and metal strapping. Whatever the hoe, do not chop with it; shave the soil. A level seedbed will make this easier. Keep all hoeing shallow to avoid bringing dormant weed seeds to the surface where they may germinate. Deep cultivation may also harm plant roots, reducing yields and the ability of the plants to withstand drought. Be careful not to cover garden seedlings with soil, which may kill them.

Most people who garden with single rows will hoe the paths first, coming as close as possible to the plants without damaging them. For widely spaced vegetables, such as broccoli, this may mean hoeing all around the individual plants. But for small, closely planted vegetables, like carrots, hoeing will have to be followed by close, in-the-row weeding by hand. When the plants are larger (have their true leaves), take this opportunity to loosen the soil around them very carefully. Often the soil becomes so hard-packed close to a plant (from watering), that absorption of water and side-dressed fertilizer becomes severely hampered. A trowel, sharp stick, or even an old table fork will help loosen the soil and remove weeds, without harming plant roots near the surface.

•Mowing and Burning

Mowing is usually reserved for border weeds, to keep them from going to seed. If you decide to gather weeds, burn them, and till them back into the soil, consider that their fertilizer and conditioning value is much greater as green plants than as ashes. It may be better to add the ashes to a compost heap, remembering to avoid too thick a layer.

Mulching to Smother Weeds

Authorities on gardening in Alaska advise against most mulching materials in most applications. Heavy mulching, as it is practiced in many warmer states, can result in special difficulties here. The main problem is that most mulches shade the soil, keeping it too cold for good plant growth. Mulching helps hold soil moisture, which is not usually an advantage, for example, in Southeastern. It can also compound the serious slug problems of Southeastern (and, increasingly, of Southcentral) gardens.

Dry areas, such as the Interior with its warmer summers, can utilize mulches, if a few modifications are made. The acknowledged authority on mulching in Fairbanks was the late Eloise DeWitt. She preferred hay, buying spoiled hay on sale when possible. Her 25 by 70-foot garden used about 10 to 12 bales per season. Straw is usable too, but is generally filled with weed seeds. The hay breaks up readily and becomes a fine shredded carpet throughout the garden. After many years of spreading mulch, Mrs. DeWitt hardly ever saw a weed in her garden, even before the mulch was spread for the year. Even the carrot bed was weed free. The years of mulching and composting turned her "Fairbanks silt" into rich, fertile soil so soft and friable that she seldom tilled in the spring.

As mentioned before, there are several modifications that must be made in order to mulch in Alaska. Mainly it is a matter of timing and amount.

How Soon to Mulch?

Mrs. DeWitt cautioned against putting down the mulch too soon. Year-around mulch is not recommended here. She usually put out her mulch in late June, after the ground had benefited from plenty of time to warm up. Peas planted May 5 are about a foot high by then. If May and June were unusually warm, she might have been able to put the mulch on in the middle of June. On the other hand, there have been times when it was not a good idea to lay the mulch until a week into July. The darkness of the exposed earth aids its warming, and you want to smother weeds, not plants, so do not get overeager. A greenhouse, because of the higher temperatures maintained, can be mulched much sooner and deeper.

How Deeply to Mulch?

Equally important with timing, is how deeply to apply the mulch. Mrs. DeWitt's experiences have shown that the six to eight inches or more used in warmer states is simply too much for Alaska. Instead, she put down a three or four inch layer of hay. More would keep the soil too cold. If a weed emerged, she simply threw on another handful of hay.

Some gardeners till in their mulch at the end of the season. Mrs. DeWitt left it, raking it back from the rows in the spring to allow the soil to warm. This old mulch is finely shredded and just right for sprinkling in the rows themselves, between tiny carrots or onion shoots, for example.

Other Mulches

Other possible mulches are wood chips, bark, sawdust, landscaping fabric (such as Weed Shield®), and paper. Compost, if it is available, makes excellent mulch, possessing as well, fertilizing and fungicidal advantages. Grass rakings and clippings are good mulching materials, especially for small seedlings. Mrs. DeWitt reported that fresh grass clippings, used to cover compost mulch on beans, heated up enough to give a real boost to plant growth.

Leaves are easy to obtain if you collect them in the fall and early spring when lawn-lovers rake them—and often bag them for you free! Do know your source well; some people rake up trash and rocks with their grass. Leaves are best used shredded; unshredded leaves tend to lie in wet soggy layers. For information on shredding leaves without a shredder, see Chapter 4.

When using any of the above organic mulches, you may need to adjust your fertilization program, because of the tie-up of nitrogen, as bacteria breaks down the mulch (again, see Chapter 4).

Plastic Mulches

If you cannot obtain enough organic materials, it is possible to use black plastic mulch around cool-weather plants such as the cole crops, if you are careful to avoid holes or cracks where light can enter. Heat-loving plants (like corn, outdoor tomatoes, and celery) will require clear plastic, or a wavelength selective mulch. Clear plastic mulches are used for soil warming (not weed control) all over Alaska (see Chapter 10).

Those using clear plastic will have three choices. Either ignore the weeds, step on the plastic to crush them (pulling by hand any that stick up out of the plant holes), or use a chemical herbicide before laying the mulch. Gardening books (written by authors in other states) often advise gardeners to cover black plastic with a layer of soil to slow down deterioration of the plastic by sunrays. Alaskans are careful **not** to cover the clear plastic with another mulch, or loose soil, knowing they would be defeating its soil warming purpose.

IRT-100® polyethylene allows the sun to warm the soil almost as well as clear plastic. The IRT polyethylene and the newest SRM Red Mulch® do a better job of stopping weeds than clear plastic. While they appear to promote similar yields, one farmer in the Interior reports that the IRT-100® has performed far better than the SRM Red Mulch® with weed suppression on his acreage. All four types of polyethylene are covered in detail in the next chapter.

Chemical Control

Herbicides are available for weed control, but should always be considered a last resort. They are designed for use in large areas with sophisticated equipment calibrated to make precise, uniform applications. Many herbicides have a low safety factor and an excess over 5% the recommended rate could well cause severe crop injury. Even more to the point, herbicides are pesticides and should be treated with the utmost respect and care. Be sure to read labels carefully and follow all safety cautions to the letter. Herbicides should never be stored with fertilizers.

Selective Herbicides

The selective herbicide classification means certain weeds are the target of the herbicide, but most other weeds and garden plants are not injured significantly. For example, a properly applied broad-leaf herbicide would kill dandelions, but not harm lawns. Another type might kill grasses, but not harm cabbages. Remember, the rate of application and other factors (such as rainfall and temperature) will play a part in determining how well the herbicide will control weeds.

Nonselective Herbicides

Nonselective herbicides are chemicals that will kill plants without regard to species. Weeds will vary in their susceptibility to amounts and types of herbicides.

Where To Apply Herbicides

Herbicides act on plants in basically three different ways:

Contact herbicides control by direct contact with plant parts. Good coverage is necessary.

Translocated herbicides move through the entire plant system, accumulating in, and affecting, the active growth centers. They are most effective applied to plant foliage.

Residual herbicides are applied to the soil and are effective on roots and emerging shoots. The length of effectiveness depends upon such factors as amount applied, soil types, rainfall, and temperature.

When to Apply Herbicides

Herbicides should not be applied when a crop is under stress, such as from frost, drought, or wind. The correct time will be determined partly by whether the weed is an annual or a perennial.

ACE staff

The missing plants in this field are the result of a double dose of premerge, an herbicide applied for weed control.

Annual Weeds

According to *Principles of Weed Control*, published by the Washington State University Cooperative Extension Service:

> Almost 100 per cent weed control of annuals is obtained when the herbicide is applied at the seedling stage of growth. When applied at the vegetative stage, control drops to about 75 per cent, and when applied at the flowering stage, below 40 per cent. Virtually no control is obtained when the herbicide is applied at the mature stage.

Perennial Weeds

With perennials, good control can be achieved either in the seedling stage, or in the fall. Fall

173

is when nutrients are moving from aboveground plant parts, down into underground parts for winter storage. These underground parts must be destroyed for control of perennial weeds.

Types of Herbicides

For chemical control of weeds in home garden plots, one must choose from three types: preplanting, preemergence, and postemergence.

Preplanting

This usually means spraying a garden plot some time before planting. Spraying is done with a nonselective spray to kill every growing thing.

Preemergence

This is the type sometimes used under plastic when planting corn or annual strawberry plants. With corn, the seeds are planted, a preemergent herbicide applied on top of the ground, plastic laid, and the weeds are killed as they emerge from the soil—while the corn is not affected.

Postemergence

These herbicides would be the contact and translocation types applied later in the summer, and would usually be selective types. Applying an herbicide to kill dandelions in an already growing lawn would be an example of the use of this type.

Cautions

Perennial weeds are the most difficult to control. Rarely will herbicides give 100% control. Be prepared to use other methods to remove weeds that regenerate or escape the chemical treatment. Contact ACE for recommendations, up-to-date bulletins on specific herbicides, and more information on specific weeds. When purchasing herbicides, as with all pesticides, check labels carefully. Cautions on a recent label always supersede information found in this or any other book.

GUIDE TO COMMON ALASKA WEEDS

The following alphabetical list is by no means exhaustive. The weeds included are just a few of the more common ones found in Alaska gardens. Pictures are included, when available, to make identification easier. When possible, a young weed is shown, as opposed to an older flowering version, because of the need to recognize the weed early and eliminate it.

Beachgrass (*Elymus mollis*)

This grass grows in clumps in the more coastal areas of Alaska. Gardeners report that it is a very persistent perennial with tough roots. One gardener tells of chopping at the roots with an axe to keep it from spreading into the garden.

Chickweed (*Stellaria media*)

The first leaves of this plant are tiny ovals with pointed tips. As the plant grows, it becomes a vine with oval leaves (pointed tips) that are set in pairs opposite each other. A creeping annual, it spreads both by seed and by branching out from leaf nodes. Chickweed roots easily at the nodes, and pieces left in the garden may re-root. This weed grows best in shady, moist areas, but Eloise DeWitt reported that it is one of the easiest to smother with the mulching method of weeding.

Georgeson Botanical Garden Collection.

Chickweed, although it is edible, is considered by many to be the number one weed in Alaska gardens. It can grow new roots from bits of stem and should be removed entirely from the garden.

ACE by Bart W.

Believe it or not, there is lettuce under that thick coat of chickweed. If not controlled, chickweed can quickly take over a garden. This chickweed in Grayling, Alaska was photographed for ACE by Bart W.

Dandelions *(Taraxacum Officinale)*

Fireweed *(Epilobium angustifolium)*

Horsetail *(Equisetum arvense)*

Georgeson Botanical Garden Collection.

Georgeson Botanical Garden Collection.

Georgeson Botanical Garden Collection.

Dandelions *(Taraxacum officinale)*

This weed grows with a rosette of toothed leaves that can be cooked and eaten like spinach, or served raw in a salad. All parts of the plant are edible, but leaves are best eaten young and tender. The bright yellow flowers should not be allowed to go to seed. The thick fleshy root will have to be removed completely, or it will send up new leaves. Some gardening books list dandelions as a good vegetable to grow in rows in the garden, overwintering them as perennials.

Scientists at Rutgers University say that if you dig up four or five inches of root immediately after the dandelions flower (this is when they have the least amount of energy) only about 20% of the plants will produce another stalk. If you keep cutting off all the leaves and as much of the stem as you can (at least five or six times during the season) the number of plants returning the next season drops to only 10%.

Dog Fennel

See pineapple weed.

Fireweed
(Epilobium angustifolium)

Fireweed is a very common weed in fields and roadsides in Alaska. It is often the first weed to appear in a burned over or newly cleared field. Fireweed can grow quite tall, but there is a dwarf variety *(Epilobium latifolium)* as well. In general, fireweed plants are quite easy to hand pull, but Dr. Dearborn, in *Potato Growing in Alaska*, labeled this weed "difficult to eradicate because of its underground spread by rhizomes."

Horsetail *(Equisetum arvense)*

Also called field horsetail, this plant is a perennial that reproduces by spores. It also spreads by underground stems attached to small tubers. It is considered one of the more difficult perennials to completely eradicate. Attempting to till it up only results in hundreds of short pieces of stem to produce more plants. This weed is considered poisonous to livestock, but most are not very interested in it anyway.

Lambsquarters
(*Chenopodium album*)
Of the goosefoot family, this weed is sometimes mistaken for prostrate pigweed, (*Amaranthus graecizans*), but they are not even of the same genus. Common lambsquarters is an erect annual that reproduces only by seed. The stems and leaves have a white mealy coating. Flowers are granular. Leaves grow in alternate positions on the stem and have slightly toothed edges. There are three main prominent leaves extending from the base. Hoeing or hand pulling is recommended. The leaves are edible as greens.

Pineapple Weed
(*Matricaria matricarioides*)
Given its common name because of the pineapple odor emitted when its green pineapple-shaped buds are crushed, this weed is sometimes mistaken for wild chamomile (*Tripleurospermum phaeocephalum*), which has similar foliage but different flowers. When very small, the weed is sometimes confused with carrots. To distinguish it, look for small lobes on one or both sides of the first long seed leaves (cotyledons), which are generally shorter and slightly fleshier than carrot cotyledons. Also, the true leaves will appear sooner and farther down on the weed plant than will the true leaves of carrots.

Lambsquarters (*Chenopodium album*)

Pineapple Weed (*Matricaria matricarioides*)

The pineapple weed hiding behind the radish is masquerading as a carrot.

177

Plantain *(Plantago major)*

Quackgrass *(Agropyron repens)*

Shepherd's Purse *(Capsella bursa-pastoris)*

Georgeson Botanical Garden Collection.

Plantain
(Plantago major)

Both pineapple weed and plantain grow well where other weeds might not. One finds them particularly in tight soil, and in lawns and heavy traffic areas. Plantain is a wide-leaf edible weed. Leaves have three or more veins running lengthwise. Older plants have a thick fleshy root system and send up a single seed stalk with rough, granular green seeds you can rub off with your hand. As with most plants, the younger leaves are best for eating; older ones tend to be stringy.

Quackgrass
(Agropyron repens)

This weed is a perennial. New plants come from joints on the running underground stems and from seed. It can be used as a pasture or hay grass. Persistence is the key to control of this plant pest.

Shepherdspurse
(Capsella bursa-pastoris)

Young weeds of this variety are often confused with dandelions, due to their rosette-like habit of leaf growth. But instead of short hollow stems with fluffy yellow flowers, they send up a single tall stalk topped with tiny white four-petal flowers. These weeds are easily hoed or hand-pulled. If it is any comfort to know it, this weed is more often found in disturbed soil areas of high fertility.

Wild Buckwheat
(*Polygonum convolvulus*)

Of the dock family, wild buckwheat is a vining annual, reproducing only by seed. Leaves resemble morning glory leaves, triangular or heart-shaped and pointed with smooth edges. Stems are red and creeping. Flowers are small and greenish-white. Hoeing is suggested, preferably when the plants are small. This weed is also known as bindweed.

Wild Buckwheat *(Polygonum convolvulus)*

Wild Mustard
(*Rorippa islandica*)

This is only one of the many mustards growing wild in Alaska. It is an erect annual or winter annual that reproduces by seed. The flowers have four yellow petals. **Caution:** *This weed is a host plant for several insect pests of Alaska gardens.* It is suggested you do not allow it to grow in uncultivated areas near your garden. There are more photographs in Chapter 8.

Yellow Rocket
(*Barbarèa orthocèras*)

Also known as winter cress. See wild mustard , above.

Wild Mustard *(Rorippa islandica)*

179

Chapter 10
Coping with Cold soil

If any of you lack wisdom, let him ask of God,
that giveth to all men liberally, and upbraideth not;
and it shall be given him. James 1:5, KJV.

Seeds germinate twice as fast at 60° F as at 50° F. Since most vegetables grow best at a soil temperature of about 75° F (a few like it considerably warmer), anything a northern gardener can do to raise the soil temperature will improve the chances of a successful crop. Soil temperatures in Alaska average about 55° F at four inches below the surface, according to Dr. Donald H. Dinkel, former researcher at the Agricultural Experiment Farm at the University of Alaska Fairbanks. The following ideas have been used by gardeners throughout the state to help warm their soil. You may wish to try one, or a combination of several, in your garden.

Directional Planting
The simplest method to warm the soil is to run garden rows in a north-south direction (greenhouses should be east/west—see Chapter 14), which minimizes shading and lets the warm sunrays reach soil on both sides of the row. Clear cultivation (weeding) will help, as weeds shade out the warm sun, too.

Planting Above Ground Level
Getting plants above the surrounding ground will help, and also may delay fall frosts since frost tends to settle in low-lying areas. Plants may be raised with built-up rows or beds (as described in more detail in the next chapter), or grown in various planters. Planters can be expensive redwood beauties, or discarded tires. The main requirements are that adequate water drainage be maintained, and plenty of room allowed for larger root systems that may result from the warmer growing conditions.

Alaskans can be ingenious when it comes to warming soil, as shown by the late Mrs. Fleugel's raised bed garden in Fairbanks. Her raised beds for tomatoes were really raised—three or four feet off the ground. But she did not stop there. She piled large bricks under the wooden frames for solar heat storage, and wrapped the frame to the ground in clear plastic. She had been experimenting with sweet potatoes in these unique beds.

Other beds in her garden, raised only a foot or so, were lined with insulation and sized to make it easy to throw a quick plastic cover over them, should frost threaten early in the season. This enabled her to plant very early—kohlrabi was golf ball size by the first of July and New Zealand spinach had been providing for the table for weeks.

Irrigating for Warm Soil

The method used to irrigate can make a big difference in the warmth of the soil. Direct watering with a hose on the plants or in irrigation furrows is not recommended, unless the water is tempered (warmed.) Water from wells all over Alaska (hot springs excepted, perhaps) is icy cold.

Mrs. Kemack, gardening in the Interior, was on city water, but still had her old well and

ACE photo by Bart W.

Styrofoam insulating boards beneath planting soil prevent loss of heat to the cold subsoil, and keep the cold below from creeping up. This photo was taken in Shageluk, Alaska, at the Shageluk High School.

pump operational. She found it less expensive to use her own well water for her garden, but she pumped it into a large barrel instead of directly onto the plants. The sun warmed the barrel, tempering the water, which could then be dipped out for watering. It would not be very expensive to add a faucet low on the barrel's side, attach a hose, and use gravity to haul the water to a garden.

For something more automatic, consider a sprinkler system. A very slow drip system would be needed to deliver tempered water to the garden, but warm air will quickly warm water from a sprinkler.

Beans are the one vegetable that should not be sprinkled. They are particularly susceptible to soil-born disease organisms, which can be spread by splattering water drops. Directions for irrigating under plastic are included with the description of the method for planting corn under plastic later in this chapter. For vegetables not under plastic, sprinkler irrigation is most often recommended for Alaska, although more and more gardeners are trying out trickle irrigation systems.

Permafrost Protection

The perennially frozen ground that underlies the topsoil in much of Alaska and Canada calls for special techniques. One such idea concerns the use of Styrofoam® insulating boards. Buried 12 to 15 inches below the surface, the two inch thick boards prevent the loss of heat to the cold subsoil, while keeping the cold below from creeping upward. See Chapter 14 for a discussion on the use of Styrofoam® under ground beds in greenhouses. In such applications, heating coils are used above the insulating board.

What Kind of Styrofoam®?

At one time, scientists at the University recommended Styrofoam® to gardeners freely, but in recent years have been more hesitant to do so. This is because of the many complaints they received from people supposedly following their advice. Investigation showed the gardeners thought that the word "Styrofoam" meant **any** type insulating board. Styrofoam® recommended is "extruded polystyrene," two inches thick (it does come thinner) and light blue or pink. Only with this board is one assured of getting sealed cells. Some other insulating boards, such as beadboard, have open cells, which moisture can penetrate. Once waterlogged, the board no longer insulates, and will have to be dug up and replaced.

OK Lumber Company in Fairbanks sells the correct boards in either two-foot by eight-foot strips, or four-foot by eight-foot strips scored in the middle to make it easy for the gardener to break them apart to make the two-foot strips. The boards come in 1", 1¹⁄₂" and 2" thicknesses, but you will probably want the thickest one. They are available from other building suppliers as well. Whichever size, the Styrofoam® can be easily cut smaller with a handsaw. Someone at the lumberyard may even be persuaded to cut it, if asked.

Solar-Heated Soil

Another soil-heating method used on a small scale by some backyard gardeners in Alaska is circulating hot water. A solar heating pad, resembling an air mattress, is put in the sun. The sun heats water in the pad, which is then pumped through pipes buried underground and back into the pad. It is the same type sometimes used to heat outdoor swimming pools.

This is initially a bit expensive, and is usually used only for a bed or two of warm-weather crops, such as melons or corn. Eloise DeWitt, who used one in her garden, reported that the pad kept the water about 10 degrees warmer, even on a cloudy day, but she did not find it warm enough for cucumbers. She preferred to use the solar pad only with corn, which she grew through clear plastic mulch as well.

Heating Soil with Clear Plastic

In Alaska, one of the most popular methods of coping with cold soil is planting through clear plastic film. This is the method pioneered in Alaska by Professor Emeritus Dr. Donald H. Dinkel beginning in the 1960's, and recommended by the University of Alaska. Soil temperatures as high as 120° F (at four inches deep) are possible beneath a clear polyethylene mulch. It should not be confused with planting through black plastic film.

Clear polyethylene allows light to pass through it into the ground, where it is absorbed by the dark soil and transformed into heat. Air under the plastic is heated, and condensation forms on the underside of the plastic. This water is also heated by the sun and then drips on the soil. Thus the soil is being heated three ways: condensate, air under the plastic, and direct heating of the soil.

This photograph shows a solar heating pad being used in Eloise DeWitt's Fairbanks garden.

The soil remains warmer during the night (which in a northern summer is very short) as the ground slowly gives up its heat, hindered a little by the plastic. The clear film even enables the soil to receive and retain the lesser heat energy present in the weaker light of a cloudy day, or when the soil is not receiving direct rays from the sun (as in early morning and late evening). It should be noted that glass would do an even better job of retaining heat, which you might want to consider if you have access to old glass storm doors and windows when building hot frames.

Why Not Black Plastic?
In many states, black plastic heats soil the little bit that plants need for optimal growing, so experts there find it hard to believe that it is not good enough for Alaska soils.

Virgil Severns reports that when he first joined the Alaska Cooperative Extension, University of Alaska Fairbanks (ACE) as an Agricultural Agent, ACE put out a paper advocating the use of black plastic. "We had to eat our words," he says now. Black plastic does control weeds better than clear, but it does not allow light to pass through to be converted into heat energy. A small amount of heat is transferred to the air between plastic and soil. The soil will be heated directly only when the black polyethylene is in direct and total contact; any little lump or pebble will foil it. Since this total contact is seldom, if ever, achieved, most of the heat is absorbed by the plastic itself, and reflected right back into the atmosphere through heat transfer with every little breeze. Either type of plastic, however, will help conserve moisture, particularly important in the Interior.

ACE staff by T. R. Grams

Beans on the back left had the benefit of growing for two weeks under clear plastic. The others did not.

In some other states, strawberry growers prefer a double-sided type of plastic. The underside is black, to stop weed production, and the upper surface is white, to hinder heat transmission (the soil is too hot where they are growing).

Clear Visqueen® is not a particularly good environmental solution to the problem of cold soil, but organic gardeners can take heart from the fact that it will grow a beautiful crop of weeds as well as it grows their vegetables. These can be tilled in as green manure after the harvest, when the plastic is removed.

The University of Alaska at one time advised using an herbicide before covering, but later tests seemed to indicate weeds kept under plastic do not set viable seed, and few gardeners bother to do anything about the weeds any more. Walking on the plastic now and then helps to keep the weeds from puffing up the plastic.

But even without viable seeds, weeds pushing up out of holes cut for plants are annoying, and they rob plants of needed nutrients and moisture. Dr. Dinkel spent several decades attempting to get polyethylene film manufacturers to develop colored wavelength selective films, to no avail. Then, in the late 1980's, the University of New Hampshire developed a wavelength selective mulch: infrared transmitting polyethylene film, or IRT-76® polyethylene. The brown/green film used now (IRT-100®) warms the soil almost as well as clear polyethylene, letting in infrared rays, used by plants for heat and reproduction, while blocking most of the light waves (photosynthetically active radiation) that weeds need for leaf growth.

How well does it heat the soil? At the Georgeson Botanical Garden in the Interior, sweet corn, grown under IRT-100® generally produces ears 3 to 5 days after the same variety grown under clear plastic. In most years, however, the IRT corn catches up and final yields are not significantly different.

Clear plastic helps heat soil for an early gardening start.

By early 1998, the US Department of Agriculture was reporting on tests of a new "red mulch" called SRM Red Mulch®. Unlike the IRT-100® polyethylene, the new material only claims to reflect back up to the growing plant the infrared rays that plants need for their reproductive growth (i.e. causing them to set flowers), thereby increasing production. In the USDA's tests, SRM Red Mulch® increased production of high grade early tomatoes by 12% to 20% over black mulch. There are similar claims for increased production in strawberries. Grant E. M. Matheke, Research assistant, Georgeson Botanical Garden, reported preliminary findings of the red film suppressing weeds about as well as black or IRT polyethylene. Further testing has downgraded this assessment.

Because what works in warmer states does not necessarily work in Alaska, University of Alaska researchers planted their own test plot in the GBG Family Food Garden in 1998, this time comparing SRM Red Mulch® to the standard IRT-100® polyethylene. Due to an unusually damp and cold July and August, tests in the Tanana Valley had mixed results, and could not be considered conclusive. In other words, there was not enough sun to reflect back on the plants and increase production. Controlled experiments will need to be repeated over several seasons to account for weather patterns. But, referring to both the IRT-100® polyethylene and the newer SRM Red Mulch®, Dr. Patricia S. Holloway, Associate Professor of Horticulture at the University of Alaska Fairbanks, states that, "This new generation of mulches holds promise for growers interested in herbicide-free production."

The researcher who developed SRM Red Mulch® stated he does not know if the film actually raises soil temperatures. There is also the question of whether or not the different angle with which sun rays arrive in northern latitudes is a factor in how well the mulch reflects the infrared rays. It could be that when the sun hits the plastic at an angle, it bounces off also at an angle and misses the plant leaves altogether.

Much more experimentation will be needed to assess how well SRM Red Mulch® heats

ACE staff

Here clear plastic warms the soil for plants. Soil covers the edges of the plastic.

soil. In the poor growing conditions of the summer of 1998, yields under SRM Red Mulch® closely approximated yields under IRT-100® film on control crops, even though it appeared the SRM Red Mulch® did not warm soil much better than black plastic. Further controlled experiments into weed suppression and soil heating with both films are planned for the Experiment Farm at the University of Alaska Fairbanks (which is located on a south facing slope), and at North Pole Acres (which is located on the much colder flats near North Pole). Tentative conclusions from the 1999 trials at both locations are that the SRM Red Mulch® did not justify the cost difference over clear plastic, and that the IRT-100® probably did, especially for organic gardeners who want warm soil with fewer weeds.

Tests at the Georgeson Botanical Gardens involving tomatoes (Sub -Arctic 25) showed no measurable increase in yield using SRM Red Mulch® as opposed to IRT-100®.

Many different vegetables are recommended for growing through clear polyethylene, but the technique varies according to whether you start with seeds or transplants. Since the use of IRT films is not yet widespread, the directions given here (except where noted) will refer to clear polyethylene. Gardeners can try either of the IRT films; they are both available in the Interior at Holm Town Nursery in Fairbanks, as well as from North Pole Acres. In Anchorage, Alaska Greenhouses carries the IRT-100® in 1000 foot rolls (four ft. wide) and they will sell it by the foot. They have plans to stock SRM Red Mulch® also.

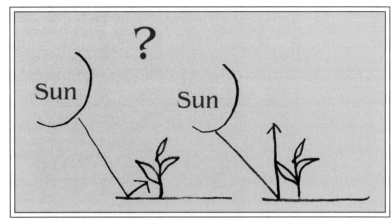

It is unknown whether the angle with which sun rays arrive in northern latitudes is a factor in the SRM Red Mulch's® ability to reflect infrared rays back onto the plants.

The addresses for all the above are in Appendix C.

Seeds Under Plastic—Corn

Corn is a good example to use in explaining the technique for planting seeds under clear plastic. It is a heavy feeder, so the plot should be well fertilized before planting.

You can make rows with string or draw lines about three feet apart with a stick. The Georgeson Botanical Garden plants their rows five feet apart ("on five foot centers") to allow room for burial of plastic at the edges.

Some gardeners save time and seed by pre-sprouting seed in wet paper towels, then planting only one kernel in each hole. If you do not pre-sprout the seed, more kernels per hole will be needed to allow for possible poor germination. The Georgeson Botanical Garden sows three seeds per hole and hopes all survive to give three plants per hole. Remember to plant several rows, for adequate wind pollination.

ACE suggests trenching as an aid to securing the plastic film. "Make a narrow trench 6 to 8 inches deep and $1^{1}/_{2}$ feet away from the center of the row the entire length of the row. Do this on both sides." A rear-tine rototiller with a furrowing attachment makes a good furrow, but should be used **before** planting. In fact, it may be better to trench and secure one edge of the plastic before planting, regardless of method. Peel the plastic back to sow the seed, or plant before laying it. A rototiller is not necessary if the ground has been well loosened; a hoe will do fine. In addition to the sides, trench across the ends.

If your soil is very sandy, a trench may not be needed. At Manley Hot Springs, the plastic is simply shoved into the ground with a square-edged shovel. For this method, plastic 4 to 6 mils thick works best and eliminates excessive tearing.

It is very important to soak the soil well before laying the polyethylene. If the soil is wet enough to begin with, the poly film will hold the moisture in and the plot will not need watering again until the plants are let out.

The next step is to lay out four-foot wide polyethylene centered over the row, with the edges in the trench. The University of Alaska recommends the less expensive 1½ mil poly-

ACE staff

A farm-scale commercial grower uses his tractor with a mulch layer to lay polyethylene. There are a variety of types, for flat or raised beds. Plastic mulch lifters can even remove your mulch at the end of the season.

ethylene, but it may be difficult to obtain in small enough quantities. It is most commonly found in 500 to 1,000 foot rolls. On the other hand, 4 mil plastic can be found locally, in 50 or 100-foot rolls, which is a good weight to use on homemade greenhouses as well. Whatever thickness is chosen, do not use less than a three-foot wide strip for maximum soil heating. Soil heating is reduced at widths less than three feet, according to GBG Research assistant, Grant Matheke.

Farm-scale planters will prefer a tractor with a mulch layer attachment. There are mulch layers for flat beds and raised rows, as well as attachments to allow the laying of drip irrigation tubing at the same time. There are even plastic mulch lifters to remove your mulch at the end of the season.

The final planting step is to refill the trenches, anchoring the plastic. Stretch the plastic while doing this, to keep it tight.

An alternate method is to use 20-foot wide film, trenching the perimeter only. Sow four or five rows and lay heavy sticks or pipes between the rows to keep the plastic flat.

Irrigating Under Plastic

An added bonus with this latter method is that it allows one to design a watering system at the same time, before spreading the plastic. Lay double-wall (or soaker) hose up one row and down another throughout the corn patch. Let one end stick out from under the plastic for attaching to a water source when needed, and plug the other (directions come with it). Another method of irrigation would be a drip system set up on top of the plastic with tiny feeder tubes going to each plant.

The owner of this boxed-in bed, with plants growing through clear plastic mulch, used poles and stones to further anchor the plastic.

Years ago, if one used the row method of planting, Dr. Dinkel recommended Chapin Twin Wall® hose, of at least 8 mil thickness, for under the plastic between each two corn rows. He believed that hose of that thickness was less apt to crack or leak in the middle of the season. Since then, there have been a lot of changes in irrigation hoses available.

The first drip tapes were simply polyethylene film folded lengthwise and sewn to form a tube, in which the water outlets were the holes formed by the stitch. They worked fairly well in small gardens, but the water pressure was not suited for long commercial rows.

A huge step forward came with the invention of the double chamber hose, allowing much longer row lengths with relatively uniform water flow. Outlet flow was regulated by the ratio of the number of inner openings between the inner chamber to the outlet openings in the outer chamber. But the water tended to squirt rather than drip, and clogging was a problem. There was also a problem when the tubing encountered a bump of soil or incline of more than .25 m (about 10 inches) high.

The twin-wall being sold now is called Chapin Turbulent Twin Wall® (by Chapin Watermatics, Inc.). The patented flow path produces a turbulent flow that reduces clogging. It is pressure compensating, which evens the flow rate over rough ground or for long rows. The flat tape is placed with the outlets on the top, and they drip, not squirt. Liquid fertilizers can be delivered through the tubing.

Now, nurseries, greenhouses, and garden supply stores carry a variety of systems, as well as individual components to build your own system. Water delivery varies from pre-spaced emitters to tiny holes all over, or no holes (apply emitters where wanted). Some are flat polyethylene tubings, some round, and many are made from recycled tires. Thicknesses range from 4 mil to 25 mil. Most can be buried with soil or mulch, or stay on the surface. Grant Matheke warns that good quality soaker hoses will water better than poor quality ones. Gardeners with heavily mineralized water supplies should also be aware that the minerals will quickly clog soaker hoses.

For those who do not want to start from scratch, complete drip irrigation kits are available with all the fittings needed. One, for example, includes 100 feet of drip tube and all components to water four rows in a 400 square foot garden, along with simple, illustrated directions. Components include sleeve tees and elbows to build a watering grid, and a regulator/screen assembly. This particular one has tubing that is thin-skinned and flat, with emitter holes every foot. It is easy to cut and close off the ends of the tubes where necessary.

Letting Out the Corn
When the corn shoots are four to six inches long, they will be growing lying on their sides under the plastic. Go down the rows, tapping the plastic. This knocks the condensation off, so you can see where the corn is growing. If you are using IRT-100® film, you will not be able to see the corn, but you can look for where the emerging corn pokes up slight bumps in the plastic. These will need to be cut out before they bend over too far, or become sunburned.

Cut two slits in the form of an X above where the corn emerges from the soil, not where the tips of the leaves happen to be lying. Slip an index finger under the bent-over stalk and lift gently to ease it out. Do not worry if the corn seems bent over or even a little yellowed; it will soon stand straight and green. Usually corn will not sunburn through the clear plastic in Alaska, but there have been cases reported in the warmer Interior, and the remedy is to cut it out a little sooner.

All other plants should be let out immediately when they sprout. Broadleaf plants sunburn very quickly through clear plastic. When cutting, slice an absolute minimum of plastic, to retain as much heat and moisture as possible.

This is the time to do any necessary thinning if more than three kernels were planted in each hole and by some miracle every single one germinated. Some believe, however, that one should not disturb the plant by pulling out the extras.

Corn germinates so fast in its flat greenhouse, that it is usually ahead of the weeds at this point, but if there are a lot of weeds, remove them from the holes now. During the summer, as the corn grows, pluck out the larger weeds as they begin to push the plastic up, a problem that may not occur when growing under IRT-100® film or SRM Red Mulch®. If necessary, enlarge the holes slightly to accommodate the thickening stalks, although corn stalks some-time show themselves to be perfectly capable of enlarging their own holes.

Add a liquid fertilizer (the late Ray Morgan, former Community Development Agent with the ACE, recommended 20-20-20) through the holes as summer progresses. If rain is sparse, and one of the drip methods mentioned earlier was not set up, slip a hose into the openings to water. If rainwater collects on the plastic film, poke a little hole in the plastic under each pool, and let it water the ground beneath.

Other vegetables that can be planted from seed under clear plastic mulch are squash, cucumbers, bush beans, and pumpkins. However, remember sunburn and let them out as soon as possible. At one time, ACE recommended growing peas through plastic in Southeastern, but heavy losses due to sunburn caused the recommendation to be dropped, according to Walt McPherson, former Southeastern ACE Agent.

Georgeson Botanical Garden Collection.

Sweet corn grows through clear plastic at the University of Alaska Fairbanks test plot.

Since IRT films block the sunrays that leaves require to grow, do not use these types when planting from seed, except for corn. The corn seed itself contains enough nutrition to see the seedling through until its true leaves emerge. It is important, however, to cut the corn out of the plastic promptly when it pushes up the film.

Beans would also have stored nutrition in their cotyledons (first non-true leaves) but they do not push up the plastic like corn. This means one must time their emergence and guess at where they are for cutting out, making IRT films more difficult to use than clear mulch with beans. Therefore, except for corn, save the IRT films for growing transplants through plastic. That way, the leaves of the plants will be above the plastic, and only weed growth will be hindered.

Transplants Through Plastic

Some vegetables need a head start before they are put outside. Since they are then too big to cover with plastic, the plastic film is usually laid first, and then holes cut for the plants. A bulb planter can be sharpened and used to cut the openings and remove dirt from the planting holes all in one operation (see Chapter 5). It is twisted as it is pushed in, and it lifts out a core of dirt very neatly. Be sure the plastic is well secured in the trenches before attempting this.

It is possible to use a knife to slit the plastic and then a trowel to dig out the dirt, but it is awkward getting the dirt back out without making the hole in the plastic too large. A posthole digger works like the bulb planter, removing the core of soil, but it too will make rather large holes in the plastic.

Some plants that have been grown successfully through clear plastic from transplants are outdoor tomatoes (see Chapter 12 about special varieties for Alaska), squash, pumpkins, cucumbers, celery, eggplant, artichokes, corn, and strawberries. The technique varies somewhat for these last two. See Part Three, **Corn**, for information on raising corn from transplants, rather than seed.

Alaska varieties of strawberries do not need plastic at all (although they often are grown that way), but the everbearing varieties grown as annuals usually are grown through polyethylene with an additional row cover of clear plastic. This mini-greenhouse can also be adapted for use with other heat-loving vegetables, such as cucumbers, as long as the cloches are opened before tender plants overheat and burn.

The last photograph in this chapter shows a slitted row cover, which the Georgeson Botanical Garden often uses over cucurbits, particularly cucumbers, if June is cold and/or rainy. Polyethylene with the slits already cut is available from some farm supply catalogs.

Row Covers—Strawberries

Dr. Dinkel, as a former Plant Physiologist at the University of Alaska, worked for years perfecting methods of growing some of the larger everbearing varieties of strawberries. He spent considerable time with Quinault, which yields enormous berries in Alaska's long days. Along with Patricia J. Wagner and Grant E. M. Matheke, he wrote a pamphlet, *Growing Everbearing Strawberries as Annuals in Alaska* (#HGA-00235) for ACE, describing his technique. The following is a condensed version of the method. Those who are serious about growing everbearing strawberriest will want to pick up the original from a local ACE office.

ACE staff

A strawberry plant (right) is being planted through clear plastic after the edges of the plastic are secured with soil.

Ed Bostrom

Prince Cambilargiu (left) cuts holes in polyethylene with a posthole digger.

This tomato plant (below) is growing through clear plastic, as well as inside a plastic cage.

ACE staff

Three strips of plastic are laid on the ground; a four-foot wide strip in the center, with 2 three or four-foot wide pieces on top, inner edges overlapping and outer edges flush with the center strip. Outer edges are secured with dirt in trenches as described earlier for corn, then the top flaps peeled back. Strawberries are planted with a bulb planter in two or three staggered rows on the center strip.

Nine gauge wire cut in about six foot lengths is arched over the row at about five foot intervals or less, and pushed into the ground through the edges of the center strip, near the trenches. In Dr. Dinkel's strawberry beds, they make an arch 30 inches wide and 18 inches high. After planting the strip, the top flaps are lifted toward the center and fastened over the hoops by rolling them together and clipping with spring clothespins.

ACE staff

The row on the left shows the plastic strips laid flat. The next row has the wires in place, and one side pulled up and fastened to the wire. The fourth row (far right) shows both sides pulled up to protect and warm the plants.

An alternate method calls for a single 10-foot wide plastic strip. Two trenches three feet apart the length of the film secure the center, but leave the outer edges, about $2^1/_2$ feet, on each long side free. The free edges are then drawn up over the hoops and fastened as above. Allowing $^1/_2$ foot of plastic for each ditch, trenches two feet apart would permit use of eight-foot wide film and three or four-foot long wires.

This row cover will protect from wind only if the ends are sealed and the hoops pressed into the ground so as to be all the same height. Hoops at the ends of rows should be lower and the ends of the plastic buried. The resulting "cloche" is quick to set up, and inexpensive enough for even a very large planting, if $1^1/_2$ mil polyethylene is used.

Interested in growing perennial types of strawberries (June bearers)? Pick up ACE publication, *Strawberries in Alaska* (#HGA-00034), by the late Dr. Curtis H. Dearborn.

ACE staff

Extra row covers are fine for everbearing varieties like Quinault. But the hardy perennial Toklat Strawberry plants are shown here (left) during field trials in 1997, planted through IRT-100® polyethylene, with no row covers.

Strawberries (below) growing in cloches. Here the top plastic strips are pulled up over the wire hoops and fastened above the plants. The plants are also growing through a plastic strip laid flat on the ground.

Commercial Plantings—Strawberries
In the Fairbanks area, Gordon Herreid has been experimenting with one acre of strawberries for a pick-your-own enterprise.

To plant on such a large scale, he mechanized his operation many years ago with a strawberry planter and a machine to lay the three strips of plastic at once. He found it worked better for him to plant the strawberries first, then lay the film over them. To cut holes for the plants to come through, he invented a special tool. Using a small propane torch and some plumbing fittings (mostly reducers), he came up with a hot plastic cutter about three inches in diameter. When the heated circular metal is touched to the plastic above a plant, a neat hole is immediately melted in the plastic with no harm done to the plant below. Using this tool, holes can be cut for 400 plants in 30 minutes, with about half a bottle of propane.

Combining Soil-Heating Methods
For growing melons, several methods may be combined to warm the soil. As mentioned earlier, the University of Alaska used Styrofoam® and heating coils in a greenhouse, but the author's cold frame (see Chapter 14 for photo and directions), with plants also growing through clear plastic laid on the ground, has produced cantaloupes, too. The following year, larger, later varieties matured in the same frame with heating cable added below the soil, but above Styrofoam® boards.

Another example of combining methods would be to grow on a raised mound, covered with clear polyethylene. This is particularly effective in areas of heavy rainfall, as the plastic helps keep the mounds from washing away. See the next chapter for more details on raised mounds.

Local gardeners in Fairbanks have adapted Dr. Dinkel's strawberry cloches to provide raised beds for other vegetables. Drip watering systems can be installed before the plants are set in. If a continuous plastic covering is used (instead of fastening two strips with clothespins), ventilation holes should be cut in the plastic, or pre-slitted plastic used.

Using Black Plastic
When attempting to find ways to warm soil, it is well to keep in mind that some plants, like broccoli and cabbage, do **not** like warm feet and are not usually grown through clear plastic. These are plants that even subarctic gardeners can mulch with black plastic for weed and moisture control. Another possibility would be to use the IRT film, which does not warm the soil quite as much as the clear polyethylene. North of the tree line (Nome for example) gardeners might wish to use the clear plastic anyway, if there are problems with these vegetables.

Master Gardeners, (from left to right) Rhonna Gilmore, Julie Hnilicka, and Lou Andreis, plant the Demonstration Garden at the Tanana Valley State Fairgrounds. Here IRT red mulch is covering raised rows, for even more heat.

Michele Hébert

A drip watering system is installed in this raised bed before an arch is put in to hold a plastic cover above the plants.

If the rows are covered tightly with plastic, be sure to cut ventilation holes as shown here.

Chapter 11

Working with Wet soil

...He maketh his sun to rise on the evil and on the good,
and sendeth rain on the just and on the unjust. Matthew 5:45b, KJV.

A few areas of Alaska, notably Southeastern Alaska, have a real weather disadvantage—extremely heavy rainfall, which itself is the cause of many related problems.

Wet soils are cold, both because the water itself is cold, and because evaporation from the soil surface has a cooling effect. Waterlogged soils cut off the air supply to plant roots, slowing plant growth. Rain erodes expensive topsoil, washes away organic matter, and leaches plant nutrients out of the topsoil. This leaching also affects soil pH, causing soils in Southeastern to be naturally acid. Certain pests, like slugs, are particularly fond of moist soil, and high moisture combined with long days favor rapid weed growth, especially such weeds as chickweed. Rainy days mean cloud cover and reduced sunlight for vegetables.

This chapter cannot stop the rain, but it will attempt to help you deal with the challenge of removing excess water from your garden, and/or raising plants up out of the water. Other aspects of the problem (such as slugs, weeds, and soil pH) have already been covered earlier in this book.

How Much Water is Enough?

According to the Alaska Cooperative Extension, University of Alaska Fairbanks (ACE), $^3/_4$ to 1 inch of water per week is required at midseason when growth is rapid. Use the lower figure if the weather is on the cool side. About half the above amount will be required when the plants are small, and later when they have reached maturity in late summer and early fall. A total of about 10 to 12 inches of water during the growing season is the maximum a garden crop in Alaska could use.

How much rain can be expected on a garden? That is hard to predict, but here are some average precipitation figures, in inches. These are precipitation averages for January through September, "based on Historical records from 1970-1997 when data available" for some Alaskan cities:

Average Precipitation Figures, January- September				
Anchorage	Fairbanks	Juneau	Kodiak	Nome
11.73 inches	8.04 inches	39.03 inches	51.49 Inches	11.98 Inches
Information from Alaska Agricultural Statistics 1998, Alaska Agricultural Statistics Service, USDA.				

If you figure that you need about 10 inches of total water for June, July, and August, it is easy to see why you would want to plan to irrigate in Fairbanks, and why you would **not** want to do so in Kodiak.

Draining "Off Garden" Water

If the garden or area around it has any slope at all, drainage may need to be provided around the garden, to prevent runoff from higher areas flooding or even washing away the plot. A V ditch above the garden is suggested to divert surface water around the garden. Do

Here terracing has been used for fruit trees in Clair Lammers' orchard. This early photo shows growing fruit trees through black plastic, which he no longer recommends. See Chapter 13 for more information.

remember to check on where you are diverting the water—you do not want to flood a neighbor's garden below.

Draining the Garden Itself

There are several ways within the garden to improve drainage, depending on how serious the problem is. Sand or fine gravel can be worked in well, in moderate amounts, to improve poorly draining soils of heavy clay or muskeg. Beach shells can be used where available. If the problem is more serious, ways must be found to keep water slowly draining away from crop rows. This can be done by mounding up rows, or using ditches or drainage pipes. Even terracing can be of help.

Drainage for Terraces

Terraced gardens are better-drained and warmer than non-terraced ones. If you noted in Chapter 2 the recommendation for minimum terraces of 20 feet wide, you should know that the narrower the terraces, the better drained and warmer they are. You may have to weigh convenience against slightly better growing conditions. The steepness of the slope may also play a part in helping determine the width of terrace to aim for. ACE suggests wide terraces with space for four or more rows on gentle slopes up to 10 degrees. They

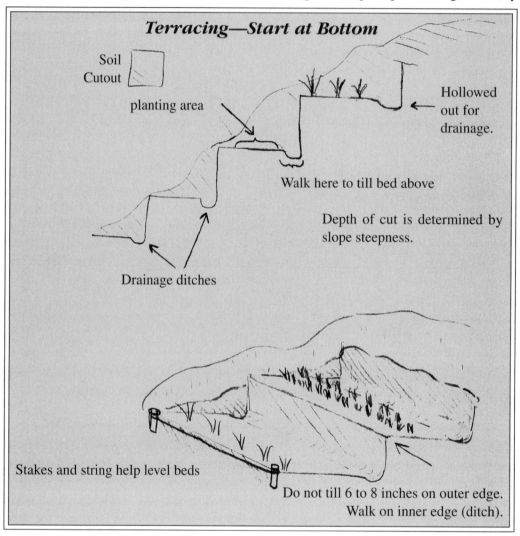

Terracing—Start at Bottom

Soil Cutout

planting area

Hollowed out for drainage.

Walk here to till bed above

Depth of cut is determined by slope steepness.

Drainage ditches

Stakes and string help level beds

Do not till 6 to 8 inches on outer edge.
Walk on inner edge (ditch).

advise that two or three-row terraces are best for intermediate slopes.

Terracing by Hand

Directions for terracing, applicable mostly for using a rototiller, were given in Chapter 2. The directions called for beginning at the top of the slope. Another method, for hand building of terraces, calls for starting at the bottom.

Set a stake and attach a cord at the level of the lowest terrace. Run it across the garden and attach the other end to another stake, to provide a level reference line. This is the front rise of the terrace. The fill used to make the soil surface come up to this line will come from the back of the terrace, digging into the hillside.

Allow ample room to walk and stand so work on the next terrace can be done easily. All types of terraces should have a flat, level surface and follow the contour of the hill. Dig a small V ditch at the base of each front rise. If a garden is terraced properly, excess water will seep through the terrace wall into the ditch. In very heavy rainfall areas, the terraces may need to be contained with boards to prevent erosion and the ditches sloped slightly so the water will have somewhere to drain.

Blind Ditches

Blind ditches are not an easy way out. They are initially a lot of work, but set deeply enough to avoid cultivating tools, can be a more or less permanent solution.

First dig deep standard ditches across the garden with a very slight pitch toward a larger ditch at the side of the garden. Fill the bottom with large rocks or poles of spruce, hemlock, or cedar (avoid rapid-rotting willow or alder) so water will move freely through them. Cover these with smaller stones and lay an old plank or roof shingles over them before refilling the ditch with garden soil. The blind ditches may need to be put as close as three to four feet apart to get good drainage.

Drainage Pipe

Perforated plastic pipe obtainable from mail-order catalogs and local hardware stores can be used for drainage. The pipe is lightweight, inexpensive, and long lasting. Put the lengths of four-inch pipe in coarse gravel-filled ditches two or three feet deep, sloping them toward a larger drainage area. The holes in the pipe should be directed downward so the water can move upward into the pipe. Rocks at the upper end of the pipe will keep it from filling with soil, and a screen over the lower end will keep out small animals.

Built-Up Rows

Built-up rows, raised rows, and ridges are terms often used interchangeably. The first two are the same, but ridges are too often interpreted as being long narrow mounds only a few inches across. To be effective, any raised mound should be about 12 inches high and 18 to 24 inches across the top. Narrower mounds will drain and dry out too quickly. There is less stress placed on plant roots when the soil they are growing in dries and warms gradually. Narrow ridges, therefore, should be avoided, and one of the two types of built-up rows used instead. The two types are raised rows, and raised beds.

Raised Rows

Raised rows are sometimes left raised year round, but are actually easier to care for when remounded each spring (or in fall if the purpose is to drain the garden early). By not planning to leave them mounded, the gardener can improve the soil by tilling in manure, organic matter, or chemical fertilizers each year. The soil is then soft and fluffy and easy to mound by hand or tiller with a furrowing attachment. Peat can be added when tilling to

201

help the soil retain moisture better in drier areas, and perhaps sand added to heavy soils in wetter areas. The drainage provided by a raised row will keep the soil in better tilth, less packed down (you will not be walking on it as much as when you garden on flat ground) and the drier soil will be warmer, as noted in Chapter 10.

The raised mounds should run north to south, with slanting east/west sides, so as to be at right angles to the sun's rays during the warmest part of the day. Since the soil absorbs the most heat from rays hitting directly, slanting sides compensate for the lower angle at which the northern sunshine arrives.

If, however, raised rows are on a slope, they should be oriented perpendicular to the slope, to avoid problems with erosion. For example, on a southern slope, the rows should run east to west.

Master Gardeners Darlene Dupont, Carol Lovejoy, Julie Hedgecoke, & Renee Lozier mark rows and prepare the soil in the Demonstration Garden at the Tanana Valley State Fairgrounds.

Raised Rows by Machine

To use a rear-tine rototiller to make raised rows, first till as usual to mix in fertilizers and soil amendments (including lime, if necessary), and to soften the soil. The last pass with the tiller should be at right angles to the direction the rows will run. This makes it easier for the machine to make straight furrows. Then put on the furrowing attachment, set the depth bar to till as deeply as possible, and till a trench the length of the proposed row. The deeper the trench, the higher the row will be. Till again about four feet away. Each furrow makes two ridges, so when finished, there will be two ridges between each furrow. Setting stakes about four feet apart to mark the rows and aiming the machine at them will help keep rows straight. Continue for one more pass than the number of raised rows desired.

If you did not fertilize earlier, or if you are using chemical fertilizers, you may want to broadcast it on the rows now, so that as you finish the rows, you will be mixing the fertilizer into the top of the mound. This is not only good for shallow-rooted plants, but is a good idea in very rainy areas where rain might quickly leach more deeply placed fertilizers beyond plant roots.

Now, with a rake, draw in the soil from the two mounds formed between each two furrows (the furrow becomes the path) and rake them smooth. Form a mound no more than two feet wide at the top, and sloping at about a 45-degree angle down to the center of the path, where you walked the tiller.

Raised Rows by Hand

Rows are raised by hand in much the same way as by furrower, except that you will use a hoe or shovel. After working in fertilizers and possibly lime, position a row of stakes across

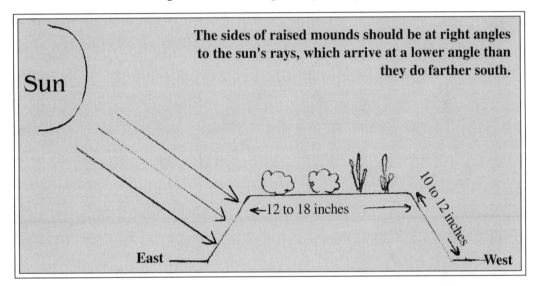

the garden to mark the center of the first ridge. Following the contour, start at the bottom of a sloping garden and work up the slope. Pull in the soil from both sides until there is a mound 12 inches high and 18 to 24 inches across the top. You can now see how wide an area you need to get the necessary soil. Set the stakes for the next row far enough from the first so there will be enough soil to make it. It usually takes a minimum of five feet, but you will be planting at least two rows of seed on each ridge, and often more.

Finally, level the tops of the mounds. Since the above method may bury the fertilizer rather deeply, you may prefer to rake the fertilizer in **after** building the mounds.

Planting Raised Rows

Planting on the raised rows is the same as with wide-row planting, covered in Chapter 2. Just be sure to tamp the seed down gently into the soil and water carefully. Good contact between soil and seed is necessary, because the surface of the mounds will dry quickly. It is not a good idea to plant in very dry mounds, as they will be difficult to wet thoroughly for germination, without washing them away. If the soil is too dry when first tilling (before mounding), water it well, wait awhile, and try again. A row cover of plastic or newspapers

ACE staff

Master Gardeners Andy McNeil, Clare Hill, Michele Hébert, and Renee Lozier pull soil up to the height of the string, making mounds 12 inches high and 18 to 24 inches across at the top.

Master Gardeners Roberta Greenlee and Lynn Cummings-Pike demonstrate how to level a raised row with a board, while Michele Hébert looks on.

Master Gardener, Missy Lieberman, demonstrates leveling the wide row with the back of a rake.

Here Missy Lieberman levels a row by gently tamping the soil down with a rake.

will help hold moisture until the seeds germinate. Just be sure to remove the cover as soon as the first sprout appears.

Each mound can be planted with a particular vegetable, but many gardeners find it more efficient to plant several types of plants on one mound. Take into consideration size and growing characteristics of your choices. For example, carrots could be broadcast on the top, where the soil is deepest for their roots, with leaf lettuce as an edging on the shoulder. Cylindrical beets do well on the sides of mounds, where they grow long and fat, hanging upside-down, unhindered by heavy compacted soil. See also Appendix A for the Companion Planting Guide.

In general, if growers plant with east-west oriented rows, the south side of each mound would be the best place for more heat loving plants, as long as they do not grow tall enough to shade the top plants. What is planted on a raised row, and how it is planted, will be partly determined by where you are growing. In Interior Alaska, raised rows will provide all the extra warmth some

ACE staff

Another way to lift your plants up out of the cold and damp is to plant in old tires, piled two or three deep.

crops need, and the seeds can be broadcast over the mound. In other areas, such as Nome, the mound may not provide enough extra warmth for some crops, and gardeners there may also want to cover their mounds with clear plastic, as discussed in Chapter 10. In a wet area like Ketchikan, the plastic film topping is desirable to prevent heavy rains from washing down and settling the mounds.

Plastic-Covered Mounds

Spread clear plastic over the mound, pinning down the uphill side with rocks, or anchoring it with soil. Bring the plastic completely over the row and anchor it on the downhill side. Cut slits exactly over the plants and pull the plant leaves through gently. For tiny plants, like young carrots and onions, you will need to plant in very straight rows on the mounds, instead of broadcasting your seed. Make lengthwise slits above the rows of seedlings, leaving a bit of plastic attached here and there (like a row of long dashes). Transplants can be set in as described in Chapter 10.

Irrigation for Mounds Under Plastic

Although it may at times be a pain to water through the holes in the plastic, the plastic will help conserve the soil moisture. Rain will get in around the plants, with excess rain being shed by the plastic like a raincoat. Sprinklers will deliver water through the holes, or you can just stick a hose down by the plants. You may want to set water-loving transplants down in a soil saucer beneath the plastic film, as described in Chapter 5.

One problem you will have to watch for when using a hose to water through holes in plastic is that the force of the water stream may wash soil away from shallow roots. Ordinarily, you would catch this happening and quickly adjust the force of the water. But the plastic tends to hide what is going on, and you may glance in the hole where celery is growing one day and find nothing but a mass of roots uncovered by the soil having been washed away. If you discover this happening, you can remedy the situation by stuffing some hay or leaves in the holes to cut the force of the water.

Michele Hébert works on raised rows. The center row has been covered with polyethylene to retain heat. In rainy areas, the plastic will shed excess rain.

Raised Beds

Raised beds are different from raised rows, in that they are permanent, often wider, and contained by something like logs, boards, or railroad ties. They are a little more work to make initially, and thus are recommended mostly for small gardens. In warmer states, the experts suggest you make the beds as wide as you can comfortably reach into the middle to weed. This would mean about a four-foot bed. ACE however, warns that this is too wide for cold climate areas, and that anything wider than two feet will not warm up as fast or as well.

For more information on this type of built-up planting, see Chapter 10. This method is particularly recommended in areas that have very shallow soils on gravel or rock, as well as high rainfall areas (some gardeners have both problems!). Good loam, topsoil, peat, fertilizers, and organic materials can be piled up around 15 inches deep to give roots plenty of room even where soils are thin and rocky. One good idea from an expert gardener in Anchorage, Lenore Hedla, is to contain your beds with corrugated fiberglass. That should help warm your bed better than dark wood, for the same reasons we use clear plastic film instead of black. Another advantage to fiberglass is that it is thinner than railroad ties or logs, thus leaving more growing space for plants.

This Anchorage garden features permanent-type raised beds.

Related Problems

In cold, wet soils, many seedlings are killed by fungi and other microorganisms. Raised beds should be filled with soil to the top (even rounded slightly above the top) of the retaining walls. This will help to eliminate poor air circulation that favors diseases such as damp off. Another way to improve air circulation is to be careful to thin seedlings before they begin to crowd each other.

Weeds are competition for plants too. If you garden where there is nearly continuous cloud cover, even without much rain, your plants cannot afford to share their "place in the sun" with weeds, so keep the soil cultivated around plants, or investigate wavelength selective polyethylene films (see Chapter 10). For more information about plant diseases, and fungicide-treated seeds, see Chapters 5, 9, and 14.

Chapter 12

Selecting Seed—

Annual Vegetables for Alaska

And God said, Behold,
I have given you every herb bearing seed,
which is upon the face of all the earth...
Genesis 2:29a, KJV.

Perhaps the only thing more important than soil warming in Alaska is variety selection. No matter how warm your soil is, your garden will be a failure if your lettuce bolts and sends up a seed stalk instead of producing a head, squash plants finally set fruit the week before the first frost, and root crops never get around to producing edible roots.

The most common failing of poorly adapted plants, however, is the production of very low yields—one very sparse picking of peas when one should be able to count on several large ones, a bean pod here and there along a row, a pint of misshapen little strawberries instead of several quarts of big ones—all this under exactly the same conditions of climate, cultivation and fertilization that made it possible for your neighbor, with well-adapted varieties, to feed a whole family from a plot the same size.

This is exaggerated, of course. You probably could not make all the wrong choices, even if you left your glasses at home the day you went to the store to buy the seed. But unless you pay very close attention to variety selection, there is no doubt at all that you are going to be disappointed with the results.

Northern Varieties

Unfortunately, many of the varieties on the seed rack at local supermarkets simply will not do well in Alaska, even though the sign on the rack or seed envelope may read "Seed especially developed for your area." The chances are that they are the same varieties offered for sale in other northern states.

Most plants grown in the contiguous United States have been bred to grow well in typical temperate climate areas—long growing seasons, hot summers, nearly equal periods of light and dark. Alaska's climate is very different—short growing seasons, summers more cool than hot, and lots of daylight with very little night.

Georgeson Botanical Garden Collection.

Chinese kale (right) does not respond well to Alaska's photoperiods, as this one shows by bolting to seed. The variety shown is Green Lance.

This zucchini (below) has succumbed to an early frost. Many gardeners listen to weather forecasts in the fall and rush to cover tender plants with plastic at night to extend the season for a few more weeks.

ACE staff photo

In addition, although most summers have about a three-month period of non-freezing weather, frosts occasionally may occur as late as June 3 or as early as July or August. These factors combine to make the selection of varieties especially important for Alaskans and other far northern gardeners.

By the way, be aware that the mere fact the word "Alaska" appears in the name of a variety does not necessarily mean the plant is at all adapted for growing in Alaska. It may mean no more than that the marigold is white, or the plant was introduced in 1959, the year Alaska became a state, or in 1867, the year it was purchased from Russia. Like Baked Alaska and Eskimo Pie, the name may have been picked, not to describe the product to us, but to capitalize on popular fantasies about our part of the world.

Photoperiodism

One of the main factors that has to be considered by scientists searching for plant varieties for Alaska is photoperiodicity—the striking effect of day length on growth and reproduction in plants. Although it is true that many plants are not particularly fussy in their requirements for a daily light-dark cycle (these are called day-neutrals), some very important ones are definitely long-day plants.

Still others are short-day plants, and it is these that present serious problems in gardens located far enough north to be exposed to constant daylight for up to a couple of months during the summer. In central Alaska, even though the sun may drop below the northern horizon for a couple of hours near midnight, it never really gets dark from early May to early August. Even at the southern tip of Southeastern Alaska, the summer nights are still very much shorter than they are in such northern states as Washington and Maine.

The fact that the light may not be very bright at night does not matter. In fact, light itself has very little to do with it. Even though we speak of long-day plants and short-day plants, it is actually the length of the **night** that counts. A short-day plant is really a long-night plant. This can be proven by flashing a light on the plant for a few minutes, in some cases for only a few seconds, in the middle of the night. Although the total amount of light involved will be negligible compared to the many hours of daylight the plant has already received in the last 24 hours, because the plant has had a short night, it will behave as though it had been exposed to a long day. Conversely, blocking off all light from the plant for a few minutes in the middle of the day will have no effect.

It seems that plants carry out some very important chemical reactions at night, and if they do not have enough uninterrupted darkness to complete these, the whole life cycle may be upset. The most striking effect is disruption of the flowering process. Even a street light outside the window will keep a poinsettia from blooming, since the night must be at least 12 hours long for this species. If you have enjoyed potted chrysanthemums during the summer, it is only because commercial growers routinely "force" these short-day (long-night) autumn bloomers by darkening their greenhouses for part of each summer day.

Most varieties of soybeans bloom much too late to mature beans in central Alaska. Some

ACE staff

Years ago (above) the Tanana Valley Community College conducted variety trials of their own. University of Alaska Horticulturist, Pat Wagner (below), plants seeds for experiments carried out at the Georgeson Botanical Garden, in Fairbanks.

Georgeson Botanical Garden Collection.

soybean plants are so sensitive that enclosing a single leaf in a black envelope can trigger early flowering of the whole plant. Many, but not all, varieties of squash and cucumbers produce only male flowers during the early part of the summer. Only when the nights lengthen in the fall are female flowers also formed, and by then it is often too late to produce mature fruit.

A few species of vegetables that are apparently short-day types are eggplant, butternut squash, watermelon, and true spinach. Most members of some other species such as beets and lettuce are adversely affected by long days but a few very satisfactory adapted varieties of these have been developed.

Variety Research

Over the years, a great deal of research and development has been conducted at the Alaska Agricultural Experiment Stations and by scientists of both the University of Alaska and the United States Department of Agriculture to find or produce varieties especially adapted to Alaska's growing conditions. This work begins with recognition that different species of plants, different varieties of the same plant, and even individual plants, vary enormously in their reactions to environmental stimuli.

The job of plant breeders is to be on the lookout for all changes that occur in a plant population; to select out plants showing features that promise to be useful—larger fruit, fewer seeds, better flavor, improved resistance to frost, a photoperiod fitting the summer day length of a given geographic region (such as the far north), resistance to certain plant diseases, etc. Usually breeders try, by means of crossing, to combine several desirable features in a single new variety.

As new varieties are developed, field trials are conducted in many different locations. That is, fairly large numbers of plants are exposed to varying growth conditions, different soils, different climates or microclimates. For example, plants might be grown in the open, in greenhouses, under plastic mulch, on hillsides, or on level land down in the valley. From the records of these trials, lists of the varieties that do best in a given geographical area are prepared.

Every year the Alaska Cooperative Extension, University of Alaska Fairbanks (ACE), cooperating with the United States Department of Agriculture, publishes the latest findings of the scientists of the University's Agricultural Experiment Stations in the form of three lists. These lists cover the major growing areas in the state: the Interior, Southcentral, and Southeast.

Many familiar varieties still grown extensively throughout Alaska were developed right here. They include Pioneer and Toklat strawberries, Kiska raspberries, Yukon Chief sweetcorn, and the Early Tanana tomato. The late Dr. Arvo Kallio was responsible for all of the above, which are still available in Alaska.

Variety trials for the Interior have been conducted, until recently, by Dr. Donald H. Dinkel. They are now conducted by the Georgeson Botanical Garden, under the leadership of its capable Director and Associate Professor of Horticulture, Dr. Patricia S. Holloway.

Georgeson Botanical Garden Collection.

Test plots in the Georgeson Botanical Garden are tended in great part by over 150 volunteers who donate close to 2000 man hours every year.

From front to back, Georgeson Botanical Garden volunteers, Judy Weber, Fran Chauvin, and Ginger Gauss help harvest plants at the University of Alaska test plots.

Neal Turner, Research Assistant for Georgeson Botanical Garden, conducts variety selection research in the lab.

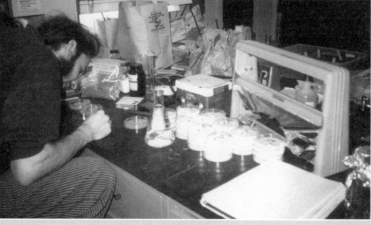

Dr. Holloway is aided by a few research assistants and over 150 volunteers who, among other things, plant flowers, weed, clean and package seeds, water greenhouse plants, propagate cuttings, mow lawns, harvest vegetables, prune trees, label plants, talk to visitors, and in general, make it all possible despite declining state financial support.

Until his retirement, Dr. Curtis H. Dearborn tested varieties for Southcentral. More recently, Dr. Don Carling has been carrying out potato trials there. In Southeast, varieties were tested by local gardeners under direction of Walt McPherson. Recently, Bob Gorman has been conducting limited trials in raised beds in Sitka. These are only a few of those who have been involved in variety testing over the years. The lists produced have become increasingly more complete over time. Once they listed only a few varieties of major types of vegetables. Now the Interior and Southcentral lists include notes on maturity, yield, growing tips, and other comments.

It is important to realize that these variety lists are not drawn up for all time. Every year, new varieties become available and some of these prove to do better than the old ones. Also, unfortunately, every so often new plant diseases appear or new insects migrate into an area and it is necessary to develop varieties of plants with the ability to resist them. Some years ago, a great corn blight seemed about to wipe out crops in several states. That particular blight is no longer a threat since new varieties of corn have now been produced which are unaffected.

The Georgeson Botanical Garden maintains a large collection of seeds and spores of Alaska native plants. It is also the repository for all horticultural crops bred at the Agricultural and Forestry Experiment Station. Seeds are tested every three or four years for germination. If germination drops below 70%, they are grown in the Garden for seed increase. Seeds are exchanged with other national and international programs, with other researchers, and used in graduate studies and other educational programs.

Appendix B includes the latest *Recommended Variety Lists* published by ACE. But, remember, next year's lists could contain important additions or deletions. In particular, the list for Southeast was in the process of a long overdue update as this book went to press. Keep in touch with a local ACE office, especially at seed ordering time.

You, as Researcher

While it is highly recommended that you use these lists as your starting point and for main crop plantings, Dr. Dinkel urges gardeners to experiment a little, too. The field trials can only test a limited number of varieties each year. The home gardener may want to try others that look good. You may also be interested in trying a few of the favorites of such local gardening experts as Eloise DeWitt, Lenore Hedla, Lee Risse, and John Holm. In addition, many commercial greenhouses and garden centers keep their own lists of favorites—just ask. And if a new variety does particularly well for you, the Georgeson Botanical Garden and the Palmer Research Center will want to know about it. You just might play a very important role in helping other subarctic gardeners all over the state, and even the world.

It's Been Done Before

John Holm started out as a homesteader off Chena Hot Springs Road in 1946, but went on to develop tomato varieties that ripen outdoors reliably without needing a polyethylene mulch. He started the Interior's first nursery in 1950, later selling his farm and opening a greenhouse and garden center. The location has changed, and Mr. Holm has passed on, but his son, Jim Holm, still runs Holm Town Nursery, selling (among other things) the seeds his father developed.

Inspired by a crop failure of a quarter acre of tomatoes, John Holm set out to breed a better tomato that would ripen fruit outdoors without plastic. He began by obtaining seed from six countries, pollinating, cross-pollinating, and gathering the resulting seed. His first big success came with Sub-Arctic 25 (named for the number of tomatoes clustered on the plant and the fact that it was 10 generations from a seed called Sub-Arctic). "Nothing surpasses the yield, fruit quality and field ripening ability of 'Sub-Arctic 25'," wrote the *Georgeson Botanical Garden Review* in 1992.

With the earliness issue solved, Mr. Holm went on to develop the Polar series, putting his effort this time into growing a **bigger** tomato. By 1995, one of them, Polar Beauty, had the largest tomato to ripen outdoors in Alaska. Denali Seed Company, in Anchorage, added some of the Holm's varieties to their seed selection, and the Georgeson Botanical Garden maintains six varieties of Holm's tomato seeds in their germplasm repository.

The late John Holm poses with his wife, Edith at the Holm Town Nursery, which still sells Alaska tomato varieties he developed.

When looking for some seeds to test, look for short season (early maturing) ones, especially those recommended for northern areas or that come from seed companies that have grown their seed stock in the north. On the other hand, according to Lee Risse, greenhouse owner in the Interior, length of season is not always the most critical factor. A long season winter squash, for example, may do better than a supposedly short season one, perhaps being more robust.

John Holm developed the Sub-Arctic 25 tomato to be grown outdoors without polyethylene mulches, although they yield even better when grown through plastic.

Compensating for Unadapted Varieties

You may also want to develop some cultural methods of your own. For instance, it takes time to develop and test plants that prefer a long photoperiod. While you are waiting for the researchers to catch up with your craving for butternut squash or eggplant, for example, you may want to experiment with altering the photoperiod on your own.

One way to do this is to devise some sort of covering to keep out light for simulated additional nighttime. This can be anything from a bag or cardboard box (as long as it cuts out every speck of light), to a complete blackout cover over a greenhouse, to a dark house on railroad tracks such as has been used by researchers in Palmer. The one in Palmer could be moved over the plants at night and easily wheeled away for sunlight by day.

If you choose to use a bag, be aware that an ordinary brown paper bag will let in too much light; a foil-lined "take-out" bag might be better. Even the tiniest bit of light will be interpreted by photoperiod-sensitive plants as daylight. Some home gardeners have put plants in a dark closet only to waste their efforts by forgetting to seal the edges of the door. Only pitch black will do! Don't forget to move plants each day to a sunny spot for their daylight allotment.

Are you interested in what is really happening when you subject the plants to longer night? The male flowers are not as particular about the length of the night, so the plant will usually produce plenty of them. But no fruit will set unless it also produces female flowers in time. The plant waits for the longer nights of fall (in Alaska) to produce the female flowers. Lengthening its night early in the plant's development stimulates the early production of the female flowers, and ensures that they will have time to "mate" with the male flowers.

Be forewarned that so little research has been done with this on a home-gardening scale, that it may be difficult to obtain information on how long to cover particular plants at night, or even when in the season to begin covering them. Remember that what you want to do is to lengthen the existing dark period. In other words, put on your cover in the afternoon or evening before dark, instead of for a short time in the middle of the day.

According to Dr. Holloway of the Georgeson Botanical Garden, sometime all it takes is a few weeks of enforced darkness for seeds to store up an inner "memory" that allows them to mature and fruit despite Alaska's short nights. One does not have to spend the summer running around every afternoon covering plants up tight. At the Georgeson Botanical Garden, plant research has involved covering the plants beginning when the seedlings are transplanted from their first flats into pots inside, and ending when they are planted outside in the garden.

Other ways to compensate for unadapted varieties would be such things as using hot frames and heating cables for melons (see Chapter 10), or starting long season varieties indoors (see Chapter 5). Whatever you do to beat the odds, keep records and you may be the one to document useful information for the gardeners of the future, or at least for yourself. While you are at it, keep records of what varieties do best in your location, with its own special microclimate. There may be too many uncontrolled variables in your garden for a tested variety to perform exactly the same way it did in its test plot. But use the latest *Recommended Variety List* as a starting point, and as you gain experience in gardening in Alaska, branch out with your own experiments. After all, meeting the challenges of the subarctic, and triumphing with a productive garden and a bountiful harvest—that's half the fun of gardening in the "Great Land"!

Jim Holm

This is one of the tomato greenhouses at Holm Town Nursery. John Holm also developed the Polar series of outdoor tomatoes.

Chapter 13
Pick Perennials for Hardiness.

And God said, Let the earth bring forth...
the fruit tree yielding fruit after his kind,
whose seed is in itself, upon the earth:
and it was so. Genesis 1:11, KJV.

Obviously, in Alaska, the first and foremost requirement for a perennial plant is that it be hardy. If it is not, it most certainly will not be a perennial. Hardiness is influenced by many factors, the most critical of which is minimum winter temperature. Alaska winter temperatures mean many plants that are perennials in other states must be grown as annuals here.

When deciding if a plant is a perennial in your locality, give it at least three years to prove itself. If it survives that long, it is a perennial. Even then, certain plants, like tulips or bleeding heart bushes, have been known to survive three winters and then suddenly die out. On the other hand, pansies, grown as annuals in many gardens north of the Alaska Range, may suddenly come back in the spring.

Hardiness Zones

Because of the existence of microclimates, which occur in small areas where conditions and temperatures vary from the larger surrounding areas, hardiness zones can only be considered as approximate guides. For many years there was no zone system for Alaska, as there was for the continental United States. But in 1980, Alan Epps, then Natural Resource and Land Use Planning Specialist, developed a hardiness system and zone map for Alaska.

Mr. Epps divided Alaska into five regions, Northern (N), Western (W), Interior (INT), Southcentral (SC), and Southeast (SE).

There is also an Alaska USDA Hardiness Zone map. Increments of 10 degrees Fahrenheit separate the zones, which set Anchorage as a zone 3, and Fairbanks as a zone 1 and 2. The zone maps have been reprinted in Appendix A, for the reader's convenience. The landscape varieties listed in *Landscape Plant Materials for Alaska,* (#HGA-00035), available from the Alaska Cooperative Extension, University of Alaska Fairbanks (ACE) are keyed to both zone maps, where known.

But, as mentioned before, zones are not perfect indicators of plant material hardiness. For example, plants hardy in zone 3 in other states are not necessarily hardy in a given spot in Anchorage. This is due to the numerous microclimates, as well as the fact that minimum temperature is not the only variable affecting plant hardiness. Other factors include day length, winter length, and desiccation (dryness).

Microclimates

A microclimate is determined by several factors: conditions such as rainfall, wind direction and force, exposure (lack of trees or other obstructions to wind), and elevation. This last (elevation) is very important in creating significant differences in growing conditions.

However, elevations seem to work differently in different parts of Alaska. For example, in Anchorage, the warmer microclimates are in the lower areas downtown, while in Fairbanks, the favored spots are often in the higher areas around town. And there are exceptions even there, with some gardens downtown in Fairbanks quite warm with a long season, and some higher areas, such as on Farmer's Loop Road, having a very short season, due in part to extreme permafrost conditions.

Short Nights, Long Winters

There is often a connection between winter hardiness and the length of the photoperiod. It is essential that plants that are to survive the winter store enough food in their roots to sustain them until the next season of active growth. It has been demonstrated here in Alaska that one of the chief differences between adapted and nonadapted lawn grasses is that the adapted grasses slow down their growth as the nights lengthen in the fall, and begin to store food in their roots. Nonadapted grasses, receiving no such signal of approaching winter, continue to grow vigorously right up to the time of frost and are completely unprepared for winter survival. It is quite possible, although not yet proven, that the winter survival of other perennials, such as strawberries, is similarly related to seasonal day length.

It may be these factors that contribute to the phenomena seen in marginally hardy plants, such as certain types of asparagus, in the Interior. Planted from healthy roots, they will seem to do well the first year or two, then begin to fail. Each year the harvest will be less, with a plant or two failing to return at all, until there is hardly anything to show for an initial large planting. Perhaps each year the plant is able to store less food for the winter, until its reserves are totally depleted.

The food storing activities of a plant in the fall are a part of what we call "hardening off" for the winter. The suddenness at which winter arrives in Alaska, with days shortening too quickly, may be a factor in winter loss of perennials which did not have time to harden off properly. All this underscores the need to choose varieties carefully, or be prepared to lose a lot of them while searching for the ones hardy to a particular area.

Low Soil Temperatures

Cold soil does not affect only annuals. Perennials, with their much larger root systems, can be severely set back by the cold soil temperatures. In much of Alaska, the temperature at 10 to 20 inches below the surface remains close to 32° F even in summer. Even inside green-houses, the temperature of soil in ground beds (unless artificially heated) remains low. Temperature probes in the Tanana Valley the winter of 1998-99 showed temperatures at three inches deep (with snow as well as 12 inches of hay mulch) dropping below 20° F, which means death to strawberry parent plants, although runners may survive.

Ed Bostrom, who grows perennials commercially at North Pole Acres, believes that one reason many perennials fail is because gardeners mistakenly follow directions given for areas farther south, planting on raised beds, for example. That is fine for annuals that are harvested before winter and replanted the following spring, but the roots of perennials will freeze quicker and harder on the raised beds than if planted flat in the ground and mulched. Mr. Bostrom recommends raised beds (and only slightly raised) for strawberries only of all the perennials that he grows, and then only to avoid drowning their short roots in wet soils.

Another problem with planting instructions from warmer states is that they often recommend planting too deeply for Alaska's cold soils, which leads to frozen roots. Ed plants asparagus only three inches deep, for example.

Soil at the surface warms slowly in the spring, delaying planting and harming trees. Fruit trees shipped in are not bothered so much by late frosts and ground heave, as they are killed by roots kept dormant by the cold soil when warm spring air temperatures cause tops to expend their energy leafing out. This is one reason fall transplanting is often more success-ful, as the ground is warmest in the fall and roots may reestablish.

Trees do not send down taproots, but rather grow their roots horizontally in the warmer topsoil. Unknowingly, homeowners seeking to landscape and raise the level of their lawns pile dirt around bushes and trees, ensuring their death in 5 to 10 years when the cold layer creeps upward.

Ed Bostrom has an interesting method of dealing with the low soil temperatures when starting perennials. He plants the first season in four-inch pots. After a full summer of growth, the plants are put in his overwintering shed, a 12-foot by 8-foot building with a slanting shed roof.

The shed is closed up tight in winter, and takes very little energy to heat. Two (one is for a back up) space heaters with thermostats keep the temperature inside the shed between 28 and 30 degrees Fahrenheit. The shed has one table and wall shelves on two walls. Plants are watered well when they are put in the shed, still in their pots. Humidity holds well, and they do not need watering again until planted out. The vents, which allow the shed to double as a smoke house in the summer, are covered for the winter.

Windows high on the tallest wall may be opened if the shed heats up too much when spring comes. The plants are held in the shed until soil temperatures reach 50° F. Then they are removed from their pots and planted in their final bed. This way, they have been helped to survive that most critical first year. For more information on helping specific perennials (other than tree fruit) survive, see Part Three.

Desiccation

Desiccation means the drying out caused by the inability of roots to take up moisture fast enough to replace what is lost through an exposed top. A tree may be dormant in the winter, but it is still living, and still needs a steady supply of water to replace what it loses, particularly when the wind is blowing.

Ed Bostrom

This overwintering shed has vents, as it doubles as a smoke house. It is heated by an ordinary space heater, with a thermostat set to hold the temperature at 28 to 30 degrees. A second complete heater/thermostat setup serves as a back up.

Clair's Cultivations, a small family-operated commercial nursery established in 1984 outside Fairbanks, advises that fruit trees need a minimum of 34 inches of rain a year, but says not to water them after July 1, except in the case of a particularly dry season. Some say it is extremely important to water well around trees just before the ground freezes in the fall, but Clair Lammers says to wait until after the first hard frost (but before the ground freezes) and then water "generously."

Late heavy watering is not necessarily recommended for small perennials, such as strawberries. While it is not considered a good idea to plant perennials in permanent pots or raised beds outdoors in the dry Interior, where their roots would be exposed to extremely low temperatures, it has been recommended by some for wetter areas. In Southeast, and some parts of Southcentral, the problem is too much water on the roots, so that when the wet ground freezes, the roots are literally imbedded in ice. In such locations, perennials are thought to survive better if lifted up out of the water by use of raised beds.

Late Growth

This last problem is actually caused more by the well-meaning gardener than the climate. In his eagerness to supply all the plant needs, he fertilizes too late in the season. This is the cause of much winter dieback in lawns. Fertilizer stimulates the plant to produce succulent new growth that is too tender when cold weather hits, not having had time to harden off properly. Avoid the problem by refusing to fertilize from midsummer through fall for all perennials. Clair's Cultivations advises fruit tree enthusiasts to never apply fertilizer to orchard plants after June 1. Those who insist on adding fertilizer, manure, or compost in the fall should wait until the plant has gone dormant for the winter.

Garden Perennials

The main vegetables considered perennials in most subarctic sections of Alaska are asparagus, chives, and multiplier onions. Fruits and berries include strawberries, blueberries (wild),

Ed Bostrom

Full of perennials well watered and still in their first year pots, the shed is closed up for the winter, vents covered, and heat turned on.

raspberries, gooseberries, currants, rhubarb (though not technically a fruit), birdcherries, and some crab apples. A few gardeners have other fruit trees they have nursed along, and which are hardy for them.

Every year, more gardeners experiment with hardier varieties of bush and tree fruits, expanding the list for particular microclimates. See Appendix B for recommended varieties, or talk with Clair Lammers or Carroll Phillips (mentioned later in this chapter). Special mention should also be made of *Landscape Plant Materials for Alaska,* (#HGA-00035), available from ACE. Entries in that publication are keyed to both of the hardiness zone maps mentioned earlier.

Be aware, a "volunteer" is not a perennial. Spinach that goes to seed one season often comes up again the next year, but that does not make spinach a perennial in Alaska. Gardeners often report strange, unexplained "volunteers". A gardener who never planted sunflowers nor fed birds has three volunteer sunflower plants in widely separated parts of his garden, and another reports tomato plants dotting his furrows like weeds. But, though wild sunflowers do grow in Alaska, no one would ever suggest that tame ones, let alone tomatoes, were perennials in Alaska.

Fruit Trees for Alaska

Most of the perennials mentioned in the proceeding paragraphs are covered elsewhere, mainly in Part Three, **Culture Clues**. But tree fruits, due to the difficulty of growing them, deserve special mention.

The only tree fruits recommended for the more challenging areas of Alaska are chokecherries (actually birdcherries), and crab apples. This is mainly because of severe winters. Occasionally several consecutive winters are very mild (for Alaska), but there are still days (or

Clair Lammers

weeks) of -30° F (-50° to -70° F for the Interior). Relatively few varieties have been bred to survive these extremes. Most fruit trees, besides being very hardy themselves, must be grafted onto very hardy rootstocks (more about them later).

Gardeners in mild winter areas of Alaska, such as Southcentral, may want to try the Summerred apple, a relative of Summerland, which was a cross between McIntosh and Delicious, with a flavor to match. Scionwood from Summerred was grafted by the late Dr. Curtis Dearborn (of the Palmer Research Center) onto a Siberian crab rootstock, *Malus baccata*, and has proven very productive. For example, as early as 1978 it

Isaac Lammers, age 2, helps himself to a September Ruby apple in his grandfather's orchard.

yielded 87 standard size ripe apples. Summerreds available for sale are usually grafted onto the less hardy rootstock, *Malus 26*. Since it takes years for a newly grafted apple tree to bear, you will have to look around for someone who bought one years earlier to see if it proved hardy enough. Chinese Golden Early is another one to try in the Anchorage area.

Gardeners in the Interior once had to be content with some of the more proven hardy crab apples. But do not look down your nose at crab apples; there are some very acceptable varieties available now. Clair Lammers calls Trailman the best "eating out of hand" crab apple. Another good one is Shafer.

Clair has been experimenting with regular apple varieties. One of his favorites is September Ruby (shown elsewhere in this chapter with the Lammers' grandchildren) followed by Westland. Clair's largest apple is PF21, measuring 5¹/₂ inches in diameter.

A favorite with his wife, Vivian, is Norland. Asked about apple flavor, she compares them to apples fresh off the tree in the Lower-48. "Most are tart," she says. Parkland is another very tasty apple, reminiscent of the Gala apple variety available in local grocery stores. It is good for eating out of hand, while the more tart varieties make good pies.

Apples for Southeast Alaska

The challenges of growing tree fruit in Southeast are different from those encountered in other parts of Alaska. Joy Orth, a Southeast gardener, described the problem as not one of cold, but "extended mild temperatures, often without even a frost, followed by temperature drops to below zero, giving the trees no period of adjustment. The lack of heat in summer is a problem in ripening, too." In the wet rainy climate of Southeast, fruit trees rot and cherries split before they can ripen.

Jim Douglas, Resource Development and Youth Agent for ACE in Juneau, describes the problem a little differently. According to him, fruit trees may be well into dormancy in January, then, as likely as not, there is an early thaw at the end of the last week in January. This is followed by frosts and thaws for the rest of the winter, sapping the trees of energy. By the time spring arrives, they no longer have the energy to put out leaves. This inability to stay dormant is a real drawback, even in an area where temperatures seldom get as low as minus 20° F. Compounding the problem is the lack of heating degree days during the summer.

Joe Orsi, hobby orchardist in Juneau (Auk Bay), offers the following recommendations for apple growers in Southeast. They are all fairly good sized apples. The first three are what he would grow if he had space to grow only three varieties.

Apple Variety	Color	Texture	Comments
Yellow Transparent (from the Sitka Station)	yellow	soft, mealy	Self-pollinator (best choice if able to grow only one tree). Not considered very good quality, but a consistent producer.
Discovery	orange-red	hard	Joe Orsi's favorite, a hard dessert type, which makes a good cooking apple as well. It has good disease resistance.
Liveland Raspberry (from the Sitka Station)	yellow with a red blush	soft	Hard to find.
William's Pride	red	hard	Newer disease resistant variety, it keeps well.
Wynooche Early	yellow-red	hard	Newer disease resistant variety. Has some immunity to scab and other problems found in wet climate areas.
Ginger Gold	yellow	hard	Susceptible to scab, but consistently scores high on taste tests.

Mr. Orsi suggests grafting trees onto a native crab. A tree grown without grafting may take four to five years to produce, while grafting it onto the right rootstock can cut that by half or more. He sees wet weather as the major challenge to Southeastern growers, though he does not see the same problem of freeze and thaw that Mr. Douglas mentioned. In his experience, apple trees are pretty late waking up in the spring, as compared with other fruit trees, but he does list moose and bears as a major challenge. He suggests electric fences (see Chapter 9) in areas where bears are prevalent.

Jerry Koener, of Jerry Appleseed Nursery in Ketchikan, adds his favorite to the list of apple varieties for Southeast. He favors Akane, a disease free, medium size hard red apple with a pure white flesh. He says sub zero temperatures are not a major concern of gardeners in Ketchikan.

Before Ordering
It is a good idea to investigate crab apple varieties before ordering. Some are very small, about the size of a large marble. Most do not keep well at all, and so must be eaten or processed right away. Then too, most apple trees are self-sterile, meaning they need the pollen of another apple to produce fruit. While it is possible to buy pollen from outside Alaska, it is certainly more convenient to have two or more trees and, of course, one would get double the apples.

When Transplanting
Anti-transpirants (chemicals sprayed on trees and shrubs to reduce water loss from leaves) are often sprayed on newly-transplanted trees to minimize transplant injury. A few are WiltPruf® and VaporGard®, which also produce a protective barrier on leaves against fungal attacks. If sprayed early in the season, (before spores reach the leaves) they can significantly reduce gray mold, leaf rusts, and powdery mildew. Unfortunately, while concentration is important, there are no recommendations to go by. You will have to experiment by treating a few leaves and waiting a couple weeks to check effects.

Tips for Hardier Fruit Trees
Those who believe it is impossible for noncommercial gardeners to grow tree fruit in the Interior, will be interested to know that Carroll Phillips, a longtime farmer in the Tanana Valley, has been doing that for decades! Almost twenty years ago, he had an orchard of over 100 trees comprising about 25 different varieties of crab apples, apples, plums, and pears. Some of them were young trees not yet bearing, but trees planted in 1956 and 1958 were loaded with fruit, despite unauthorized pruning by mice and rabbits some years previous. (They nibbled the trees right to the ground.) He built a high rabbit fence to enclose the orchard, and metal barrels surrounded many of the trees for protection from mice.

From his over 40 years of experience growing (Dawn is one variety he favors, bearing slightly small, beautifully rosy apples—with a taste similar to Granny Smith apples—quite acceptable to eat right off the tree) and reading about growing fruit trees, Mr. Phillips has come up with four principles that might help the novice be successful growing them.

One important factor for success is elevation. Mr. Phillips' orchard is about 500 feet above Fairbanks. He believes very strongly that the side hills are the best places to try fruit trees, at least in the Interior. This may not be true, for instance, on the hillside area of Anchorage, where winds make the difference. It would especially be a problem in any area where winds blow away the snow cover.

Secondly, fruit trees should be on Siberian rootstocks, by far the hardiest obtainable anywhere. Mr. Phillips believes the secret of the success of these rootstocks is revealed in how quickly the leaves turn yellow in the fall, indicating that the sap has moved to the roots for winter. Fruit trees he has had which kept their green leaves into winter usually did not survive. Siberian rootstocks tend to be slower growing than other types, so if ordering from a nursery, you may discover your tree was grafted onto another rootstock so it would grow faster and look nicer for the customer. Specify what you want, and hope they listen.
Tree branches are usually hardier than trunks, so "bushing" your trees is what Mr. Phillips recommends. This means to cut off the leader (the part growing up in the center, destined to

Fourteen-month old Bayly Lammers can't be bothered with waiting to pick this September Ruby apple growing at her grandfather's nursery.

be the main trunk) and let the tree branch out into a bush.

For fertilizer, he recommends well-rotted cow manure (not chicken or horse, but cow), preferably made into compost. Carroll Phillips also believes in planting grass around the trees when they are about five or six years old, letting it grow long in wet seasons, but cutting it when the weather is dry, to keep it from stealing moisture from the trees.

Clair Lammers, at his commercial tree nursery near Fairbanks, used to put black plastic around the base of his trees. He stopped doing that when he found that the soil was at least 3° colder under the plastic. He now keeps the soil bare. He does not plant grass because of problems with voles, (rodents, like large mice) which hide in grass (even if cut) and damage the trees. Instead, he surrounds the trees with composted manure (one inch, applied under the tree's drip line). He prefers rabbit manure he gets from a commercial rabbit farm, but suggests if that is not available, well-composted cow manure could be used. He mixes two parts rabbit manure to one part processed sludge from the City of Fairbanks (after he screens the sludge).

Some of his other suggestions for success differ a bit from Mr. Phillips. For one thing, he uses the Ranetka crab apple rootstock that produces a genetic semi-dwarf tree. If you are having problems overwintering trees in your area, try the very hardy Rescue, actually an apple-crab.

Mr. Lammers advises planting trees 12 to 14 feet apart, since they will top 12 to 14 feet

Clair Lammers of Clair's Cultivations shows off a Norland apple tree.

when mature. The tree that first produced for him (Rosthern 18) is now 12 feet tall, and 14 feet wide. Most apple varieties will start to bear by the fourth year. He finds it most important to protect the trees from moose, which he does with a high fence.

He does not bush his trees like Carroll Phillips, but prunes only crossing or touching branches, waterspouts (branches that grow straight up), and any deadwood. Some trees, especially if stressed the previous year, will send up suckers. Cut them off at ground level.

In 1998 Clair harvested a total of 1239 pounds of apples (he did not weigh the other fruit). As of 1999, he had ripened 93 varieties of apples, 10 cherries, 8 plums, 5 pear and 3 apricot.

Quarantine

Complicating the problem in regards to fruit trees is the law requiring quarantine on some types of foreign-grown nursery stock before shipment to the United States. Only "virus indexed" trees can be shipped into the United States. Normally trees must be sent to a plant introduction station in the contiguous United States for a time until it can be ascertained that they do not have any diseases, notably nematodes and fireblight. (Never mind that nematodes are no problem in Alaska's cold soils!) The stresses caused by a holding period in a warm-winter state result in frequent losses.

There is little that can be done about low winter temperatures, except to be constantly on the lookout for hardier introductions, and to order nursery stock from as far north as possible. Mr. Lammers orders much of his stock from Canada, where, for a fee, his supplier will handle the paperwork.

Clair Lammers

The PF21 apple tree has produced the largest apples in Lammer's orchard, with a diameter of 5¹/₂ inches.

When asked for a recommendation for varieties that might survive in the Interior, at lower elevations than the hillsides of Clairs Cultivations, (on the "flats") Clair listed Rescue and Trailman. And while you are waiting for the researchers to come up with a better variety, why not plant some apple seeds?

Chapter 14

The Green-Thumb Greenhouse

Let the people praise thee, O God; let all the people praise thee.
Then shall the earth yield her increase;
and God, even our own God, shall bless us. Psalm 67:5,6, KJV.

Accprding to Dr. Donald H. Dinkel, who operated green-houses for the University Experiment Station in Fairbanks for many years, Alaska has a "superior greenhouse environment for six months of the year, and a good environment for three or four more months." The major problem of greenhouse growers in more southerly states, high summer heat, is never an insurmountable problem here, although the cost of supplemental heat during colder periods is a problem, unless some reasonable heating source is available.

ACE staff

This greenhouse at the University of Alaska, Fairbanks is the site of research to benefit all Alaskan growers, from bush gardeners to commercial greenhouse operators.

From March 15 to September 15 there is excellent light for greenhouses, especially in the Interior where cloud cover is not a major problem most years. The combination of long days of sun and cooler summer temperatures gives Alaska a nearly ideal climate for green-house production, something many local gardeners are just discovering.

The University of Alaska has long taken advantage of the superior climate with a greenhouse devoted to research to benefit Alaskan growers. In the 1970s and 1980s space was given to a study of hydroponics—experiments involving growing plants in a nutrient film without soil. At one time, a whole greenhouse was devoted to tomatoes, and a waste heat project studied the feasibility of commercial greenhouse production of roses year round. The experiments were very successful—a commercial greenhouse near Fairbanks is even now successfully raising roses.

The University of Alaska has moved on, and is now using their greenhouses to study the re-

ACE staff

Early experiments studied the feasibility of growing roses year round using waste heat from the University of Alaska.

sponses of flowering plants to different light and temperature levels. Out of these trials, Meriam Karlsson, an Associate Professor conducting research in the greenhouse, hopes to discover varieties which thrive in cooler than normal greenhouse temperatures, to conserve fuel.

While most greenhouses are shut down for at least a few months of the year (for reasons discussed later) there are advantages even then, with insect and disease control courtesy of the low winter temperatures.

Site Selection

In locating a greenhouse, first consideration should be given to sun exposure, even if it means putting the greenhouse on a roof to avoid shade (and many do just that!). Try to find a protected place that cuts down as little as possible on sunlight for plants.

Attached greenhouses are especially recommended in windy areas such as along the major mountain ranges, with the protecting building to the north (not because the winds are from the north, but because the sunlight is not). If given the choice, a slight (about 10 degrees) southeast orientation for the major face of the greenhouse is actually better than a perfect southern exposure. (This does not mean magnetic south.) This way, the greenhouse will be exposed to morning light, and the west wall of the greenhouse (which should be glazed as well) will pick up the afternoon light. Research has shown there is little point in glazing the north wall of a greenhouse. It would be better to insulate and build the north wall with a northward slope at the top of 65 or 70 degrees from vertical, even if the greenhouse is freestanding. A vertical north wall is a good compromise.

ACE staff

This rooftop greenhouse can take full advantage of the sun. Note the fan located near the peak of the roof, to vent excess heat that rises in the greenhouse.

Considerable heat is lost through greenhouse walls in heavy winds, and greenhouses made from wooden framing and polyethylene sheeting are easily damaged and torn by high winds. If strong winds usually blow in your area, an attempt should be made to shield the greenhouse with something such as a row of evergreens beyond the shade zone, or a clear barrier such as a wall of rigid clear plastic. Double covering of the greenhouse itself seems to provide some resistance.

Other things to consider in locating a greenhouse are the accessibility to water, and the types of heating or ventilation planned.

Framing
While aluminum or steel framing is recommended for commercial growers, wood will serve well for the home gardener, if care is taken in treating it. Warmth and moisture can

cause rapid deterioration of wood, so posts, wall planks, and benches in contact with the ground should be treated. For a wood preservative, water-based solutions of copper, chromium, and zinc are recommended. Some preservatives, like creosote and pentachlorophenol, are toxic to plants and should never be used around a greenhouse.

Above ground wooden parts, except benches, should be painted with a high quality light color that reflects light well. Aluminum paint is suggested for wood and metal parts. Zinc paints will also do. As suggested in Chapter 5, flat white is superior to metallic surfaces (such as foil) for reflecting light. Reflectors such as aluminum foil (called specular reflectors) soon lose much of their reflecting ability and can also create hot spots which can harm plants. Flat white paint is not only less expensive, it tends

ACE staff

These greenhouse benches were photographed in a greenhouse in Eagle, Alaska.

to diffuse the available light more evenly to the plants, brightening the whole greenhouse. Insulated north walls, in particular, should be made reflective, which will make the rear wall slope less critical.

Foundations

Depending on how long a greenhouse is expected to last, and how much money will be invested, consider putting in a foundation of poured concrete, concrete block, stone, or wood. A treated wooden foundation would be the cheapest and should last for 10 years or longer, depending on soil conditions. If ground beds in particular are planned, the foundation should be insulated. It is suggested that the insulation be extended a foot or two below the bottom of the foundation.

The foundation ties the greenhouse to the ground and supports the weight of the structure. Consider the weight of snow and ice, and the wind direction and force. If the greenhouse is a permanent structure, the foundation should extend below frost level or at least to a solid footing so the house does not settle or heave. For a temporary structure, a frame box covered with plastic film and not attached to a foundation can be quickly moved to other ground for crop rotation, but will probably need to be recovered yearly. Built-in benches will add to the weight and make movement less feasible.

Remember that wood foundations and wooden benches will be subjected to nearly constant moisture. You will want to either line your beds with plastic sheeting, or paint them

Tomatoes are grown in ground beds in this greenhouse with board paths.

with a wood preservative. Alaskan garden author and Master Gardener, Pat Babcock, warns against using creosote or penta that, as mentioned before, are poisonous to plants. According to her, "Copper naphthenate is the only wood preservative to use on wood which comes in contact with plants!"

Beds Versus Benches
Decide whether to plant in beds or raised benches, or a combination of the two. It is even possible to plant in pots and tubs set into the beds or benches.

Benches cut down on vertical space for tall cucumbers, pole beans, or tomatoes. They also increase the initial cost of the greenhouse and will need to be replaced periodically. In order to tend the plants, construct benches no more than five feet wide (if there is an aisle on both sides) or 2¹/₂ feet wide (if there is an aisle only on one side, or between two benches).

Benches for tall plants should be built near the floor and contain a minimum of 8 to 12 inches of soil. Because of these height limitations, the Alaska Cooperative Extension, University of Alaska Fairbanks (ACE) recommends use of ground beds (planting directly into the ground) where possible.

But there are advantages to benches, especially in Alaska. Benches are recommended on cold wet soils, or on permafrost soils. The soil in benches will warm up faster in the spring and the plants will be higher and easier to care for. Since heat rises, higher means warmer, too. If one accidentally overfertilizes, it is easy to leach out excess fertilizer by flooding the soil with water.

Snow Loads/Roof Slope

Most greenhouses are designed for a snow load of 10 pounds per square foot—fine for areas where greenhouses are heated all year, melting what snow falls. But in Alaska, it is not very practical to heat a greenhouse through the winter just to melt snow.

One construction detail that may help is roof slope. The slope of the south-facing roof of an Alaska greenhouse should be as steep as is practicable, according to an early ACE publication, which recommended a slope of 30° to 45°. Advantages of a steep slope are more than simply having the snow slide off easily. A roof with a good

ACE diagram

At least the south-facing roof of an Alaskan greenhouse should be as steep as is practicable to allow snow to slide off easily, and to transmit more sun during periods of the year when the sun is low in the sky.

slope transmits more sun in the early spring and late fall, when the sun is low in the sky. Another advantage of a steep slope is that moisture condensing on the inside tends to run down rather than drip on the plants.

Reinforcing for Snow Load

Designing a greenhouse frame for a heavier load would increase the size (and cost) of framing members, with a corresponding decrease in available light for the plants. Instead, the recommendation for Alaska is to use temporary supports. Install a row of movable columns down the center under each frame. This can increase the design snow load to as much as 40 pounds per square foot. Hinge the supports to each frame and swing them against the roof during the growing season. Lumber or concrete footers or pads are suggested to keep the posts from settling into the soil. If using lightweight pipe columns, reinforce them against buckling. Since a snow load of 50 pounds per square foot is possible, especially in areas such as Valdez, plan to occasionally shovel snow off the roof if it is a snowy winter.

If the greenhouse is a temporary wood frame structure covered with polyethylene film, there will be no need to worry about snow loads; the film will most likely need replacing each spring anyway. This is due to wind damage and degradation caused by ultraviolet rays in summer, and freezing in winter. To prevent frame collapse, slit the roof film in case, for some reason, it fails to be torn soon enough by the weight of the snow accumulation.

ACE staff

Inexpensive polyethylene covers this greenhouse. It should be removed in the fall to prevent collapse of the structure due to snow load.

Covering a Greenhouse

The part of a greenhouse covering designed to let light in, whether plastic or glass, is called glazing. A minimum thickness of 6 mils is recommended for greenhouse glazing. Although many greenhouse owners recover a temporary structure each season with 4 to 6 mil polyethylene, the material has an extremely low heat resistance (meaning heat leaves quickly whenever outside temperatures are lower than inside temperatures) compared with other glazings, particularly glass. Manley Hot Springs has one of the few remaining glass greenhouses in the state. It is much more efficient in trapping heat, and so must be well ventilated to avoid baking the plants.

For permanent buildings, choose from glass or various plastics, rigid or nonrigid, corrugated or flat. Building supply stores can give specific information on more recently developed plastics.

Glass is permanent, but is heavy to ship and needs heavier framing. In Alaska, a double or even triple layer with dead air space between is probably best, for reasons discussed later. It is important to know, however, that even with clear glass, the thicker the covering, the lower the light transmission. With glass, the loss runs between 10 and 15% for each layer. One must balance this fact with a need to retain supplemental heat in early spring and late fall. If planning to use a greenhouse only from June through August, for example, take advantage of the higher light transmission of thinner glazings. The ideal to aim for is 90% light transmission.

ACE staff

This greenhouse at Circle Hot Springs, Alaska uses rigid corrugated plastic panels. It will last better than polyethylene, but will not transmit as much light as clear glass, nor retain as much heat.

Rigid plastics can be purchased flat or corrugated for extra strength. Be warned that many plastics, especially acrylics, ignite readily and support combustion, though some tend to be self-extinguishing when heat is removed.

Whether choosing glass or plastic, always look for as clear a layer as possible. Green-tinted coverings may be nice for patios, but plants in a greenhouse will suffer. Also, plan to replace plastics eventually. Some have a longer life than others, but all will tend to cloud over gradually. There are special coatings available that help extend the life of plastic coverings. Some are applied on the inside and some on the outside, so read the labels to ensure the proper side faces out.

Dr. Dinkel recommends that if using two layers with an air space between, the space be no more than eight inches deep. This is obtained by fastening glazing to both sides of framing members eight inches or less in thickness. Inside layers will not discolor as fast as the outside layer, and it can be a cheaper plastic film because it will not be subjected to the same climate extremes as the outer layer. To save money on replacement costs, one might cover the roof with the heavier corrugated type plastic. For other reasons why Dr. Dinkel recommends layering, see **Glazings**, later in this chapter.

Be vigilant in keeping glazing spotless. Dirt, dust, and algae will cut down on the amount of light reaching plants. Remember, too, that whatever is used will deteriorate over time, reducing light transmission.

Lighting

Most gardeners in Alaska (especially in the outlying areas and places such as Nome where

Virgil D. Severns

This prefabricated greenhouse was erected in Kotzebue, Alaska.

garden centers are not available) start plants early under grow lights. This is quite practical since the lights can be located only a few inches above the tiny seedlings. However, it is not economically feasible to put lights in the greenhouse for winter use with plants larger than seedlings. In fact, it is not considered practical to operate a home greenhouse in the colder winter months at all, due to the short period of daylight and extremely low outside temperatures. Even if heat were available at low cost, the cost of supplemental light in winter would be prohibitive.

While a few fluorescent lights might make the greenhouse seem well-lit to your eyes, plants require a great deal more light than you might think to carry out photosynthesis, the conversion of light, water and carbon dioxide to plant foods. Providing adequate lighting could cost much more than the price of the same vegetables at the store.

Incidentally, the previous paragraph refers to enough light for growth. As mentioned in

Chapter 12, even light of very low intensity may be sufficient to cause a plant to produce flowers (or not produce flowers). In these cases, light is merely serving as a stimulus, not as a source of energy for growth.

In general then, in Interior Alaska, the home greenhouse season extends from April through October, with some type of supplemental heat needed during parts of the first and last two months. South of the Alaska Range, you might be able to make an earlier start.

Michele Hébert

This photograph of the ceiling area of Risse's greenhouse shows commercial lighting. Most home greenhouses will not require lighting in the summer in Alaska, due to long days.

Ventilation

"Ventilation is more important than heat in a seasonal greenhouse operation," states Dr. Dinkel. Given a choice of spending money on a heating system or a ventilation system, he recommends the money be spent first for ventilation. A good ventilation system will control excessive temperature and moisture that is often a contributing cause of plant diseases, such as gray mold and powdery mildew. A greenhouse will generally be 30 to 50 degrees warmer than outside when the sun is shining, meaning that if it is 70° F outside, it may easily be above 100° F inside.

In the home greenhouse, a manually operated wall ventilator may be adequate, but constant monitoring will be required. A thermostatically controlled fan is much more reliable. Many large commercial greenhouses in the state use a perforated plastic duct system for distribution of heat, and it can double for ventilation. A complete change of air every 1 to 1$^{1}/_{2}$ minutes is considered adequate for warm-weather ventilation.

Aim for the total square footage of outside vents to equal one-sixth the total floor area of the greenhouse. To promote good air circulation, locate a low vent on the windward side of the greenhouse, and a high vent one-third larger on the downwind side, especially if not planning to use a fan. With benches, vents can be located under benches that are next to the glazing. If ground beds in the greenhouse are next to low vents, provide deflectors so wind will not blow directly on the plants. Heat activated vent openers add convenience.

With an exhaust fan, a multispeed motor or adjustable pulley will make it easier to reduce the ventilation rate during cold weather. The fan should have a thermostat with a temperature differential of not more than one degree Fahrenheit, meaning that if it is set to come on at 70° F, it will shut off at 69° F. A good setting for greenhouse ventilators is somewhere between

70° and 75° F. Whatever the setting, the ventilator thermostat should be set to come on at about 10 degrees above the heater thermostat setting, to avoid having them run simultaneously.

To determine requirements for airflow, use this formula: Multiply length times width to obtain greenhouse floor space. Multiply this number by eight. The result is the required capacity of the fan or fans to cool and distribute the air in the greenhouse. Another method is to multiply the square footage by the height of the greenhouse to get the total greenhouse volume in cubic feet.

According to ACE bulletin *Controlling the Greenhouse Environment* (#HGA-00336), an exchange rate equivalent to ³/₄ of the greenhouse volume (as just figured above) should maintain an inside temperature of about 11° to 13° F above the outside temperature. An

These greenhouse windows are made to open for venting excess heat. Venting a greenhouse is very important. When the sun is shining, greenhouse temperatures may easily rise above 100° F inside, even though it may be only 70° F outside.

exchange of one volume per minute should keep the temperatures from 10° to 12° F above the outside temperature. The bulletin mentioned above has a chart to help ensure the purchase of the right size fan for each situation, which has been reprinted in Appendix A.

Humidity
Humidity should not be allowed to fall below 30 or 40% to avoid plant wilt. Most plants (except germinating seeds) grow well with up to 70% relative humidity. Excess humidity in the greenhouse, as evidenced by condensation on the walls, may not harm very young plants, but if present during flowering, will hinder fruit set. This is because high humidity will keep

pollen damp and sticky, so that it is less likely to be transferred from one flower to another. Research has determined that the relative humidity for optimum pollination, fruit set, and fruit development of tomatoes is 70%. In addition to problems of pollination, powdery mildew is encouraged by high humidity and excessive use of nitrogen fertilizers.

Ventilation reduces humidity as it removes excess heat from the greenhouse. To help reduce humidity problems, a porous floor will allow excess water to drain away quickly. An instrument called a psychrometer can be used to check relative humidity.

Heating

Many factors enter into determining heating requirements for a greenhouse and in selecting appropriate equipment. The temperature range recommended by ACE for most greenhouse plants is between 50° and 85°F "for best photosynthetic efficiency". Tomatoes espe-

Jim Holm

These square heaters and round fans were photographed during installation into the new Holm Town Nursery in Fairbanks. The fans distribute the warm air from the heaters, and operate on their own to cool a too-hot greenhouse. Not shown are the plastic ducts mounted lengthwise under the roof ridge, which direct the air down, forcing circulation as hot air rises again along the inside of the outer walls.

cially should not be grown in temperatures above 90° F. This section will only summarize some general principles and options available.

A heating system is usually designed on the basis of the lowest possible outdoor temperature during the particular growing period. Getting the heat into the greenhouse does not guarantee an even distribution to all plants in the building. As mentioned before, perforated plastic ducts are often used in larger greenhouses to distribute heat. Fans and cross-ventilation from doors, windows, and other vents can also help.

Types of Heating Systems

According to Alan C. Epps, former Program Leader, Agriculture and Natural Resources/

Community Resource Development, and Axel R. Carlson, Extension Engineer (now re-tired), the ultimate in greenhouse heating is a combination of hot-water or steam baseboard radiation (fin tubes) and unit heaters.

Oil and gas-fired ventilation systems are available for heating as well, and space heaters fueled by wood, oil, or gas may be used in small structures with an adequate heat distri-bution system. Propane heaters have the added advantage of supplying carbon dioxide for the plants' use, which is also true of air supplied directly from the home in the case of attached greenhouses.

This heated greenhouse can extend the season by many months, but will be too expensive for the dead of winter.

A home's hot water furnace may be used, but it may not be practical to tie domestic hot air systems into greenhouses, due to possible overheating of the residence. This can be avoided by zoning the hot-air ducts and providing separate cold-air returns. Electric space-heating equipment may be inexpensive and easy to install, but will be very expensive to operate. Soil-heating cables, especially for seed starting, may be more practical. When using an oil burner, be sure it does not get out of adjustment. Tomatoes are very sensitive to oil fumes.

With whatever system chosen, it is desirable to install a battery-operated, low-temperature alarm that activates a bell in the home to warn of low temperatures or failure of the green-house heating system.

Fuel
Oil, coal, wood, and natural gas are the most common fuels used in greenhouses. Each

has its advantages and disadvantages. Oil and natural gas, where available, are generally the most expensive, but the most dependable and best adapted to automatic control. Coal and wood are usually cheaper, with wood being the easiest to obtain in many outlying areas, but both require more work. Coal involves work to supply the heating unit and remove ashes. Wood requires the same, with either continuous attention or automatic draft controls to reduce temperature fluctuations.

Utilizing Solar Heat

In a sense, all greenhouses utilize solar heat to some extent. But by planning ahead, you can greatly enhance the solar capabilities of a greenhouse, even though you may not be able to depend on complete solar heating for the entire greenhouse season. Naturally, your own microclimate will determine just how much solar heat will be utilized.

There are several aspects of solar heating to be considered. Passive systems are the simplest, and just require designing a structure to take advantage of what solar heat is available. Active systems involve technology to move heat into storage and out for delivery to the plants when needed. Most active systems are more complicated and expensive and are beyond the scope of this book. Check a local library for more information. The following are some of the easier, mostly passive, things that can be done to improve a greenhouse's solar potential. ACE also has a flyer, *The Attached Solar Greenhouse* (#400G-01259).

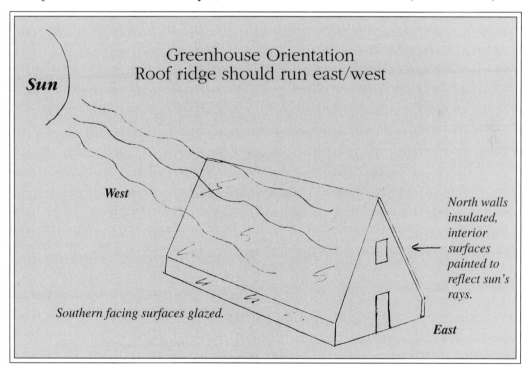

Orientation

Research shows the ridge should run east/west, even though very little heat will be provided by the north roof. Many greenhouse owners line up their greenhouses north/south, in the erroneous belief that the plants will better receive sun from both sides. Because the greatest amount of light is transmitted through a surface oriented perpendicular to the sun's rays, it is important to have as much glazing slanted that way as possible. Vertical end walls are directed to the south when a greenhouse is oriented north/south. (Note, this is not necessarily bad in the early spring and late fall when the rays arrive from such a low angle in most of Alaska.)

Orienting the greenhouse east/west, and then insulating the north wall and roof heavily will save considerable heat. In addition, the inside of the insulated portions can be painted a light color to reflect sunlight onto the back side of the plants, thus achieving the same goal as the north/south oriented greenhouse, with a net heat saving. Similarly, long narrow greenhouses, with more south-slanted glazing, will be more energy-efficient than square buildings. The general rule is a length of twice the width. If the south side has a knee wall, even though vertical, it should be glazed as well as the roof.

Glazing

Starting at the outside of the greenhouse, the next item to be considered is the glazing. The thinner and clearer the glazing, the more light will be let in to change to heat, but also the more heat will be able to escape back out. Flat plastics are better than corrugated ones in this respect, because corrugated ones have more area through which heat can escape.

All glazings lose heat, no matter how thick. What actually offers the most resistance to heat loss is not the glazing itself. It is the air film on the surface of the glazing, and the air space created by layering the materials. In other words, two layers of glass with an air space between will trap considerably more heat than one layer the total thickness of the two layers, but with no air space. If this sounds as though you should rush out and install eight layers of glazing with air spaces between, don't. Not only will light levels in the greenhouse be lowered with each additional layer, but the increment in heat retention will be less with each subsequent layer. Research has shown there is not much point in using more than two or three layers, even in Alaska.

Using double-glazing, however, is suggested for other reasons than heat retention by the air space. Condensation on the glazing lowers light levels in the greenhouse, besides dripping on the plants. Water also directly contributes to heat losses. When water evaporates from plants and soil and then condenses on cool glazing, heat is removed from the greenhouse. By installing a second layer of glazing, the inside layer will be warmer, cutting down on the condensation problem and resulting heat losses. Many large commercial greenhouses, such as Ann's greenhouse in Fairbanks, find it worthwhile to use, on the inside of their glazing, a chemical coating which has been especially developed to reduce condensation problems.

Before purchasing glazing materials, do a little research. Materials vary widely in ability to transmit light, ability to retain heat, weatherability, and ease of installation. When buying plastic products, be sure they are sold for greenhouse use, and if planning a glass roof, be sure to get tempered glass (a minimum thickness of $1/8$ inch), not just double-strength glass. Panes of glass should never be butted together with no space between, and both plastic and glass should have room to expand and contract with temperature changes.

Wind

Wind contributes greatly to the heat loss problem, especially if special attention has not been given to making the greenhouse airtight. Many a gardener with a heated greenhouse has lost an entire supply of early-started seedlings on a windy day when he found it impossible to keep heat in the greenhouse.

Wind currents around the structure create imbalances of pressure on different sides of the building. Warm air from the greenhouse is sucked out to low-pressure areas on the side away from the wind, causing lower pressure inside. This low pressure, in turn, sucks in cold air from the high-pressure area on the windward side of the greenhouse. The stronger the wind is, the greater the infiltration of cold air into the greenhouse. Currents set up inside the greenhouse on a windy day speed up water evaporation from soil and plants, which also causes a loss of heat, as explained under the section on **Glazing**.

A suitable location will probably contribute most to reducing the problem of wind. Read again the earlier section in this chapter on **Site Selection**.

Minimizing Heat Leakage

Even without the wind factor, it is very important to build greenhouses as airtight as possible. Caulk joints and use weather stripping. Large pieces of glazing will reduce the amount of sealing necessary. (This is one disadvantage of glass, which is usually installed as small panes, for strength). There can also be excessive heat losses through framing members. Aluminum conducts heat more readily than glass, so if using an aluminum frame, figure a way to insulate the members.

Insulating concrete slabs and edgings can minimize heat losses through floors, because concrete conducts heat faster than soil. For reasons discussed earlier in Chapter 13, it is a good idea to insulate ground beds in Alaska a foot or two below the surface with Styrofoam® (the kind described in Chapter 10).

At the University of Alaska Agricultural Experiment Station, Styrofoam® has been used under ground beds in greenhouses. There they are combined with heating coils with a thermostat setting of 80° F. The coils are laid on top of the insulating board. Drainage is no problem, as the edges are not sealed, of course, and any excess water just runs off into the soil. Heat loss is greatest at the perimeter, so be sure the foundation is insulated as mentioned earlier.

An arctic entry or air lock for the greenhouse will cut down on cold air entering the greenhouse directly. A handy place to store greenhouse paraphernalia, it need not be very large. An attached greenhouse can be entered from the house. If neither idea is practical in your situation, at least locate the greenhouse door away from prevailing winds.

Heat losses increase with increases in temperature differences. In other words, the colder the outside air and the hotter the inside air, the greater the heat loss. Since warm air collects at the peak of a greenhouse, temperature differences are greater at the peak, and heat loss is accelerated there. By using a fan to circulate the warm air, plants will benefit even though the total heat loss may not be particularly affected.

There are two other ways to maintain the heat in a greenhouse. One is to keep it from escaping on cloudy days by use of a night blanket, and the other is to store some of the heat from the day for release on cloudy days, or cool nights.

Night Blankets
Thermal shutters, or movable nighttime insulation, can help trap precious heat. With the sky lit all night from early spring to late summer, it may be difficult to decide when to use the insulation on clear days. Be sure to remove it early in the morning

Styrofoam® insulating board is being put a few feet under the soil of this bed in a greenhouse at the University of Alaska Fairbanks.

when the sun reaches the greenhouse. On very cloudy days of early spring and late fall, insulation can be left on and supplemental artificial light provided for the plants. Tight fitting insulation batts or boards are more effective than drapes. Be sure to provide a way to fasten them securely, especially in areas subject to high winds. Plan a place to store them when not in use.

Heat Storage
Here again there are many options. Research seems to indicate the most efficient storage medium is water, but only if in small containers with good contact between them. Many

246

people use black 55-gallon drums. Water in that large a container tends to stratify, the warmer water being near the top. Round drums waste space. A wall of 5-gallon square metal cans of water is better, if the cans are stacked on their sides and painted a dark color.

One-gallon clear or semi-clear plastic jugs containing water colored black with ordinary fabric dye are also effective if stacked on their sides in layers at least three high. To obtain more mass, shelves may have to be built to help support the weight of the jugs. If planning to leave them in the empty greenhouse through winter, empty them or fill them with an antifreeze solution to avoid replacing cracked jugs that have frozen. Experiment with just leaving headroom for freezing expansion, but it will mean a white area in the top of the jug, which may cut down on efficiency.

You may want to add a bit of antifreeze or rust inhibitor to the metal cans also, to extend their lives. If the only choice is the 55-gallon drums, at least insulate the back and sides not directly heated by the sun, and stack them more than one layer high. Improving contact between the top and bottom barrels may help, too.

Heat can be stored in cement or rocks, but due to natural currents set up in water when it is heated, water is much more efficient at taking up heat than solid materials. Water will also hold over twice the amount of heat by volume as solid materials. Fans to circulate the hot air through rocks will help improve the situation somewhat.

Whatever the storage material, try to locate it in the greenhouse where the sun will shine directly on it (although it would pick up some heat as secondary storage even if it were not in direct light). This usually means in front of an insulated north wall, or any wall that is not glazed. Darkening the material, with black paint or dye, for example, will improve its heat-collecting properties.

What this is, essentially, is a trade-off between the need for light-colored reflecting surfaces for additional light, and the need for dark-colored collectors for additional heat. A compromise might be to locate collectors against the lower half to two-thirds of the wall, and use a reflecting surface above. If the collector must be located in the front part of the greenhouse, near the glazing, the collecting side can be painted black, with a white surface turned toward the plants. In this case, do not put the collectors too close to the glazing, or too much heat will be lost back out the glazing.

Other Types of Greenhouses

Types of greenhouses are limited only by the imaginations of gardeners. Most common, besides freestanding and attached, are pit greenhouses, cold frames, and hot frames.

Pit Greenhouse

Because of permafrost problems in many parts of Alaska, pit greenhouses are often impractical. But what the term means is building a greenhouse with very low headroom, then digging the pathway down into the ground a few feet so you can stand in the greenhouse and work without stooping over. This is sometimes done in other states to increase the heat storing mass of the greenhouse, by insulating several feet into the ground around the perimeter so the soil of the greenhouse can be used for heat storage.

Cold Frame

A cold frame is also without headroom. It is used in mild climates to grow cool-season crops, often through winter. In some places, it is used to grow early starts for the garden. Usually it consists of a box of some type, with a removable or hinged sash on top. The top sash is often slanted toward the sun. Cold frames can be purchased ready-made, complete with automatic ventilators. But they are really quite simple to make, requiring, for example, an old storm door or screen window frame with polyethylene stapled to it, set on a simple framework of two by fours.

The author's hot frame grows cantaloupes in Fairbanks, planted through clear plastic and using Styrofoam® beneath the soil, topped with heat tapes. Gallon jugs of water act at solar heat collectors on the south wall of the house. The top is an old screen door fitted with plastic and set on a simple frame. The light bulb adds extra heat when needed, helping to extend the growing season.

Hot Frame

Add heat to a cold frame; it then becomes a hot frame. To grow very warm-weather crops such as melons in a frame, add soil-heating cables. A small battery heater, car interior heater, or even a light bulb can help to extend the season without too much expense. Gallon water bottles for solar collection may also be located behind the plants.

The author's hot frame, used to grow cantaloupes in Fairbanks, utilized a doorframe hinged to the south wall of the house. Three narrow boards formed a box, with the wall for the fourth side, and two pieces of scrap wood as legs for the front corners. Then plastic was wrapped around the sides from the frame to the ground. A rope could have been rigged up to tie the door in any position for venting or working in the hot frame. In the case of this frame, the cantaloupes also grew through clear polyethylene stretched on the ground inside.

Soil and Fertilizer for Greenhouses

Soil used in a greenhouse is nothing special. Aim for the same type of good soil anyone would want in a garden. See Chapters 3 and 4 for more information on soil. If a problem should develop with soil in a small greenhouse, it would not be too difficult to completely change the soil, which may be a good idea to do every few years anyway, in lieu of crop rotations.

To properly fertilize in a greenhouse, learn something about the needs of the plants you wish to grow. For example, experienced gardeners keep peppers away from crops such as tomatoes and cucumbers because peppers require much less fertilizer than the other two crops. Tomatoes like a more alkaline soil than cucumbers, which might influence applications of lime. Also, the pH of 6.8 recommended for tomatoes is not very low, and if you try to grow them with a cucumber pH, you will run the danger of a low calcium supply, which contributes to blossom end rot. As mentioned in the section on **Tomatoes** in Part Three, Holm Town Nursery solves that problem by using a pH of 7 to 7.2 for tomatoes.

Many pelleted commercial fertilizers cause a salt buildup in a greenhouse over time, so it is recommended that you always use soluble fertilizers in greenhouses to avoid this problem. Do not use regular garden fertilizer.

Obtaining the highest yields of tomatoes and cucumbers in a greenhouse requires large quantities of fertilizer. To avoid plant injury or the buildup of excessive salts in the soil, use fertilizers that contain no chlorides, sodium or sulfates. Fertilizers without these are available as diammonium phosphate, monopotassium phosphate, calcium nitrate, potassium nitrate, urea, and mixtures of these compounds. They should be applied before planting (preplant), as well as by adding some to the irrigation water during the growing season. The out-of-print ACE bulletin, *Soil Fertility for Home Garden and Greenhouse*, contained a suggested fertilization program for tomatoes in a summer greenhouse operation, and said that:

> If calcium nitrate and potassium nitrate are not easily obtained, you may substitute approximately equal quantities of 10-52-17. If the manure is unavailable, substitute 1 lb. of 10-52-17 per 100 sq. ft.

> Cucumbers require additional nitrogen, which can be supplied by adding 1/2 lb. ammonium nitrate (33-0-0) per 100-sq. ft. every 10 days after fruiting begins.

ACE has available up-to-date flyers on fertilization programs for both cucumbers and tomatoes. Addresses for ACE offices are in Appendix C.

Organic matter is also important in a greenhouse, helping to maintain soil tilth, which in turn improves soil aeration and water-holding capacity, and helps reduce problems of excessive fertilizer salts. The organic matter should be mixed thoroughly with the soil. Peat will increase the acidity of the soil, as discussed in Chapter 4. Lime may be added to bring the soil pH back to a desirable range. If no pH determination has been made for the greenhouse soil, about 10 pounds of ground limestone may be incorporated into the soil-peat mixture for each cubic yard of peat added, or follow the formula given in Chapter 4. But a soil test is always preferable (see Chapter 3).

More information on starter solutions for when transplanting into the greenhouse, and side-dressings of fertilizer for later in the season, can be found in Chapters 5 and 4, respectively.

Watch greenhouse plants carefully. If they show signs of poor growth and if their leaves change to a lighter color, more fertilizer may be needed. The growth of plants is the best indicator as to when and how much to fertilize. Study your plants to learn their requirements.

Carbon Dioxide

Air outside a greenhouse contains about .03% carbon dioxide. This is a minimum requirement for healthy plants, and they can easily benefit from 10 times that (3 or 4% carbon dioxide). Carbon dioxide is essential for photosynthesis, and is a plant's only source of carbon, which makes up around one half its total dry weight.

In a nearly airtight greenhouse, the plants will quickly deplete the carbon dioxide supply. Attached greenhouses will be able to supply much of the needed carbon dioxide from the residence, but other types of greenhouses may need other sources. A few possibilities are dry ice, ventilation, decaying organic matter, and the exhaust from a propane heater. Care must be taken when ventilating for carbon dioxide in cold weather. A commercial greenhouse, if venting for adequate carbon dioxide, may require a complete change of air every 10 minutes, which can add up to a large heat loss.

Watering

Every summer the problem of blossom end rot shows up in greenhouse tomatoes all over the state. This disease in tomatoes (and poor growth in other plants) can often be traced to poorly timed or too light applications of water, which contributes to, or accompanies, a low calcium supply. One thorough soaking a week (which is preferred to frequent light watering) is usually enough for ground beds. But benches tend to dry out too quickly. Edges dry faster than centers, and even if the surface looks damp, the soil a few inches down may be powder dry. Commercial greenhouses sometime use a combination of double-wall and capillary watering systems (see Chapter 5).

Because greenhouse plants are growing rapidly and the greenhouse is warmer than outside, they usually require more frequent watering. Larger plants, or fruiting ones, will need more water, perhaps daily. On very hot days, water more than usual. On the other hand, water less in cool, cloudy weather. The goal is for the soil to have all the water it can hold without being soggy. Dr. Dinkel says, "Plants should be watered on demand—not on a schedule. Thoroughly water, then let dry to a near wilting point."

Greenhouse Insects

Greenhouses that are closed down and allowed to freeze for a few months in winter seldom have serious insect problems. Occasionally, aphids may infest a greenhouse during summer, particularly if birch trees grow nearby (the birch tree aphid is the most common aphid pest in Alaska).

The two other major greenhouse pests, whiteflies and red spider mites, can be prevented more easily than they can be controlled. These two pests are introduced into the greenhouse on purchased plants, or plants that have overwintered in the home. Red spider mites are native to Alaska and can be introduced from spruce

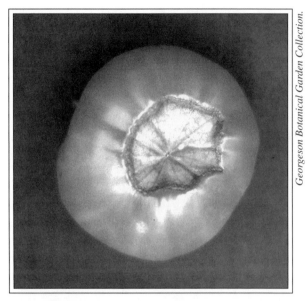

Tomato blossom end rot can usually be prevented by maintaining an even moisture supply.

trees allowed to grow near the greenhouse. It is strongly suggested that greenhouse owners treat plants before putting them in their greenhouse. If possible, eliminate spruce trees near the greenhouse. Close up easy entry points. Increasing humidity can discourage spider mites, as well as continuously removing the webbing they use for scaffolding.

Try hand picking, hand vacuuming, sticky traps, and spot killing with a cotton swab dipped in rubbing alcohol and rubbed on stationary pests. A predatory mite, the Encarsia mite, can be used if you have a very high infestation. See Chapter 8 for more help in controlling these and other insect pests.

Greenhouse Diseases

The major diseases found in Alaska

This tiny whitefly has been magnified many times. Whiteflies, aphids, and red spider mites are the major insect pests in Alaska greenhouses.

greenhouses are damping off, leaf mold, gray mold rot, powdery mildew, and mosaic. Damping off is covered in Chapters 5 and 9.

Leaf Mold

A disease of tomatoes, leaf mold is brought into the greenhouse as fungal spores on seeds. The spores are dry and spread rapidly through the air from leaf to leaf and plant to plant. They may survive in the soil indefinitely.

Symptoms of leaf mold are irregular yellow spots less than $\frac{1}{2}$ inch in diameter on the upper surfaces of the leaves. Directly under these spots, on the undersides of the leaves, will be a brown, felt-like splotch of fungal spores. If the infestation is severe, foliage may dry up completely, and the plant eventually dies.

Leaf mold spores need very high humidity for germination and infection. The disease will usually become serious in Alaska greenhouses in late summer when temperatures begin to drop and cloudy cold days are the rule. Tomato plants are large by then, and transpire large quantities of water. In greenhouses with poor ventilation, humidity is high, and moisture condenses on plant leaves, keeping them wet.

Control of leaf mold consists of two steps. One is to keep the humidity down by ventilating. The other is to provide supplementary heat to keep the greenhouse temperature from dropping below 60°F.

Georgeson Botanical Garden Collection.

Gray mold rot on strawberries.

Gray Mold Rot

This very common fungal disease, also known as *Botrytis*, may attack any plant when humidity is very high. Control is similar to control of leaf mold. The strawberries shown at left were probably not grown in a greenhouse, but they give an excellent illustration of gray mold rot, or *Botrytis*.

Powdery Mildew

Powdery mildew is not widespread in Alaska greenhouses, but can cause heavy damage to cucumbers when present. The fungus grows on leaf surfaces, and feeds on the plant. In fact, it is thought to grow only on living plants.

Symptoms are white spots on older leaves. The spots have a powdery flour-like appearance. The abundant spores do not require high humidity for germination, but in greenhouses, powdery mildew is encouraged by high humidity and excessive use of nitrogen fertilizers.

ACE recommends controlling powdery mildew with fungicides. Sulfur controls mildew, but cucumbers are sensitive to sulfur, so it should be applied sparingly.

Georgeson Botanical Garden Collection.

Powdery mildew on Lathan Raspberries.

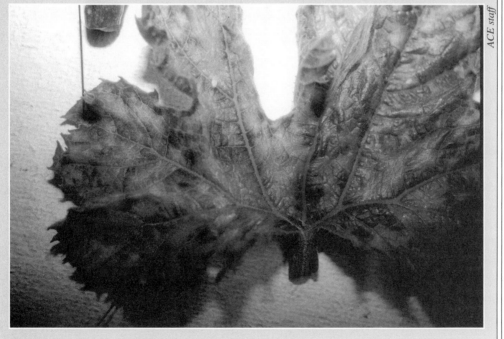

ACE staff

Zucchini leaf with cucumber mosaic virus.

Dusting sulfur is available from seed supply stores. The sulfur may be applied with a duster, or placed in a cloth bag to shake gently over the plants.

Mosaic

This is a viral disease occurring regularly in Alaska. Tobacco mosaic is carried on tobacco and the hands of smokers, and is easily passed on to tomato plants. See Chapter 9 for more information on this disease. If you smoke, it is strongly recommended (when working with tomatoes) that you wear rubber gloves that have not handled tobacco.

Chapter 15

Culture Clues

So then neither is he that planteth
any thing, neither he that watereth; but
God that giveth the increase. I Cor. 3:7, KJV.

This section gives specifics about particular vegetables (plus melons and a few berries). Where it would be beneficial to read other sections of the book concerning a particular plant, the chapter numbers have been given. Do not forget to consult Appendix B for the *Recommended Variety Lists* from Alaska Cooperative Extension, University of Alaska Fairbanks (ACE). See Chapters 12 and 13 for an explanation of the process of variety selection in Alaska.

ARTICHOKE, globe
Family: Compositae
Optimum pH: 6.5
Annual In Alaska

Artichokes are actually derived from thistles and seed sometimes tends to revert to thistles, as well as taking longer to produce a crop, so these are best grown from roots or suckers from older plants. Try California Nursery Company (Niles, CA 94536) or Stribling's Nurseries (Merced, CA 95340) for roots. Several companies listed in the Appendix A carry seed.

Georgeson Botanical Garden Collection.

Artichokes do not have much of a chance in Alaska unless grown through clear plastic (see Chapter 10). Do not count on a very high yield, as production is very low the first year of this "perennial," and there is not likely to be a second year. The best available is said to be Green Globe, an Italian artichoke. Grand Buerre is another with a good flavor.

SOIL AND SITE: Climate is the most important thing for growing artichokes. Even in

255

warmer states, they are called tender perennials. They will not survive a very cold winter, but they like cool, foggy summers. Artichokes are heavy feeders, and like a high nitrogen fertilizer. They need a moist but well-drained soil with plenty of humus and compost or manure. They should have a sunny location.

SOWING: If growing from seed, start indoors early. If growing from roots, set them about four feet apart, burying the old woody stalk in a vertical position and putting growing points or shoots just above the ground.

CULTIVATION: Keep weeds under control and soil moist but not soggy.

CHALLENGES: Aphids, slugs, and *Botrytis* (a fungal disease), may be problems. Do not use chemical sprays for aphids, because of the difficulty of removing spray residue from the buds. See Chapter 8 for other ways to control aphids and slugs. For information on *Botrytis*, see Chapter 14 under **Gray Mold Rot**.

HARVESTING: Cut buds before blossoms begin to open, keeping about 1$\frac{1}{2}$ inches of stem attached. The buds will be from 1$\frac{1}{2}$ to 4 inches across. In states where they are grown as perennials, foliage is cut down to the ground in the fall and a box or basket inverted over the plant to keep out moisture. Then manure is piled thickly over all.

Georgeson Botanical Garden Collection.

ASPARAGUS

ASPARAGUS
Family: Liliaceae
Optimum pH: 6.5
Perennial

Asparagus has not been widely grown in Alaska (at least north of the Alaska Range) due to a lack of adapted varieties.

The old standard, Mary Washington, has been available for many years, but has a poor survival rate in Alaska, and an increasingly lower yield with age, although Ed Bostrom of North Pole Acres believes that planting depth is the culprit, rather than poor quality of the variety. Recently, better success has been noted with the Fairbo Hybrid, Howard's Green. The latter much improved variety may be difficult to obtain, and is usually grown only from seed. If you can obtain the seed, you will discover that asparagus is quite easy to start, in spite of a rather long germination period (it can take weeks).

Other varieties showing promise at the Fairbanks Experiment Station are Viking, Viking 2K, and Ceto. The recommended variety for the Interior is now Super Male Jersey

Knight, — an early variety with good yield. It has been reported that seed-grown asparagus will outproduce crown plantings after about five years, even though they begin producing edible stalks later.

The sexes are separate on asparagus plants. Female plants have a lower survival rate and lower yields than male plants, so if you want a really productive bed, remove all female plants. This can be done in a nursery bed if you grow them there long enough to bloom. Asparagus flowers look like tiny yellowish-green bells. A hand magnifying glass will help you identify the females. Female flowers have 6 poorly developed stamens and a well-developed pistil with three lobes. The plant later produces berries. The male flower is larger and longer, with 6 well-developed stamens and a rudimentary pistil. Ed Bostrom reports that if you plant Jersey males and happen to find a plant with seeds, they will most likely not be viable.

SOIL AND SITE: One of the most important considerations for this plant is good drainage. Standing water on roots is one of the quickest ways to kill asparagus. University researchers theorize that Ed Bostrom's phenomenal success with asparagus might be related to factors such as soil type or water table depth at North Pole Acres.

Full sun, preferably against a south wall, is best, because the spears will grow tougher in the spring if they are subjected to a late frost. Asparagus is very sensitive to zinc deficiencies in the soil. As with all perennials, the permanent bed should be in the best possible condition when plants are set out, since it will not be dug up each year.

SOWING: Seed can be started indoors in peat pots with an air temperature between 75° F and 80° F for fastest germination. Another way to speed germination is to soak the seeds in water for 12 to 24 hours, or pre-sprout them between moist paper towels as described for corn (Chapter 10). Seedlings will be thick straight shoots that develop fine fernlike foliage difficult to see.

The seedlings should be transplanted into a nursery row or permanent bed by the time they are 12 inches high (in full sun) but may be set out when much smaller. Ed Bostrom does not believe they should be set in the garden until the soil temperature at three inches deep is 50° F. Handle the delicate seedlings carefully. Set them only a few inches deep and fairly close together, to allow for some mortality.

Crowns, or plantings of one to three-year-old roots, are spaced somewhat differently. Most authorities recommend a deep trench, which is gradually filled in as the plants grow. This was originally partly for blanching (to whiten) the stalks, which is no longer as popular as it once was, and a lot of trouble besides. But there is another reason growers plant deeply in warmer states. Deeply planted roots (about 10 inches deep) produce thicker stalks, although yield is slightly lower and emergence delayed. Thicker stalks are more tender, and therefore more desirable, but Alaska's soils are cold at 10 inches.

In spite of this, Dr. Dinkel was successful with deep planting. He started seeds in March. Trenches were dug one foot deep with two inches of peat (aged manure would be good too) in the bottom. The trench was filled in as the plants grew, with care being taken never to cover the growing points. This is probably a better method to use in Southeast than in the Interior.

In the Interior, Ed Bostrom has had excellent results growing his Jersey Knights from seed.

He overwinters them in three- or four-inch pots in a shed heated to from 28° F to 30° F, and then plants them into the garden when the soil is 50° F, at the depth they are growing in the pot. For more information on his method, see Chapter 13.

Ed believes that phosphorus is very important for asparagus, and generally lacking in Alaska soils (see Chapter 4). He suggests digging a hole or trench and working in a handful of compost and a tablespoon of 8-32-16 fertilizer. He also sprinkles one tablespoon of triplesuperphosphate in the hole and sets the plant directly in it. This way the phosphorus will be immediately available to the roots. Don't worry, it is **nitrogen** in fertilizer that you hear about burning plants, not phosphorus. The triplesuperphosphate is 0-45-0, meaning it has **only** phosphorus.

There are several ways to extend your asparagus harvest, but the one probably best for Alaska (except perhaps north of the Alaska Range) is to vary the planting depth. More deeply planted crowns produce later in the season, with lowered yield, but better sized stalks. By planting some of your crowns at four or five inches, some at six to eight inches, and some at 10 inches, you will stagger their emergence, and hence, your harvest.

Asparagus has a large root system, but most of the roots (especially in Alaska) will spread laterally, so do not put manure, etc., too deep. Dr. Dinkel reports a three to four inch spacing of seedlings in rows two feet apart, but recommends six inches for in-row spacing. One to three-year-old roots are usually planted farther apart. Ed Bostrom recommends rows four feet apart for them.

Research has shown that crowns do better when planted on ridges, instead of flat in the bottom of the trench. This means mounding two inches of fertile soil (compost, aged manure, etc.) in the bottom of the trench, placing the crowns on top of this ridge, and spreading the roots gently over the mound. Cover with about two inches of soil and water well. In a few weeks, add more soil to cover weeds, pinching off any low branches in the way. As the years pass, soil should be added to keep the roots at the proper depth, since the crowns (at least in warmer states) grow upward at a rate of as much as one inch per year.

CULTIVATION: Asparagus needs plenty of water for the tenderest spears. This vegetable, in particular, does poorly in competition with weeds, and spear size suffers. Fertilizers, compost, and manure should be carefully worked in each spring, and later right after harvesting is discontinued.

CHALLENGES: There have been no major pests of asparagus reported in Alaska.

HARVESTING: Do not harvest at all the first two years for crown-planted asparagus, or the first three years for seed-grown plants. The first year you harvest, cut just for a week or two, taking only the thickest spears (at least thumb size) five to eight inches long. Harvest morning and night. If you have never grown asparagus in Alaska, with its long days, you may be astonished at its rapid growth on hot days!

Then let the bed go to fern. Do not remove the ferns. They produce food the plant stores in its roots for the winter, and for increased production the following year. Ed Bostrom advises fertilizing with a nitrogen fertilizer (1 pound per 100 square feet) when the spears have ferned out, but never after the middle of July in the Interior.

In later years, harvest can extend a little longer, but Interior gardeners still should not harvest after July 15 at the latest. Spears not harvested will leaf out into foliage (they can reach 6 feet high) that should not be removed. While you might be able to cut them down after they are killed by frost, in some areas they serve the useful function of holding snow cover over the roots, aiding winter survival. See Chapter 4 for information on winter mulch.

It used to be recommended that spears be cut below the soil surface. The recommended procedure now is to snap the stalk off above the ground (with your hand) at the lowest point at which it snaps easily. Below that point the spear will probably be too tough anyway, since spear tenderness increases toward the tip.

BEANS
Family: Leguminosae
Optimum pH: 5.8 to 6.5
Annual

Most beans are considered "warm season vegetables." The most often grown are bush beans (or snap beans), but pole beans (grown in a greenhouse) are growing in popularity due to their heavy yield, in spite of large space requirements. Broad beans (fava or faba beans) are also grown in some areas. Broad beans are not closely related to other beans and, in fact, are a cool season vegetable. Unlike bush or pole beans, it is the seeds that are eaten, cooked like lima beans (which are very difficult to grow in Alaska).

Some of the green bean varieties are listed by ACE as snap beans. No pole beans are listed.

Georgeson Botanical Garden Collection.

BEANS

SOIL AND SITE: Bush beans can be grown with no special provisions in the Interior, but even there, they will do better on raised beds to help warm the soil. In wetter areas, clear plastic on raised beds is definitely recommended (see Chapters 10 and 11), and so is pre-sprouting seed. Do not crowd plants; air circulation is needed to discourage fungal disease, although researchers in Canada in 1995 concluded there was no advantage to spacing plants farther apart to improve air circulation in order to prevent white mold or cottony rot. Avoid heavy clay soils; the plants will mature faster in warm sandy soils.

High nitrogen will encourage foliage at the expense of pods. Pole beans, on the other hand, are heavy feeders and will need a richer soil and plenty of water. Beans are legumes (note family name) and return nitrogen to the soil, at least where soils are warm enough for bacterial activity (see Chapter 4, **Nitrogen**). Overfertilizing will cause blossoms to drop off the plant.

SOWING: The most critical thing about planting beans is soil temperature. If you cannot get the soil temperature up to 60° F the seeds will rot instead of germinate. Putting down clear plastic ahead of time will help warm the soil. If unable to pre-sprout, at least soak the seed overnight. Beans are frost-tender and should not be planted until all danger of frost is past.

As mentioned before, pole beans are usually grown in a greenhouse, due to needing a longer season than bush beans. They should be grown in ground beds since they can easily reach 10 feet in height. Vertical support for the vines is best, the vines twining counter-clockwise as they climb. One good variety is Kentucky Wonder, which has foot-long pods and a very heavy yield.

CULTIVATION: Beans succumb easily to fungal diseases, so be especially careful to keep weeds (which hold moisture) away from the plants to improve air circulation. Anything done to warm air (like row covers) or soil (like polyethylene on raised beds) will help get a crop to mature in time for a harvest. (See Chapters 10 and 11.) ACE discourages cultivating after blossoms appear.

CHALLENGES: The disease problem mentioned earlier is the most serious problem with beans, if you do not count poor weather (see Chapter 2, **Irrigation**). Alaska is blessed with a lack of Mexican bean beetles.

HARVESTING: Snap and pole beans are picked when pods are nearly fully-grown, but before the pods show outlines of the seeds. Tips of pods should be soft and pods should snap easily. Most bush beans of recommended varieties (see Appendix B) can be picked several times in the season, at about three-day intervals, especially in the Interior. But it is reported that Spartan Arrow produces its pods nearly all at one time. The earliest producing variety that is recommended in all three major growing areas in Alaska is Provider.

BEETS
Family: Chenopodiaceae
Optimum pH: 6 to 6.8
Annual in Alaska

Grown as an annual, beets are actually bi-ennial, a fact that is only important to those planning to grow their own seed, but which can become important if one plants a non-adapted variety. Variety is particularly important for beets, as many poorly adapted varieties are sensitive to the long photoperiod (see Chapter 12) and will bolt to seed in one year instead of two. Recommended varieties have done well as far north as the Interior, but may bolt in cooler areas. Late planting, as well as thinning, reduces bolting. Recommended varieties include both the usual ball type, and cylindrical beets, good for uniform slicing.

SOIL AND SITE: Because this is a root crop, soil should be deep and friable. Do not overfertilize with nitrogen, or you will be growing beet greens instead of beets. This crop particularly resents an acid soil. It enjoys full sun, but will not grow well in very hot weather.

SOWING: Each beet seed is actually a cluster of two to six seeds in a dry fruit husk, which makes thinning a must. Plant seed one to three inches apart. The seeds will germinate faster if soaked for 12 hours before planting. Beets can be started inside and transplanted to the garden in very poor climate areas. Being a cool-weather plant and able to germinate in cool soil, beets can be planted as much as a month before the last expected frost—a little frost will not harm the plants. In some areas, a second planting can follow in early July.

CULTIVATION: Plants should be thinned early, first so leaves do not touch, and later (when six to eight inches tall) to about four inches apart. Inadequate thinning can cause roots to be tough and woody. If you plan to side-dress fertilizer, this is the time to do it. Thinnings can be cooked or added to salads. Watch moisture levels carefully, as beets become tough and stringy when allowed to dry out, or become too hot. In the Interior, mulch may be called for to keep the soil moist.

CHALLENGES: Beets are quite pest and disease-free. They have no very serious enemies, although slugs can be a problem in coastal areas, and mice sometimes find beet greens tasty. See Chapters 8 and 9 for suggestions on slug and mice control, respectively.

HARVESTING: Most beets are best when young, and pulling can begin anytime after they reach about $1^1/_2$ inches in diameter. When cutting, leave about $1^1/_2$ inches of stem, to cut down on "bleeding" when cooking. You do not have to be very picky about cleaning them. Boil in a pot of water until tender (usually no more than 45 minutes), switch them to cold water, and the dirty skins and rootlets will slip right off. Beets make good pickled beets. See Chapter 6 for other storage methods.

BROCCOLI
Family: Cruciferae
Optimum pH: 7 to 7.5
Annual

ACE staff

Only grown widely in America since 1900, sprouting broccoli is sometimes known as Italian asparagus broccoli. The plants grow as high as two feet, and nearly as wide. Green flower heads develop at the top of a central stalk. When the central or terminal head is cut, other smaller heads, called laterals, develop from leaf axils. Both stalks and flower heads are eaten, cooked or raw with a dip. Stalks are also good dipped in tempura.

SOIL AND SITE: Broccoli does well in Alaska because of its preference for cool nights. It needs a steady moisture supply. The equal of one inch of rainfall is preferred each week. "Ricing," which refers to the blossoms separating into individual florets (which means lower quality) is encouraged by an overdose of hot weather.

Soil should contain plenty of moisture-holding humus. This plant's high calcium requirement can be met by compost incorporated into the soil at the rate of one pound per plant. If your plants are not doing well, check the soil pH; it may be too acid. If there is no lime available, wood ashes watered in well will do double duty by also discouraging root maggots.

SOWING: Broccoli is usually started early indoors and set out after the first true leaves are formed. It should be sown in flats four weeks before planting-out time. Tiny seedlings can be transplanted into individual containers after one week. One packet of seed will yield over 100 plants. The crucifers in general are so hardy they may be set out as much as a week before the planting-out time of most other vegetables. In fact, many gardeners find they can plant broccoli from seed directly in the garden.

CHALLENGES: In Alaska, only two insects are any real problem. Cutworms sometimes attack this plant, and root maggots are often a challenge (see Chapter 8). Damp off when young can also be a problem (see Chapter 9).

HARVESTING: Terminal heads must be cut before the yellow flowers break open, or even begin to show any color at all. Up to eight inches of stalk can be cut with the head. Beneath the second set of leaves is a good place to cut. As long as the smaller secondary heads are forming, they should be cut promptly, or the plant will stop producing. This means if any shoots are missed and begin to flower yellow, they should be immediately removed, even if this means discarding them. There should be no need for prolonged soaking in salt water to destroy insects, as in some warmer states. A brief rinse, drying, and refrigeration is all that is necessary for fresh eating. For longer storage, freezing is recommended.

BRUSSELS SPROUTS
Family: Cruciferae
Optimum pH: 6 to 7
Annual in Alaska

A slow-growing hardy biennial, some varieties grow to four feet high. A tuft of cabbage-like leaves grows at the top of a tall stalk, with other leaves spaced farther apart down the stalk. Sprouts or buds growing in the axils of lower leaves are the edible portion (tasting somewhat like cabbage). Generally one or two inches in diameter when harvested, they are usually eaten cooked. There are not very many varieties available. The one recommended for anywhere in Alaska is Jade Cross.

SOIL AND SITE: A touch of frost improves flavor. In fact, the ideal is sunny days with nights of light frost. A sandy loam is recommended, with good drainage. This plant is a heavy feeder of nitrogen.

Georgeson Botanical Garden Collection.

BRUSSELS SPROUTS

SOWING: Brussels sprouts must be started indoors to mature in most parts of Alaska. All stages of the plant grow best in cool temperatures. Plants to be set should be about seven or eight inches tall. When setting plants out, pinch off a few leaves from the bottom.

CULTIVATION: This plant needs plenty of moisture, so mulch might be advisable in the dry Interior. A high nitrogen fertilizer should be side-dressed about two weeks after the plants are put into the garden, and again when sprouts start to form. As buds sprout, lower leaves are removed to make room for them to grow, and to direct the plant's energy into maturing the sprouts. Be sure not to remove top leaves. Plants are sometimes staked when they are about one foot high.

CHALLENGES: Brussels sprouts may need to be protected from cutworms and root maggots.

HARVESTING: Pick sprouts before they change color. Lower sprouts are picked first, although ones higher up on the plant will often form firmer heads. Break off the leaf below the sprout, (if still present), then twist the sprout off. A well-grown plant should supply about one quart of sprouts. In late fall, plants may be taken from the garden and "planted" in a cool area of a garage or basement. Buds will mature in storage for another month or two. Be sure to keep the soil around the roots moist.

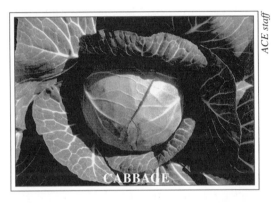

CABBAGE
Family: Cruciferae
Optimum pH: 6 to 7
Annual in Alaska

A biennial if you want to save your own seed, cabbage comes in many sizes and shapes. The head may be conical, round, pointed, or flat; the leaves smooth or crinkled (Savoy), green, or red. Leaves are eaten raw, cooked, or pickled as sauerkraut. You may also want to try the O-S Cross Hybrid, available from Denali Seed Company, which produces the giant heads the Matanuska Valley is famous for (but which grow elsewhere in Alaska, too). Savoy types are not good storage cabbages. Oriental vegetables (Chinese cabbage for example) tend to bolt in Alaska and must be planted late and harvested early before seed stalks emerge.

SOIL AND SITE: Rich moist loam is recommended, with good drainage and large amounts of humus. Cabbages will grow well on sand, muck, or other heavy soils, but the earliest crops will be those grown on sandy soils. Cabbage likes full sun, but is a hardy vegetable. Even when frozen in the garden, it may often still be harvested, thawed, and eaten as if it had never frozen.

This field of cabbage has been decimated by root maggots.

SOWING: In other states, late cabbages are put in the garden in mid-July. Do not make the mistake of planting that late in Alaska. Early cabbage can be grown from seed planted directly in the garden in early spring, but late varieties, such as Storage Green, will not mature from seed. So start them indoors and plant them out early. If hardened-off well, newly set-out plants will withstand light frosts (see Chapter 5). If planting O-S Cross Hybrid cabbages, be sure to give them plenty of room. Some gardeners plant them in old truck tires laid on the surface of the ground and filled with soil. This has the effect of considerably warming the soil.

Place cabbage seedlings lower in the soil than they sat in their flat—right up to the first leaf. Otherwise, the stem above the ground may break from the weight of the growing head. Side-dress cabbages two or three weeks after setting them out.

CULTIVATION: All cabbages need a constant water supply, but the O-S Cross needs a tremendous amount of water to grow prize-winning heads. If gardeners allow plants to dry out, and then resume proper watering, the heads may break open. In the fall, when heads are large, drying winds may have the same effect. It is suggested you break a few feeder roots to prevent this. At the first sign of splitting, pull the head up slightly until you hear the slight cracking sound of the feeder roots breaking. This will slow growth and (temporarily at least) stop splitting. If you want to instead, you can shove a sharp hoe or knife into the soil on two sides of the cabbage, to sever some roots.

Those serious about growing a prize winning O-S Cross might want to try some suggestions from Michele Hébert, Land Resources Agent for ACE in Fairbanks. Dig 3-foot holes, fill them with fresh manure up to six inches from the top, then finish with regular soil. Plant the transplants and fertilize weekly when watering.

Remember that even moisture levels are essential. Since fertilizer is also critical, you might even want to grow your giant cabbage on a compost heap.

CHALLENGES: Cabbages are susceptible to cutworms and root maggots. ACE can supply information on chemical insecticides used for root maggots in cabbage. For non-chemical control, ACE, in an out-of-print publication, *Alaska Grown Cabbage*, suggested marigolds (the odor to discourage the adult fly), and stated that ashes and garlic water have also been used by some gardeners with varying success. See Chapter 8 for more information, and the Companion Planting Guide in Appendix A. Moose enjoy cabbages (see Chapter 9).

HARVESTING: Pick cabbages before they have over-matured. Late varieties are improved by a slight touch of frost. Store cabbage away from other produce (and living quarters) because of odors that develop in storage.

A final note on the O-S Cross Hybrid: if your head weighs less than 50 pounds, you are not even in the running for a first prize at the fair. Leslye Dinkel's 1990 entry of a 98 pound cabbage still holds the record for the Palmer State Fair.

CANTALOUPE
(See Melons)

CARROTS
Family: Umbelliferae
Optimum pH: 6.5 to 7
Annual in Alaska

A biennial when grown for seed, this plant can send roots down over two feet deep in warmer soils than Alaska has. In general, short stubby

CARROTS

carrots will mature faster than long tapered types. The best varieties will have the smallest central core, as sugar and carotene are stored in the outer portion of the root. Nantes types are perhaps the best for market sales, but the Chantenay and short French forcing carrots are better suited to Alaska's cold soils. The Chantenay is a good storage carrot. Alaska carrots are considered very high quality compared with those grown in other states, because of their high sugar content.

SOIL AND SITE: Because this is a root crop, soil should be a sandy loam with a high humus content, and free from lumps. If manure is used, it should be dug in the previous year. Fresh manure stimulates root branching, and the main root becomes rough-skinned and soft. ACE reports yields drop off rapidly at lower pH readings than 6.5. Fertilizer should be incorporated during seedbed preparation, as well as side-dressed before the early summer growth-decline period. Uniform, rapid growth is needed for high-quality carrots. Carrots grown in too much peat may develop a bitter flavor. A soil deficiency of manganese or boron can turn the carrot core black.

SOWING: Carrot seed germinates slowly—in about 18 days in 50° F soil, and 12 days in 60° F soil. They can be transplanted, but this is not recommended. Raised mounds are good for carrots in Alaska. Although carrots grow well in cool climates, they do not like cold soils.

Carrot seeds are tiny, and difficult to broadcast evenly. As an aid in spreading them out more uniformly over the ground, some gardeners recommend mixing (i.e., "diluting") with fine sand (about one cup of sand per packet of seed). To obtain sand fine enough, run it through a sieve. Another idea is to soak the seed to swell it larger, pre-sprout, and plant as soon as the root appears. A more expensive way to go is to purchase pelleted seed. Since carrot seeds are so tiny, they must be planted quite shallow. To keep them moist, cover the planting with clear plastic just until the first seed germinates. The plastic will also help raise soil temperature. If you plant in rows, you may want to mix in some faster germinating radish seed so you will know sooner where the rows are.

CULTIVATION: Careful cultivation is important for carrots. Weeds must not be allowed to compete with the tiny seedlings. Weeding may need to begin even before carrots emerge. Most weeds look different enough from carrots to make this easy, but watch out for pineapple weed (see Chapter 9 for description). Consult ACE for recommendations for herbicides on carrots, and the safest time to apply.

Plants need to be thinned eventually to at least two inches apart, but it can be done in stages and you can eat the tiny thinnings. Keep carrots evenly moist, but remember that watering will cool the soil. Another thing to keep in mind when cultivating is to be sure that the shoulders of the carrots are covered by soil. Uncovered, whether by rain or growth of the carrot, they will turn green and bitter, as potatoes do.

CHALLENGES: Carrots have very few enemies in Alaska. The only noteworthy one is often almost invisible. It is a larva found (with careful searching) lying on the rib of the leaves. Often on the same plant will be found tiny black dots tangled in webbing, which many gardeners mistake for the culprit. Where the larva feeds, the fronds turn brown and dry, and growth slows. Diazinon has been used with success by one gardener, while another just pulls off and destroys affected fronds as soon as detected. Before using chemical pesticides, be sure to consult a local ACE office for the latest control recommendations, and follow label directions carefully.

Alaska carrots are not bothered by Aster Yellows, a virus disease that often causes bitterness in carrots grown elsewhere.

HARVESTING: A good commercial yield of carrots is described as being 2 to $2\frac{1}{2}$ pounds per foot of row. A 1976 report put Alaska's yields at half that amount, but Alaskan carrot growers can meet or exceed the $2\frac{1}{2}$ pounds with good management. Commercial carrot production, since 1988, has been decreasing in the Tanana Valley, but steadily increasing in the Matanuska Valley.

Carrots grown on mounds are easy to pull. They should be cooled rapidly to 32° F. Humidity should be 90 to 95 percent. If that humidity cannot be maintained, it may be best to store in sand, as described in Chapter 6. Carrots may be washed when harvested, but should not be wet when they enter storage. Cut tops short for long-term storage. If boxes are used, wooden ones are recommended. Carrots should be kept in the dark to avoid greening.

CAULIFLOWER
Family: Cruciferae
Optimum pH: 6 to 7
Annual in Alaska

Once called cauliflower broccoli, this biennial herb is more tender than most of the brassicas. The edible portion is the flower head called the "curd," which can be eaten raw or cooked.

SOIL AND SITE: Cauliflower prefers a cool, humid climate, but is very frost tender (unlike most of its close relatives). It will need plenty of moisture, so requires fertile soil with a lot of humus. It may not form heads at all if the weather is too hot.

Cauliflower is very sensitive to boron deficiency and may develop whiptail. It also requires large amounts of calcium, which can be supplied by lime if the soil is too acid. It needs large quantities of potash and nitrogen, making well-rotted manure particularly good for it, if dug in the previous fall.

SOWING: In some areas of Alaska direct seedings may mature, but for reliable crops, early starting indoors is advised. If anything disturbs growth until they are set in the garden, heads may be tiny.

CULTIVATION: A constant water supply is a must, with the most water needed while heads are forming. When heads begin to

Here whiptail shows up in the head of a mature cauliflower in a garden in Aniak, Alaska.

form, many gardeners cover them to keep them white, either by tying leaves over the heads (a spring clothespin will do), or breaking a large leaf and laying it over the head. Water well at this time, also. Be sure to leave plenty of leaves to manufacture food for the plant.

CHALLENGES: In Alaska, the main problems are cutworms and root maggots, especially the latter. Of all the brassicas, cauliflower seems to be the one most bothered by root maggots. See Chapter 8 for suggestions on control. Do not forget to rotate this crop to a new area of the garden each year.

HARVESTING: Harvest the flower as soon as it is large and solid; it will not grow larger, only looser and branched (called ricing), and flavor will deteriorate. For about a month of storage, the plant may be pulled up by the roots and hung in a cool place. In any case, roots should never be left in the ground to harbor root maggots. Remove and destroy even plants that became over-mature and unfit to harvest.

ACE staff

The cauliflower on the left has curled leaves typical of whiptail, a micronutrient deficiency disease.

CELERY
Family: Umbelliferae
Optimum pH: 6
Annual in Alaska

Celery grows 12 to 18 inches tall and has a very shallow root system. It is biennial in many places. Stalks and leaves are eaten, and two varieties are grown: green, easiest to grow; and golden, or self-blanching, although it does need blanching too. In Alaska, Utah 52-70 (a green type, shown early in the season in the photograph right) is the standard variety, although Ventura has been the highest yielding in the Interior. Both are considered midseason varieties.

Georgeson Botanical Garden Collection.

CELERY

SOIL AND SITE: Celery needs a very rich soil high in potash. It would be difficult to make it too rich. Well-rotted manure is good, or compost and dried chicken manure. Celery is a marsh plant, and, as such, needs a cool climate with plenty of moisture. Lots of humus will help keep the moisture content high enough for quick-growing crisp stalks. It needs a fairly long season, so grow it in a spot protected from early frosts. In other states it is grown on muck, but Alaska muck soils are too cold. Here, silt or sandy loams are better.

SOWING: Celery takes so long to germinate and mature, that it is always started very early inside. To speed up germination, try soaking seed or pre-sprouting. Although seed will germinate slowly at 40° F soil temperature, an air temperature below 50° F for very long will cause seedlings to bolt without forming stalks. Be sure to provide seedlings with plenty of fertilizer, as they will be inside a long time.

When planting out, set no more than very slightly below the level at which they were growing, and be careful to keep soil from between leaf stalks. Each time celery is transplanted, shade it from sun until growth begins again. Celery grows very slowly at first, but growth speeds up as plants become larger.

CULTIVATION: About 1¹/₂ inches of water per week is recommended for celery. Do not even bother planting it in the Interior if you are not able to irrigate. Planting in a slight depression will provide a basin for watering. Organic growers recommend manure water one week after planting out, and twice more at 10-day intervals.

For blanched celery, blanch three to four weeks before harvest. Cover with soil (but be careful of getting soil into centers), boards, or large cereal boxes opened at both ends and pulled over the plants. Leave the four to six inches of top leaves out for sunshine. Cereal boxes are not a good idea for wet areas like Southeast, where one will be constantly replacing them. A plasticized cardboard gallon (or larger) milk container would work better there. Heavy building paper can also be tied around stalks. Many people prefer the flavor of unblanched celery.

CHALLENGES: Damp off can be a problem with just-emerged seedlings. Watering from the bottom and maintaining good air circulation may help. Aphids are sometimes a problem, getting inside where they are hard to wash out.

HARVESTING: Plants may be harvested lightly all summer by pulling outer stalks from plants and letting centers keep growing. When ready to harvest the plant (before it freezes), cut just below the ground for fresh eating.

For storage, lift the whole plant with its roots and closely pack upright in moist sand, in a box with a cover to maintain humidity. Prune roots and tops a little, but do not wet the leaves or stalks. Keep in a cool, dark place (just above 32° F), and it will blanch itself. Remove a plant or two at a time and refrigerate.

CHARD

Georgeson Botanical Garden Collection.

CHARD, Swiss
Family: Chenopodiaceae
Optimum pH: 6 to 7
Annual in Alaska

An ancestor of the beet, Swiss chard is grown in warm areas of the United States as a substitute for spinach. Its leaves are eaten raw or cooked. In warmer states, it has a very extensive root system, which, however, never gets thick like regular beets. There is a red variety, called rhubarb chard, but green chard seeds are easier to obtain. Rex is the variety shown here. Fordhook Giant is perhaps the one most widely grown in Alaska. Another variety to try is Lucullus.

SOIL AND SITE: Grown like beets, chard will grow in any soil that grows good lettuce. It is more tolerant of acidity than beets.

SOWING: Swiss chard can be started indoors ahead, but most gardeners plant it from seed outside, because it is quite hardy and can be planted before the last frosts of spring. To speed germination, you can soak seed for 24 hours before planting.

CULTIVATION: Swiss chard tends to go to seed, especially when planted early and crowded in the row. While still in the seedling stage, thin to a minimum of six inches apart in the row—8 to 10 inches would be even better. Mrs. DeWitt recommended 12 to 14 inches apart for transplants.

CHALLENGES: There are no major insect pests or diseases of Swiss chard in Alaska. Poultry enjoy chard.

HARVESTING: Harvest begins when the largest leaves are about seven inches high. Pick outside stalks (leaving inner ones to continue growing), strip leaves, and treat as a salad green or cook like spinach. The juicy stalks are sometimes cooked as for asparagus. Freezing is recommended over canning as a storage method.

CORN, Sweet
Family: Graminae
Optimum pH: 6 to 7
Annual

Corn is difficult to grow in Alaska, due to lack of enough hot summer days and warm soil. Where it is grown, in favorable years, it does best through clear polyethylene mulch. This section is only a summary—more complete information on growing corn in Alaska is included in Chapter 10, where it is presented to illustrate the use of clear plastic mulch.

Georgeson Botanical Garden Collection.

The best varieties for cool soils and short seasons are Yukon Chief (developed in Alaska by the late Dr. Arvo Kallio) and Polar Vee, from Canada. Canadian seed catalogs contain other promising varieties as well.

Where seasons are longest, or where greenhouse protection is afforded, Earlivee and Earliking are better quality hybrids that respond satisfactorily in Alaska's photoperiods. There are a few other borderline varieties, but in general, most corn varieties grown in other states are poorly adapted to day length in Alaska, and while they might grow extremely tall, may not produce ears. Adapted varieties, on the other hand, tend to be rather short. When checking the variety lists in Appendix B, look under S for sweet corn, rather than C.

Georgeson Botanical Garden Collection.

SOIL AND SITE: Corn is a heavy feeder, and demands much moisture-holding humus. Manure, spread on the planting site in the fall, can be incorporated in the spring to provide the humus. After plastic is laid, fertilizer side dressings will have to be liquid. Pick the warmest site for corn, and if soil can be heated any way (with cables, hot water pipes, etc.), so much the better.

SOWING: Corn is wind pollinated, so should be planted in blocks of rows. See Chapter 10 for details on sowing seed under plastic. Another way to lengthen the season is to use Mrs. DeWitt's transplant method. Start corn inside in cup-sized individual containers. Corn should be given only a 10 day head start. Peat pots are not recommended, because the roots grow so fast that in this time they penetrate the pots too far and dry out. Expect corn started inside to germinate much faster than unsoaked seed planted outside.

Dig deep trenches for the transplants so that the plant will be lower than the surface when planted. Lay the plastic over the rows and let the corn continue to grow taller under the plastic canopy. When they finally get too tall for their tent, cut slits (as for seed corn), and let them out. With this method, corn can be put in the garden earlier, and will have the greenhouse benefit longer, before it is subjected to the cooler outside temperatures.

Some other gardeners feel transplanting is unnecessary, and that pre-sprouting is the way to go. When pre-sprouting, be very careful not to break the tender root or sprout, and set it in a slight depression in the soil beneath the plastic. Seed can also be planted in raised beds for soil warmth, but be aware that tops of narrow mounds will dry out very quickly, which can affect germination of non-sprouted seed.

Judy Weber's Corn Method
Judy Weber, a Georgeson Botanical Garden volunteer and organic gardener, manages to break all the usual rules for growing corn in Alaska, yet succeed magnificently. All winter she saves $1/2$ gallon cardboard milk cartons and large frozen yogurt containers. In early April she punches holes in the bottom of each with an ice pick and fills them with starting soil. Each box gets three corn kernels of an under 70-day variety. She likes to grow four containers each of four different varieties, both white and yellow, so with three kernels in each, she will have 12 plants of each variety if all survive.

After germination, the corn plants are kept indoors under grow lights. When the weather warms a bit, they are set in a greenhouse with a propane space heater (for night heat) with fans running constantly for air circulation. Since they did not start in flats, they do not need to be transplanted.

When the soil is warm enough, usually just before the end of May, they are about two feet high, and are planted outside. Her only fertilizer consists of bags of chicken manure tilled in before planting. Judy splits the containers very carefully and slips out the block. She does not disturb the roots by trying to remove any of them, even if all grew. Note that she does not plant through polyethylene at all, yet she is feasting on corn on the cob by the end of July from plants only $4^1/2$ feet tall!

CULTIVATION: See Chapter 10.

CHALLENGES: In a very few areas, the seed corn maggot may be a problem. But, for most of Alaska, there are no insect pests of corn.

HARVESTING: Hot weather causes corn to mature quickly, a problem you are not likely to encounter in the fall in Alaska. But there is a perfect time to pick—when the silk is brown and dry, the tips of ears rounded but not too hard, and the kernels exude milk when dented with a fingernail. Over-mature corn is tough, and the milk doughy and starchy. The sugar in the kernels continues to turn to starch after picking, so it is very important to cook corn as soon after harvesting as possible—experts recommend having the water boiling before picking. If there must be a delay, chill the corn immediately (still in the husks) in the coldest part of the refrigerator.

CUCUMBERS
Family: Cucurbitaceae
Optimum pH: 5.5 to 6.8
Annual

ACE staff

CUCUMBERS

Cucumbers are a member of the gourd family, and grow on a trailing or climbing vine. Male and female flowers grow on the same plant, with the males outnumbering the females. It is a warm-season crop, easily injured by frost, so is usually grown in greenhouses. Some varieties (such as Victory) will mature outside in the Interior through clear plastic mulch. See Appendix B for other varieties.

SOIL AND SITE: Since cucumbers are over 95% water, humus is needed to hold moisture. Cucumbers are heavy feeders. In fact, Lenore Hedla, Anchorage gardening authority, recommends fertilizing cucumbers every other day with a high-nitrogen, soluble fertilizer to promote bloom production. Provide support for greenhouse vines, and plan to help the vines around it.

SOWING: In the Interior, seeds of certain varieties can be grown through clear plastic. But the best crops will come from plants started inside and planted out in a greenhouse. Cucumber roots are easily damaged, so start seeds in individual pots to avoid the need to move them more than once (into the greenhouse). Be sure to set them at the same level at which they grew in their pot, as the stem is very susceptible to fungal diseases at soil level. If plants do well for a short time, then wilt and die, suspect root damage when setting out. If there are no replacements for them, do not pull them up and discard too soon, they may yet recover and produce something.

CULTIVATION: Dr. Dinkel recommends four square feet of sunshine for every greenhouse cucumber plant (including paths). Low light levels will cause cucumbers to shrivel. Since this is a greenhouse plant, refer to Chapter 14 for more information. As mentioned before, give them plenty of food (especially if noticing a lack of female blossoms) and plenty of water. It is perfectly normal, however, for male blossoms to be produced first. Female blossoms follow later when days are shorter (see Chapter 12).

Cucumbers need higher temperatures than tomatoes, so plant them in the sunniest spot, water with tempered water, and even lay a plastic mulch over the soil of unheated ground level greenhouse beds, to help warm the soil. While it can be inconvenient (if you like both tomatoes and cucumbers), it is even recommended that cucumbers and tomatoes not be grown in the same greenhouse, so that cucumbers can be kept warmer, without jeopardizing fruit set of tomatoes.

There are two main types of cucumbers grown: standard American, and the long European self-pollinating types (called gynoecious). The latter are growing in popularity due to lack of seeds, smaller more compact vines, and most of all, because of the lack of any need to hand pollinate.

In fact, it is said they develop better unpollinated. They are heavier feeders than the American kind, but usually do not develop the bitterness toward the stem end that others sometimes do.

If you grow the standard variety, you will need to know the difference between male and female flowers, so you can hand pollinate them. You will also need at least two plants, as they need cross-pollinating. Male flowers have stamens, and females an ovary that looks like a mini-pickle. This is located just behind the petals. You can see this in the picture at the beginning of this cucumber section.

You can pick a whole male blossom, tear off the petals, and then insert the center into a female flower growing on another plant. If you leave it there, you can tell which flowers have been pollinated. Or you can use a paintbrush, brushing first a male center, then a female center. Wind and insects should take care of outside cucumbers, but if the bees seem more interested in other plants, you may want to hand pollinate outside, too.

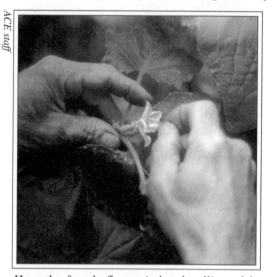

ACE staff

Here the female flower is hand pollinated by inserting the center (stamen) of a male blossom. A paint brush will do too—brush the male center, then the female.

CHALLENGES: If plants set one cucumber at a time, increase fertilizer. If they are bitter and slow growing, Mrs. DeWitt advised adding lime—your soil may be too acid. For insects and diseases, see Chapters 8, 9 and 14. If flowers and cucumbers rot, you may need to raise the temperature and lower the humidity.

HARVESTING: The main thing to remember is that leaving a cucumber on the vine, in hopes of it getting very large, will slow or even stop production of other fruits on that vine. Keep them picked. Remember that some varieties are for pickling, and are picked small. Slicing ones are generally harvested larger.

CURRANTS
Family: Saxifrage
Optimum pH: 6 to 8
Perennial

Currants are hardy, and in fact, grow wild in Alaska. They need damp, cool summers. In some states, the growing of black currants is discouraged (and in many states, outlawed) because they are an alternate host for a fungal disease called white pine blister rust. All currants are self-fertile, meaning you will need two plants for cross-pollination.

Georgeson Botanical Garden Collection

It is estimated that a well-grown mature bush can yield up to three quarts of fruit. Recommended varieties are Holland Longbunch (also called Long Bunched Holland), displayed above by Horticulturist Pat Wagner in Jim Cox's garden in the Interior. If you want a black currant, look for Swedish Black. North Pole Acres prefers Ben Nevis Black and Viking Red. All currents (white, red, and black) do well in Southeast.

SOIL AND SITE: Currants do not do well in very warm soils, so a fertile, heavy clay soil may be better than a light sandy one. Since rooting occurs near the surface, the soil needs humus to hold its moisture. But good drainage is necessary, too. The plant does well in full sun, if that does not mean high heat.

SOWING: Currants begin to bear in their third year, so two-year-old stock will produce fastest. If setting bushes in the spring, plant while the bushes are still dormant, but Ed Bostrom says they can be planted up until near the first of August. Set bushes four to six feet apart and slightly lower than they were growing in the nursery. If they arrive bare-rooted and dry, soak for a few hours first. Then trim off any damaged or too-long roots. In other states, growers cut the top back to 6 to 12 inches, especially if the root system is poor.

CULTIVATION: Pruning is important for the best yield from currants. Two and three-year-old canes produce best. Older canes should be cut out completely. A two-year-old bush should have about six to eight canes. The next year, prune to three strong three-year-old canes. The object is to have about three one-year canes, three two-year canes, and three three-year-old canes on a bush, by pruning out old and weak canes. However, Ed Bostrom says no pruning is needed for two to three years. Then you can prune dead canes (lying on the ground) and about $^1/_3$ of the old growth canes. He says **not** to prune cane ends. Prune in early winter.

Starting new bushes is very easy, as currants can be propagated from current wood. Ten-inch cuttings are planted (while still dormant if possible) with no more than two buds above ground. Provide shade and keep the soil moist.

CHALLENGES: There are some pines growing in Alaska (Lodgepole Pine is native). If you know of a white or 5-needled pine, be sure not to plant your currants within 900 feet of it. Although black currants are more susceptible to white pine blister rust, red currants can also be attacked by it. Do not take any chances.

ACE staff

EGGPLANT

HARVESTING: Currants left on the bush after ripening will become sweeter, but also lose their pectin. If picking for jelly, pick a little green. Berries should be picked a cluster at a time, by the stems. Stripping berries from the stem will make a mess, and the berries will not keep well. Incidentally, commercial dried "currants" (that look and taste similar to little raisins) are not really currants. They are actually raisins made from a special type of grape.

EGGPLANT
Family: Solanaceae
Optimum pH: 6 to 7
Annual in Alaska

In the tropics, eggplant is a perennial, but here it is grown as a tender annual. A long, hot growing season (days of 80° F to 90° F, and nights of 70° F or 80° F) is preferred, which leaves out most of Alaska, except in greenhouses. In the Interior, Dusky can, in a favorable year, be grown outdoors through clear plastic.

Eggplant has a photoperiod problem. You may need to artificially lengthen its nights, in order to force the plant to produce fruit. The large lavender blossoms will fall off without fruiting if there is too much daylight. See Chapter 12 for more information on photoperiodism, and what can be done about it.

SOIL AND SITE: If weather is cool too long, plants will be stunted and produce poorly, if at all. For this reason, most successes have been in greenhouses. Unfortunately, eggplants are a favorite with aphids, which will not do your greenhouse any good. Many seasoned gardeners banish eggplant from the greenhouse and provide a plastic coat for them outside. See Chapter 10 for directions on growing through polyethylene .

Eggplant is another heavy feeder, and needs rich, moist, well-drained soil. Sandy loam is better than clay, as it will be warmer. Be sure to incorporate plenty of humus. If using rotted manure or compost, figure on at least two pounds per plant. Be sure no tobacco stems are in any soil amendments you might use, since tobacco is death to all members of the *Solanaceae* (nightshade) family. If you do not want aphids in your greenhouse, and your season is too cold and wet even for clear plastic to help much, consider planting in tubs you can move inside at the first hint of cool weather.

SOWING: Start seed indoors 8 to 10 weeks ahead, presoaking overnight first. They will germinate best at a soil temperature of 85° F, so apply bottom heat if you can. In your house, air temperatures of 65° F to 70° F by day and 50° F to 55° F by night are recommended for the young seedlings. Watch for insects that can stunt growth and cause the seedlings to become woody.

Do not plant outside or even start to harden plants too soon, to avoid setback. Allow two to three feet of space between plants, planting at least two. Protect from wind and use a starter solution. Begin regular feedings of fertilizer about a month later. If using liquid manure, do not allow it to touch the stem itself.

CULTIVATION: Moisture is a must, especially when plants are fruiting. Best quality fruit will be borne on plants that are not allowed to set more than about six fruits. Pinch off terminals and extra flowers.

CHALLENGES: Aside from eggplant's long season and high-heat requirements, the main problem will probably be aphids. See Chapter 8 for control suggestions. It is also suggested you not grow eggplant where any of its other family members grew the previous year.

HARVESTING: Eggplant can be picked like cucumbers, at almost any size. Usually you can plan to begin picking as soon as glossy fruits are $^1/_3$ grown, but be careful not to leave any until the skin begins to dull and lose its shine. Seeds in overripe fruits will be bitter. **Warning**: *Do not consume any part of the eggplant other than the fruit. Other parts can cause a toxic reaction.*

ENDIVE
Family: Compositae
Optimum pH: 6 to 6.5
Annual in Alaska

Endive has curly, narrow leaves, and is used as a salad green. Another variety, with broad leaves, is known as escarole. Green Curled is one endive variety listed on the recommended list for Southeastern. Endive is sometimes grown as a substitute for lettuce because it can take more heat and will grow faster in cold, rainy weather than lettuce.

Theresa Perteet
ENDIVE

SOIL AND SITE: Any soil that will grow lettuce will do well for endive.

SOWING: For the best, most mature heads, sow indoors about four weeks before the frost-free date. Set seedlings 12 inches apart. If you plant from seed, thin to this spacing and use the thinnings in early salads.

CULTIVATION: Endive is usually blanched for three weeks before harvesting, which removes color and bitterness from the inner leaves, and makes them more crisp. Unfortunately, it also removes vitamins—especially vitamin A.

Plants should be nearly fully grown, about 12 to 15 inches in diameter, before blanching is begun, which is why the early start. Pull outer leaves together and tie above the plant's heart with soft string or strips of cloth. IMPORTANT: Do this only when plants are perfectly dry; no water should be allowed into the hearts or they will rot. If they do get wet, you will have to open them to dry them out and then tie them closed again. You can also blanch with two boards set in tent fashion over the plants.

CHALLENGES: Slugs are particularly fond of endive (see Chapter 8).

HARVESTING: Before the first hard freeze, plants can be lifted with soil and stored in a tub in a cool, frost-free cellar. Check for slugs before storing. Cut back on watering, keeping the soil nearly, but not quite, dry.

HERBS
Family: varies
Optimum pH: varies
Annuals/Perennials

Herbs can be grown in Alaska, but you may not find varieties listed in Appendix B, except parsley. Most need a very early start indoors, and it does not take very many plants to overflow your kitchen with more dried leaves and seeds than you can use or give away. For these reasons,

Jim Holm
HERBS

many find it much easier to buy a few starts each spring at the garden center. If you do start your own, remember that parsley, fennel, borage, and coriander need dark to germinate, and lemon balm, summer and winter savory, and dill all need light for germination.

A few herbs, like chives, are perennial. Chives do well here, especially when started from plants. There is even a wild chive native to Alaska. The best way to start chives is from a division of a friend's healthy but overgrown clump.

Lenore Hedla, garden author in Anchorage, suggests this timetable for early starting of herbs: four to six weeks ahead: basil, dill, lemon balm, marjoram, oregano, sage, summer savory, thyme: eight weeks ahead: mints.

She also suggests growing tarragon from purchased plants because seed racks carry Russian tarragon, which is a weed "of no value for seasoning"!

Georgeson Botanical Garden herb garden.

Barbara Fay, an Interior gardener who taught classes on herbs for many years at the Georgeson Botanical Garden, developed an herb chart for her classes. It is reprinted in Appendix A with her permission.

CHALLENGES: Related to onions, chives might have a root maggot problem (see Chapter 8).

HARVESTING: Harvesting from the growing tips will encourage a more compact growth. Begin to clip dill when it reaches eight inches in height. Full-grown mature herb plants do not do well when brought into the house for the winter. If you have a grow-light setup, start new plants mid-season and bring them in young. According to garden columnist, Linden Staciokas (writing for the Fairbanks Daily News-Miner), sweet basil, rosemary, chives, borage, and oregano all have tasty flowers.

JERUSALEM ARTICHOKES
Family: Compositae
Optimum pH: 6.5
Annual in Alaska

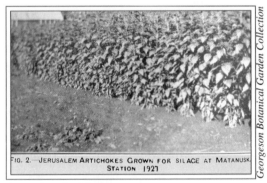

A very long-season plant, Jerusalem artichokes are for the avid experimentalist. It was difficult to even find a photograph of one growing in Alaska. The one shown right was taken in 1923 when they were grown for silage in the Matanuska Valley.

FIG. 2.—JERUSALEM ARTICHOKES GROWN FOR SILAGE AT MATANUSK STATION 1927

Jerusalem Artichokes

In warmer states, spreading roots make new plants that quickly become weeds. Unlike standard artichokes, the edible portion is an underground tuber. You are on your own as far as variety selection goes.

SOIL AND SITE: A rich, sandy loam is required, and heavy soil should be avoided.

SOWING: Jerusalem artichokes are planted much like potatoes, from whole tubers or pieces of tubers. Pieces weighing less than two ounces make smaller plants with lower yields. Little has been written on growing this plant in Alaska, but it is possible in favorable areas if grown through clear plastic (see Chapter 10). In other states, tubers are planted four inches deep, two to four feet apart.

CULTIVATION: Plants grow quite tall, and need plenty of nutrients and water.

CHALLENGES: These plants have not been identified with any particular diseases or insect pests in Alaska.

HARVESTING: Tubers are dug any time after the first frost. They may not keep well in storage, and seem to need high humidity levels to keep them crisp.

KALE
Family: Cruciferae
Optimum pH: 6 to 6.5
Annual

A member of the cabbage family, kale is seldom eaten raw in salads because of its rather tough, coarse leaves. It is easy to grow in Alaska, and most kinds do well here.

SOIL AND SITE: Kale needs plenty of calcium, so it would do well to plant it in soil that was recently limed. Sandy or clay loam is fine, as long as it has plenty of nutrients, to keep it growing fast. Quick growth produces the most tender and flavorful leaves. While it does best at a pH of 6 to 6.5, it also does well to 8.

SOWING: Kale is a short-season vegetable, and as such can easily be grown from direct seeding in the garden row.

CULTIVATION: Thin to give plants at least 12 inches of elbowroom. Fertilize frequently to keep it growing fast.

CHALLENGES: While technically subject to the same insect pests as cabbage, (cutworms, root maggots, and occasionally aphids), kale does not seem to be bothered much by anything.

HARVESTING: Harvest outer leaves to cook like spinach (before they get too old and tough), leaving the center to grow. For salad greens, pick plants whole and use the more tender inner leaves.

KOHLRABI
Family: Cruciferae
Optimum pH: 6 to 7
Annual in Alaska

The edible part of this plant is a swollen bulb-like main stem, which sits on top of the ground and from which leaves arise. The stem

277

is eaten raw with a dip, or cooked, like a turnip. You will not often see this vegetable in a grocery store, as it is not the most economical to grow, in terms of space and time in the garden. Each plant produces only one edible globe, which must be picked at less than three inches in diameter or it will be woody and poorly flavored.

Early White Vienna is perhaps the easiest to obtain seed for locally and freezes well; but Grand Duke, an earlier variety with high yield, may be worth hunting for.

SOIL AND SITE: The tenderest bulbs are grown in rich loam with lots of humus.

SOWING: Plants mature soon enough to be planted from seed directly in the garden, but if the spot you have reserved for them is not the best, you may have more success starting plants ahead inside. Rather hardy, kohlrabi can be planted quite early in the spring.

CULTIVATION: Moisture is probably the most important consideration for a good crop of kohlrabi. Thin seedlings to six inches apart for ease of harvesting (roots of closely planted ones tend to intertwine), or a bit closer for maximum yield.

CHALLENGES: Kohlrabi is often grown as a substitute for turnips, as the edible portion is above ground out of the reach of root maggots which can riddle turnips with holes. But protection may be needed, anyway, for the underground roots.

HARVESTING: Harvest when only about two inches across if possible. If they are closely planted, cut off at the soil surface, leaving roots in the ground to avoid disturbing roots of others. Kohlrabi can be trimmed and stored like cabbage for a long time.

LETTUCE
Family: Compositae
Optimum pH: 6 to 7
Annual

There are four main types of lettuce, all of which grow well in Alaska, and all of which can be started from direct seeding in the garden. There is loose-leaf, the easiest and quickest to grow; Cos (romaine); Butterhead; and the cabbage head type (iceberg), which is the head lettuce most popular in grocery stores.

ACE staff
LETTUCE

If you check seed catalogs and experiment a little, you will find there are some delicious kinds you may have never tasted because they do not ship well. For example, one of these, Oak Leaf, is best eaten the same day as harvested (the same hour, if possible). There are varieties listed in Appendix B for all four types of lettuce.

SOIL AND SITE: Lettuce is not a very fussy plant, and any good garden soil should do well. There are more likely to be problems with the temperature than the soil. Lettuce is a cool-weather plant, meaning it will not do well (especially heading varieties) in hot weather. But that does not mean you should plant it in the shade in Alaska. Even in the warmer Interior, it needs its sunshine to grow quickly.

SOWING: While any lettuce sown early in the garden will have a good chance of maturing, head types are often started inside. Succession plantings are a good idea for all kinds, as lettuce does not store well. Lettuce seeds need light to germinate.

CULTIVATION: Quality is improved by quick growing, and plenty of room in the row. Most garden books say thin to six inches. An ACE bulletin (#300G-00134) recommends a 12-inch spacing for both leaf and heading types, although their planting guide, in Appendix A, lists a closer spacing for leaf lettuce. If you have had problems with wet, soggy, molding leaf lettuce, try the wider spacing to improve air circulation and help the plants dry out after a rain. It sometimes helps to remove large drooping outer leaves from head lettuce before they rot. Removing old leaves will also cut down on hiding places for slugs. Lettuce needs plenty of water, particularly if the weather is warm. However, too much water will make lettuce heads puffy instead of firm.

CHALLENGES: Slugs and aphids will sometimes be a challenge, depending on location. Cutworms can be avoided with collars as described in Chapter 8. Stem rot (*Sclerotinia sclerotiorum*), a soil-born disease, may be a problem where crops are not rotated.

HARVESTING: Loose-leaf types are harvested from the outside, leaving the small inner leaves to grow, or the plant can be cut off just above ground level and new leaves will grow from the roots. Removing too many outer leaves lowers the quality of head lettuce, and these are best harvested whole when heads are mature. However, if you do not happen to care for leaf lettuce, you can grow more heads than you will want to harvest in the fall, and harvest the extra before maturity to use like leaf lettuce.

MELONS
Family: Cucurbitaceae
Optimum pH: 7
Annual

ACE staff

The only two varieties of melon usually attempted in Alaska are cantaloupes and watermelon. What we call cantaloupes are not true cantaloupes (*cantalupensis*), but are *reticulatus* (netted or nutmeg melons). *Indorus* is the label for the winter melons (honeydew and casabas), which will ripen in cooler weather than the others, but which require a very long season. Most melons begin with little or no netting, and the netting develops later. Some varieties have deep ribs, some shallow, and some none at all. Watermelon is covered separately later.

SOIL AND SITE: Cantaloupes need light clay loam or sandy loam. Avoid heavy clay, muck, or peat. Acidity should be near neutral, so have soil tested to see if lime needs to be added.

SOWING: You will have the best choice of varieties if you start your own ahead, instead of purchasing seedlings. You cannot sow melons directly in your garden. The cantaloupes shown in the picture above were grown in Fairbanks through clear polyethylene. Gardening books recommend setting plants out before they have grown more than three true leaves, as they do not transplant well when roots are larger. See

Chapter 12 for information that may help you ripen melons in spite of their photoperiod sensitivity.

Varieties which are known to have ripened in the Interior are Minnesota Hybrid 16, Sweet'n Early Hybrid (Burpee), and Alaska Melon (called Melon Brode by the Alberta Seed Co. in Canada).

All of the above were grown through plastic, and most under additional protection such as row covers or hot frames (see Chapters 10 & 14).

CULTIVATION: Melons need warm roots. Soil-heating cables can be set as high as 100° F without harming the plants. But 80° or 90° F will probably do fine. The plants need a lot of water until the melons begin ripening. Then, withholding water a bit will improve melon flavor. Excess melons, or those set after mid-July, should be removed to speed ripening and improve size and quality of remaining melons.

CHALLENGES: Many melon varieties are sensitive to the photoperiod (see Chapter 12). Fungal diseases that attack cucumbers also attack melons. Good air circulation is important, and melons should be raised from the ground. Some gardeners use boards, but heavy-weight black plastic seedling containers put upside-down work well, as the black color provides a little extra heat for ripening.

HARVESTING: Most melons will be ripe when the stem pulls away from the melon easily as the melon is lifted and twisted slightly. Sometimes a crack will show all around the stem where it is attached to the melon, called "full slip." Some varieties are best picked at "half slip." Some varieties do not leave their stems. For these, you will have to tell by the color (some yellow when overripe), or softness (soft is usually overripe).

ONIONS
Family: Liliaceae
Optimum pH: 5.5 to 6.5
Annual/Perennial

ONIONS

There are three main types of onions. American onions are yellow, strong flavored, medium size, and store well. European or other foreign varieties (like Bermuda, Spanish, and Italian) are usually milder flavored, sometimes quite large, and do not store as well. Egyptian onions are the perennials, forming sets (bulbils) instead of flowers. They are also called multiplier onions or top onions. Any of the three types can be picked small (before bulbs swell) as bunching onions. Onions grown as annuals are actually biennials—they will send up seed stalks the next year if replanted.

SOIL AND SITE: Onions do best in a sandy loam, silty loam, or peat. Avoid heavy clay, coarse sand, or gravelly soils. Organic matter, as well as nitrogen, should be high.

SOWING: Onions can be grown for bunching from seed, sown quite early because they will germinate at a low soil temperature, and are relatively frost hardy when young. However, care must be taken to keep weeds away, or the delicate seedlings will quickly be overwhelmed. Onion seed should be fresh; it does not retain its viability long. Leeks will need a three or four-month head start inside, green onions only one or two months.

Many gardeners grow their onions, both green and dry, from sets (small bulbs). Either plant them a few inches apart or, as Eloise DeWitt once suggested, plant one large bulb, then three small, one large, and so forth down the row. Thin later by pulling the small ones for green onions, while the larger ones continue to grow for dry onions. ACE recommends planting in a very shallow trench, spacing two or three inches apart. Cover the sets to their necks, but do not bury them completely.

CULTIVATION: Onions are very shallow rooted, so cultivate carefully, and water frequently. When 10 to 12 inches tall, mulch to preserve the moisture that is necessary while bulbs are swelling. Do not be alarmed if the bulbs tend to swell above ground (as seen in the photograph of ringmaker onions on the previous page).

CHALLENGES: Root maggots. See Chapter 8.

HARVESTING: Damp fall weather, common in much of Alaska, will slow down maturing of dry onions. ACE's publication, *16 Easy Steps to Gardening in Alaska* (#300G-00134), advises pulling, shaking off dirt, and then letting bulbs dry. They may take a month to complete curing. Until then, keep them at room temperature, spread out so they do not touch. When dry, rub off tops and roots. Store in a cool dry room.

Small onions can be stored by braiding tops and hanging by the braids (large onions are too heavy for this and the tops may break). Plastic net bags are fine too. Mrs. DeWitt kept her onions spread out at room temperature until January, when some began to sprout. Then she stored them in paper bags (not plastic) in the refrigerator, where they kept well until the new spring crop was in.

PARSLEY
Family: Umbelliferae
Optimum pH: 6 to 6.5
Annual in Alaska

Georgeson Botanical Garden Collection

PARSLEY

There are two kinds of parsley, curly-leaf parsley and, as shown to the right, plain-leaf (turnip-rooted) parsley. The former is the most popular in Alaska gardens. The plain-leaf type (pictured right) has edible roots (cooked like parsnips, the flavor is more like celery) and a stronger flavored leaf.

SOIL AND SITE: Plants do best in full sun, with good, moist soil.

SOWING: Parsley needs to be started indoors fairly early, due to a rather long germination period. Germination can be speeded up somewhat by soaking seeds for 24 hours before planting. They require 24 hours of dark to germinate, so cover seed flats well to keep out all light for that period.

CULTIVATION: If started from seed in the garden, thin to at least four inches apart. Set plants out four to six inches apart, depending on variety. Parsley can be mulched lightly to keep down weeds, as cool soil will not bother the plants once they are beyond the seedling stage.

CHALLENGES: Parsley is quite trouble-free in Alaska.

HARVESTING: Older stems are on the outside and may be picked, leaving inner stems to grow. Parsley can be dried, but much flavor and nutrition is lost. You can freeze parsley in bags without blanching (either whole stems or chopped). To bring a plant in for the winter, pick the youngest one, or start one late in the season just for that purpose.

PARSNIPS
Family: Umbelliferae
Optimum pH: 6 to 6.5
Annual in Alaska

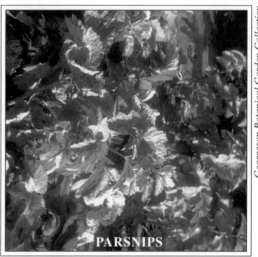

Actually a biennial, parsnips are both slow to germinate and slow to grow. Their edible roots can be several feet long, and three to four inches in diameter. Flavor improves with freezing, which turns the plants' starch to sugar. Hollow Crown is easily the most popular variety.

SOIL AND SITE: Like carrots, parsnips need a light-textured soil for the best-formed roots. Raised rows will help provide deep soil for roots. Fresh manure should be avoided since it will cause roots to divide.

Georgeson Botanical Garden Collection

SOWING: Even when fresh, parsnip seed does not germinate well or fast. Do not attempt to save the seed for another year. Soak seed overnight and sow thickly. Radishes in the row will help mark it until the parsnips make their appearance.

CULTIVATION: Thin to at least three or four inches apart in the row. If you have never grown parsnips before, you may be surprised at how large they can grow and how much room well-thinned plants can take up. Supply them with plenty of moisture.

CHALLENGES: There have been none reported in particular, but if any insects or diseases bother your celery or carrots, look for the same problems to occur with parsnips.

HARVESTING: While you could pull parsnips as soon as they are large enough to cook, allowing them to stay in the ground until they have spent a few weeks at near-freezing temperatures will greatly improve their flavor. If they should freeze, do not thaw until ready to cook. Some gardeners leave some in the ground until spring, digging them before the tops begin to develop. If stored in a root cellar, it should be very cold and they should be covered with moist soil to prevent shriveling.

PEAS
Family: Leguminosae
Optimum pH: 6.5
Annual

ACE photo by Bart Z

PEAS

Peas are one of the best vegetables for Alaska. The young seedlings are quite frost hardy, prefer cool, moist weather, and are not bothered by diseases or insect pests. In Alaska they bloom early due to the long days of sunlight.

SOIL AND SITE: Peas require lots of phosphorus and potassium but, being a legume, are not so fussy about nitrogen. You may want to inoculate your seed to assist the plant's roots with nodulation, or nitrogen "fixing." See Chapter 4, **Nitrogen**, for a more detailed explanation of this, and directions for inoculating. A light sandy soil will produce the earliest crop, though just about any soil will grow peas.

SOWING: Peas can be one of the first crops planted in the spring because of seedling hardiness. There are two types planted: smooth seeded (earliest and hardiest) and wrinkle seeded (later and sweeter). You can also choose between regular garden peas, sugar pod peas (you eat the pod without shelling, while the peas are still immature) and sugar snap peas (you eat the pods without shelling just about any time). In addition, you have the choice of dwarf varieties that do not need trellising, tall ones that need fencing but bear more heavily, and even pole peas.

Peas are directly sown in the garden, perhaps after soaking overnight. Do not soak if planting in very wet ground, as the seeds may rot. Peas are not usually thinned, so plant seeds about an inch apart in a trench opened with the point of a hoe. If planning a fence, make two drills about four to six inches apart, plant, then erect the fence between (see Chapter 5). You could also put up the fence first, and use it to make your rows straight. Do not put fence supports too far apart, or the fence will sag too much in the middle from the weight of the vines. A more permanent fence on the edge of the garden can be made of chicken wire, or you can buy less expensive plastic netting, which, with care, will last you three or more seasons. String nettings have a shorter life in sun and rain.

Be aware that most sugar snap peas grow very tall, and will need an especially high fence, or you will be folding the vines over the top and growing them down the other side. ACE publication, *16 Easy Steps to Gardening in Alaska* #(300G-00134), suggests only growing on the south side of fences going east-west, but do not waste the north side of the fence; you may get enough production to be worth planting there in spite of the lower light levels.

CULTIVATION: The publication mentioned earlier, #(300G-00134), advises putting two pints of a complete fertilizer per 100 feet of row in the bottom of the furrow when planting. This is covered with soil and the peas planted above. The seed is covered with another $\frac{1}{2}$ inch of soil, tamped down and watered. The publication further recommends the same amount of fertilizer be spread down the row when the vines are six inches high. Then push soil up against the vines to lean them toward the fence. Another side dressing of fertilizer is recommended for early August. Be sure no dry chemical fertilizer ever touches roots, vines, or leaves.

CHALLENGES: Chickweed can be a real challenge, especially when vines are young. They are vines themselves and often try to climb pea vines and supports. They grow matted at the base of plants and rot vines completely off in severe cases during wet autumns. Control must begin early by hand in the rows. Later in the season, when the soil has warmed up thoroughly, you might try mulching.

The author experimented one summer with mulching to smother chickweed, said to be one of the easiest weeds to smother. A three or four-inch mulch of grass clippings or leaves did not completely eliminate the weed, but the few weed vines remaining grew thick and tender, becoming extremely easy to pull. The grass mulch seemed to work better, being easier to tuck in around pea vines, than the whole leaves, but shredding the leaves might have helped.

ACE staff

Sugar snap peas won an AAS Gold Medal in 1979 when they were introduced. Their pods are as delicious as the peas, and they are eaten raw or cooked.

Another problem, which is sometimes encountered, is vines that do not cling tightly enough to the supports, due to a heavy load of pods. To reinforce them, start when the vines are only about a foot tall. Loop heavy string from one support, outside the vines, to the next support and tie securely. Repeat this every foot or so that the vines grow.

HARVESTING: Peas need plenty of water while pods are filling. Begin picking from the bottom of vines, as pods fill. Once begun, vines will usually need picking every three days. To keep them producing, remove all full pods, even over-mature ones that were missed earlier. But keep these latter separate; they will be past their prime, and may not even be edible. You could leave them to dry on the vines, to use in soup or like dried beans, but that would slow or even stop production of new peas on the vines.

Process peas quickly—within two hours of picking their sugar begins to change to starch. If unable to process immediately, chill and refrigerate. Avoid washing peas after they are shelled, as they quickly lose nutrients and flavor in water. Freezing is the recommended storage method, though some people prefer canned peas.

Harvest can be spread over a longer season by growing two varieties; an early-bearing one and a later one. Good combinations include Sparkle or Freezonian for early picking, and Green Arrow for a late variety. Green Arrow is a heavy-bearing variety, with beautiful long smooth pods, good for a fair entry. But if it is all you plant, you will have a long wait for peas. By planting Sparkle, you will be eating peas while you wait. Freezonian is listed on one list as late, and another as early (see Appendix B), but it bears several weeks before Green Arrow, on shorter vines, which keep climbing and bearing because it is an "indeterminate" variety (see **Tomatoes**, later).

Mrs. DeWitt wrote that peas can often be made to bear a second crop by slacking up on watering while harvesting ("Too much water slows the filling of the pods" she noted), then watering well, "almost drowning the plants," fertilizing, and then watering again. This, with the shorter fall days, simulates spring and the vines send out new growth and blossom again.

PEPPERS
Family: Solanaceae
Optimum pH: 6.5
Annual

Peppers are actually perennials from the tropics. A tender annual here, they are grown either in a greenhouse, or outside through clear plastic. There are two kinds, sweet and hot. Sweet ones (like bell peppers) are green, and may turn red when older, but are always sweet. Hot ones (chili peppers) are green (or yellowish), turning red when mature, but they are always hot. The hot ones are smaller than the sweet peppers. The one pictured here is Park's Early Hybrid Pepper.

SOIL AND SITE: Peppers grow faster on sandy soil, with bell peppers liking a lighter soil than hot peppers. Peppers are usually grown away from tomatoes, because (although climate requirements are similar) they use less fertilizer than tomatoes. The neat, upright plants are ornamental and lend themselves well to tub culture.

SOWING: Peppers should be started ahead in individual containers. Disturbing them too much will lower yield, so transplant only once, into the greenhouse or outside through polyethylene (see Chapter 10.) Plants are set 12 to 18 inches apart. Do not plant sweet and hot peppers near each other, or you may wind up with all hot peppers, due to cross-pollination. Set plants deeper than in their pots; about an inch or two below the lower leaves.

CULTIVATION: Peppers need a lot of water when young. Later their roots will be longer and they should not need any more water than tomatoes. Peppers in a greenhouse can be pollinated the same way as tomatoes—by flicking the flowers.

CHALLENGES: Aphids are the major pest of peppers. Mrs. DeWitt protected hers by squirting soapy water on them each day as she cared for her greenhouse plants. This must be repeated daily since it does not destroy the eggs. (See Chapter 8 for more ideas on controlling aphids.)

HARVESTING: Pick green peppers before they change color, when they are firm and heavy. Wait for red peppers to be fully red before picking. Cut stems $\frac{1}{2}$ inch from the pepper cap to avoid breaking the brittle stems of the plant. To keep green peppers fresh for a little over a month, store as close to 32° F as possible, with very high humidity (98%). Hot peppers can be dried by pulling plants and hanging them upside-down. Remove pods when dry and store dry until used.

POTATOES
Family: Solanaceae
Optimum pH: 5.4
Annual

POTATOES

ACE staff

The *Solanaceae* (nightshade) family includes eggplant (a close relative) and tomatoes (a more distant cousin). Many members
of the family produce poisonous alkaloids.
These are produced in the potato stems,
leaves, and berries, but the edible portion,
the tuber, does not contain the poison. (Tomato leaves also produce alkaloids.)
Alaska's climate is nearly perfect for growing potatoes, which need cool temperatures
and adequate moisture. Temperatures should
average slightly below 70° F during the growing season, and it should be cool in particular
when the tubers are forming. An average of one inch of water per week should be maintained, but the soil should be well drained.

There are essentially four types of potatoes to choose from, depending mostly on how they
are to be served. They are all-purpose, baking, breeding, and new potatoes. Baking potatoes have a mealy texture and are light and fluffy when baked, but they tend to fall apart
when cooked other ways. All-purpose potatoes have a waxier texture, so they hold their
shape better when boiled. They are a good choice for potato salad.

Both of the above types lose some moisture in storage and become more absorbent, so they
are then good for dishes where liquids are added (such as mashed potatoes). Any potatoes
freshly picked at golf-ball size or smaller, and cooked quickly with skins on (boiled) are
"new potatoes." Served with butter and parsley, they are delicious and one of the best reasons to "grow your own," since they do not store well (two weeks at the most) and have
such thin skins that they will not stand a trip to the supermarket. Breeding potatoes are
grown especially for processing: round tubers with high solid content for potato chips, and
long tubers for French fries.

Many years ago (before variety testing) Alaska had a poor reputation for potatoes, producing
mostly watery, poor quality tubers. Now there are many excellent varieties to choose from,
available locally or by mail order. Several good varieties were developed in Alaska. Alaska
114 is a standard now—a late variety with a tough skin, producing some of the heaviest yields
in the Interior, although many gardeners still swear by the thin-skinned Kennebec. Bake King
is the recommended baking variety, with Snowchip or Denali good ones for Southcentral. A
good all around potato grown commercially in Southcentral is Shepody, which was not developed in Alaska but is known for its high dry matter and large size.

SOIL AND SITE: Potatoes bear well in soils with a pH of 4.8 to 6.5, but you are advised
not to plant in soil above 5.6. A pH of 5.6 or lower inhibits the spread of scab, a very
common disease in potatoes. A pH below 5 destroys the disease. If you cannot lower the
pH enough, look for a scab-resistant variety.

Potash is an important element for potatoes; a deficiency produces potatoes that are soggy after cooking, but you will have mealy potatoes (the best kind for baking). An excess of nitrogen will produce lush foliage and vines at the expense of tuber formation, and may make the tubers watery.

SOWING: Potatoes are subject to many different diseases, some of which are seed-borne. It therefore becomes extremely important to use seed potatoes certified free from disease. Grocery-store potatoes should never be used as seed. First of all, it may be impossible to tell what variety they are (which may be important). Worse still, most will have been treated with anti-sprout chemicals, which will delay the crop, if indeed, they sprout at all. Finally, and most important of all, you may import a potato disease not present in the state before.

You can order whole potatoes (try about one pound per five feet of row), or eyes that are pre-cut with a scoop of potato left on (sold by number, not weight). With eyes, you can calculate exactly how many you need if you know your in-row spacing, but allow some extra for "blind" eyes.

If you bought whole potatoes, cut medium-sized tubers into about four sections with no more than three eyes on each. If the potato is small, use it whole. Generally, an egg-sized piece will give the best results, supplying the plant with enough food until it produces roots to feed itself. Pre-cut eyes are smaller, but have the advantage of being healed and ready to green, plus their shipping weight will be less. Freshly cut surfaces should be healed before planting, both to avoid rot, and to keep other disease organisms from entering. Air drying at about 70° F for 24 hours is all that is needed, although some suggest covering with damp burlap for four or five days. Be sure pieces do not touch each other or mold may occur.

Pre-sprouting, or greening, a process by which eyes are allowed to sprout $1/4$ inch, will significantly speed up the development of your crop and is highly recommended. To do this, spread potatoes on trays, eyes up, in light, about four to six weeks before planting. You must not allow any water to touch the pieces during the greening period, so if they green outside be sure to bring them in if there is any chance of rain. Before planting, discard any blind eyes that did not sprout. If you cut the potatoes yourself, break off any long spindly, weak sprouts.

There are other methods. For instance, De Armoun Greenery, in Anchorage, recommends sprouting the pieces out of light, in a closed paper bag, at room temperature. Some people just let the bag of seed potatoes stand at room temperature until sprouting occurs. Whatever method works best for you can cause your plants to break through the surface of the ground up to two weeks before they otherwise would, giving them a real head start.

Some years ago, there was a significant breakthrough in potato research. A plant breeder, Dr. Scott Trees, developed Explorer, the first successful open-pollinated potato from seed. It has at least an 80% germination rate, and is without the wide variations of earlier varieties that made it impractical to use true potato seed for propagation. The seeds may be started indoors four to six weeks early, and were available for the first time in 1982 from Burpee, Park, and Stokes seed companies, to name just a few. It was believed that if seeds worked out, the savings in shipping costs over seed potato eyes would be impressive.

Since then, there has been much experimentation with the production of minitubers from *in vitro* tissue cuttings, a process that promises to produce pathogen free tubers with a 95% germination rate. The method was tested with the cooperation of the University of Wisconsin's Plant Pathology Department, which maintains a tissue culture lab.

Assuming the use of seed potato eyes, plant in trenches about four inches deep, covering with only about one or two inches of soil. Trenches should be two or three feet apart (the larger distance for machine cultivation). Pieces may be spaced anywhere from six inches to 14 inches apart, depending on what authority is consulted. Kennebec tends to develop hollow heart if planted farther apart than about nine inches.

CULTIVATION: Dr. Charles Logsdon of Agresources, Palmer, an expert on potato culture and diseases, feels proper hilling is very important. Hilling is to cover the tubers from light (which causes the greening that makes potato tubers inedible), to prune roots, and to provide room for the tubers to grow. Pruning causes branching in the hill, meaning more potatoes. Fertilizer is good at the time of hilling, but increase potash while decreasing the nitrogen that delays maturity.

As sprouts appear, most authorities advise gardeners to cover the stem with more soil (leaving tops out), adding more as the plants grow, until a broad mound is formed. Dr. Logsdon advises **not** hilling until the plant flowers, which usually is one indication that tiny potatoes are forming. According to him, the potatoes are formed in relation to the soil surface, not the seed piece. By hilling after tuber formation begins, plants are encouraged to produce more stolens, and more potatoes form. **Note**: *Under certain weather conditions, some varieties do not bloom, even though there may be potatoes growing.*

The shape of the hill is important. A concave top will direct water to sink in around the stem, thus avoiding rotting of the potatoes in the rest of the hill. Steep sides will dry out too quickly, and too little slope will drain poorly.

A potato is more than 75% water, so moisture is very important. If the soil is allowed to dry out, the tops may look fine, but the tubers will stop growing as the plant waits for more favorable conditions. Then, when watering is resumed, knobs are formed. Oblong potato types are more apt to form knobs than round types.

CHALLENGES: The only insect pests you will probably have trouble with are wireworms, leafhoppers, and aphids, none of which are considered much of a potato problem here. Aphids suck plant juices, but they also carry diseases such as potato mosaic virus. See Chapter 8 for more information on these three insect pests.

Potato Diseases

There are four classes of diseases found in potatoes: nonparasitic, fungi-caused, bacteria-caused, and virus diseases.

Nonparasitic Diseases

Nonparasitic diseases include those caused by:
- uneven moisture,
- too much moisture after the tuber is formed,
- frost and freeze damage,

- bruising and mechanical cracking from improper harvest methods,
- internal black spots caused by low potash,
- pressure bruising caused by piling potatoes too deeply in storage
- greening caused by exposure to light in storage, or in the garden when not properly hilled, or hilled too late. Kennebec, in particular, greens easily.
- Black heart caused by excluding oxygen from the tubers. It can usually be traced to storing the potatoes with too much soil.
- Scald, where tubers shrink, discolor, and lose water. The problem is caused by harvesting and leaving the tubers out in wind. This is a particular problem in the Matanuska Valley, and can be avoided by covering newly dug potatoes with a tarp to protect them. See more on frost damage under **Harvesting**.

Fungus

It was a fungus that caused the potato famine in Ireland. Called potato late blight, caused by the fungus *Phytophthora infestans*, it has never been reported north of the Alaska Range. It may have occurred in Alaska in Ketchikan around the turn of the century. Bill Campbell, of the state's Division of Agriculture Plant Material Center, confirmed an outbreak in 1995 that involved only one field and one variety. Dr. Jenifer Huang McBeath, representing the state's Export Enhancement program (formerly the Virus Free program), identified potato late blight in the Matanuska Valley in 1998. Since the first two farms

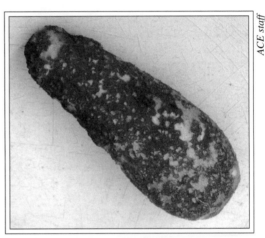

This potato has a bad case of scab.

where the disease was identified had their seed source in common, she believes that was the source of the disease, although there was no official determination of cause.

Dr. McBeath's recommendation was to kill the vines (this was late in the season) with a desiccant. Those who opted to use a fungicide instead found their potatoes rotting in storage (this fungus has a high tolerance to fungicides, which are not as effective as they used to be). Those who killed their vines may have had smaller harvests, but their potatoes had a better storage survival rate.

These fungal attacks were unusual for Alaska. Potato late blight needs warmth and especially humidity. Below 18° C (about 64.4° F), growth is slowed considerably, even if high humidity is present. The best prevention is provided by gardeners who are careful to purchase locally produced seed potatoes that have been certified disease-free. See Chapter 9 for more information on this serious seed-born disease of potatoes that can also spread from tomato seedlings (not seed).

A few related fungal diseases that have occurred in other areas of Alaska are leak, *Rhizoctonia solani* (also known as rhizoc or black scurf), early blight, powdery scab, and *Sclerotinia sclerotiorum* (also known as white rot or cottony rot). Some of the fungal diseases only disfigure tubers, and do not rot them.

Leak was a problem in 1979, when the fall was warm and dry. It spreads rapidly in dry soil.

The affected potatoes rot in storage. When you cut a potato open you will see that the whole inside is gray to light brown with a black rim around it. If squeezed, a clear "water" runs out. Leak does not carry over on seed because it destroys the seed.

Rhizoc (the most common fungal disease, resulting in the most losses), attacks stems, restricting food to the tubers, thus causing small tubers. Like *Sclerotinia* described below, rhizoc can generate black sclerotia (fruiting bodies about the size of mouse droppings), but it is the only one of the two which produces disfigured tubers. This pathogen is a problem for many potato varieties, but the peanut potato (also called Swedish peanut) is the most susceptible, according to Dr. McBeath.

Powdery scab is not bad in Alaska yet, but Southeast has reported some. It looks like common scab. According to Dr. McBeath, this disease is very rarely found in the western region of the United States, including Alaska.

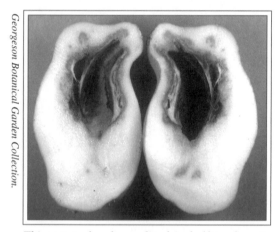

Georgeson Botanical Garden Collection.

This potato has been sliced in half to show its hollow heart. This one also has a secondary infection. Kennebec needs to be planted no farther apart than 9 inches to avoid hollow heart.

Sclerotinia sclerotiorum is a not a serious problem here in potatoes (although it has been reported with Kennebec in very dry conditions), but it can become a problem when potatoes and cabbages are planted in rotation. Other vegetables are affected as well. The disease forms cottony white masses on the outsides of vegetables either in the field or in storage, giving it the common names of white rot or white mold. It is quite common on beans and carrots. The white mold stage is often found on salad greens where gardeners practice a cabbage and lettuce rotation. Advanced stages of the disease produce black sclerotia, described above. Dr. McBeath has seen these sclerotia on cabbages when the heads are quite rotten. Dr. Holloway, of the Georgeson botanical Gardens, has noticed them most often on carrots in storage.

Bacteria

The four main bacteria-caused diseases include black leg, soft rot (both considered native to Alaska), ring rot, and common scab. For the first three, it is recommended that you be sure to start with high quality certified seed, and if the last (ring rot) has been a problem in the past, to destroy all leftover potatoes and old potato bags, sterilize tools and storage areas, and start over with clean seed. There is no need to disinfect the soil. ***Important note for those who want to sell their seed; the state of Alaska has a zero tolerance regulation regarding bacterial ring rot. If even one plant has the disease, the entire lot will be disqualified for sale as seed.***

For common scab, there is no really good control. The recommendation is not to plant potatoes in newly cleared soil in Alaska. Farmers are advised to plant grain for three years first. After three years, complex bacteria (such as produce this disease) decline and simple bacteria take over. Crop rotations are also recommended. Keep soil pH low, as well.

Viruses

Viruses are 100% seed-borne, according to Dr. Logsdon, so using certified seed is the best defense against them.

Do not let all this discourage you from raising potatoes. It is highly unlikely that you will ever see more than a few of the diseases mentioned above. They are discussed here mainly to help you prevent a problem, to diagnose your problem if you should have one, and in a few cases, to cope with it. Most local gardeners will tell you that they have never been bothered by anything worse than common scab or frost damage.

HARVESTING: New potatoes may be dug as soon as the plants begin flowering. But remember that the more you dig at this time, the lower your total yield will be later. In more southern states, potatoes mature and vines die before harvest. When the vines die, the potato skins toughen prior to digging. This seldom happens in Alaska, as vines are usually still growing when hit by the first heavy frost. If you wish to toughen your tubers in advance of digging, cut off the vines about two weeks before digging, to create artificial frost conditions. **Warning**: *Heed the notes at the beginning of this article on the dangers of eating other parts of potato plants.*

Proper harvest methods can prevent many diseases. Avoid bruising the tubers. Bruised or cut ones, as well as small tubers, should be put in a separate container for immediate table use. Potatoes that have been frosted in the garden may not show any damage at first, but they will not keep long. Storage time for them can be lengthened slightly by storing at near freezing; colder than is usually recommended for potatoes.

Potato hilling is clearly shown in this photograph of potato harvest.

Potato skins are toughened (and cuts healed) after digging by a process known as suberization. To suberize, store at room temperature (the ideal is 60° F with relative humidity at 90%) for at least 10 days. If this humidity cannot be held, raise the temperature to 70° F, hold the humidity as close to 90% as possible, and cure for only 7 days. If you can only raise the temperature a bit above 55° F, you will have to cure them for at least three weeks, as healing will be slower. Then potatoes are cooled to from 38° F to 40° F (33° F to 37° F for seed storage, and 45° F to 48° F for potatoes meant for processing). High humidity reduces moisture losses.

Remember that potatoes in storage will produce heat through respiration. Air circulation is very important, whether or not the area needs ventilation. Do not attempt to lower temperatures too fast (you can take a month), or the sudden cold air may cause condensation on the potatoes. If storage should get too cold, starch will change to sugar and the potatoes will taste too sweet. This can be remedied by bringing them into room temperature for 10 days before using, being sure to keep them in the dark. This will cause the sugar to be turned back into starch.

PUMPKINS
Family: Cucurbitaceae
Optimum pH: 5.3 to 7.5
Annual

Georgeson Botanical Garden Collection

Pumpkins need a long hot summer to do their best, but they do not need hot nights like melons, so it is possible to grow them in Alaska by starting them ahead and growing them through clear plastic. Vines can get very large, so you will not want to plant too many in a small garden. Male and female flowers grow on the same plant, so if the insects do not pollinate them, you will have to hand pollinate. As with cucumbers, female flowers can be recognized by miniature fruits (pumpkins in this case) growing behind the petals. You will have many more male flowers than you need. Try picking some of these blossoms while still fresh, dipping in batter, and deep-frying .

SOIL AND SITE: The main soil requirement for pumpkins is lots of humus, to hold the immense amount of moisture they will need. Large exhibition pumpkins can be grown in pure compost, and spent mushroom manure is also recommended, although this might be a bit difficult to find in Alaska.

Virgil D. Severns

Pumpkins and various squash are being harvested from Virgil Severns' garden in the Interior.

SOWING: Seed must be started indoors, but the plants do not transplant well, so exercise care. The Interior variety listings in Appendix B suggest a four or five-week head start, and others recommend even less. As you do with other cucurbits, set the plant at the same level at which it grew in its first container. Set in through clear plastic, as described in Chapter 10, and water with tempered water if possible. See Chapter 12 for ideas on compensating for unadapted varieties by altering their photoperiod.

CULTIVATION. When enough fruits have set, remove fruits that will not mature before frost, and pinch back vines so nutrients will go toward maturing the fruit you have left.

CHALLENGES: In Alaska, weather will be the main problem.

HARVESTING: Handle pumpkins carefully, due to their tender skins. Cut stems about one inch from the fruit. In warmer states, this cutting is done after the first frost, and the fruit is left to cure in the field for two or three weeks. Green pumpkins should continue to ripen indoors. They do not keep as well as other winter squash, but can be stored at a cool room temperature (from 55° F to 65° F). Do not refrigerate. You may, however, steam them, and can or freeze the strained pulp.

RADISHES
Family: Cruciferae
Optimum pH: 6
Annual

RADISHES

Radishes grow rapidly and go to seed early here with our long days. In America, three types are grown. The small red globes (like Cherry Belle) are spring radishes; long white ones (like White Icicle) are summer radishes; and fall storage radishes can be black or white, round or long (like Chinese White). See Appendix B for recommended varieties in Alaska.

SOIL AND SITE: Most radishes grow best in cool weather. Since feeder roots are very short, fertilizer should be concentrated near the surface. Never use fresh manure. Radishes are always sown outside. It is said that the best radishes will come from the largest seeds, and some gardeners even sift their seeds and discard smaller ones. Radishes are often sown with members of the slower growing *Umbelliferae* family (such as carrots) so rows will be marked. See more information on when to plant under **Challenges**. Those who really like radishes, may want to space plantings every two weeks.

CULTIVATION: Radishes that grow slowly will be woody and tough, so it is important to keep them growing fast. In the Interior, mulch will help keep the soil cool and moist in midsummer. Radishes need a lot of water, and thinning to suit the variety (an inch or two for smaller ones; as much as four to six inches apart for the larger fall varieties).

CHALLENGES: The only real insect pest for radishes in Alaska is the root maggot. See Chapter 8 for details on this pest. With radishes, the best solution seems to be a matter of timing. Since they do mature so quickly, you can often plant around the middle of July and get a crop of perfect radishes with no maggot damage whatsoever, and without the use of pesticides. If you do go for an herbicide solution, it should not be applied after the roots have begun to swell. Consult your local ACE agent for the latest recommendations before trying chemical controls.

HARVESTING: Pull radishes promptly, before they go to seed, or they will grow large and woody. Winter radishes can be stored in a root cellar like carrots or parsnips.

RASPBERRIES

RASPBERRIES
Family: Rosaceae
Optimum pH: 5 to 6.5
Perennial

This perennial produces biennial canes that grow in the first season, bear fruit the second summer, and then either die or bear very poorly and must be pruned away. New canes are growing while the old canes are fruiting, so care must be taken not to prune these new canes until they, too, have borne fruit.

SOIL AND SITE: Plan ahead for raspberries, being aware that they spread like weeds. It is a good idea to leave room for a tilled swath on both sides to contain them to rows about 18 inches wide. Raspberries do well on the heavier soils, from sandy loams (that will hold moisture), to well-drained clay loams. They do best with an acid soil, but if the pH is lower than 5, you will need to apply lime to raise it to that.

Raspberries respond well to organic fertilizers, but some research in other states has seemed to indicate that slightly better results are obtained from decomposed vegetable matter (compost) as opposed to animal manures. Straw, rotted leaves, etc., can be applied as a mulch to help conserve moisture in the Interior.

SOWING: One-year-old certified (disease-free) bushes are recommended. In the case of red raspberries, this means number one sucker plants. You will get a crop the first year if you plant full bushes (not bare-rooted) in early spring, while canes are still dormant. If you plant in the fall, wait until leaves have dropped, and have the planting completed by late October. North Pole Acres suggest their Kiskas can be planted "from as early as you can work the soil until about the first of August."

Georgeson Botanical Garden Collection

New canes of Kiska raspberry.

If bare-root stock arrives looking dry, soak two or three hours before planting. Keep roots covered with damp burlap or peat to protect them from drying sun or wind, until they are planted. Dig holes a foot wide and two and a half to three feet apart—deep enough to contain the roots without crowding.

Enrich the holes well, since this is a perennial and will not be disturbed later. Publication #38, of the ACE, recommends "an annual application of a good commercial fertilizer, such as 8-32-16 at the rate of 2 pounds per 100 square feet." It goes on to recommend barnyard manure "as it adds to the soil not only nutrients but also organic matter which is needed, particularly in sandy soils." Mr. Epps (see Chapter 13) suggests you prune canes to six or eight inches in height, at planting time. If green shoots, rather than dormant plants, are set out in June, wait until the end of the first season, then cut them back to about 24 inches.

CULTIVATION: Weeds need to be kept down, so this is one you may want to grow through IRT-100® polyethylene. The most water will be needed between blossom-time and harvest. Raspberries spread by sucker growth. Suckers that grow up in paths should be removed promptly, or dug and transplanted where you want them. In addition to the above points, there are two major considerations in the cultivation of raspberries: staking and pruning.

The most common method of staking is used when planting in rows or hedges. Pound in two sturdy posts three to four feet apart at each end of the row (more in the row if the row is very long). String sturdy wire from one post to the next, outside the canes, around the end posts, and back to the first post again. Secure well. In the long box you have thus made, some canes may be leaning over and threatening to slip under the wire. Here and there along the row, fasten canes to the wire so they are upright. Paper-covered wires (twist-ties) work fine, or use a string. You will need the bottom wire a foot or two from the ground, then another wire every few feet up to the top of the posts. Pruning time is a good time to check your wires and make sure the bushes are all contained and reasonably upright.

Pruning can mean the difference between a few berries here and there, and a berry crop next year. When the harvest is over, cut off (flush with the ground) all canes that have borne fruit this year. These canes, if they live at all, will never bear well again, but they will steal light, water, and soil nutrients from the good canes. You can tell an old cane by dried traces of the fruit you have picked, and the bark will be rough and shaggy instead of smooth. You can also remove any very thin, weak-looking canes, aiming for about 4 or 5 canes per running foot of row 15 to 18 inches wide. As mentioned before, canes should be cut all the way down to ground level, as stubs can harbor diseases and interfere with weeding and later pruning. Then cut all the remaining good canes back to shoulder height.

This may seem pretty drastic. You may think all you have left are a few sticks. Not to worry! Next spring a mass of branches will appear on each cane, and it will be these that will bear fruit. Except for the first one or two laterals, the best fruit is said to be produced low on the bushes. Buds are progressively weaker the farther they get from the roots, and tips of canes often winter-kill. Incidentally, prune only in the fall, or at the very latest, early spring before the buds have begun to grow, otherwise you may destroy the very parts of the plant you want to save.

CHALLENGES: Your main challenge will probably be aphids, but birds like raspberries, too. See Chapter 8 for ideas on aphid control. Ed Bostrom warns that Kiskas should be kept away from wild raspberries, since insects can spread wild raspberry diseases to the tame ones. Raspberry leaf rollers may be a problem (see Chapter 8).

HARVESTING: You will need to pick every three days to avoid the loss of ripe berries, which will fall off if not picked. Handle fruits carefully to avoid crushing. The correct way to pick raspberries is to get as low as possible under the bushes and pick, looking up where the berries are hidden by foliage. You will miss a lot of berries if you try to pick while standing, looking down.

RHUBARB
Family: Polygonaceae
Optimum pH: Various
Perennial

Rhubarb is a vegetable, used in desserts as a fruit. It is often called pie plant. It cannot be grown without a cold period of dor-

Georgeson Botanical Garden Collection

RHUBARB

mancy, preferably below freezing (certainly no problem here). According to ACE, "plants with deep dark red leaf stalks are superior to green ones." The photograph at the start of this section shows the plant, and one stalk, which has been properly harvested by pulling, not cutting.

SOIL AND SITE: The optimum pH for rhubarb has been variously reported as 7 to 7.5, 5 to 6.8, and 5.5 to 6.5. Take your pick. The site should be well drained but not gravelly. You may find it advisable to plant rhubarb outside the garden area, perhaps as a house foundation planting, as it can become so large that it interferes with garden chores. Since it will occupy its space for many years, you will want it in a place that will not be disturbed by garden tilling, and you will want to enrich the site as much as possible before planting.

Ed Bostrom

Rhubarb should be planted with four feet of space in every direction, as plants can grow quite large.

SOWING: Rhubarb seeds cannot be trusted to come true to type, and it takes much longer for seeds to develop to the production stage. Because of this, most gardeners plant crowns or roots from a nursery or neighbor. Crowns are cut through, leaving half undisturbed. The other half is lifted out and divided into pieces containing one to three eyes and some root. Dig large holes (about a foot wide and a foot deep) about four feet apart. Fill in with rich soil, and if possible, manure. Commercial fertilizer can be substituted for the manure if humus is added as well. ACE recommends a cupful in the bottom of the hole. Fill the hole so the crown is slightly above the surface. Pack soil around, leaving a depression to hold water. Pour on a bucket of water and mound remaining soil over the crown.

ACE photo by T. R. Grams

This rhubarb plant is suffering from root rot and insects.

CULTIVATION: Rhubarb needs lots of nitrogen. ACE recommends a fertilizer side dressing of two cups of a complete commercial fertilizer scattered over a three foot area in early May, another cup in early July, and another in late August. Ed Bostrom advises a side dressing of a high nitrogen fertilizer (around $1/4$ pound per plant) when the plant reaches approximately 8 to 10 inches in height. Water is very important for juicy stalks. Plants should not be allowed to dry out even during the after-harvest period. Remove flower stalks when they appear; do not let them go to seed.

About every four years, an abundance of thin stalks will tell you it is time to divide crowns and share with a neighbor.

CHALLENGES: The main insect pests have been climbing cutworm. See Chapter 8. Also note harvest cautions later.

HARVESTING: The leaves of cultivated rhubarb contain oxalic acid, a poison. Only the leaf stalks should be harvested and eaten, but the leaves may be put on your compost heap. Stalks are usually eaten cooked, in pies, cakes, and jellies (making an especially good extender), but some like them raw, too. Do not harvest until your plant's second year, and then take only stalks (not counting the leaf) that are at least 10 inches long and one inch thick. Ed Bostrom advises taking only $1/3$ of the stalks in that second year, and never more than $2/3$ after that.

Pull the stalks; do not cut them, which will leave a stump to rot. Take the stalk near the base and twist away from the plant. Most authorities caution against ever removing all stalks from a plant, but a gardening expert in Fairbanks, the late Mrs. DeWitt, noted that stalks can be harvested just before killing frost, when stalks and leaves have done their job. She also harvested her older plants completely two or three times throughout the summer.

A late 1999 *Master Gardener Update* reveals an interesting way to extend the rhubarb harvest. Directions are to choose a healthy plant that has been grown with lots of water and extra manure. Dig a large chunk of root up before the ground freezes, planting it in a 20 inch deep (at least) pot or box filled with compost and dirt. The buds should be planted just below the soil surface. Water well, but do not bring it inside until it has frozen. Then put it in a dark cellar with a temperature of 35° to 40° F. According to the article, if it is kept moist, it can be harvested in six to eight weeks (even though it is kept in the dark).

See Chapter 6 for preservation methods suitable for rhubarb .

RUTABAGAS
Family: Cruciferae
Optimum pH: 6 to 6.5
Annual in Alaska

Actually a biennial, rutabagas have also been called Swedes, Swedish turnips, and winter turnips. Hardier than turnips, they may take a month more to mature. They are quite similar to turnips, and can be prepared in many of the same ways, but their leaves more nearly resemble other members of the cabbage family. The plant shown above is Long Island Improved.

Georgeson Botanical Garden Collection

SOIL AND SITE: Heavy clay can cause root branching. Soil pH may be as low as 5.5 and as high as 7. Do not plant where other cabbage family members have grown in the past three years (including turnips and radishes), to avoid feeding root maggots.

SOWING: Seed is planted outside early. The seed is very fine, so refer to the section on **Carrots** for ways to make sowing easier. Germination is generally quick.

CULTIVATION: Rutabagas need to be thinned more than turnips, about 8 to 10 inches apart in the row.

CHALLENGES: Root maggots may attack rutabagas. See Chapter 8 for help.

HARVESTING: Rutabagas can take a light frost, but do not allow them to freeze. They will not keep well frozen. Quality improves in cool, moist storage (just above freezing.) Either store in damp sand, or clean and wax them. This latter method is preferred, and is described more fully in Chapter 6.

SPINACH
Family: Chenopodiaceae
Optimum pH: 6 to 6.7
Annual

SPINACH

Georgeson Botanical Garden Collection

Spinach needs cool weather and short days. Alaska has little problem with the first requirement, but short days in summer are another matter. So far, only two varieties have been found that have some light resistance to "bolting" (going quickly to seed): Melody for the Interior (shown at right), and Marathon for South-central. Late crops (when days are shorter) may be worth a try, since spinach matures so quickly.

SOIL AND SITE: Spinach is rather choosy about soil pH. It will not thrive in a soil more acid than 6, and you will have to add lime. Yet if it gets too much lime, it may develop a manganese deficiency and the leaves will turn yellow and grow pointed. For best growth, provide a fertile loam high in nitrogen and humus.

SOWING: Spinach seeds should be fresh, as they do not remain viable long. If you plan to harvest with the whole-plant method (see **Harvesting**), make succession plantings to insure a continuous harvest. Seed can be pre-sprouted inside (in the refrigerator), or plants started ahead, although few gardeners bother with either.

CULTIVATION: Keep the soil moist and, if necessary, shade from hot sun.

CHALLENGES: There may be some damp off if planting weather is cold and wet. If slugs are a problem, be careful not to put mulches up close to the plants. See Chapter 8 for more information on slugs. Chapter 5 covers treating seeds to prevent damping off.

HARVESTING: With the whole-plant method, one harvests by cutting the entire plant when mature, but before it goes to seed. A plant is mature when half a dozen leaves are seven inches long. A slower way, for a higher total yield, is to cut the outer leaves carefully (to avoid damaging the plant) and leave the inner ones to continue growing.

Do not soak leaves when washing, and cook in as little water as possible, just until leaves wilt. Because this plant is not really adapted to Alaska's photoperiod, it tends to bolt to seed quickly, which is why many gardeners prefer to grow New Zealand Spinach instead (covered next).

SPINACH, New Zealand
Family: Aizoaceae
Optimum pH: 8 to 7
Annual

Not really spinach at all, this plant has a flavor very similar to spinach and is often grown as a substitute for that vegetable. Rather than being an upright plant like true spinach, it spreads over the ground as far as four or five feet. It can take more heat than true spinach, and long days do not cause it to bolt to seed. It does take longer to mature than true spinach.

SOIL AND SITE: This plant grows well in a more nearly neutral soil, enriched with manure and lime.

SOWING: The seed germinates very slowly. Try soaking in hot water for three or four hours, or cold water for 24 hours before planting. Plants can be started inside and set out when all danger of frost is past. Do not sow seed outside until soil has warmed up a bit or the seeds may not germinate.

CULTIVATION: Plants are generally thinned to about a foot to a foot and a half apart, but can be grown closer if kept harvested.

CHALLENGES: There do not seem to be any major pests of New Zealand Spinach.

HARVESTING: Unless thinning, do not pull or cut whole plants. Break off young (three or four inches long) tips of branches (forget the old tough leaves), and new branches will grow from nodes. Harvest in this way right up to frost. Eat fresh in salads, cook, or preserve just like spinach.

Georgeson Botanical Garden Collection

SPINACH, New Zealand

SQUASH
Family: Cucurbitaceae
Optimum pH: 6 to 6.5
Annual

There are two types of squash; quick-growing summer squash (including zucchini) that is eaten immature and does not store well, and winter squash that spends its summer growing a shell hard enough to enable it to store through winter. Summer types can be obtained that grow on compact bushes, but most winter types grow on sprawling vines. Squash needs hot days, although it can tolerate cool nights better than some things, like cantaloupe.

Kathy Kollodge & ACE

SQUASH

SOIL AND SITE: A sandy soil will be warmer for squash than a heavier type. Squash will still grow well with a pH up to 8. Soil should be well drained, but able to hold a lot of water, since squash is composed mostly of water.

SOWING: Squash in Alaska should be grown through clear polyethylene (see Chapter 10). If seeded outside, plant summer squash in hills with five or six seeds per hill. Space hills four feet apart (from the center of one to the center of the next). If you plant in rows, space only two feet apart. Winter squash will need an area of up to eight feet by eight feet for each hill. More of a head start can be obtained by starting plants inside. Early starting is the same as for pumpkins, so turn back to that section for more information.

Butternut squash, as well as many other squash and cucurbits, are sensitive to the photoperiod. Try the technique given in Chapter 12 under **Compensating for Unadapted Varieties**, shading plants from any light at all for eight hours every night from the time they are transplanted from their flats until they are put out in the garden or greenhouse (or at least 10 days if not transplanted).

A researcher at the University of Georgia, D.S. NeSmith, believes he has discovered the ideal age for summer squash transplants—21 days. He reports that all plants grown from transplants produced fruit 10 to 15 days earlier than direct-seeded squash.

Virgil D. Stevens

Virgil Severns, former Extension Agent for ACE, grows his squash through clear plastic.

CULTIVATION: If you plant vining squash near the edge of the garden, you may be able to train the vines outside the garden and save space. Gently pick up the vines and lay them where you want them to grow. Since squash is a heavy water-drinker, you may want to arrange a saucer or dike around them for watering. If so, train the vines away so they will not lie in water. If you find the vines running heavily to leaf and stem, slack up on nitrogen, and pinch back the tops. You may need to do this more than once.

CHALLENGES: The main problem you can expect will be cold, wet weather. You may (especially in the case of zucchini) have a problem with an overabundance.

HARVESTING Summer squash should be harvested while still immature. Mature summer squash will have poor flavor, large tough seeds, and leathery skin. A rule of thumb is to pick when your fingernail easily breaks the skin when pressed only lightly. More specifically, long varieties (even zucchini!) are picked smaller than eight inches; patty pans when between one and four inches in diameter. Pick them even when you cannot use them, if you want the vines to keep bearing.

Winter squash is cut as late as possible, but before frost. If you have two weeks of frost-free weather after cutting, leave the squash out to cure. If not, bring them inside and keep for several days at about 70° F to toughen the skin. Incidentally, to avoid stem-end rot, always cut (do not break) stems at least one inch from the fruit. Wash and dry gently, being careful not to bruise the skin. Store in a single layer in a dry place at a temperature of about 50° F. Check every week or two for mold. If you discover mold, wipe it off with an oily cloth before it spreads too deeply into the squash.

STRAWBERRIES
Family: Rosaceae
Optimum pH: 5.7 to 6.5
Perennial

Considerable research has been done in Alaska in recent years, directed toward developing improved varieties and cultivation methods for strawberries. There are only two species of strawberry native to Alaska. The Sitka Hybrids, developed (not in Sitka, or even in Alaska!) in the early part of the century, can still be found growing in many parts of Alaska. But according to the late Dr. Curtis H. Dearborn, formerly Research Horticulturist in Palmer, "none compares favorably with good strawberry fruits of other states."

Dr. Dearborn, working with Matared, Susitna, and Skwentna cultivars; and Dr Dinkel, working with the everbearing Quinault as an annual, have each presented findings of considerable importance to prospective strawberry growers in Alaska. These were published by ACE in *Strawberries in Alaska* (#HGA-00034), and *Growing Everbearing Strawberries as Annuals in Alaska*, (#HGA-00235), respectively. Information for this section is drawn largely from these two sources.

Dr. Dearborn made the statement quoted above some years ago, and he and other scientists have been working ever since to find or develop strawberries that equal the best of other states. One variety has shown great promise. It is the Toklat strawberry, a delicious midseason high yielder with large fruit, which can be grown with or without plastic and appears to be quite hardy. It was developed by the late Dr. Arvo Kallio, who was a horticulturist at the Fairbanks Agricultural Experiment Station for 18 years, beginning in 1950. Dr. Kallio's introductions include the Alaska Pioneer strawberries as well (see Chapter 12).

SOIL AND SITE: The best site is a gentle southerly slope, with light, well-fertilized soil that holds moisture well. Most important, it needs to provide maximum winter protection, especially protection from prevailing winter winds. If trees are used as windbreaks, extra irrigation must be provided for, as tree roots can grow under the bed and create drought conditions. In the wet soils of Southeast, raised beds or drainage ditches may be needed to permit good aeration of the root system. Fortunately, red stele disease (a fungus disease which infects roots on wet ground) is not prevalent in Alaska. Plants should not follow sod, but rather a clean-cultivated crop (meaning well weeded), to lessen competition from weeds and grass, which can be a real problem in strawberry plantings.

Ed Bostrom maintains a "pick your own" strawberry field in North Pole. Strawberries are the only perennials Ed grows that he puts on a slightly raised row. This is to lift the shallow rooted plants out of water, and would probably be a must in Southeastern Alaska. For weed suppression, he plants through the IRT-100® polyethylene, setting plants 12 to 18 inches apart. He keeps runners trimmed, though if he planted without plastic, he would move runners into the row for matted rows. In that case, he would rototill between the rows, keeping them about 18 inches wide.

Newly set plants should not be fertilized heavily with nitrogen or potassium. Dr. Dearborn recommended two and a quarter pounds of 8-32-16 per 100 square feet, worked in thoroughly before planting. Excess nitrogen results in reduced yield, increased rot, late ripening, and poor quality. Because of leaching, however, sandy soils will need more nitrogen than heavier ones. Mr. Bostrom recommends fertilizing with a high nitrogen fertilizer when berries set, and after harvest.

Dr. Dearborn listed the signs of nutrient deficiencies in strawberries as follows:

- Low nitrogen: leaves light green, plants and fruit small, leaves turn bright red just before or while fruits ripen.

- Low phosphorus: slow plant growth, small plants, bluish color in older leaves.

- Low potassium: reddish-purple tint appears at the tips of serrations of older leaves, progressing from margins of these older leaves inward in a narrow band, the edges where the color first showed becoming eventually brown, dry, and crisp in severe cases.

SOWING: Plants for transplanting usually arrive "bare-rooted" and should be set in a few inches of peat (roots covered with peat) in a plastic tub, at a temperature near 70° F (ideally, your greenhouse) until planting time. Water periodically and allow to grow. Dr. Dinkel recommends a liquid fertilizer solution (2 tablespoons of 9-45-15 per gallon of water) be applied about 10 days before and again at time of transplanting.

ACE staff

Many varieties of June-bearers grow numerous runners which must be removed to preserve the main plant's strength.

For information on treating everbearing strawberriest as annuals, and planting through clear plastic mulch with row covers each year, you are referred to Chapter 10.

For hardy June-bearers, which you do not plan to plant through plastic, contact ACE for more information. Of particular interest would be various planting patterns (single hill, matted row, and solid plantings). Some varieties are very prolific when it comes to making runner plants and some provision needs to be made for removing runners that sap the mother plant's strength and lead to smaller berries the next season. The crowding that an overabundance of runner plants would cause would also lead to poor air circulation and increased fruit rot.

When planting June-bearers in most states, gardeners are cautioned to remove all flowers the first year so the plant will become well established before production is required of it. Dr. Dearborn wrote that this is not necessary in Alaska, unless plants are very weak or recover poorly from transplanting. He maintained that "In this northern environment, a good transplant, well managed, will produce several ripe fruit the first season and also develop good runner plants."

When planting any strawberries, space plants no closer than 12 inches apart, and pour a cup of water into the planting hole. Set the plant so the base of the bud is at soil level (no roots exposed, no crown covered), spreading the roots out. If, with your other hand, you squeeze a bit of dirt to make a tiny mound in the planting hole, it is easy and quick to spread the roots over this and firm the soil carefully about them to eliminate air pockets which might allow them to dry out. Planting on cloudy days or after midday is preferred to planting on sunny or windy days.

CULTIVATION: The main thing to remember is that it is much easier to remove a weed when it is young than after it has taken over a strawberry patch. Start weeding early and keep it up. Hoe shallowly, to avoid disturbing the shallow roots.

ACE staff

CHALLENGES: Weeds are an ever-present challenge. Some of the animal pests Dr. Dearborn listed were shrews, field mice, rats, rabbits, porcupines, birds, dogs, and moose. For moose, he suggested a fence at least seven feet high. Rodents are particularly troublesome under winter mulches or crusted snow-

This hardy Toklat strawberry plant produces larger berries than Alaska Pioneer.

drifts. He advised putting a four-foot-wide tilled strip around the planting in summer, and trampling down the snow around the bed in winter, to expose rodents to their predators.

Insect pests listed by Dr. Dearborn include springtail, thrips, cutworms, water lily beetle, aphid, spider mite, weevil, wasp, wireworm, June beetle, grub-type insects, and slugs. See Chapter 8 for information on many of these. One pest which seems to be the most common is a small black weevil which he referred to as the Alaska strawberry snout beetle. It is recognized by its distinct snout. It bores into and destroys ripening fruit, and is a particular problem when fruits lying on the ground are left on the plants until fully ripe.

Slugs can be a real problem in coastal areas where damp leaves and plants are more often the rule than the exception. Coastal areas also have earwigs which "may be both damaging and a nuisance." Chapter 8 includes a section on slugs, which may be of some help.

Ed Bostrom

The only disease that has been any real problem in Alaska has been *Botrytis* rot of the fruits. It is mainly a problem in prolonged periods of wet weather. Mold or rot of strawberries in the test plots at the University of Alaska's Fairbanks campus has been controlled with the application of fungicides, but you should consult ACE for the latest recommendations. See Chapter 9 for an organic suggestion.

The large berry on the right, under a leaf, shows typical signs of Botrytis.

HARVESTING: Most strawberries display their ripeness by turning red. Usually the whole cluster of berries will not ripen all at once. You will need to pick every few days during the harvest season—every day if temperatures are high, which causes fruit to ripen rapidly. Pick while still firm, as soft berries rot quickly.

If picking for sale, Dr. Dearborn advised leaving the hull and some stem attached; the former to guard against rot organisms entering the open flesh; the latter to avoid accidentally pulling off the whole cluster, some of which may not be fully ripe. Pick into shallow containers carefully, to avoid bruising fruit. Store in a cool, well-ventilated room. Just before a hard frost, pick large berries that have not ripened. Some may yet ripen, and you will be surprised at how good tasting you will find even still-white berries.

Even with berries that have been bred for winter hardiness, a winter mulch of six inches (oat straw is particularly recommended because of its tubular stems) applied around the end of September is advised. Hay and grass form too tight a mat, but thin foam roll-out matting (such as is used on golf greens) has given excellent protection. All mulches should be weighted down with netting or coarse mesh wire, especially in windy areas. In areas subject to late frosts, leave the mulch on to delay flowering. You can remove it in April in most areas and broadcast a light application of fertilizer.

TOMATOES
Family: Solanaceae
Optimum pH: 6.8
Annual in Alaska

TOMATOES

Sometimes it seems as though there are as many greenhouse tomato varieties as there are tomato lovers. Your choices for outdoor culture are more limited. Fruits range in size from large, weighing over a pound, to small cherry tomatoes. Vines grow all over the place (indeterminate), or stop when they reach a predetermined height (determinate). There is also ISI (indeterminate short-internode, or dwarf indeterminate). Shapes and colors vary as well. Start with the recommended varieties, then expand with some others the seed catalogs are so good at tempting you with.

SOIL AND SITE: Despite the recommendation above, Jim Holm of Holm Town Nursery says their tomatoes seem to do best with a pH of 7 to 7.2, and Linden Staciokas prefers a pH of 6 to 6.5. If you look on the pH Chart in Appendix A, you will note there is a wide range possible.

While the addition of fertilizer will encourage the best yields, too much nitrogen will lead to the overproduction of vines, and may hinder fruit set. There is some thought now that night temperatures may have a more significant effect on fruit set than excess nitrogen. It is important that the soil, as well as air, be warm, which is why most tomatoes in the state are grown in greenhouses, and the rest through clear plastic, even though the popular Sub-Arctic 25 was developed for outdoor culture without polyethylene (see Chapter 12).

SOWING: Plants are started indoors eight to ten weeks before they are to be set outside or into the greenhouse. To lessen the chances of damp off, lighten the starting mix with sterilized soilless mixtures. Still indoors, they are transplanted one or more times, each time setting them deeper than they were growing before. This is to encourage new roots to form, which will happen all along the buried stems. When finally set outside or into the greenhouse, plants may be put on their sides and most of the stems buried. (Do not do this if you are getting a very late start).

Dr. Donald H. Dinkel, former Plant Physiologist at the University of Alaska, recommends three square feet of sunshine for each tomato plant. In a large greenhouse of tomatoes, that translates to plants a foot apart in rows three feet apart. What is important is the amount of light, not root space. More crowded, the plants will be harder to tie, and there will be little or no increase in total yield in spite of the extra plants. When figuring for a smaller greenhouse, remember that paths count in the total square footage of light for the plants.

CULTIVATION: Pollination is simple with tomatoes. The flowers are "perfect," meaning each one contains both male and female parts. If bees and breezes are scarce, as in your greenhouse, you can pollinate them yourself simply by snapping the blossoms. Some commercial greenhouses, with hundreds of plants, use electric or battery vibrators. You can substitute an electric toothbrush. To be on the safe side, snap or vibrate once a day, in mid-morning or at noon (flowers should be dry so pollen will fly).

Tomatoes have a shallow root system, so cultivate carefully. Keep the soil evenly moist. A long period of drought followed by adequate watering can contribute to blossom end rot of the fruits.

ACE staff

To increase the size of tomatoes and keep indeterminate vines under control, pruning is recommended. Recommendations vary on pruning, to one vine, or to one main vine and one or two secondary vines. There are two kinds of shoots. The shoots that bear

These are Pixie F1 Hybrid tomatoes.

fruit grow from the stem. The shoots that grow in the axils of leaf and stem are the ones to pinch off while they are still small. Left alone, they will grow into more vines. Although it is true that they will also bear fruit as well as leaves, if you leave very many, one plant will soon make a jungle of your greenhouse. Many fruits will be set, but they will be smaller fruits than if each root system had to support one, or at most, a very few vines. Pruning should start early, and continue throughout the season, as the little shoots grow amazingly fast and will soon reach the point where they are too thick to risk removing.

In any case, you will probably want to cut off the tops of indeterminate vines completely in early August, to force the plants energy to go toward ripening fruit that is already formed, rather than setting more fruit from flowers.

Many stems on greenhouse tomatoes will need to be supported. Plastic clips that fit around the plant's stem and clamp to supporting strings are used commercially and may be available at garden supply stores and nurseries. Horizontal wires can be used, with twist ties to fasten the plants at strategic points. Vertical strings (heavy weight twine or cord) are fine. Tie the bottom of the cord around the base of the plant and occasionally help the top of the plant twist itself around it. There is no need to fasten the bottom of the cord to a stake in the ground—the plant will soon pull the cord tight itself. Fasten the cord to roof beams, cup hooks in the ceiling frame, or whatever is available. Some growers leave extra string.

When indeterminate plants reach the ceiling, letting out a little more string lowers the plant enough to enable it to grow some more (letting the plant sag down a bit). Another way to handle the problem is, as mentioned above, to pinch off the growing stem when it reaches the top of the greenhouse. Then the plant's energy can be channeled into ripening its fruit.

Increasing Tomato Yield

Georgeson Botanical Garden has been conducting experiments with Amisorb®, a biodegradable chemical called polyaspartate that promotes nutrient uptake by plants. By promoting the uptake of fertilizer, it was said to result in a 10 to 15 percent increase in yield, and promote early maturity. The chemical is not absorbed by the plants, acting instead as an extension of the plants' root hairs. Each molecule carries a negative charge that attracts positively-charged nutrients, making them more available to the plant. The Georgeson Botanical Garden had been hearing about this chemical of Amilar International since 1996, but wanted to see how it would work on our cold soils.

The Garden obtained a sample and ran tests. First results were discouraging, but after consultation with company representatives they changed their application method, and began applying the Amisorb® concurrently with a solution of a complete soluble fertilizer (15-16-17), instead of separately. Used on Sub-Arctic 25 tomatoes grown through IRT polyethylene mulch with trickle irrigation, the response was amazing, and immediately visible. The treatment was a June drench of half the application followed by the rest in a second midsummer application.

Plants treated with the drench yielded nearly eight pounds of tomatoes per plant, as opposed to untreated plants, which averaged 6.3 pounds per plant. This translates to a 25% increase in tomato yield with Amisorb®, much greater than what had been reported from other states! The increase was seen in **more** tomatoes, rather than **larger** tomatoes. The Georgeson Botanical Garden plans to extend their experiments to other vegetables.

A novel idea comes from the University of Colorado, which increased their tomato yields by applying carbonated irrigation water through their trickle irrigation system. The carbonation adds CO_2. Home gardeners can try the same by filling a plastic jug (with a small hole in the bottom) with carbonated water. The cap on the jug can be tightened and loosened to help regulate the flow, though it is not clear how much carbonation would be lost through a loose cap.

CHALLENGES: Aphids may be a problem, especially when growing eggplant or peppers in the same greenhouse as tomatoes. See Chapters 8 and 14 for more information on problems and solutions for tomatoes.

HARVESTING: Tomatoes develop their best flavor if allowed to fully ripen on the vine before picking. Leave a little stem on when picking. Never refrigerate a tomato until fully ripe (some say never at all) for the very best flavor. Cooling the fruit destroys flavor that can never be restored by rewarming. **Warning**: *Ingesting tomato vines can cause a toxic reaction.*

If your gardening experience is typical, the season's end will find you with vines full of green tomatoes. Covering vines with plastic will hasten ripening of the fruits. You should also pinch off any new flowers, and the growing points of the plants, as mentioned under **Cultivation**. Ripening may also be hurried by root pruning. Stress (caused by sinking a shovel in the ground around part of the plant to sever some of the roots) causes the plant to speed up ripening of the seedbearing fruits, to insure survival. Green tomatoes can also be picked as late as possible and brought in for ripening inside, but do not bother with small, hard, dark ones, which will more likely dry up and shrivel than ripen. The whole plant may be brought inside to hang upside-down (see Chapter 6).

TURNIPS
Family: Cruciferae
Optimum pH: 6.5
Annual in Alaska

There are three types of this biennial grown, one for its leaves, and two for roots (one white-rooted, and one yellow). They need cool weather to grow well, quickly becoming hard and woody when the weather is too hot. Excess heat will also cause them to bolt to seed. Turnip greens are eaten raw in salads or cooked like spinach. If you grow a variety developed specifically for its leaves (like Seven Top), do not expect too much in the way of edible roots. Follow the *Recommended Variety Lists* (see Appendix) to avoid quick-bolting plants.

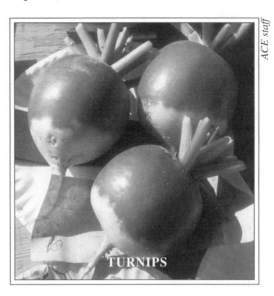
ACE staff
TURNIPS

SOIL AND SITE: Turnips are not heavy feeders, but feeding will speed maturity and improve quality.

SOWING: Sow seed directly in the garden early (light frost will not hurt them), or plant in mid-June for winter storage turnips. Purple Top White Globe is a recommended storage turnip.

CULTIVATION: Thin young turnips to a minimum of four inches apart in the rows.

CHALLENGES: Turnips are quite susceptible to root maggots. See Chapter 8 for information on varieties to plant, which may help. Red turnip beetles may also present some problems, especially if you allow wild mustard to grow near your garden.

HARVESTING: For best winter storage, pull, clean, and wax them before they turn woody. See Chapter 6 for more details on waxing vegetables.

WATERMELON
Family: Cucurbitaceae
Optimum pH: 5.5 to 6.5
Annual

Watermelons pictured here were grown in College, Alaska through clear plastic, with extra heat and Styrofoam® insulation.

Heat (the lack of it) is the limiting factor for watermelons. Watermelons will not ripen off the vine and they require months of hot weather, day and night, to ripen on the vine. There also seems to be a photoperiod problem (see Chapter 12), so it may be

Georgeson Botanical Garden Collection.
WATERMELON

difficult to get it to set female blossoms. Some who have managed to obtain the female blossoms report difficulty keeping them—they shrivel and fall off, apparently unpollinated. If you are still not discouraged, and decide to try them anyway, refer to Chapters 10 and 14 for additional help.

SOIL AND SITE: Watermelons need a sandy soil, or at the least, a very light loam. They require a more acid soil than most other members of the cucurbit family.

SOWING: You will find no mention of watermelon on the *Recommended Variety Lists* for Alaska, but you may be able to find Sugar Baby plants at a local garden center. It is a midget variety with a relatively short "days to maturity" listing. If you start your own plants, sow indoors no more than eight weeks before planting out (less if you have to grow with poor lighting).

CULTIVATION: Try to provide a greenhouse or hot frame for them all summer. Remember that this is a vine plant and vines can take up a lot of room. Midget varieties are a little less space robbing. As you probably can guess, watermelons need a lot of water.

Linden Staciokas, garden columnist for the Fairbanks Daily News-Miner, recommends trellising greenhouse watermelons on 36-inch tall old metal welded fencing (not chain link, but the kind with two inch by four inch squares), to avoid the damage to vines, leaves and fruits often caused by contact with wet soil. Cut the fencing into five-foot segments and shove the short side about a foot into the soil against one inside wall of your planter, bend it over and shove the other end into the soil against the other inside planter wall. The planter walls will help hold the resulting 36-inch wide trellis in place. The watermelon transplants are then (or before might be easier) planted in the soil under the humps, and pulled through squares in the fencing (gently!) when they are tall enough. In addition to protecting the plant from wet soil, the trellis provides support for the heavy melons so their weight does not pull them off the vines.

CHALLENGES: Since few gardeners in Alaska grow watermelons, little is known about specific problems that would be encountered here, other than those already mentioned. Much that is written elsewhere about cucumbers probably applies here as well. See Chapter 14 on greenhouse problems, and **Melons**, discussed earlier in Part Three.

HARVESTING: Few ever get this far, but if you do, avoid letting vines set more than two fruits per vine, for larger fruit and earlier ripening. At one time, Dr. Dinkel placed small pieces of Styrofoam® (approximately one inch thick and four to six inches square) under watermelons and cantaloupes to protect them from the cold soil and to help in uniform ripening (speeding up ripening of the side that faces down). Indications of ripeness vary with the variety, but most experts suggest thumping with the knuckles—a hollow sound indicating a ripe melon. Also look under the melon. The white patch where the melon rests usually becomes a creamy yellow and slightly rough as the melon matures.

ZUCCHINI
(See Squash)

Appendices

Who says gardening is all work and no play? This is Marsha Brewington's bed of potatoes.

APPENDIX A
Charts and Helps for the Gardener

APPENDIX B
Alaska Cooperative Extension Recommended Variety Lists

APPENDIX C
Addresses

Planting Guide

Suitable for a family of four allowing some extra for home processing.
(Adjust to family's needs, likes, and dislikes)

Vegetable	Length of Row	Plants or Seed Needed	Depth to Plant	Row Space (inches)	Plant Space (inches)	Days to Mature	Approx. Yield
Beans	100	3/4 lb	1/2"	36	6-8	65-90	50 lb
beets	50	1/2 oz	1/4"	24	2-4	60-80	50 lb
Broccoli	50	25 plants	transplant	36	18-24	50-100	30 lb
Brussels sprouts	50	25 plants	transplant	36	24	100-120	30 lb
Cabbage	60	30 plants	transplant	30	18-24	50-130	90 lb
Carrots	100	1/8 oz	1/8"	18	2-4	50-90	100 lb
Cauliflower	50	35 plants	transplant	24	18	65-75	75 lb
Celery	25	40 plants	transplant	24	6-8	100-120	45 lb
*Corn, sweet	100	1/8 lb	1/2"	30	12-14	75-115	100 ears
Chard, Swiss	25	1/4 oz	1/4"	24	6	60-75	25 lb
*Cucumber	25	25 plants	transplant	36	12	60-80	50 lb
*Eggplant	12	8 plants	transplant	36	18	80-100	15 lb
Endive	25	1/8 oz	1/8"	20	10	60-80	15 lb
Kale	25	1/8 oz	1/8"	24	10	70-130	25 lb
Kohlrabi	50	1/8 oz	1/8"	18	4	50-75	50 lb
Lettuce, head	25	1/16 oz	1/8"	18	10-15	50-80	25 lb
Lettuce, leaf	25	1/16 oz	1/8"	18	3-6	40-70	20 lb
Mustard greens	25	1/16 oz	1/8"	16	6	50-75	15 lb
Onion, scallion	10	1/8 oz	1/4	14	1-3	50-70	10 lb
Onion	25	10 lb	Sets	14	2-4	45-70	25 lb
Parsley	10	1/16 oz	1/8"	16	4	50-75	5 lb
Parsnips	50	1/16 oz	1/4"	24	3	100-150	50 lb
Peas	150	1 1/2 lb	1/2"	30	2	100-120	40 lb
*Peppers	25	15 plants	transplant	24	18	90-130	25 lb
Potatoes	150	30 lb	1"	30	10-14	90-110	200 lb
Radishes	25	1/16 oz	1/4"	12	1	25-35	18 lb
Rutabagas	50	1/16 oz	1/4"	20	4	50-75	75 lb
Spinach	25	1/8 oz	1/4"	24-36	18-24	60-80	20 lb
*Squash, summer	10	4 plants	transplant	36	30	60-75	75 lb
*Squash, winter	25	6 plants	transplant	60	48	120-135	60 lb
*Tomatoes	75	25 plants	transplant	36	24-36	90-110	150 lb
Turnips	50	1/16 oz	1/4"	18	3	50-75	75 lb

*Grown through clear polyethylene
From *16 Easy Steps to Gardening in Alaska* (#HGA-00134), ACE

Companion Planting Guide
Plants That Attract Beneficial Insects

Caraway
Carrot family (*Umbellifierae*)
Catnip
Daisy family (*Compositae*)
Dill
Fennel

Hyssop
Lemon Balm
Lovage
Mint family (*Labiatae*)
Parsley
Queen Anne's Lace

Rosemary
Snapdragons (to attract bees for pollination)
Thyme
Yarrow

General Repellent Crops

Garlic .... repels most insects
Catnip and tansy .... repel aphids, squash bugs
Radishes... repels cucumber beetles from cucumbers, squash
Sweet alyssum .... repels aphids, from even peppers and basil
Wormwood and southernwood .... repel flea beetles from cabbages

Specific Repellent for Particular Pests

Ants (& aphids they bring) — pennyroyal, spearmint, tansy

Aphids — the above, plus garlic, chives, coriander. Sweet alyssum has been used very successfully in the Interior. Nasturtiums and basil are used as trap crops to attract aphids away from other plants. Use nasturtiums & petunias around fruit trees.

Borers — garlic, tansy, onions

Cabbage moths — mint, rosemary, thyme, sage, celery, catnip, nasturtium

Cutworms — tansy

Leafhoppers — petunia, geranium

Mice — mint

Mites — onion, garlic chives

Moles — spurge, castor beans

Nematode — marigold (African & French) salvis (Scarlet sage) dahlia, calendula (pot marigold)

Rabbits — Allium family (a type of colorful onion)

Red spider mites — Oriental garlic chives (*Allium tuberosum*)

Root maggots — mint, tomato, rosemary, sage for cabbage. Yellow turnips attract less than white.

Slugs — prostrate rosemary, wormwood

Squash bugs — tansy, nasturtium

Tomato hornworms — borage (also attracts bees), marigold, opal basil (Use dill for an attractant or trap crop to attract away from vegetable crop)

White flies — nasturtium, marigold, nicandra (Peruvian ground cherry)

Wireworms — white mustard, buckwheat.

Special Notes:

Tansy: Be sure you get *Tanecetum vulgare*. Some tansies are poisonous to livestock or turn into weeds. In good soil tansy may grow to 5 or 6 feet tall, so it is best grown with crops that can hold their own, or as an ornamental border plant. One variety, crispum, is shorter and, some think, more ornamental.

"Good Neighbors": Some plants are complimentary because of different nutritional needs, such as corn and lettuce, because of different space requirements, or because of different harvest times, such as radishes and carrots. Legumes add nitrogen, and for some reason basil enhances almost anything growing near it.

Allelopathic plants: Some plants hinder other plants. For example, the roots of a cover crop of rye will secrete a substance that inhibits the germination of small seeded plants and weeds. But don't let the rye go to seed!

Table of Optimum Crop Soil pH ranges.

Crop	Optimum pH range[1]	Crop	Optimum pH range[1]
alfalfa	6.5-8.0	lupine	5.5-7.0
apples	4.8-6.5	oats	5.5-7.0
apricots	4.8-6.5	parsnips	5.3-6.8
barley	6.5-8.0	peas	5.8-6.8
beets	5.8-8.0	peppers	5.3-6.8
blackberries	5.7-6.5	potatoes	4.9-6.5[2]
blueberries	4.0-4.8	pumpkins	5.3-7.5
broccoli	6.0-7.5	quackgrass	5.5-6.5
Brussels sprouts	6.0-7.5	radishes	5.8-7.0
cabbage	5.8-8.0	rape	6.0-7.5
carrots	5.3-6.8	raspberries	5.7-6.5
cauliflower	5.8-6.8	red fescue	5.5-6.5
celery	5.8-6.8	reed canary grass	6.0-7.0
cherries	4.8-6.5	rhubarb	5.8-7.0
Chinese cabbage	6.0-7.5	rutabagas	5.3-6.8
chives	5.8-7.0	rye	5.0-7.0
clover,		snap beans	5.3-6.8
Alsike	5.5-7.5	spinach	5.8-7.5
red	6.0-7.5	strawberries	4.8-6.5
white	6.0-7.5	summer squash	5.8-7.5
cucumbers	5.3-6.8	timothy	5.5-7.5
currants	5.8-8.0	tomatoes	5.3-7.5
gooseberries	5.8-8.0	turnip	6.0-7.0
horseradish	5.8-7.0	wheat	6.0-8.0
Kentucky bluegrass	5.5-8.0	vetch	5.5-7.0
lettuce	5.8-7.0		

[1] These ranges are estimates only: they are for mineral soils (not mucks or peats).
[2] Potatoes grown at the upper end of this range may be more susceptible to potato scab than those grown at lower pHs.

Table by J. L. Walworth, Soil Scientist, Agricultural & Forestry Experiment Station, Palmer Research Center, University of Alaska Fairbanks.

Plant Nutrients in One Ton of Different Manures
Figures given in pounds/ton. Includes solid, liquid, and bedding

Animal	Nutrient Content (lb/T) Dry Weight Basis				
	% Moisture	Tons per year, fresh, normal bedding	Nitrogen (NH_4+)	phosphate (P_2O_5)	Potash (K_2O)
Cow	86	15.0	11	3	10
Goat	65	—	16	10	17
Duck	61	—	22	29	10
Goose	67	4.5	22	11	10
Hen	73	0	22	18	10
Hog	87	18.0	11	6	9
Horses	80	10.0	13	5	10
Sheep	68	7.5	20	15	8
Steer	75	8.5	12	14	11
Turkeys	74	—	26	14	10
Rabbit	6	6.0	45	27	16

Micronutrients in Animal Manure (pounds/ton)

Animal	Boron	Calcium	Copper	Iron	Magnesium	Manganese	Mo	Sulfur	Zinc
Horses	.03	15.7	.01	.27	2.8	.02	.002	1.4	.03
Cattle	.03	5.6	.01	.08	2.2	.02	.002	1.0	.03
Sheep	.02	11.7	.01	.32	3.7	.02	.002	1.0	.05
Hogs	.08	11.4	.01	.56	1.6	.04	.002	2.7	.12
Laying Hens	.12	74.0	.03	.93	5.8	.18	.011	6.2	.18
Broilers	.08	29.0	.06	2.00	8.4	.46	.007	—	.25

The above two charts are from *Animal Manure as fertilizer* (#100G-00340), by Jerry Purser, Agriculture Resource Management Agent, Matanuska-Susitna-Copper River District, ACE.

Chemical Composition of Fish By-Products Used on Agricultural Crops

fish by-products	Nitrogen (%)	Phosphorus (%)	Potassium (%)
fish meal	9.79	2.88	0.7
crab meal	5.15	1.58	0.45
fish scrap	1.87	0.15	0.32
fish compost	0.6-1.2	0.1-0.5	02.-0.5

Source: Wyatt, B. & G. McCourty. 1990. *Use of Marine By-Products on Agricultural Crops.* International By-Products Conference, April, 1990. AK.

SEED SOURCES FOR NORTHERN VARIETIES

A   Asgrow Seed Company, (888) 441-5985, 1905 Lirio Avenue, Saticoy, CA 93004; www.svseeds.com

A&C   Abbott and Cobb, Inc., (800) 345-7333, P.O. Box 307, Feasterville, PA 19053; www.acseed.com

Ag   Agway, Inc. Seed Plant, (800) 952-7333, 1225 Zeager Rd., Elizabethtown, PA 17022, www.seedway.com

Ah   Ahrens Nursery and Plant Labs, RR1, Huntington, IN 47540

Al   Alberta Nurseries & Seeds Ltd., (800) 733-3566, Box 20, Bowden, Alberta T0M 0K0, Canada, www.gardenersweb.com

Ar   Arco Seed Company, Box 181, El Centro, CA 92244-0181

B   Ball Seed Company, (800) 879-2255, 622 Town Road, West Chicago, IL 60185-2698; www.ballseed.com

Br   Burgess Seed and Plant Co., (309) 663-9551, 905 Four Seasons Road, Bloominton, IL 61701

Bu   W. Atlee Burpee & Co., (800) 888-1447, 300 Park Ave., Warminster, PA 18991; www.burpee.com

CG   Cook's Garden, (800) 457-9703, Box 5010, Hodges, SC 29653-5010; www.cooksgarden.com

D   Denali Seed Co., (907) 344-0347, Box 111425, Anchorage, AK 99511-1425; www.denaliseed.com

Di   Dinkel's Greenhouse, (907) 357-8733, HC 31 Box 5193, Wasilla, AK 99687

Dr   DeRuiter Seeds, Inc., (614) 459-1498 Box 20228, Columbus, OH 43220; www.deruiterusa.com

Dv   D.V. Burrell Seed Growers Co., (719) 254-3318, Rocky Ford Seedhouse, Box 150, Rocky Ford, CO 81067; burrellseeds@rminet

F   Farmer Seed & Nursery Co., (507) 334-1623, 818 NW 4th Street, Faribault, MN 55021

FM   Ferry-Morse Seed Co, (800) 283-3400, Box 1620, Fulton, KY 42041 online catalog only; www.ferry-morse.com

G   H.G. German Seeds, Inc., Box 398, Smethport, PA 16749

GC   Garden City Seeds, (406) 961-4837, 778 Highway 93 North, Hamilton, MT, 59840; www.gardencityseeds.com

Gu   Gurney Seed & Nursery Co., (605) 665-1671, 110 Capital Street, Yankton, SD 57079; www.gurneys.com

H   Harris Moran Seed Co., (800) 514-4441. Box 22960, Rochester, NY 14624-2960; www.harrisseeds.com

HG   Hydro-Gardens Inc., (800) 634-6362 Box 25845, Colorado Springs, CO 80936-5845; www.hydro-gardens.com

J   Johnny's Selected Seeds, (800) 437-4290 (USA), Foss Hill Rd., Albion, ME 04910; www.johnnyseeds.com

L   Liberty Seed Co., (800) 541-6022, Box 806, New Philadelphia, OH 44663-0806; www.libertyseed.com

M   Mountain Seed & Nursery, Box 271, Rt. 1, Moscow, ID 83843

N   Nichols Garden Nursery, (541) 928-9280, 1190 Old Salem Road NE, Albany, OR 97321; www.gardennursery.com

NK   NK Lawn & Garden (formerly Northrup King Co.), (800) 328-2402 ext 2989, Box 24028, Chattanooga, TN 37422 no catalog; www.nklawnandgarden.com

P   Park Seed Co., (800) 845-3369, 1 Parkton Ave., Greenwood, SC 29647-0001; www.parkseed.com

PS   PetoSeed Co., Inc., (800) 647-7386, Box 4206, Saticay, CA 93007-4206; www.svseeds.com

RS   Royal Sluis, Inc., 1293 Harking Rd., Salinas, CA 93907

SB   Seeds Blum, (800) 528-3658, 27 Idaho City Stage Rd., Boise, Idaho 83716; www.seedsblum.com

Se   Seedway, Inc., (800) 952-7333, 1225 Zeager Rd., Elizabethtown, PA 17022; www.seedway.com

Sh   Shepherd's Garden Seed, (860) 482-8926, 30 Irene St., Torrington, CT 06790; www.shepherdseeds.com

SoC   Seeds of Change, (888) 762-7333, Box 15700, Santa Fe, NM 87506-5700; www. seedsofchange.com

S&G   Sluis & Groot of America, 124A Griffin St., Salinas, CA 93907

St   Stokes Seeds Inc., (716) 695-6980, Box 548, Buffalo, NY 14240-0548; www.stokeseeds.com

TG   Tomato Growers, (888) 478-7333, Box 2237, Fort Myers, FL 33902; www.tomatogrowers.com

Tr   Territorial Seed Co., (541) 942-9547, Box 157, Cottage Grove, OR 97424-0061; www.territorial-seed.com

T&T   T&T Seeds, Ltd., (204) 895 9962, Box 1710, Winnipeg, Manitoba R3C 3P6, Canada; www.ttseeds.mb.ca

T&M   Thompson & Morgan, (732) 363-2225, Box 1308, Jackson, NJ 08527, for catalog, email catalogue@thompson-Morgan.com; www.thompson-Morgan.com/tm/home.html

Tw   Otis S. Twilley Seed Co., Inc., (800) 622-7333, 121 Gary Road, Hodges, SC 29653; www.twilleyseed.com

V   Vesey's Seeds, Ltd., (800) 363-7333, York, Prince Edward Is., C0A 1P0, Canada; www.veseys.com

VB   Vermont Bean Seed Co., (888) 500-7333, Garden Lane 0250, Fair Haven, VT 05743-0250; www.vermontbean.com

WD   William Dam Seeds, Box 8400, Dundas, Ontario L9H 6M1, Canada

Note: The inclusion or exclusion of names on this seed source list does not constitute endorsement or lack thereof.

Early Seed Starting Dates

The following is based on a June 1st date for planting outside. Remember that your own microclimate will determine when to start your plants. In this book will be found suggestions by other growers that are different. This chart is really for the convenience of the beginning gardener. As you grow in gardening experience, feel free to adjust these dates and develop your own chart.

March 16 (11 weeks ahead) .... Celery, Leeks
March 23 (10 weeks) .... Greenhouse tomatoes*
March 30 (9 weeks) .... Brussels sprouts, Peppers*
.... Eggplant,* Sweet corn using
.... deep pot method
April 6 (8 weeks) .... Tomatoes (outside)* Transplant
.... when near bloom. Do not
.... subject to frost.
April 13 (7 weeks) .... Parsley, Herbs
April 27 (5 weeks) .... Cabbage, Cauliflower. Broccoli
.... Melons**
May 3 (4 weeks)................................ Cucumbers,** Pumpkin,** Winter
.... Squash, Head Lettuce
May 10 (3 weeks).............................. Summer squash**
May 22 (10 days).............................. Sweet corn

Vegetables which can be direct seeded in the garden between May 15 and June 1 with little danger of loss due to frost are:***

| Beets | Lettuce | Potatoes | Carrots | Mustard | Radishes |
| Chard | Parsnips | Spinach | Dill | Peas | Turnips |

*Seedlings should be transplanted to a pot after first true leaves develop.

**Since roots should be disturbed as little as possible, plant 3 or 4 seeds in a 3-4" pot. Before or after planting into the garden, thin to one plant.

***Corn and a few other plants can be started from seed before June 1 if they are under plastic.

Storage Table for Common Vegetables Grown in Alaska

This table gives the recommended storage conditions and duration, as well as the highest freezing point for common garden vegetables in a root cellar.

Item	Temperature in °F.	Relative Humidity	Average Storage Life	Highest Freezing Point, °F.
Beans (green)	45°	85-90%	9 days	—
Beets	32°	90-95%	1-3 months	30.3°
Broccoli	32°	90-95%	14 days	—
Brussels sprouts	32°	90-95%	3-5 weeks	30.5°
Cabbage	32°	90-95%	3-4 months (early varieties only, 6 weeks)	30.4°
Carrots, tops removed	32°	90-95%	4-6 months	29.5°
Cauliflower, leaves removed	32°	85-90%	2-4 weeks	30.6°
Celeriac	32°	90-95%	3-4 months	30.3°
Celery, transplanted	32°	90-95%	3-4 months	31.1°
Chinese cabbage	32°	90-95%	1-2 months	—
Cucumbers, waxed	50°	85-90%	3 weeks	—
Endive	32°	90-95%	2-3 weeks	31.9°
Garlic	32°	65-70%	6-7 months	30.5°
Horseradish	30-32°	90-95%	10-12 months	28.7°
Jerusalem artichoke	31-32°	90-95%	2-5 months	—
Kale	32°	90-95%	10-14 days	31.1°
Kohlrabi	38°	90-95%	3 months	30.2°
Leeks	32°	90-95%	1-3 months	30.7°
Onions	32°	55-70%	5-8 months	30.6°
Parsnips	32°	90-95%	2-6 months	30.4°
Peppers, dry	32-50°	60-70%	6 months	—
Peppers, sweet	45-50°	90-95%	8-10 days	30.7°
Potatoes	38-40°	85-90%	5-8 months	30.9°
Pumpkins	50-55°	70-75%	2-3 months	30.5°
Radishes, winter	32°	90-95%	2-4 months	30.7°
Rutabaga	32°	90-95%	2-4 months	30.1°
Salsify	32°	90-95%	2-4 months	30.0°
Small Fruits	32°	85-90%	7 days	—
Squash, winter	50-60°	55-75%	3-6 months	30.5°
Sweet potato	55-60°	85-90%	4-6 months	29.7°
Tomatoes, mature green	55-60°	85-90%	2-6 weeks	31.0°
Tomatoes, on vine	60°	55-60%	8 weeks	—
Turnips	32°	90-95%	4-5 months	30.1°
Turnips, waxed	38°	90-95%	3 months	—

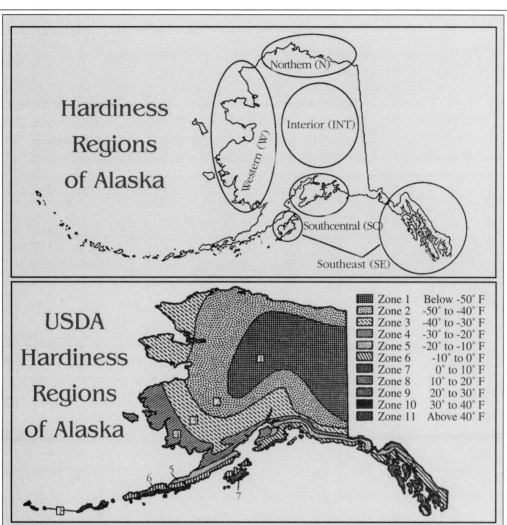

Hardiness Regions of Alaska

USDA Hardiness Regions of Alaska

Zone 1	Below -50° F
Zone 2	-50° to -40° F
Zone 3	-40° to -30° F
Zone 4	-30° to -20° F
Zone 5	-20° to -10° F
Zone 6	-10° to 0° F
Zone 7	0° to 10° F
Zone 8	10° to 20° F
Zone 9	20° to 30° F
Zone 10	30° to 40° F
Zone 11	Above 40° F

Approximate Fan Air Delivery Capacities

Fan Size	Motor Size (H.P.)	Air Delivery @ 0.125A" S.P. (Cu. Ft./min)
24 inches	1/4	4,400
	1/3	5,000
	1/2	5,800
30 inches	1/4	5,600
	1/3	6,500
	1/2	7,800
36 inches	1/4	7,000
	1/3	7,800
	1/2	9,300
42 inches	1/3	9,200
	1/2	10,600
	3/4	13,200

From *Controlling the Greenhouse Environment*, (#HGA-00336) by Wayne Vandre, Horticulture Specialist, Alaska Cooperative Extension.

Growing Culinary herbs in Fairbanks
SEED AND PLANT INFORMATION

HERBS	Annual Bi-Annual Perennial	Direct Seed	Easy to Start	SEEDS Seed Start Date	SEEDS Re Seeds Itself	PLANTS Propagate By	PLANTS Order From Catalog	OVER WINTER Outdoors	OVER WINTER Indoors	CULINARY CATEGORY Flavor/Function	SCIENTIFIC NAME
Anise hyssop	P		X	April 13	X	S		X	X	Anise	Agastache foeniculum
Arugula	A	X				S				Savory	Eruca vesicaria sativa
Basil	A		X	April 20		S,C	(8)			Savory*/Accent	O. basilicum
Borage	A		X	April 20	Readily	S				Cucumber	Borago officinalis
Calendula (1)	A		X	April 14		S				Savory	Calendula officinalis
Cilantro (2)	A	X				S				Savory/Character	Coriandrum sativum
Chervil (2)	B	X			X	S				Anise /Accent	Anthriscus cerefolium
Chives	P		X	March 12	Readily	S,D		X		Savory/Accent	A. schoenoprasum
Dill	A	X		April 27	X	S				Savory/Accent	A. graveolens
Fennel	A	X		April 13		S,D				Anise	Foeniculum vulgare
French tarragon (3)	P		Does not set seed			C,D			X	Anise /Character	Artemisia dracunculus sativa
Lemon balm	P		X	April 13		S,C,D			X	Lemon	Melissa officinalis
Lemon thyme	P		Does not set seed			L,D			X	Lemon	T. x citriodorus
Lovage	P		X		X	S,D		X		Celery	Levisticum officinale
Marigold (4)	A		X	April 24		S				Savory	T. tenuifolia
Marjoram	P		X	April 13		S,C			X	Savory/Character	Origanum majorana
Mints	P		X (7)	April 13		C,D	(8)	X	X	Mint*	Mentha
Mitsuba	P		X	April 13		S		X		Savory/Accent	Crptotaenia japonica
Nasturtium (5)	A	X		April 27		S				Spicy	Tropoeolum majus

Herb	Propagation	Start date	Propagation Methods		Flavor	Botanical name
Oregano (6)	P	X (7) April 13	S,C,L,D	X	Savory/Character	Origanum heracleoticum
Parsley, curly	B	April 13	S		Savory/Accent	Petroselinum crispum
Parsley, flat leaf	B	April 13	S		Savory/Accent	P. crispum neopolitanum
Rosemary	P	slow March 25	C,L (8)	X	Savory/Character	Rosmarinus officinalis
Sage	P	April 13	S,C,L (8)	X	Savory*/Character	Salvia officinalis
Silver thyme	P	April 13	C,L,D	X	Savory/Character	T. vulgaris 'Argenteus'
Sorrel	P	X	S,D	X	Lemon	Rumex acetosa
Savory, summer	A	X	S,C	X	Savory/Character	Satureia hortensis
Savory, winter	P	April 13	S,C,L	X	Savory/Character	Satureia montana
Sweet cicely	P	X	X		Anise	Myrrhis odorata
Sweet woodruff	P		C,D	X	Anise	Galium odoratum
Thyme	P	April 13	S,C,L,D (8)	X	Savory/Character	Thymus vulgaris
Lemon verbena	P		C,L	X	Lemon	Aloysia triphylla

1. 'Kablouna' best variety as herb
2. Look for "slow bolt" varieties
3. DON'T buy Russian tarragon
4. Gem varieties have best flavor
5. 'Empress of India' has best flavor
6. Greek oregano is best
7. Plant recommended
8. For widest selection of varieties

Propagation Methods
S= Seed
C= Cutting
L= Layering
D= Division

NOTES

Savory Herbs
Have a distinctive, characteristic flavor
*Some varieties may have an undertone of fruit or other flavors

Accent Herbs
Give subtle background note to a dish
Can be used in combination with each other
Are added to food at the last moment

Character Herbs
Impart a strong dominant note to dishes
Do not marry happily with each other
Are usually cooked for some time with the foods they flavor

© Barbara Fay 2000 Chart developed for use in herb classes taught for the University of Alaska Fairbanks, Georgeson Botanical Garden.

Vegetable and Fruit Varieties for Interior Alaska

By Michele Hébert Land Resources
Agent and Grant Matheke Research Assistant

Growing vegetables in Alaska can be easy and rewarding. In this land of the midnight sun, there are few pests to compete with and plants grow quickly. Annually at the Palmer State Fair 80 pound-plus cabbages are brought in for weighing. During the long days, plants photosynthesize, building size. During cool nights, respiration is slow and plants retain the sweetness unlike anywhere else.

Selecting the right varieties is important because of the latitude and unique climatic conditions. The long day-lengths can be a challenge, causing beets, spinach and radishes to bolt or go to seed prematurely. The many hours of sunlight signal some types of plants to flower. The cold soil can slow down root growth and require special soil-warming techniques for warm season crops such as tomatoes and corn. Soil warming techniques are described in publication #HGA-00132, *Raised Bed Gardening in Alaska*. Varieties can be selected to reduce bolting and withstand cool soil temperatures. Varieties can also be selected for the intended use.

Individuals entering vegetables in the State Fair can select varieties for their large size. It is ultimately determined by the genetic makeup of the variety. Varieties such as O-S Cross cabbage and Shogun broccoli have the potential to utilize the sun and grow to champion sizes. If winter storage is desired, it is best to select a late maturing variety and harvest as late as possible. Refer to the comment sections of this publication to find the varieties good for storage.

In Alaska, gardening is also easy because there are few pests with which to share our crops. The most common is the root maggot that is the larval form of a small fly. It attacks cole crops and onions. Understanding its life cycle can help the gardener avoid this pest. Ask for a copy of publication #PMC-00330, *Root Maggots in Alaskan Home Gardens*, for suggestions on control.

Many of the varieties listed in this publication were field tested by research Horticulturists at the Agricultural and Forestry Experiment Station at the University of Alaska Fairbanks. Additional testing has been conducted by Extension agents and specialists, Master Gardeners, and growers.

Most of the varieties have been selected after years of successful trials and evaluation. There are a few, however, that have been included because they have shown exceptional promise after only one or two years of testing.

For additional information on gardening, contact your district Alaska Cooperative Extension office.

Vegetable and Fruit Varieties for Interior Alaska #HGA 00030

Vegetable and Fruit Varieties for Interior Alaska
Garden Vegetables

	Variety & Source	Maturity	Yield	Comments
Asparagus	Super Male Jersey Knight, F	Early	Good	Plant shallow, winter mulching
Snap Beans*	Provider, D, GC, J, L, P, SoC, ST, Tw, V	Earliest	High	Good quality, good freezer
	Spartan Arrow, H	Early	Good	Good quality, good freezer
	Bountiful, VB	Early	High	Good quality, flat
	Roma II, Bu, L, P, Sh, Tw	Intermediate	High	Italian type, flat
	Royalty Purple Pod, J, St, L, Br.	Early	High	Does well in cool soils
	Contender, ST, P, Tw, D	Second Early	High	Good quality, good freezer
Yellow-wax	Rocdor, GC, H, J, Sh, St, VB	Early	Good	Reliable, early
Beet	Formanova, St	Intermediate	Good	Resists bolting, long uniform growth
	Detroit Dark Red, Bu, F, FM, GC, H, Se, SoC, Tw, V, VB	Intermediate	Good	Globe shaped
	Cylindra, Bu, CG, F, L, P, T&M, Tw, VB	Intermediate	Good	Resists bolting, tender sweet, long
	Sangria, F, Sh	Early	Very gd	Good quality
	Burpee Golden, Bu, L, St, T&M, V	Intermediate	Fair	Yellow, round, high quality
Broccoli	Green Duke, Tw, VB	Intermediate	High	Large laterals, excellent quality
	Green Comet, CG, D, FM, GC, H, L, T&M, Tw, VB	Intermediate	High	Large heads
	Emperor, Se, St, Tw, V	Intermediate	High	Good commercial quality
	Green Valiant, J, Tw, Tr, V	Intermediate	High	Good quality
	Premium Crop, GC, H, L, P, Sh, Sr, Tw, V	Intermediate	High	Large lateral production
	Shogun, Tr, D	Late	Highest	Large heads to 14" in diameter
Brussels Sprouts	Prince Marvel, CG, GC, H, P, St, VB	Earliest	Highest	Excellent quality
	Jade Cross E, Bu, L, P, Sh, St, Tw, V	Early	High	Very good, dependable
Cabbage	Earliana Hybrid, Bu, SoC	Early	Fair	Small heads, good quality
	Golden Acre, D, F, GC, L	Early	Good	Solid heads, stores well
	Dynamo, H, P, Sh, Tw, V	Early-mid	Good	Small heads, dense
	Baby Red Early, T&T, S&G	Mid-season	Good	Red
	Regal Red, J, St	Mid-season	Good	Good storage type
	Savoy Ace, Bu, CG, F, H, L, Tw	Mid-season	Good	Best savoy type
	Ruby Ball, AL, T&M, Tw, Tr, VB	Mid-season	Fair	Red, small head
	Ruby Perfection, CG, J, Tw, VB	Late	Good	Red, storage type
	O-S Cross, D, T&M	Late	High	Giant cabbage capability
	Stonehead, Br, GC, F, L	Late	Good	Small compact heads
	Lasso, GC	Late	Good	Stores well, red
Cauliflower	Snow Crown, St, CG, GC, H, J, Tw, Tr, VB	Early	Good	Dependable, good quality
	Extra Early Snowball, St	Early	Good	Good quality

Variety & Source	Maturity	Yield	Comments
Cauliflower Andes, Se, V,	Mid-season	High	Good quality, self blanching
Dominant, GC	Mid to late	High	Very dependable, good curd
White Sails, St	Mid to late	Very high	Excellent
Carrots Scarlet Nantes, D, GC, J, L, P, SoC, St, Tw, VB	Early	High	Stores well, good quality
Touchon Deluxe, St	Early	High	Flavor excellent, Nantes type
Minicor, CG, GC, F, J, St, Tr, V	Early	High	Baby carrots, pull @ 2-3"
Thumbelina, Bu, GC, FM, J, L, P, Tr, Tw, V	Early	Good	Small, round, gourmet type
Royal Chantenay, Bu, D, H, L, P, SoC, St, Tr, WD	Late	High	Storage type
Celery Ventura, J, GC, St, Tr	Mid-season	Highest	Good quality
Utah 52-70, Bu, D, P, Se, St, Tr, Tw, V	Mid-season	High	Dependable
Florida 683, St	Mid-season	High	Good quality
Chives *Nearly all kinds do well*			
Cucumber* *Grow through clear polyethylene*			
Early Pride, Bu	Early	High	White spine (slicer)
Fanfare, Bu, F, FM, L, P, St, Tw, V, VB	Early	High	Bush, white spine (slicer)
Sweet Success, Bu, GC, L, P, Se, Tw, WD	Early	High	White spine (slicer)
Little Leaf, J, P	Early	Good	Compact, easy to pick (pickler)
Northern Pickling, GC, SoC	Early	High	Black spine (pickler)
Eggplant* *Grow through clear polyethylene, but all varieties marginal in the Interior*			
Dusky, F, GC, H, L, P, St, Tw Tr, V		Poor	
Ichiban, P, Se, Tw		Poor	
Mini-finger, P, St		Poor	
Greens Bak Choi, CG, J, Sh, St, Tr	Mid-season	Good	Very nice, holds well
Green Wave, J, L, SoC, VB	Mid-season	Good	Showy & hot
Tendergreen, VB	Mid-season	Good	Good mustard
Rhubarb Chard, Bu, H, J, L, SoC, Sh, St, Tr, Tw, V, VB	Mid-season	Good	Attractive, smaller than white types, tends to bolt
Bright Lights Chard, Bu, FM, H, J, L, St, Tr, VB	Mid-season	Good	All America Selection, multicolored
Vates Collards, D, L, SoC, St, Tw	Late	Good	Good quality
Kale *Nearly all kinds do well*			
Kohlrabi Grand Duke, Bu, F, H, St, T&M, Tr, Tw, VB	Earliest	High	Very nice, early
Kolibri J, Se, Sh	Early	High	Very nice, purple
Leeks Pancho J, SoC, Sb	Late	Good	Good quality, cold tolerant
King Richard, CG, GC, J, Tr	Late	High	Nice long neck

Variety & Source	Maturity	Yield	Comments
Lettuce			
Head			
Ithaca, GC, H, L, St, Tw, V	Mid-season	Good	Good quality and flavor, reliable
Minigreen, Bu, F, St, T&M, Tw, V	Earliest	Good	Good quality and flavor, short core
Butterhead			
Ostinata, St	Early	High	Bolt resistant, dependable
Kagran Summer, J, SB	Early	Good	Bolt resistant, dependable, good quality
Sangria, J	Mid-season	Good	Red-tipped, good quality
Romaine			
Paris Island Cos, Bu, D, FM, GC, L, Se, St, Tw, V, VB	Mid-season	High	High quality, dependable
Kalura, J	Mid-season	High	High quality
Looseleaf			
Salad Bowl, CG, D, F, FM, H, J, L, St, T&M, Tr	Early	High	Excellent, bolt resistant
Red Salad Bowl, Bu, CG, GC, J, L, St	Early	Good	Good quality, bolt resistant
Oak Leaf, Bu, F, J, L, T&M	Early	Good	Very nice quality and appearance
Royal Oak Leaf, Cg, H, P, Sh, VB	Early	Good	Excellent
Grand Rapids, F, L, St	Mid-season	Good	Fair quality
Merlot, CG	Mid-season	Good	Intense deep burgundy
Ruby, St, SB, D	Mid-season	Good	Red, good quality
Onion			
Bunching			
He-shi-ko, F, VB	Mid-season	Fair	Good quality
Evergreen Hardy White, FM, GC, J, P, SB, Tw	Mid-season	Fair	Good quality
Sets	*Any kind should do well*		
Parsley	*Nearly all kinds do well*		
Parsnip			
Hollow Crown, Improved, Bu, D, L, St, Tw, V, VB	Late	Good	Good quality, most dependable
Peas			
Maestro, J, P, St	Early	High	First early Green Arrow type
Oregon Giant, J, St, Tr	Early	Good	Edible podded
Oregon Sugarpod II, H, Tr, Tw, V	Early	Good	Edible podded
Sugar Ann, St, Tr, J, D	Early	Good	Edible podded, like snap bean, doesn't require support
Dwarf Grey Sugar, D, F, SB, Tw	Early	Good	Edible podded, dependable
Lincoln, St, VB, F	Mid-season	High	Good quality
Novella II, CG, GC	Mid-season	High	Semi-leafless
Sugar Snaps, J, P, Tw	Mid-season	Good	Edible podded, like snap bean
Green Arrow, F, P	Late	Highest	Outstanding quality, long pods
Freezonian, F, D	Late	High	Indeterminate type, good quality
Peppers*	*Grow through clear polyethylene*		
Hot Thai, CG, H, P, VB	Early	High	Excellent quality
Fajita Bell, J, L, P, Te, VB	Early to Mid	High	Hot Bell pepper
Park's Early Thickset, P	Mid-season	High	Good quality
Gypsy, Bu, H, FM, L, P, St, T&M, Tw, V	Early	Good	Pointed, yellow

Variety & Source	Maturity	Yield	Comments
Peppers (cont.) Hungarian Yellow Wax, P, St, J	Mid-season	Good	Hot yellow
Karlo, J	Mid-season	Good	Hot yellow
Italian Sweet, St, Tr	Early to mid	High	Italian sweet type
Super Chili, FM, L, P, Sh, Tw	Mid-season	Low	Very hot
Super Cayenne, H, P, T&M, Tw, V	Mid-season	Low	Very hot
Potato** Rote Erstling	Early	Good	Red, tough skin, yellow flesh, good quality
Alaska Red	Early	High	Red, tender skin
Kennebec	Early	High	Tender skin
Green Mountain	Late	High	Good quality
Swedish	Late	Low	Home garden type
Bake King	Mid-season	High	Good quality, baking
AK 114	Late	High	Good quality, even size, tough skin
Norgold Russet	Late	High	Good quality, attractive
Pumpkin* *Grow through clear polyethylene (use transplants 4-5 weeks old)*			
New England Pie (Small Sugar) Bu, J, P, SoC, St, Tr, VB	Mid-season	Good	Small, good baking quality
Connecticut Field, CG, F, H, J, L, St, Tw, WD	Mid to late	High	Good size
Lumina, Bu, F, H, L, P, Se, St, Tw, V, VB	Mid to late	Good	Medium size, white skin
Radish Cherry Belle, Bu, D, F, FM, L, SoC, St, T&M, Tr, Tw, V, VB	Early	Good	Good, but doesn't hold
Scarlet Globe St, Tr, VB	Early	Good	Holds better then Cherry Belle
Burpee White, Bu	Mid-season	High	Holds longest without bolting
Snow Belle H, Tw, V	Mid-season	High	Nice round white radish
White Icicle, Bu, D, F, J, L, St, Tw, V	Late	Fair	Long
Rhubarb *Perennial–plant comes back every year.*			
McDonald, Bu	Early	High	High quality
Canada Red, Ah	Early	High	High quality
Rutabaga York Swede, J, V	Mid-season	High	Club root resistant
American Purple Top, Bu, D, Tw	Mid-season	High	Good storage type
Spinach Melody, Bu, H, L, St	Early	High	Plant early, excellent quality, most bolt resistant
Squash* *Grow through clear polyethylene*			
Summer Zucchini Elite, H	Early	High	Excellent quality
Greyzini, F, RS, T&M	Early	High	Striped, nice flavor
Goldrush, CG, L, P, St, T&M, Tw, VB	Early	High	Striking yellow zucchini
Peter Pan, B, FM, H, I, P, Se, Tw, VB	Early	High	Green scallop
Sunburst, CG, GC, J, L, P, Se, Sh, St, Tw, V, VB	Early	High	Bright yellow scallop

	Variety & Source	Maturity	Yield	Comments
Summer	Sundance, Br, CG, L, St, Tw, VB	Mid-season	High	Yellow crookneck, excellent Hand pollinate in Interior for best response
	Early Prolific, Bu, Dv, GC, FM, L, VB	Early	High	Straight neck
	Seneca Prolific, Bu, J, P, Tw	Mid-season	Fair	Yellow, Botrytis resistant
Winter	Gold Nugget, CG, J, SB, Tr	Earliest	Good	Good quality, dependable, bush type, small size
	Tivoli, GC, H, J, Se, T&M, Tw	Mid-season	Good	Spaghetti squash, dependable
	Sweet Mama, F, P, St, Tw, V, VB	Early	High	Good quality
	Ambercup, Bu, FM, H, J, L, Se, St, Tw, VB	Mid-season	High	Bright orange buttercup
	Buttercup, F, FM, J, SoC, St, Tr, Tw, V, VB	Mid-season	High	Dark green, excellent quality
	Improved Green Hubbard, St	Late	High	Very large, avg. 20 lbs in trials
	Pink Banana, L	Late	High	Large, elongate
	Golden Hubbard, St, Tw, Se	Late	High	Excellent quality
Sweet corn*	*Grow through clear polyethylene*			
	Yukon Chief [1]	Early	Fair	Dependable for cool soils, open pollinated
	Grant, St	Early	Fair	Sugary enhanced hybrid, replaces Polar Vee
	Polar Vee, D, GC, V, VB	Early	Fair	Dependable for cool soils
	Earlivee, F, GC, St, V	Mid-season	High	Best quality, nice ears
Tomato	*Best results when grown through clear polyethylene*			
	Early Tanana[1], D	Early, Indeter	Good	Ripens well when picked green
	Bush Early Girl, Bu	Determinate	Excel	Early and medium sized
	Sub-Arctic 25, D	Earliest Indeter	Good	Small fruits
	Sub-Arctic Maxi, St	V. Early Indeter	Good	Largest fruit for subarctic type
	Taxi, J	V. Early Deter	Good	Medium yellow fruit
	Lemon Boy, TG	Early Indeter	Good	Large yellow fruit
	Black Plum, TG	Early Indeter	Good	Small prolific purple fruit
	Gold Nugget, J	Early Deter	Good	Cherry
	Red Robin, TG	Early Deter	Good	Small $^1/_2$ inch fruit, prolific
Turnip	Tokyo Cross, Bu, F, T&M	Early	Good	Use for small turnips, high quality
	Purple Top White Globe D, J, F, FM, GC, SoC, St, Tr, V	Late	Heavy	Keeps well throughout winter

[1] Developed at the Agricultural and Forestry Experiment Station, University of Alaska Fairbanks.
*Crops for Production through Polyfilm: Warm season crops will benefit by planting them through a clear or wavelength selective plastic mulch. The plastic hastens soil warm-up by allowing the sun's rays to penetrate the soil and prevents heat from being dissipated by the wind. Caution is required, however, since most seedlings sunburn if not released from beneath the plastic as soon as they emerge from the soil. Sweet corn may remain under the plastic until 4 to 6 inches tall before being released. Transplants may be planted under plastic by cutting an X or by making a hole through the plastic with a bulb planter.
** Potato Sources: Always use certified disease-free seed purchased locally in Alaska. This will keep out diseases that exist in the Lower-48, but have not yet entered the state of Alaska.

Greenhouse Vegetables

	Variety & Source	Maturity	Yield	Comments
Cucumber	*All are long European type and are gynoecious -- having only Female flowers*			
	Carmen, V	Early	High	Good quality
	Corona, St	Early	High	Consistent, good keeper
	Uniflora-D, T&M	Early	High	Even size, good quality
	Fidelio, Dr, HG	Early	High	Large size
Tomato	Vendor, St, J, V	Early	High	Good quality
	Caruso, St	Early	High	Good quality
	Sweet 100, Bu, H, St, T&M, Tw	Early	Good	cherry type, many fruits, good quality

Fruit Varieties

Some fruit varieties may only survive in the more favorable sites. Carefully selecting a growing site, observing successful gardeners, and testing trials with several varieties will increase fruit growing success. Your local nursery is a good source for recommended varieties.

	Variety & Source	Maturity	Yield	Comments
Strawberry	Alaska Pioneer[1]	Early	High	Hardy, yield is high when well fertilized and watered
	Toklat[1]	Mid-season	High	Hardy, larger fruit than Alaska Pioneer
	Quinault, Ah	Mid-season to frost	Highest	Grow as an annual through polyethylene
Raspberry	Latham, Ah, Bu, F	Late	Good	Good quality
	Boyne, Ah, F	Late	Good	Good quality
	Kiska[1], Di	Early	Good	Most hardy
Currant	Red Lake, Ah, P, F	Late	Good	Hardy in higher elevations
	Holland Longbunch	Late	Excell	Hardy in higher elevations
Gooseberry	Pixwell, Ah, Br	Late	Good	Hardiest, for higher elevations
Apple	Heyer No. 12	Late	Fair	Marginally hardy
	Parkland	Late	Good	Marginally hardy
	Westland	Late	Good	Marginally hardy
	Nor-series (10)	Late	Good	Marginally hardy
	Golden Uralian	Late	Good	Marginally hardy
Apple-crab	Rescue	Late	Fair	Marginally hardy
Crab apple	Adam			Marginally hardy
	Sylvia			Marginally hardy
	Jacques			Marginally hardy
	Columbia	Late	Fair	Marginally hardy

[1] Developed at the Agricultural and Forestry Experiment Station, University of Alaska Fairbanks

Vegetable and Fruit Varieties for Southcentral Alaska
Garden Vegetables

Variety & Source	Maturity	Yield	Comments
Snap Beans* Contender, ST, P, Tw, D	Earliest	Heavy	Pods may become splashed with purple
Provider, ST, P, Tw, J, D	Early	Heavy	Good quality, good freezer
Strike, St	Mid to late	Heavy	Good quality
Top Crop, Bu, F	Mid-season	Moderate	Good quality and dependable
Roma, Bu, V	Mid to late	Moderate	Straight, flat wide pods, good flavor
Royal Burgundy, Tr, St, L, Tw	Mid-season	Moderate	Good quality and dependable
Beet Boltardy, T&M, D	Intermediate	Heavy	Does not go to seed, solid dark red, and round
Ruby Queen, NK, D	Early	Heavy	Uniform and smooth
Cylindra, F, T&M, SB	Intermediate	Fair	Long, cylindrical
Burpee Golden, St, Bu	Intermediate	Fair	Round gold instead of red flesh
Broccoli Shogun, S, A&C, Tr, D	Late	Heavy	Large central heads to 14"
Packman, J, St	Early to Mid	Heavy	Medium central heads
Green Comet, T&M, L, D	Early	Fair	Large central heads
Cruiser, J, St	Mid to late	Heavy	Medium central heads
Waltham 29, SB, Se, D	2nd Early	Heavy	Medium central heads, many laterals
Emperor, J, St,	Mid to late	Heavy	Medium central heads
Green Duke, NK, Tw, VB	2nd Early	Moderate	Medium central heads, many laterals
Brussels sprouts			
Jade Cross, J, St, NK	Early	Heavy	Uniform size sprouts, good quality
Prince Marvel, P, St, VB	Early	Heavy	Uniform size sprouts, excellent quality
Cabbage Early Jersey Wakefield, L, Bu, SB	Earliest	Good	High quality, pointed heads burst early
Castello, St	Late	V Heavy	Round heads
Early Marvel, St	Early	Good	Good quality, round head; all heads mature over a short period
Emerald Acre, St	Early	Good	Nice shaped heads
Hybrid Golden Acre, L, F, D	Early	Good	Fair quality, round head, long core
Darkri hybrid, P	Early	Good	Small frame plant
Stonehead, L, Bu, V, St	Mid-season	Heavy	Firm uniform head, long core
Fieldsport, Se	Mid to late	Good	Dark green heads, oval, very firm
Survivor, St	Late	Heavy	Storage type
O-S Cross, D	Late	V Heavy	Has potential for very large size
Early Red Meteor, Tr, St, D	Mid-season	Heavy	Stores well until early spring, high quality
Multikeeper, St	Late	Heavy	Storage type
Chinese Hybrid, St	Early	Good	Harvest early to avoid seed stalk emergence

Variety & Source		Maturity	Yield	Comments
Carrot	Nantes Coreless, F	Early	Fair	Medium cylindrical, sweet, tender, stores well
	Kazan, Se	Mid-season	Heavy	Large diameter, commercial type
	Gold King, PS, NK, D	Mid-season	Heavy	Long, cylindrical, tapered point
	Spartan Bonus, F, T&T, A	Late	V Good	Long tapered commercial type, high quality
	Klondike Nantes, St	Late	Good	Consistent quality
	Gold Pak, Bu, St, F, D	Mid to late	Heavy	Long tapered commercial type, high quality. Needs deep soil
	Nantes Scarlet, PS	Mid to late	Good	Consistently large
	Royal Chantenay, St, WD, Tr, D	Late	V Good	Large diameter, large core, fair quality
Cauliflower	Super Snowball, F	Very Early	V Good	Light heads, do not get ricy or purple
	Early Snowball, PS	Early	V Good	Medium heavy heads, fair leaf cover
	Snow Crown, St, NK, J	Early	Good	Dependable early variety
	Andes, St, J, V	Mid-season	Heavy	Self-wrapped type
Celery	Utah 52-70, V, Tr, L, Bu, D	Mid-season	Good	Long stalks, dark green
Chives	Nearly all kinds do well	Early	Good	Perennial, onion like flavor
Cucumber*	Victor, St	Early	Heavy	Sets 1st 4 or 5 fruits without pollination, no male flowers produced (slicing)
	Slice King, St	Early	Good	Gyneocious, hybrid slicer
	Early Pride, Bu	Mid-season	Good	High quality (slicing)
	Gemini 7, V, PS, D	Mid-season	V Heavy	Sets 1st 4 or 5 fruits without pollination, no male flowers produced (slicing)
	Liberty, Bu, L, PS	Early	Good	Black spine, uniform, fairly blocky (pickler)
	Saladin, Bu, F, P	Mid-season	Heavy	White spine, uniform (pickler)
Kale	**Green Curled Scotch**, St	Early	Good	Medium size plants
Kohlrabi	**Early Purple Vienna**, L, Bu, St	Early	Good	Substitute for turnip where turnip root maggot control is impossible
	Early White Vienna, L, Bu, St	Early	Good	Both keep well into late winter in common storage
Greens	Fordhook Giant Chard, SB, J, D	Late	Heavy	Vigorous, large leaf and petiole
	Green Wave Mustard, St, D	V Early	Good	Distinct mustard flavor
	Seven Top Turnip, S&G	Early	Good	Use turnip and tops when root is one inch diameter
	Vates Collards, St, Bu, D	Late	Heavy	Mild mustard flavor

	Variety & Source	Maturity	Yield	Comments
Lettuce				
Head	Salinas, J, Tr, PS	Mid-season	Good	Tipburn resistant, firm head
	Ithaca, St, Se, PS	Mid-season	Heavy	Less likely to tipburn than others
	Great Lakes 659, L, Se, PS	Late	Heavy	Tolerates more cold than others
Butterhead	Buttercrunch, L, Bu, Tr, D	2nd early	Good	Excellent quality, withstands some frost, long season of use
Looseleaf	Salad Bowl, Tr, J, PS, D	Early	Good	Does not go to seed as early as others
	Grand Rapids, St, F, L, D	Early	Heavy	Best adapted to low light intensities
Onion				
Bunching	Evergreen Bunching, Bu, SB, D	Early	Good	Bulb area enlarges more than others
Sets	Ebenezer, P	Early	Good	Yellowish flesh, very mild, stores well
	White Portugal, St	Earliest	Good	White flesh, mild
Parsley	Curlina, St	Mid-season	Good	Suitable for garden or indoor culture
Parsnip	Hollow Crown, F, St, Bu, D	Late	Good	May be left in garden if winter is mild
Green Pea	**Spring**, St	Earliest	Good	10 day picking period-trellising unnecessary
	Sparkle, Tr, J, F	Early	Heavy	8 day picking-trellising unnecessary
	Dwarf Gray Sugar, F, SB, D	Early	Good	Flat edible pod pea-trellising unnecessary
	Alaska, L, Bu, SB, J	Early and Continuous	Good	Small pod, small pea, light color
	Freezonian, F, Bu, Br, D	Early and Continuous	Heavy	Continuous but only a few at a time—**must trellis**
	Sugar Ann, D, L, Br	Early	Good	Plump edible pod, trellising unnecessary
	Patriot, P, St	Early to mid	Heavy	Trellising desirable
	Progress No. 9, Bu, Se	Mid-season	Heavy	Trellising desirable
	Green Arrow, St, J, F, L	Mid-season	Heavy	Continuous-trellising unnecessary
	Sugar Snap, St, P, Tw, D	Late	Fair	Plump edible pod pea-trellising desirable
Potato	Alaska Red[1] (red skin)	Early	Heavy	Uniform shape for market gardening
	Allagash Russet	Mid to late	Heavy	Round tuber, medium to heavy russeting

Variety & Source		Maturity	Yield	Comments
Potato (cont.)	Kennebec	Early	V Heavy	Space seed 7 to 9 inches tubers green quickly when exposed to light
	Alasclear[1]	Early	Good	Very resistant to common scab disease
	Superior	Early	Good	Processing quality, heavy yield when irrigated
	Shepody	Mid to late	Heavy	Long white, high dry matter, large size
	Alaska Frostless[1]	Mid to late	Good	Grows after others are killed by frost, no need for hilling
	Denali[1]	Mid to late	Good	Baking and chipping quality
	Snowchip[1]	Mid to late	Heavy	Baking and chipping quality
	Alaska 114[1]	Mid to late	Good	Tough white skin
	IditaRed	Mid-season	V Heavy	Tough red skin
	Green Mountain	Mid to late	V Heavy	Widely adapted, tender skin, boiler
	Bake King	Mid to late	Heavy	Uniform tuber shape, good baker
	Highlat Russet	Mid to late	Good	Good texture and flavor baked
	Yukon Gold	Mid to late	Good	Good quality
	Butte	Mid to late	Good	Long tuber shape
	Lemhi Russet	Mid to late	Good	Long tuber shape, baker
Pumpkin*	Spirit, St, Ps	Late	Good	May mature if transplanted through polyethylene film
	Autumn Gold, J, L, A&C	Late	Good	Turns from yellow to deep orange
Radish	Cherry Belle, St, F, L, D	Early	Good	Small top, round root, crisp
	Burpee White, Bu	Early	Good	Tender, mild and crisp
	Chinese White, Bu, St	Mid-season	Heavy	Long large diameter, for winter storage
	Champion, L, SB, F, D	2nd Early	Heavy	Uniform roots, good quality
Rhubarb	**MacDonald**	Early	Heavy	Cooks red, high quality
Spinach	Melody, T&M, St, D	V Early	Good	Excellent quality, resists early bolting
Squash *summer**	Gold Rush, St, P, Tw	Early	Good	Slender, gold colored
	Elite, H, J	Early	Heavy	Dark green zucchini
	Seneca Prolific, P, Tw, Bu	Early	Good	Yellow straight neck
	Black Jack, St, PS, D	2nd Early	Good	Produces over a long period
	Greyzini, St, PS	2nd Early	Good	Light green, slender
	Aristocrat, T&M	Early	Good	Excellent quality
Squash *winter**	*Grow under clear polyethylene to lengthen growing season*			
	Gold Nugget, J, SB	Late	Fair	Small fruit

Variety & Source	Maturity	Yield	Comments
Squash (cont.) Sweet Mama, St, P, Tw	Late	Fair	Buttercup type, compact vines
*winter** Golden Hubbard, St, Se, Tw	Late	Good	Long fruit
Improved Hubbard, St, K, WD	Late	Good	Thick flesh, dark green
Spaghetti squash, J, Tr, Tw	Mid-season	Heavy	Novelty squash
Sweetmeat, Tr, H, Ar	Late	Good	Short blue hubbard type
Sweet corn* *Growing season must be lengthened by growing with clear polyethylene*			
Polar Vee, St, V, T&M, D	V Early	V Good	Short cob, short plant
Earliking, T&M	Early	Good	Long cob, good quality
Earlivee, St, V, J	Early	Good	Excellent quality
Tomato* Sub-Arctic 25, D	Early	Fair	Good ripe fruits
Early Tanana, D	Early	Poor	Several fruits mature per plant
Turnip Tokyo Cross, St, F, Bu	V Early	Fair	May bolt to seed
Purple Top White Globe, St, J, F, Bu ,D	Mid-season	Heavy	Mild flavor

Greenhouse Vegetables

Variety & Source	Maturity	Yield	Comments
Cucumber Uniflora D, T&M	Early	Good	Attractive, Long, European type
Gemini 7, V, D	Very Early	Heavy	Standard type, sets 5 fruit without pollination
Sandra, St	Early	Heavy	European type, excellent quality
Superator, St	Early	Heavy	European type, excellent quality
Sweet corn Polar Vee, St, V, T&M	Earliest	Good	Small ears, good quality, plants 6 feet tall
Earliking, T&M	2nd Early	Good	Medium ears, very good quality
Super Sweet, St	3rd Early	Heavy	Very long ears, superb quality, plants 8 feet tall
Earlivee, St, V, J	2nd Early	Good	High quality, medium ears
Tomato Tropic, PS	Early	Heavy	Desirable for hydroponics
Vendor, St, J, V	Early	Heavy	Short vine for low ceiling houses
Early Girl, L, Bu	Very Early	Heavy	Good resistance to grey mold
Ultra Girl, St	Early	Heavy	Attractive fruit

[1]Originated at the Agriculture Research Center, Palmer, Alaska

* **Crops for Production through Polyfilm**: Bean, cucumber pumpkin, summer squash, winter squash, sweetcorn and tomato have a much better chance of maturing fruit when seeded under clear plastic, or wave length selective, than when planted in the open. Row covers are also an added benefit. As the seedlings grow, make slits in the film just above the plants so they can grow above the plastic film. For very short growing season areas, the following varieties are suggested: Provider bean, Victory and Liberty cucumber, Elite summer squash, Gold Nugget winter squash, spaghetti squash, Polar Vee sweet corn and Tanana tomato.

Small Fruits

	Variety & Source	Maturity	Yield	Comments
Strawberry	**Matared**[1]	Very early	Heavy	Deep red fruits, excellent quality, winter hardy if mulched
	Susitna[1]	Mid-season	Heavy	Medium red, holds shape when frozen, winter hardy if mulched
	Pioneer	Earliest	Low	Low quality, prolific plant maker, frequently survives without mulch
	Skwentna[1]	Mid-season	Good	Medium red, distinctive flavor, excellent frozen
Raspberry	Latham, Bu, F, Ah	Early	Good	Excellent quality and flavor
	Festival, N	Mid to Late	Good	Large fruits
	Boyne, Ah, F	Early	Good	Excellent quality and flavor
	Reveille, N, Ma, W, Bs	Mid to late	Good	Excellent quality and flavor
	Indian Summer, Bu	Mid-season	Good	Excellent quality, very mild
	Kiska, Di, Lo	Early to Mid	Good	Very hardy, small fruit
	Titan, Bu, Ah	Mid-season	Heavy	Large fruits, mild flavor, winter hardy to -15°F
	Golden Amber, Bs	Mid-season	Good	Yellow fruit
Gooseberry	Pixwell, Br, Ah	Late	Fair	More winter hardy than Champion
Currant	Red Lake, P, F, Ah	Late	Heavy	Very large fruits and seeds
	Holland Longbunch, Di, Lo	Mid-season	Good	Large fruit, reliably hardy
	Stevens #9	Late	Heavy	Large fruits, medium size seeds
	Boskoop Giant, Wh, E	Mid to Late	Heavy	Large fruit, excellent quality
	Swedish Black	Late	Heavy	Large fruits, excellent quality

Tree Fruits

	Variety & Source	Maturity	Yield	Comments
Apple	Chinese Golden Early	Very early	Fair	Sweet, pleasant, ripens in late August
	Rescue	Early	Heavy	Crisp, juicy, sprightly, red, early September
	Yellow Transparent	Mid-fall	Good	High quality, for eating and culinary uses
	Summerred	Mid-fall	Good	Crisp, juicy, sprightly, red, late September
Crab apple	Quality	Late	Good	Small, yellow astringent, good preserving
	Jacques	Late	Fair	Firm, yellowish-red, remove calyx and bake whole

[1]Originated at the Agriculture Research Center, Palmer, Alaska

* Crops for Production through Polyfilm: Bean, cucumber pumpkin, summer squash, winter squash, sweetcorn and tomato have a much better chance of maturing fruit when seeded under clear plastic, or wave length selective, than when planted in the open. Row covers are also an added benefit. As the seedlings grow, make slits in the film just above the plants so they can grow above the plastic film. For very short growing season areas, the following varieties are suggested: Provider bean, Victory and Liberty cucumber, Elite summer squash, Gold Nugget winter squash, spaghetti squash, Polar Vee sweet corn and Tanana tomato.

Vegetable Varieties for Southeastern Alaska

Garden Vegetables

BEANS
Contender
Provider
Royal Burgundy

BEETS
Formanova
Little Egypt
Early Wonder
Little Ball
Cylindra

BROCCOLI
Waltham #29
Green Comet
Green Goliath
Premium Crop

BRUSSEIS SPROUTS
Jade Cross
Dwarf Improved

CABBAGE
Early Jersey
Wakefleld
Earliana
Stonehead
Hybrld Golden
  Acre
Copenhagen Mkt.
  (Early)

CARROTS
Danvers Half Long
Nantes Coreless
Scarlet Nantes
Royal Chantenay
Red Cored
  Chantenay
Nantes Half Long

CAULIFLOWER
Super Snowball
Early Snowball
Snowcrown
Extra Early
  Snowball

CELERY
Utah 52-70

CHIVES
Nearly all do well

ENDIVE
Green Curled

KALE
Nearly all do well

KOHLRABI
Early Purple Vienna
Early White Vienna
Grand Duke

GREENS
Bok Toy Mustard
Seven Top Turnip
Vates Collards
Green Wave Mustard

LETTUCE
Heading
  Premier Great Lakes
  Minilake
  Ithaca
Butterhead
  Butter Crunch
  Bib
Loose Leaf
  Grand Rapids
  Salad Bowl
  Oakleaf
  Black Seeded
    Simpson
Cos Romaine
  Little Gem
  Paris White

ONIONS
Bunching
  Evergreen White
  Beltsville Bunching
Sets
  Any kind

PARSLEY
Nearly all do well

PARSNIP
Hollow Crown Improved
All American

PEAS
Alaska
Sparkle
Green Arrow
Freezonian

Edible Podded
Dwarf Gray Sugar
Sugar Snaps
Sugar Bon

Pole Peas
Tall Telephone

POTATOES
Kennebec
Alaska 114
Green Mountain
Netted Gem
Red Pontiac

RADISH
Cherry Belle
White Icicle
Champion
Scarlet Globe
French Breakfast
Easter Egg

RHUBARB
Canada Red
McDonald

RUTABAGA
Laurentian Neckless
American Purple Top

SPINACH
New Zealand
Bloomsdale
Longstanding

SQUASH
Summer
Zucchini Select
Aristocrat
Greyzini

SWEETCORN
(Grown through
  polyethylene)
Polar Vee

SWISS CHARD
Fordhook Giant
Lucullus

TOMATOES
Early Tanana
Sub-Arctic 25
Sub-Arctic Maxi

TURNIP
Tokyo Cross
Purple Top
White Globe

Greenhouse Vegetables

CUCUMBERS
European Type
Superator
Faribo
Standard
Slicemaster
Bush Champhon
Sweet Success

TOMATOES
Tropic
Fantastic
Vendor

Jim Douglas - Jill Thayer
Selected because of favorable performance through growth trials conducted by Master Gardeners and other experienced gardeners in Southeastern Alaska. As of publication, this list was being up dated—contact ACE for the latest list.

Alaska Cooperative Extension Offices

Anchorage District
(907) 279-5582, fax 279-2139
2221 E. Northern Lights Blvd., #118
Anchorage, AK 99508-4143

Anchorage State Office
(907) 279-6575, fax 279-2139
2221 E. Northern Lights Blvd., #118
Anchorage, AK 99508-4143

Bethel District
(907) 543-4553, fax 543-4551
Box 556/ Kuskokwim Campus
Bethel, AK 99559

Delta Junction District
(907) 895-4215, fax 895-4210
P.O. Box 349/Jarvis Bldg.
Delta Junction, AK 99737

Fairbanks State Office
(907) 474-7246, fax 474-6971
University of Alaska Fairbanks
P.O. Box 756180
Fairbanks, AK 99775-6180

Fairbanks—Tanana District
(907) 474-1530, fax 474-6885
Room 138 University Park Bldg,
1000 Univ. Ave.)
Box 758155
Fairbanks, AK 99775-8155

Juneau District
(907) 465-8749, fax 465-8742
1108 "F" Street, Suite 130
Juneau, AK 99801

Ketchikan District
(907) 225-3290 fax 247-3200
2030 Sea Level Drive, Suite 210A
Ketchikan, AK 99901

Nome—Northwest District
(907) 443-2320, fax 443-2150
Box 400 Northwest Campus
Nome, AK 99762

Palmer—Copper River/Mat-Su District
(907) 745-3361 fax 745-5479
809 South Chugach Street, Suite # 2
Palmer, AK 99645

Soil Testing Laboratory
533 Fireweed
Palmer, AK 99645

Soldotna—Kenai Peninsula District
(907) 262-5824 fax 262-3939
43961 K-Beach Road, Suite A
Soldotna, AK 99669-9728

Tanana Chiefs Conference
1-800-478-6822,
local (907) 452-8251, fax 459-3936
1302 21st Avenue, Suite 100
Fairbanks, AK 99701

Hotlines
Energy & Building
1-800-478-8324
Food Safety & Preservation
1-888-823-3663

**Visit the Alaska Cooperative
Extension Home Page at:
http://www.uaf.edu/coop-ext**

**Alaska Cooperative
Extension Locations**

Addresses for Polyethylene Films:

Alaska Greenhouses
1301 Muldoon Road
Anchorage, Alaska 99504
Web site: http://www.mochamadness.com/agi
(907) 333-6970

Holm Town Nursery Inc.
1301 30th Avenue
Fairbanks, Alaska 99701
Web site: http://www.ab-biz.com/holmtownnursery
(907) 451-TREE (8733)

North Pole Acres
PO Box 56822
North Pole, Alaska 99705
[Located at 6 1/2 mile Eielson Farm Road]
Web site: http://www.primenet.com/~sonia/npa
(907) 488-3940

Index